POETIC COMMUNITY

Poetic Community: Avant-Garde Activism and Cold War Culture

STEPHEN VOYCE

UNIVERSITY OF TORONTO PRESS
Toronto Buffalo London

ISBN 978-1-4426-4524-0 (cloth)

Printed on acid-free, 100% post-consumer recycled paper with vegetable-based inks.

Library and Archives Canada Cataloguing in Publication

Voyce, Stephen, 1978–
Poetic community : avant-garde activism and Cold War culture / Stephen Voyce.

Includes bibliographical references and index.
ISBN 978-1-4426-4524-0

1. Poetics – History – 20th century.   2. Literary movements – History –
20th century.   3. Cold War – Influence.   4. Poetry – Social aspects.
5. Community activists. I. Title.

PN1081.V69 2013   809.1'9358   C2012-906889-6

This book has been published with the help of a grant from the Canadian
Federation for the Humanities and Social Sciences, through the Aid to
Scholarly Publications Program, using funds provided by the Social
Sciences and Humanities Research Council of Canada.

 Canada Council **Conseil des Arts**
for the Arts **du Canada**

University of Toronto Press acknowledges the financial assistance to its
publishing program of the Canada Council for the Arts and the Ontario
Arts Council.

University of Toronto Press acknowledges the financial support of the
Government of Canada through the Canada Book Fund for its publishing
activities.

for Shannon and Justin

Contents

Acknowledgments

Several colleagues and friends deserve my sincerest gratitude for their probing insights, generosity, and inspiration. I reserve special thanks for my mentor and friend Marcus Boon, who provided invaluable guidance and enthusiastic encouragement; Irene Gammel, for her discerning commentary and generosity; Lesley Higgins and Arthur Redding, for their commitment and support; and for my dear friend and collaborator Shannon Meek, with whom I spent many nights plotting this book. I would also like to offer my gratitude to Richard Ratzlaff, Barbara Porter, Charles Stuart, and the reviewers at the University of Toronto Press for their thoughtful analysis and editorial rigour.

Thanks also to my colleagues, friends, and family for their unwavering support: Nathan Brown, Andrew Griffin, Suzanne Zelazo, James Papoutsis, Pierre Joris, Robert Stacey, Alana Wilcox, Angela Rawlings, Melinda Mortillaro, Jed Rasula, Jason Demers, Christian Bök, Dee Morris, Jon Winet, Nicki Saylor, Greg Prickman, Peter Balestrieri, Garrett Stewart, Blaine Greteman, Jennifer Wolfe, Adam Hooks, Jennifer Buckley, Loren Glass, Derek Flack, Lori Emerson, Barbara Godard, Steve McCaffery, John Wrighton, Chris Nealon, Joshua Clover, Juliana Spahr and the 95 Cent Skool, the staff at the Victory Café, Justin Voyce, David Voyce, May Voyce, and Linda Pashak. I greatly acknowledge the helpful librarians and staff members at the Modern Literature and Culture Research Centre, the Getty Research Institute, the Thomas Fisher Rare Book Library, the George Padmore Institute, Simon Fraser Library Special Collections, the Charles Olson Research Collection at the University of Connecticut, the Digital Studio for the Public Humanities, and the University of Iowa Special Collections.

This book was supported generously by the Social Sciences and Humanities Research Council of Canada, the Ontario Graduate Scholarship Program, the Canadian Federation for the Humanities and Social Sciences' Aid to Scholarly Publications Program, the Modern Literature and Culture Research Centre, and the University of Iowa's Office of the VP for Research Subvention Fund. Sections of chapter 5 appear in *Open Letter* 13, no. 8 (Spring 2009) and 14, no. 7 (Fall 2011).

The author and publisher greatly acknowledge permission to reprint material from the following sources:

Kamau Brathwaite, *The Arrivants* by Brathwaite (1973), ninety-three lines from "Ananse," "Caliban," "Cane," "The Cracked Mother," "Eating the Dead," "Jah," "Jou'vert," "Legba," "Negus," "Ogun," "Veve," pp. 162–3, 165–7, 174–5, 184, 192, 221–2, 242–3, 264–6, 269–70. By permission of Oxford University Press; Kamau Brathwaite, "Interview with Edward Kamau Brathwaite" (by Anne Walmsley). Papers of the Caribbean Artists Movement, 6/9. Courtesy of the George Padmore Institute; Jo Carrillo, "And When You Leave, Take Your Pictures With You." Reprinted by permission of the author; Robert Creeley, "Song (Were I Myself)," "The Memory," "Hart Crane," "The Immoral Proposition," "The Conspiracy," "For Rainer Gerhardt," from *The Collected Poems of Robert Creeley, 1945–1975*, by Robert Creeley, © 1982 by the Regents of the University of California. Published by the University of California Press; Judy Grahn, "The Common Woman Poems" and "She Who continues," from *Love Belongs to Those Who Do the Feeling: New and Selected Poems, 1966–2006*. Reprinted by permission of Red Hen Press; Dick Higgins, Letters to Steve McCaffery, dated 14 July 1976 and 13 April 1979, Dick Higgins Papers, Getty Research Institute, courtesy of Hannah Higgins and Jessica Higgins; John La Rose, "Fantasy in Space" and "Connecting Link," from *Foundations*; "Prosepoem for a Conference," from *Eyelets of Truth Within Me*. Reprinted with permission by Sarah White and New Beacons Books; John La Rose, "Interview with John La Rose" (by Anne Walmsley). Papers of the Caribbean Artists Movement, 6/44. Courtesy of the George Padmore Institute; Philip Larkin, "This Be the Verse," from *Collected Poems* by Philip Larkin. Copyright © 1988, 2003 by the Estate of Philip Larkin. Reprinted by permission of Farrar, Straus and Giroux, LLC for U.S. rights. Reprinted by permission of Faber and Faber, Ltd., for World excluding U.S. rights; Denise Levertov, from *To Stay Alive*, copyright © 1971 by Denise Levertov. Reprinted by permission of New Directions Publishing Corp.; Steve McCaffery, "The Body: In Light," "An Afterthought," and "Seasons,"

Reprinted by permission of the author; "The Letter 'a' According to Chomsky," *Kommunist Manifesto: Wot We Wukkerz Want*, and "A Translation of Sir Philip Sidney's Sonnet XXXI from 'Astrophel and Stella,'" from *Seven Pages Missing*. Reprinted by permission of the author and Coach House Books; Honor Moore, "Polemic #1." Copyright © 1975 by Honor Moore, used by permission of The Wylie Agency, LLC; Robin Morgan, "Pass the Word, Sister." Reprinted by permission of the author; bpNichol, "Bilingual Poem" and "Seasons." Reprinted by permission of Eleanor Nichol; Charles Olson, "Culture and Revolution," 29: 1522, Prose No. 45, Typescript, Charles Olson Research Collection. Archives & Special Collections at the Thomas J. Dodd Research Center, University of Connecticut Libraries; Charles Olson, *The Maximus Poems*, by Charles Olson, © 1983 by the Regents of the University of California. Published by the University of California Press; Sylvia Plath, "Daddy," from *Ariel*. Copyright © 1963 by Ted Hughes. Reprinted by permission of HarperCollins Publishers for U.S. rights; Reprinted by permission of Faber and Faber, Ltd., for World excluding U.S. rights; Adrienne Rich, lines from "A Walk by the Charles." Copyright © 1993, 1955 by Adrienne Rich; lines from "November 1968." Copyright © 1971 by W.W. Norton & Company, Inc, from *Collected Early Poems: 1950–1970* by Adrienne Rich. Used by permission of W.W. Norton & Company, Inc.; Ben Shahn, "A Glyph for Charles," Art © Estate of Ben Shahn / Licensed by VAGA, New York, NY.

Figures

Abbreviations

A	Brathwaite, *The Arrivants*
BB	Duncan, *Bending the Bow*
C	Salkey, "Chile"
MP	Olson, *The Maximus Poems*
PV	Olson, "Projective Verse"
RG	McCaffery and Nichol, *Rational Geomancy*
SA	Levertov, "Staying Alive"

POETIC COMMUNITY

1 Introduction

In the case of a cultural group, the number of people involved is usually much too small for statistical analysis. There may or may not be organized institutions, through which the group works or develops, but even the most organized institutions are different in scale and kind from those of large groups. The principles which unite the group may or may not be codified … But there are many important cultural groups which have in common a body of practice or a distinguishable ethos, rather than the principles or stated aims of a manifesto. What the group itself has not formulated may indeed be reduced to a set of formulations, but some effects of reduction – simplification, even impoverishment – are then highly probable.

    The social and cultural significance of all such groups, from the most to the least organized, can hardly be doubted. No history of modern culture could be written without attention to them. Yet both history and sociology are uneasy with them. We find histories of particular groups, but little comparative or analytic history.

– Raymond Williams[1]

Art's a peculiar division of labors.

– Robert Creeley[2]

Poetic Community investigates the relationship between poetry and community formation among several groups collaborating during the Cold War era. Although the phrase "literary movement" is more likely to conjure images of the numerous avant-garde groups in existence during the first decades of the twentieth century, consider a shortlist of poetic groups operating in the years after 1945: the Black Mountain poets, the Iowa Writers' Workshop, the coterie of British poets known as the Movement, the Beats, the San Francisco Renaissance, the New York School, the Caribbean Artists Movement, the Concretists, Fluxus, the Black Arts Movement, the Toronto Research Group, Naropa, the St Mark's Poetry Project, the Dub poets, and the Language Group. Certainly these communities differ drastically. Each one posits a very distinct relationship to national and racial identities; the groups named write in remarkably different geographical locations, ranging from the rural environs of the American Midwest to the cosmopolitan milieu of London, England. That they are variously affiliated through creative writing programs, performance venues, alternative colleges, and self-styled artistic laboratories also suggests that decidedly different forms of organization enable their creative practice and shape their political commitments. Some have a poetics clearly defined by political agendas or common aesthetic principles, while others value collaborative interaction as a more unsystematic cultural activity. And although one may object that not all of the "members" of such communities self-identify under the collective nouns that have since come to designate an aspect of their work, evidence that these writers share with one another methodologies, resources, and institutions certainly warrants an investigation of the relationship between community formation and the development of artistic practices. I will expand on my terms shortly, but as provisional definitions, I take *community* to mean the network of poets, cultural spaces, and institutional frameworks that enable a group's collaborative work. By *practice*, I mean the methods and texts that evolve generatively among a group of authors to form an approach to writing.

There is something in this commitment to community formation that is at odds with the dominant critical assessments of mid-century poetry and poetics. The editors of the *Norton Anthology of Modern and Contemporary Poetry* echo the often stated remark that contemporary poetries typify a shift from objective to subjective sensibilities (2:xlv), advancing a neo-Romantic aesthetic in opposition to Eliot's objective correlative. Helen Vendler describes the function of contemporary verse as the "mirror" of one's "feelings," laying bare the "voice of the soul itself"; she asserts that the "lyric desires a stripping-away of the details associated with a socially specified self" (*Soul Says* 2–3). The gifted critic Charles Altieri characterizes post–Second World War poetry in terms of a transition to a poetics of "immanence." Having no recourse but to declare the failure of modernism, contends Altieri, poetic imagination shifts radically to the epiphanic disclosure of "numinous experience" (*Enlarging the Temple* 31).[3] Perhaps surprisingly, the equally talented Marjorie Perloff takes a similar view, albeit from a position that denigrates this paradigm. The poetry of the 1950s, 1960s, and 1970s, she argues, reveals an "authenticity model" in search of "the 'true voice of feeling'" (*21st Century* 4). Perloff insinuates that the previously heralded poetries of open form, Personism, and Beat aesthetics might be a more suitable object of study for critics of the lyric tradition who probe in order to determine what, in fact, the soul says. Yet this view of poetic practice, even among those critics who judiciously acknowledge the shift towards process (over product) in contemporary verse, tends to emphasize the inward (if not passive) exploration of the writer's own consciousness. As a result, this approach ignores the social nature of aesthetic production. It is important that many of the most significant practices in contemporary poetry – projectivism, "nation language," concrete and sound poetries, the "new sentence," aleatoric and constraint writing, even confessional verse – occurred generatively and collectively, through a process that involved many poets adapting and transforming a poetics to which they contributed. The solutions of modernist authors may indeed have become untenable for poets during the Cold War era, but a resultant "inward turn" to the self is at best a partial history of the varied cultural contexts of aesthetic production after 1945.

Intriguingly, a poetics of the "private self" as an alternative to the copious number of totalizing notions of community – be they neoliberal, fascist, or otherwise – would have been understandable. For historian Eric Hobsbawm, "[i]t was not a crisis of one form of organizing societies, *but of all forms.*" Indeed, "[t]here was no other way left to define group identity, except by defining the outsiders who were not in it" (*Age of Extremes* 11). Categories designating group formation, regardless of political orientation – the people, the masses, the crowd – seemed reducible somehow to the "hoard," the "*volk,*" the "*mêlée,*" as any collectivity will invariably become violently unhinged or else will totalize, fix, and exclude.[4] W.H. Auden's "unintelligible multitude" stands poised to become

A million eyes, a million boots in line,
Without expression, waiting for a sign[.]

("The Shield of Achilles" [1952] 14–15)

Any philosophical affirmation of community expressed after the Second World War would seem to share the same fate as poetry, according to Adorno's admonishment, that to speak of it is disingenuous, if not barbaric. Hence, we have come to accept that a preoccupation with alienation and the cult of the outsider are central themes in post-war poetry. Philip Larkin's "This Be The Verse" (1971) is exemplary:

> They fuck you up, your mum and dad.
>   They may not mean to, but they do.
> They fill you with the faults they had
>   And add some extra, just for you.
>
> But they were fucked up in their turn
>   By fools in old-style hats and coats,
> Who half the time were soppy-stern
>   And half at one another's throats.
>
> Man hands on misery to man.
>   It deepens like a coastal shelf.
> Get out as early as you can,
>   And don't have any kids yourself.   (1–12)

To be fair, Larkin's poem is meant to be ironic and funny, but its fatalism is at best typical of an age surging with Eliotic "whimpers."

Other poets express a more complex and ambivalent view of the poem's role in constructing communal identities. The now-famous opening lines of Allen Ginsberg's "Howl" (1956) seem to promise a similar disintegration of restrictive bonds, yet his persistent idealism is incompatible with Larkin's defeatism. The lines "I'm with you in Rockland / where we are great writers on the same dreadful typewriter" (104–5) challenge the poem's earlier dissolution, intimating a nascent counterculture's celebration of a communal and participatory culture. Had Larkin, who was living in Hull when he composed his poem, been present to witness the genesis of the West Indian Student Centre in London during the same period, he would have encountered a very different approach to community building among an eclectic consortium of expatriate Caribbean writers. These poets, who dubbed themselves the Caribbean Artists Movement (CAM), understood the founding of a community to be the necessary precondition of their artistic and social existence. Thus, the speaker of Kamau Brathwaite's *Islands* (1969) announces:

It is not
it is not
it is not enough
to be pause, to be hole
to be void, to be silent
to be semicolon, to be semicolony;

...

So on this ground,
write[.]   ("Negus" *A* 72–7; "Vèvè" *A* 51–2)

A poet and feminist activist like Adrienne Rich articulates a similar "drive to connect":

imagining the existence
of something uncreated
this poem
our lives

...

I have to cast my lot with those
who age after age, perversely,

with no extraordinary power,
reconstitute the world.
                    ("Incipience" [1973] 18–21; "Natural Resources" [1978] 173–6)

In an interview conducted for *The New Woman's Survival Sourcebook* (Ramstad and Ronnie, 1975), Rich records that the "poetry of many of [her] male contemporaries" conveys the sense that "we're all doomed to fail somehow, in human relationships, politically, you name it" ("Poetry and Women's Culture" 108). "It's not as interesting," Rich insists, "to explore the condition of alienation ... as it is to explore the condition of connectedness" (108). Gloria Anzaldúa, author of *Borderlands/La Frontera*, claims similarly that "some of us are still hung- / up" on the notion "that the poet / is forever alone. / Separate. / More sensitive. / An outcast." Yet "[w]e don't want to be / Stars," she writes, "but parts / of constellations" ("The New Speakers" 22–8, 45–7 c. 1975). Contrary to claims that poetry after 1945 functions according to a paradigm of expressive individualism, community persists as a problematic of central importance for innumerable post-war poets, both as experiments in social action and in the invention of poetic forms. *Poetic Community* argues for an inexorable relation between the two; like any social collectivity, one should analyse the structure of poetic texts for the emancipatory projects they potentially embody and enact. Among writers as diverse as Rich and Brathwaite, Charles Olson and Steve McCaffery, Judy Grahn and Robert Duncan, the poem constitutes a space in which to imagine alternative forms of social existence. Following the speaker of Rich's text, this book examines the various ways that mid-century poetic communities aim to "reconstitute the world."

The momentous political, economic, and cultural changes enacted during the Cold War era cannot be overstated. This study addresses groups of poets who were writing from 1950 to 1980, an era often described by the stark contrast between the cultural conservatism, conformity, and consensus politics of the 1950s and the dissent directed against prohibitions on sexual, aesthetic, and political freedoms a decade later. This somewhat arbitrary division obfuscates significant underlying continuities, while it arguably focuses too strictly on the Cold War's impact on American culture. The recognizable organs of a global economic apparatus – the World Bank and the International Monetary Fund, for instance – appear during the late 1940s and expand radically throughout the subsequent decades. As so many historians observe, the Cold War generated a violent either/or logic of West versus East, and the United States and the Soviet Union were the chief sites of this conflict, but both its physical and ideological violence would reverberate throughout the world – in the policy of innumerable governments, and by war of proxy in Vietnam, Cuba, Grenada, Afghanistan, and elsewhere. If the post-war condition is marked by a rapid expansion of mass industrial production, one also encounters the emergence of a logic variously termed "late-capitalist," "post-industrial," or "post-Fordist," dominated by multinational capitalism, new and diverse forms of consumption, the saturation of media, the exploitation of Third World labour, and an unprecedented displacement of peoples across the globe. Of course, this period of history is also notable for the post-colonial independence won by several nations throughout Asia, Africa, and the Caribbean, yet many critics observe that it is also the beginning of a "neocolonial"[5] enterprise, in which empire operates under the guise of political interference, military-industrial collusion, and humanitarian debt relief. And although esoteric matters of copyright policy may seem trivial when placed alongside the death toll of the Vietnam War, the Cold War period also marks the nascent formation of a global "intellectual property" regime bent on consolidating control over culture and information by corporate concerns in the West (the consequences of which we are only now beginning to realize fully).

Marxist critics often identify the period of 1978 to 1980 with a new phase of capitalism,[6] signified in the political sphere by the ascendency of Ronald Reagan in the United States, Margaret Thatcher in the United Kingdom, and Deng Xiaoping in China, the last of whom would take the first steps in liberalizing the largest economy on earth. The economic policies set into motion in these nations especially and throughout most of the West at the end of the 1970s were intended to further abolish trade unionism, deregulate manufacturing industries, exploit ecological resources, and liberalize global financial markets. A history of the 2008 economic crisis would find a convincing point of departure in the radical changes implemented by these policymakers during this fateful period of history. Nevertheless, although it is true the securitization schemes and futures markets of today make Thatcher's iron-fisted union-busting look old-fashioned by comparison, it is more instructive to understand this increasingly ubiquitous totalization of capital as a slow-moving process rather than a decisive breach. It has been said of Olson that he is America's first "postmodern poet."[7] Whether this claim is accurate or not, one may say with certainty that he is one of the first poets of the post-war era to recognize the stakes of what Marxists call "total subsumption." He writes in 1952: "[i]nside totality, where are we, who are we?" ("Culture and Revolution" 4). Throughout *The Maximus Poems*, Olson warns of a totalizing interiorization of our social relations to capital, such that its mode of production comes to saturate the intimate texture of our everyday social existence – our desires, our affects, our knowledges, indeed, our "mu-sick": "where shall you find it, how, where, where shall you listen / when all is become billboards, when, all, even silence, is spray-gunned" by those "who use words cheap" ("I, Maximus" [1950] *MP* 1:2). It is perhaps now a truism to say that capitalism possesses a unique ontological status. Every other socio-economic system in history involved some founding exclusion, some elemental site that could not be absorbed by the dominant social order. An emancipatory politics had at least the possibility to launch from this exterior position. In a word, one can no longer draw a clean distinction between what used to be called base and superstructure, economy and ideology, the production of commodities and the manufacture of desires and ideas. Rather than characterize the Cold War era in the Manichaean terms typically reserved for this period of history, one might instead interpret its several terrains of struggle as so many shifting *fronts* of contestation. The dividing line between West and East is joined by those separating the rich North and the exploited South, the policies of global institutions and the consequences for local populations, the entitlements of citizens and the treatment of refugees, and so on.

These developments signal the emergence of new identities, subcultures, and social movements. For instance, the civil rights movement, the anti-war movement, the Women's Liberation Movement, and the environmental movement in the United States and abroad; the protests of immigrant communities in Britain; and the May 1968 revolution in France mark occasions in which the previous solidarities of economic class needed to make room for the concerns of racial, gendered, and sexual identities. These events, which no doubt produced disagreement among the Left, also created new possible alliances and collective subjects, initiating a crucial re-evaluation of citizenship, subjectivity, and institutions capable of either suppressing or enabling social action. The four case studies constituting this book – Black Mountain College (BMC), the Caribbean Artists Movement (CAM), the Women's Liberation Movement (WLM); and the Toronto Research Group (TRG) – may appear at first glance to represent an eclectic sampling of the many aesthetic-social movements to emerge during the Cold War era. Yet *Poetic Community* seeks to be representative in a somewhat different sense. I shall expand on these choices at the end of this introduction, but, for now, it suffices to say that each case study situates a shared body of writing at a crucial site of antagonism or "cultural front" of the post-war era.[8] The book begins at Black Mountain College, where Olson, Robert Creeley, and others collaboratively develop open form writing; a significant context for what Olson calls "works in OPEN," I will argue, involved commitment to alternative forms of local community building. CAM consists of a group of Caribbean poets living and working in London during the 1960s, just as the British government eliminated "common citizenship" for Commonwealth subjects. The work of Kamau Brathwaite, Andrew Salkey, and John La Rose articulates an anti-racist poetics at the crossroads of the so-called Immigration Question, and, in so doing, anticipates many comparable migrant struggles (e.g., the *sans-papiers* in France, "Mexican illegals" in the United States). Returning stateside, poets associated with the WLM, including Adrienne Rich, Judy Grahn, Audre Lorde, and Robin Morgan, challenge the gender oppression implicit in conservative America *and* among proponents of the civil rights and Black Power movements. For readers less familiar with the TRG, the work of Steve McCaffery, bpNichol, Dick Higgins, Robert Filliou and others can be found at the intersection of an international grouping of sound and visual poetics, Fluxus, and language-based conceptual art. Their elaborate multi-authored poems, collages, appropriations, and performances anticipate and challenge a growing intellectual property regime threatening access to information and culture. In this sense, each chapter documents the generative development of a poetic movement's body of practice as it encounters and negotiates questions of collective local autonomy and state intervention, the post-war diaspora and race discrimination, feminist formations and gender division, and the changing status of cultural property amid an increasingly mobile and manifold system of state and corporate power.

For several decades now we as critics have dutifully rehearsed our incredulity towards "master narratives." This now canonical axiom of postmodern thought challenges modernity's intransigent monumentalism and its myth of a universal selfhood by conceiving of subjectivity as something provisional, transitory, nomadic, and diasporic, wherein a position of permanent displacement is said to register an ideal of ideological flexibility.[9] Yet members of a collective such as the Caribbean Artists Movement never celebrated rootlessness in such ways; the highly structured organization they formed created stability for members disenfranchised by systemic racism. One of the Women's Liberation Movement's most adept thinkers warns against the "tyranny of structurelessness." Radical feminist Jo Freeman coined this term to describe a tendency among the New Left to promote "leaderless, structureless groups as the main – if not sole – organizational form of the movement" (285). Rather than eradicate hierarchies of power, structureless movements may indeed create disparity among their participants by concealing the rules, procedures, and practices designed to reveal the power dynamic of collectives. I am indebted to the network theory of Michael Hardt, Antonio Negri, and Bruno Latour, insofar as this study attempts to trace the "types of connection" between the elements composing a "group formation" (Latour, *Reassembling* 5, 27). The task of this book is to determine, in a specifically literary context, how an "internally different, multiple" collective subject "acts in common" to invent new modalities of social existence (Hardt and Negri, *Multitude* 100). One should, however, be sceptical of the inchoate energies that are said to bring such contingent networks into being. Hardt and Negri's *multitude* would seem to perpetuate postmodernism's valorization of a transitory collective, defined in the final analysis by the spontaneous and unpredictable formation of a social subject, whose constitution, they argue, draws its power from the very fact that its coalescence cannot be anticipated or sustained. Alain Badiou argues instead for a prescriptive politics, such that only an axiomatic claim can initiate the formation of a collective subject.[10] Yet one need not transpose the dictates of twenty-first-century Continental philosophy onto the activities of post-war cultural movements, since they, too, were preoccupied with such questions. The following passage from Pamela Kearon's "Power as a Function of the Group" is instructive:

> [T]he group creates its own reality and its own truth. Knowing that reality is whatever is agreed upon by society, the group creates its own society and thereby its own power. Power is the organization of many wills with a common purpose and a common interpretation. The group through its many individuals working together creates an interpretation and then stands collectively behind it. (109)

Radical feminism is often criticized for its ostensible promotion of a universalizing female subject, yet for Kearon even equality is not an essential truth discoverable in human nature, nor is community founded on autochthonic or tellurian presuppositions. Simply put, truth is a *production*, not an essence. Collective subjects are formed by the construction of axiomatic claims – for instance, "radical equality must exist" – at which point the group is invented coextensively with such a claim. One need only state this position, commit to it, and mobilize in its realization. Attention to a litany of Cold War–era literary cultures indicates that if poets were suspicious of the Enlightenment's essentialist conception of a social totality, then they were equally doubtful of an impermanent community defined merely by a refusal of totalizing ideologies. From the vantage point of the twenty-first century, it is precisely this prescriptive politics that we are most uneasy with, yet it is this aspect of mid-century poetic culture that is most neglected.

To this end, a number of pressing questions emerge: do Cold War–era poetic groups challenge or establish continuities with the modernist avant-gardes? How do they conceive a collective modality that neither makes concessions to liberal-humanist abstract universality nor an atomized individualism suspicious of any group formation as the inevitable erasure of personal freedoms? How do poets respond to and operate within institutions such as the college writing program and how did they negotiate the role of poetry within political movements? In addition, what role is given to collaboration and collective artistic production? Poetic practice shifts to an emphasis on process, strategies of appropriation, polylingualism, and interdisciplinarity, thus politicizing aesthetics and contesting the New Critics' claim for the poem's aesthetic autonomy. To what extent might these formal operations be understood to problematize authorship not by erasing the originator of texts but by "communalizing" literary artefacts?

An impetus towards collectivism among poets writing after the Second World War certainly has its precursors. Critics who take seriously the influence of collaboration and community as a formative aspect of aesthetic process have typically focused on the proliferation of "-isms" that dominated the literary and artistic landscape of high modernism. To be certain, the phenomenon is not a high-modernist invention either, but it may be argued without reservation that the early decades of the twentieth century demonstrate an unparalleled intensification of this tendency, causing critics Jerome Rothenberg and Pierre Joris to declare that the "exploration of new behaviors and the opening of new possibilities" was chiefly expressed in "movements ... some tightly organized, some hardly so" (*Poems for the Millennium* 5). The "movements of those first two decades," they argue, "functioned also as collaborative *vortices* ([Ezra] Pound's term), bringing together many individualities in a common push toward a new dispensation, aimed at a drastic change of poem and mind" (5).

Yet the concept of the avant-garde "movement" as a process of self-definition through polarization has arguably overdetermined notions of literary community during the twentieth century.[11] Renato Poggioli offers the most comprehensive definition of avant-garde community formation in his pivotal work, *The Theory of the Avant-Garde*. The "movement's" chief distinguishing trait, according to the Italian critic, is that, unlike other terms such as "school" or "circle," it is a "term which not only the observers, but also the protagonists, of that history use" to describe a "group of artists intent on a common program" (17–18). The formation of a movement is essentially agonistic; it is defined "*against* something or someone" – and typically the academy, tradition, or the public (*Theory* 25). Though agonism has complex associations with Greek, Christian, and Romantic traditions, "avant-garde agonism" refers to an extreme form of antagonism, a paradoxical affirmation of "self-sacrifice" by a "collective group" on behalf of the principles it advances (*Theory* 67–8). Poggioli's agonistic model is suggestive of Harold Bloom's filial and patently male-centred presentation of literary tradition: the author as a rebellious *son* who rejects the parental imposition of the *father*. In this case, the avant-garde becomes the "band of brothers" who together forge an alliance of siblings to usurp control of the household. The Italian Futurists "glorify war – the world's only hygiene," exalting that there are "beautiful ideas worth dying for" (Marinetti, "Manifesto of Futurism" 187); the Russian Constructivists pledge "to stand on the rock of the word 'we' amidst the sea of boos and outrage" (Burliuk et al., *A Slap in the Face* 223). This combative stance establishes the moral superiority of the "we" and the banality of the "they."[12] Of course, several critics take issue with such claims, in particular, the temerity of the avant-garde's opposition to a bourgeois culture that, in fact, aided its formation.[13] But for the purposes of the present study, I would prefer to highlight the function of avant-garde community formation, understood by Poggioli and others,[14] as a militarized and masculinized *en-closure* with clearly demarcated boundaries between members and non-members, practitioners and non-practitioners.

It is also worth pausing to consider that such a model of group practice offers an explanation of a collective identity forged in relation to external factors only (usually the public). The internal dynamic of Imagism, Surrealism, or Vorticism was fiercely hierarchical, orchestrated by controlling ideologues. Pound made no secret of his opposition to Amy Lowell's proposal "to turn 'Imagism' into a democratic beer-garden" (*Selected Letters* 48). To become a Surrealist, one had to pledge his or her allegiance to André Breton, the self-appointed "Pope" who reserved the right to excommunicate members. Perhaps no one puts the question of a group's internal hierarchy more succinctly than Wyndham Lewis in his discussion of Vorticism in *Blasting and Bombardiering*: "I concluded that as a matter of course some Romantic figure must always emerge, to captain the 'group.' Like myself! How otherwise could a group get about, and above all *talk*. For it had to have a mouthpiece didn't it?" (46).[15] Although it is beyond the scope of this book to address the political affiliations of such writers as Pound and Marinetti, the following observation by Paul Morrison in *The Poetics of Fascism* is instructive:

> Communism collectivizes the means of production and the fruits of labor; fascism provides the illusion of collective experience through aesthetic means ... [by] respond[ing] to real needs with a pseudocommunity of the *Volk*[,] ... respect[ing] the basic sanctity of capitalist property relations even as it labor[s] to provide ... an aestheticized version of the Marxist promise. (6–7, 8)

This characterization of fascist politics helps to illuminate the "pseudocommunity" promised by numerous avant-garde leaders, a promise, namely, for a "true" communal experience, without any change to the property ownership of ideas and artistic practices, or without change to the material conditions that would facilitate collective artistic production.

Two observations deserve emphasis: first, a study of contemporary poetic communities cannot and should not take the modernist avant-gardes as its proverbial strawman. Second, the heterogeneity of group formations during the first decades of the twentieth century is a debate far from being over. Critics like Stuart Hall and Raymond Williams emphasize that modernism "was always composed of many different projects, which were not all integratable or homogenous with one another" (Hall, "On Postmodernism" 132). Poggioli's agonistic model provides an effective description of the historical formations and militaristic tropes favoured by the Italian Futurists, Imagists, Vorticists, or Surrealists – movements notably dominated by male authors – yet, as I argue elsewhere, it fails to characterize the comparatively more inclusive gender politics of the Bloomsbury Group, New York Dada, or the salons of Paris.[16] Neither does the self-destructive logic of avant-gardism describe the cultural poetics of the Harlem Renaissance, a group whose political goals seem somehow trivialized by Poggioli's claims. In this regard, more recent scholarship on modernist communities offers invaluable instruction. Shari Benstock's groundbreaking *Women of the Left Bank: Paris, 1900–1940* and Emily D. Bilski and Emily Braun's *Jewish Women and Their Salons: The Power of Conversation*, for instance, call attention to the impressive literary production of female communities of authors that also shaped high modernist aesthetics. Although neither study explicitly contests Poggioli's now-canonical definition of the avant-garde movement, the breadth of their historical research exposes a much more heterogeneous array of communal practices and political commitments. Similarly, in *The Poetic Avant-Garde: The Groups of Borges, Auden, and Breton*, Beret E. Strong argues convincingly that far from aspiring to realize the groups' own dissolution, movements during the interwar period advance a politics of survivalism.

Studies of literary community in the post-war era often focus (consciously or not) on generating alternatives to Poggioli's agonistic model. Hoping to retain the avant-garde as a concept, a critic such as Achille Bonito Oliva proposes a "trans-avant-garde": "these artists," he insists, "no longer seek head-on confrontation" ("The International Trans-Avant-Garde" 257). Whereas the modernist avant-gardes, according to Oliva, advanced a fiercely dialectic conception of art "as a means of overcoming and reconciling contradictions and differences," the trans-avant-garde "is an indefinite area that groups artists together … its family stock extend[ing] fan-like over precedents of diverse descent" (257–8). According to this view, the avant-garde comes to stand for a zone of interaction and convergence, rather than a strict adherence to aesthetic principles. Ron Silliman redefines avant-garde collectivism in similar terms, offering a useful distinction between *scenes* and *networks* – a lexicon that notably avoids the term "movement." While a scene is specific to a place, the network is transgeographic. He states further that "neither mode ever exists in a pure form. Networks typically involve scene subgroupings, while many scenes (although not all) build toward network formations" (28–9).[17] In contradistinction to Poggioli's notion of the movement, Silliman has in mind a more open system of affiliations and aesthetic intersections.

Notably, studies such as Michael Davidson's *The San Francisco Renaissance*, Daniel Kane's *All Poets Welcome: The Lower East Side Poetry Scene in the 1960s*, and David Lehman's *The Last Avant-Garde: The Making of the New York School of Poets* demonstrate a conversion to Silliman's preferred terminology as a means to jettison agonism as the defining trait of avant-garde community formation. The title of Kane's book – *All Poets Welcome* – epitomizes this tendency. Davidson argues that poets congregating in San Francisco during the late 1950s and 1960s (among them Jack Spicer, Robert Duncan, Robin Blaser, and Michael McClure) forged a literary community that refused "to propose an institutionally 'correct' ideology." A commitment to pluralism, he claims, distinguishes the project of these poets from W.H. Auden and Stephen Spender, adherents "to a single humanist ideal and a series of accompanying institutional and doctrinal supports (Marxism, the Catholic Church, existentialism)" (*The San Francisco Renaissance* 31). Davidson goes further than any other critic of contemporary verse to theorize the importance of community for mid-century poetics, but the absence of female authors and ethnic diversity among the San Francisco poets makes Davidson's claim for an "essentially plural society" debatable, nor can one say that the Bay Area was representative of the period.[18] Did not radical feminist poets propose an axiomatic politics as the foundation of its aesthetic work, an uncompromising, if not totalizing, commitment to unqualified emancipation?

It is worth noting that an attempt to amend the avant-garde is a specific trend among those poets and critics cognizant of the avant-garde tradition in the first place. Frank O'Hara writes in his "Personism" manifesto that the "movement" was founded at a particular place and time ("lunch with LeRoi Jones on August 27, 1959"), on "a day in which I was in love with someone (not Roi, by the way, a blond). I went back to work and wrote a poem for this person. While I was writing it I was realizing that if I wanted to I could use the telephone instead of writing the poem, and so Personism was born. It's a very exciting movement which will undoubtedly have lots of adherents" (499). Given O'Hara's emphasis on cosmopolitanism, his campy homoeroticism, and the politics of interracial friendship, it is hard not to read his description of a "movement" as parody of the avant-garde's canonical definition. The omission or ironic use of the term "movement" among bohemian-cosmopolitan poets is telling. Notice that where the term enjoys continued currency, especially among groups such as CAM, the WLM, the Black Arts Movement, or Situationism, it typically loses its associations with aesthetic elitism, positing instead an affinity with the collective struggles undertaken by proponents of the civil rights movement, Black nationalism, radical feminism, and so on. That is, the term "movement" forges links with political rather than strictly aesthetic discourses. Attempts by bohemian literary communities to reformulate avant-garde community make significantly less sense in these contexts.[19] The politico-aesthetic project of a group such as CAM is articulated within a diasporic context, and should be understood as a synthesis of the African-Caribbean literary traditions they sought to revive and the new social movement activism underway in London. Groups like CAM also demonstrate that the creation of literary community is not merely the consequence of voluntary "self-exile" (Fredman, *The Grounding of American Poetry* 69); according to this view, the alliance forged by avant-garde artists is the consolation of individual alienation from a dominant culture. Like the WLM in America, members of CAM found themselves *involuntarily* excluded from the political apparatus of British society. Their work as

writers and activists often focused on overcoming exclusionary policies that disenfranchised immigrant communities in England.

One should examine seriously whether an attempt to reformulate
community without agonism is desirable to begin with. What would
it mean if contemporary poetic communities simply rejected high-
modernist agonism in the name of a non-adversarial pluralism? A
consensus-driven criticism that rebukes oppositional cultures simply
for being oppositional would no doubt curb artistic exploration and
pacify political dissent. Members of the WLM and CAM, for instance,
were unapologetically militant in their opposition to race and gender
oppression and capitalist exploitation. They zealously sought to hege-
monize radical equality. By evading the overt politicization of poetry
that the term "movement" announces, terms like "scene" and "network" risk a degree of political quietism. At the very least, none seems
wholly appropriate when applied to the multiplicity of social identities that emerge in the decades after the Second World War. There
is no reason to delete the term "avant-garde" from the vocabulary of
cultural analysis, but to avoid the inevitable dead ends perpetrated
by the modern/postmodern (read: agonistic versus inclusive, mono-
lithic versus pluralistic) dichotomy, one should reserve descriptions of
avant-garde activism specifically for those experimental practices that
embody and advance emancipatory projects. Hence, the question one
should ask is this: how do experimental literary forms propose novel
social modalities?

Notably, all of these words – avant-garde, movement, scene, and
network – bear the trace of the word *community*, a term that, in turn,
remains the broadest and least theorized. One speaks of national or
ethnic communities, counter-communities, community-building or
-outreach. Indeed, among those critics who give explicit attention to
the term in their examinations of poetry and poetics, it often modifies
another term more actively pursued, or else it contrasts against a comparatively more rigid system of social organization: community *and*
performance, *and* coalition, *instead of* institution.[20] Raymond Williams
astutely notes that the term "community," unlike "society," "state,"
or "nation," has managed to retain a "favorable" sense throughout
modern history.[21] Yet community is almost always defined favourably
insofar as it remains undefined. I mean by this paradoxical statement
that the word is evoked in opposition to what it purportedly is not:
community is not society, not the state, not the nation, and hence it
is assumed to be something comparatively unbureaucratic and less

structurally rigid. Community then denotes tactile and immediate personal relations between subjects in opposition to objective (often oppressive) structures that purportedly confine, bind, and exclude individuals. Readers of nineteenth-century German social philosophy will likely infer the source of Williams's terms; the sociologist Ferdinand Tönnies first formalizes this general distinction as *Gemeinschaft und Gesellschaft* (1887). (Significantly, Tönnies's book was not translated into English until 1957, featuring the appropriate title *Community and Society*.)[22] To be sure, this categorical separation of community and society is a consummately modern idea. If the abbreviated appellation "post-WWII" names an aftermath – "after" Nazism, "after" the Holocaust, "after" an unprecedented fusion of technology and death – then it also signals a further polarization of Tönnies's terms, marking a spectacular rupture in the West's understanding of social existence. After 1945, community could only signify affirmatively by naming an unrepresentable absence, a structureless outside solely defined by its withdrawal from whatever was inside. One encounters an unparalleled reverence for individualism, which would come to represent the only antidote to the failure of all social forms. That poetry in popular culture is so often thought to represent the apotheosis of individualistic expression only serves to underscore the principal task of mid-century literary groups: to defend community from its very definition as negation.

Hence, I will argue, mid-century poetry advances a very different understanding of *community*. I take this term to mean *not* the absence of structure but the productive invention, multiplication, and arrangement of social formations. For the literary critic, this means tracing the associations between elements of cultural production – actors, materials, technologies, methods, spaces, and texts – in order to determine what sort of social model it invents. Terms like "group" and "institution" are coextensive rather than antithetical, since it is impossible to theorize social formations apart from the structures that enable organized collaboration. By *practice*, I propose a term to denote the work of the community. A practice may entail a common set of aesthetic goals, but this is not its defining feature. Instead, a practice denotes what a community *shares*: its tactics, procedures, conceptual models, and resources. One might usefully contrast the concept of a practice with a *style*. The designation of a style involves a theoretical abstraction: it imagines a quantifiable and static taxonomy of characteristics specific to it. A style describes the features of a finished cultural artefact and is therefore a formalist concept. A practice, conversely, has both a social-historical and an aesthetic-formal dimension, insofar as it names a cultural artefact and its characteristic traits, but also a process of construction, a social space in which such construction is carried out, those who participate in the process, and the political project it enacts. In this sense, the object of study is not a particular author or work, but instead the ensemble of agents, locations, techniques, and texts that together come to constitute practices of community.

Polemics directed at the institutionalization of poetry too often impede rigorous analysis of the relation between community and practice. Those who complain of poetry's co-optation by the academies tend to believe that participation in such organizations invariably rarifies and homogenizes creative output. Christopher Beach remarks of academic writing programs that what is now needed are studies that "analyze the phenomenon from ... historical, sociological, pedagogical, or even philosophical perspective[s]" (*Poetic Culture* 54). Yet perhaps a preliminary step is needed, since there is certainly debate as to what constitutes an "institution" in the first place. While the BMC has come to designate a site of one of the most radical poetic innovations at mid-century, the Iowa Writers' Workshop is now synonymous with the type of "academic lyric" that has incited so much inflammatory response, especially among critics associated with the Language Group. It is intriguing that movements like CAM and the WLM do not receive similar criticism. During the rebellious 1960s, Brathwaite, Salkey, and La Rose were busy organizing meetings and conferences. Members of the WLM published lists of feminist presses in almanac-style sourcebooks alongside information about health services and legal resources. They viewed this institutionalization of their work, if one chooses to call it that, as a necessary tactic to render such resources more available to women without access to education. Having said that, I do not mean to exonerate all poetry produced within academies, or any other site of artistic production. Rather, I would caution against the pejorative sense imposed on such words as "institution." It bears asking what the actual impact a given organization has on the creative production of its members. If one accepts the premise that all social interactions (meetings, movements, etc.) and the artefacts produced by such encounters (poems, stories, etc.) indeed possess an organizing logic, then we will have to refute the validity of Tönnies's distinction between society conceived as the imposition of order (*Gesellschaft*) and a structureless community of purely lived relations (*Gemeinschaft*). Instead we should examine the structure of poetic texts the same way we examine the structure of cultural movements, recognizing, as Jacques Rancière does, that poetry has its own metapolitics – its capacity for "proposing to politics re-arrangements of its space" (*Dissensus* 119). In addition to questions regarding content, a text's processual logic and its formal innovations may imitate and enact novel forms of social existence.

If questions of community pervade theoretical discussions in mid-century poetics, then one finds a commensurate thematic preoccupation in countless creative texts – for instance, the formulation of "polis" in Olson's *Maximus Poems* (1953); diasporic community in Brathwaite's *Arrivants* trilogy (1967, 1968, 1969); critiques of governmentality in Duncan's *Bending the Bow* (1968); and social activism in Levertov's *To Stay Alive* (1971), Adrienne Rich's *A Wild Patience Has Taken Me This Far* (1978), and Audre Lorde's *Between Our Selves* (1976). In addition, it is striking that so many major developments in mid-century poetic writing emerge from intensely collaborative poetic cultures: the situationist *détournement*; feminist writing as re-vision; Caribbean creolizations of "standard" English and the signifyin(g) practices of Black Arts; open form's mutually adaptive modes among Black Mountain, the Beats, and the New York School; along with the innumerable creative misprisions of Fluxus, Concrete, the TRG, and the Language Group. These experimental forms of writing are inexorably linked to experiments in forms of collective life and action. On the relation between form and the social formations they embody, Olson was never more candid

> that no line must sleep,
> that as the line goes so goes
> the Nation!   ("I, Mencius" [1954] 31–3)

An experimental poetics for Olson is nothing other than an "initiation / of another kind of nation" tested out in the discursive space of the text ("I live underneath" [1969] *MP* 3:228).

Yet how might one discuss specific poetic texts for the collectivities they enact? Following Gilles Deleuze and Félix Guattari's contention that "every politics is simultaneously a macropolitics and a micropolitics" (*A Thousand Plateaus* 213), this would entail an analytic approach focusing on the political structures that poetic forms articulate. Take Steve McCaffery's *The Kommunist Manifesto: or Wot We Wukkerz Want* (1977) as an example. The text rewrites Marx and Engels's manifesto in the dialect of the author's native Yorkshire slang:

It's abaht buddy time thut kommunizum spoouk its orn mind, unwarrit-sehbaht, un edder reight set-too we awl this youngunz stuff ehbaht boo-ergy-misters, wee uh bitter straight tawkin onnitsoowun.

Un soourt kommiz frum awlort place uv snugged it up dahn I Lundun, un poowildahl the buk lernin tehgither un cummupwithisser Manifesto, unnitz innuzoowun un int' froggy, unt' jerry, un i-ti, unt flemmy unt da-yunish. (171)

[It is high time that Communists should openly, in the face of the whole world, publish their views, their aims, their tendencies, and meet this nurs-ery tale of the Spectre of Communism with a manifesto of the party itself.

To this end, Communists of various nationalities have assembled in London, and sketched the following manifesto, to be published in the English, French, German, Italian, Flemish, and Danish languages.] (33–4)

The idea for a translation of the *Communist Manifesto* was inspired by a conversation between McCaffery, Allan Kaprow, and Robert Filliou during a trip to Robert's Creek, British Columbia, in the mid-1970s. To-gether they conceived of an "Eternal Network" (a concept Filliou had developed years earlier with George Brecht) as the shared artistic tech-niques and conceptual models that anyone can use and adapt. The group thus proposed this text as a poetic expression of the network. Si-multaneously local and global, micro and macro, the idiomatic transla-tion constitutes a singular, local expression that nonetheless preserves communism's axiomatic claim: that class subjugation is not inevitable, that a form of collective organization based on the freely associated la-bour of producers is possible. Hence, Marx's *Communist Manifesto* in never universal in the liberal-humanist sense of an abstract general-ity applied to any situation, but universally transferable, in that it may be taken up eternally by communities that choose to incorporate (and adapt) its principles as their own.

It might be alleged, however, that such a reading strategy is ap-propriate only for a selective range of texts, in particular, experimen-tal poetry that demystifies the artifice of artistic construction. Yet one can apply this analytic approach to decidedly different poetic tradi-tions. The following passage is taken from Sylvia Plath's famous lyric, "Daddy" (1962):

Daddy, I have had to kill you.
You died before I had time –

Marble-heavy, a bag full of God,
Ghastly statue with one gray toe
Big as a Frisco seal

…

An engine, an engine
Chuffing me off like a Jew.
A Jew to Dachau, Auschwitz, Belsen.
I began to talk like a Jew.
I think I may well be a Jew.

…

Not God but a swastika
So black no sky could squeak through.
Every woman adores a Fascist,
The boot in the face, the brute
Brute heart of a brute like you.   ("Daddy" 6–10, 31–5, 46–50)

Read in its entirety, the poem's private references to a father/husband figure are filtered through a series of signs (god, Nazi, devil, vampire, teacher). It is not simply that Plath's father and husband are patriarchal figures presiding over the household; they also represent precise references to state, religious, cultural, and educational apparatuses and historical events. One could map these relations, drawing lines that link private reference to public symbols and institutions.

It is not at all that Plath confines her focus to a domestic sphere, while turning inward towards the private psyche. Rather than oppose private to public experience, Plath exposes the common patriarchal logic structuring both social spaces. And although critics sometimes argue that Plath depicts a victimized female subject, the daughter/wife figure of "Daddy" identifies potential alliances of resistance between women, minoritarian communities, and artists. Hence, the poem contrasts two competing social formations: one generating oppressive bifurcations and hierarchies (man/woman, public/private, etc.) and a collective that might potentially subtend these dominant relations (woman – Jew – artist).

Studies of poetic culture usually take the form of cultural biography, assessments of canon formation, or critiques of poetry's institutionalization. Whereas biography attempts to capture the ethos of a group's personal relations, studies of canon formation and literary professionalization examine the pedagogical frameworks of literature and criticism, the dissemination of texts, and the criteria of literary taste. These modes of study have produced an abundance of fruitful inquiry. My goal is not to take issue with these approaches and themes, which in many respects frame and guide this book. Rather, *Poetic Community* argues for a crucial intersection between social formations and the invention of poetic forms. Nichol and McCaffery's description of their work as a *"we-full*, not an *I-less* paradigm" applies equally to group formation and literary texts (*RG* 11). Hence, this study charts the connections between the cultural organizations that authors build, the poetic techniques they jointly develop, and the poetic texts such collaborations generate. I am indebted to scholars such as Barrett Watten, Adalaide Morris, and Rachel Blau DuPlessis, who examine the reflexive relation between poetic forms and their cultural contexts. Additionally, I find common cause with critics Joshua Clover, Chris Nealon, and Nathan Brown, whose work on poetry and political economy informs this study.

Chapter 2, "Black Mountain College: A Poetic of Local Relations," examines the literary production at the college in North Carolina between 1949 and 1956, during which time Olson had become its rector. The work of Olson and Creeley develops amid intensive discussions about how to forge a local, autonomous artistic community unaffected by state authority. It was also at this time that John Cage, Merce Cunningham, and Robert Rauschenberg were present at the college, and participated in several performance art projects. Although the college is typically associated with the abstract expressionists who worked there during the late-1940s, Olson had collaborated with Cage, while Creeley worked with an expansive range of artists affiliated with Fluxus, mixed media, pop, and abstract art. A wealth of correspondence and archival materials indicate that "open form" poetries should be read as an extension of Black Mountain's localism and its interdisciplinarity.

Chapter 3, "The Caribbean Artists Movement: A Poetic of Cultural Activism," investigates the emergence of a pan-Caribbean community of authors in London, England, during the late 1960s. The three principal members of CAM, Kamau Brathwaite, John La Rose, and Andrew Salkey, together with an expansive group of writers, artists, and critics, viewed their activities as a collective effort to preserve Caribbean cultural history. Yet the group also participated in struggles for migrant rights in the British capital. The chapter reads the work of Brathwaite and his collaborators within this context of Black British activism, situating the development of "nation language" (Brathwaite's term for Caribbean English) in relation to La Rose and Salkey's Marxist commitments and their tireless work as activists in London.

Chapter 4, "The Women's Liberation Movement: A Poetic for a Common World," examines a network of American feminist poets involved with the movement during the 1960s and 1970s. Like members of CAM, poets such as Adrienne Rich, Audre Lorde, Judy Grahn, and Robin Morgan mobilized around a formative counter-culture linking a social poetics with political work. Denied a place in the counter-public spheres of the New Left, radical feminists devised comparatively more dispersed networks of small press organizations anchored by an axiomatic politics of female emancipation. The chapter traces a much-misunderstood poetic of the "common," a term that Rich, Grahn, and others use to denote cooperation, shared resources, and an accessible "common world." Given the considerable attention to the commons in recent social theory (including the work of Hardt and Negri, Paolo Virno, Slavoj Žižek, and Alain Badiou), it is telling that the prescient work of WLM poets and theorists remains largely unacknowledged.

In contrast, chapter 5, "The Toronto Research Group: A Poetic of the Eternal Network," addresses a cosmopolitan grouping of Canadian, U.S., and European poets experimenting with multi-authorship, appropriative writing, and creative translation during the 1970s. Although readers of U.S. and British poetry are likely less familiar with the TRG, its members were active in artistic movements such as Fluxus, conceptualism, and mail art, such that their work might be thought of as a poetic constellation drawing from these various traditions. Steve McCaffery and bpNichol, along with other members of the Four Horsemen, Paul Dutton and Rafael Barreto-Rivera, constituted the core group in Toronto, Canada, but their collaborative experiments also involved Dick Higgins, Robert Filliou, Dieter Roth, and George Brecht, among others. The group designed their network of shared "conceptual models" in order to discredit proprietary notions of authorship and the nascent emergence of an intellectual property regime, the consequences of which have since become an imperative concern for twenty-first-century writers, musicians, and artists. "For a time, in the 60s and 70s," remark historians Steven Clay and Rodney Phillips, "Toronto might well have boasted the largest number of avant-garde poets per capita of any city on the face of the earth" (*A Secret Location* 51). Despite comments like these from several critics, there is little sustained engagement with the Toronto scene outside of a small group of dedicated writers publishing in *Open Letter*. Suffice it to say, Steve McCaffery's participation in the Language Group and Nichol's role in the international concrete movement is just the tip of the iceberg.

No doubt alternative case studies were possible. For instance, while Black Mountain is the first major post–Second World War poetic movement in North America, the San Francisco Renaissance or the first-generation New York School would also have provided succinct histories of open form writing's development. Had the book featured a chapter on the Black Arts Movement instead of CAM, it would have undoubtedly joined with the WLM to produce a more dialectically driven study of American open form writing's emergence and transformation. Likewise, a more conventional history of Fluxus instead of the Toronto Research Group would have made for a tidier national study of U.S. poetry. Yet the book would then have to jettison its attention to the diasporic shifts, post-colonial expressions, local experiments, and international alliances forged *elsewhere* in response to the Cold War's *global* ideological enclosures. The study of Cold War literature too often perpetuates its own "politics of containment" by focusing on American literature exclusively. *Poetic Community* begins in the rural United States; it then moves to cosmopolitan London (while assessing the post-war Caribbean diaspora en route); it circles back to America, this time to its urban centres; and then over to Toronto (a city positioned at the borderline of its super-power neighbour). These geographical movements in and out of America, from the rural to the urban, and through the West and its Others, confront so many ideological borders – be they gendered fronts, racist divisions, or proprietary walls. In the end, however, we visit these sites of exclusion to encounter those willing to trespass against them.

Since the Enlightenment, Duncan remarks, "in poetry as in government or religion, the goal is system or reason, motive or morality, some set of rules and standards that will bring the troubling plenitude of experience 'within our power'" ("Ideas" 102–3). Instead, he remarks, we must remake the poem as a "co-operative" (90). Duncan's contention appears in "Ideas of the Meaning of Form," an essay devoted to the premise that formal decisions – those regarding grammar, syntax, style, etc. – manifest themselves as political choices. Critics often argue that the formal elements of a text shape its ideology; yet a poem's formal politics has the capacity to reflect alternative ideologies as well as dominant ones. It can reiterate a culture's hegemonic presuppositions, or it can expose and disrupt them, opening up new spaces in which to imagine other possible worlds. A valuable consequence of this work, I hope, will be to establish points of connection between several disparate traditions that comprise the field of contemporary poetry. The collaborative projects that this book documents point finally towards a "we-full, not I-less" aesthetics shaping current performance poetries, intermedial activities, conceptual writing, and digital cultures. *Poetic Community* looks forward to a tradition of literature tasked with defending communal culture from the enclosures that threaten it.

2 Black Mountain College: A Poetic of Local Relations

Inside totality, where are we, who are we?

– Charles Olson[1]

We were trying to think of how a more active sense of poetry might be got …
We were trying in effect to think of a base, or a different base from which to
move … The form an actual writing takes is very intimate to the circumstance
and impulses of its literal time of writing[,] … that the modality conceived and
the occasion conceived, is a very similar one.

– Robert Creeley[2]

Assembly Point of Acts

In contemporary discourse on American poetry, the term "Black Mountain" has come to denote a significant site of literary production undertaken during the first half of the 1950s. First and foremost, it is the
name of a college that opened in the isolated environs of southwest-
ern North Carolina in 1933. For literary scholars, in particular, the term
marks the era of the college between 1951 and 1956,[3] at which time
Charles Olson acted as its rector, and a number of poets transformed
the institution into a central site of poetic experimentation – in particular, the development of "open form" or projectivist writing. Sharing its
namesake with the *Black Mountain Review*, the term is also a metonym
for a "little magazine" edited by Robert Creeley, and a variety of allied
publishing venues that include Jonathan Williams's Jargon Press, Cid
Corman's *Origin*, and Creeley's own Divers Press. Yet despite this complex of associations, perhaps the most lasting of its connotations refers

to a category in Donald Allen's groundbreaking anthology, *The New American Poetry, 1950–1965*. Hence, these various uses of the signifier in critical discourse speak simultaneously to a set of personal relationships, organizing institutions, and canonical categories. Black Mountain College (BMC) combined elements of a "scene" and a "network" (Silliman's terms); the physical site occasioned a great deal of interdisciplinary and collaborative practice, while it anchored a network of correspondence and publishing activities through which poets associated with the college theorized their practice.

In an essay entitled "Advance-Guard Writing" composed for the *Kenyon Review* in 1951, Paul Goodman argues that the role of the avant-garde must shift: "society" has become "'alienated' from itself, from its own creative development, and its persons ... estranged from one another," thus "the essential present-day advance-guard is the physical reestablishment of community" (375). It is difficult not to attribute these assertions, at least in part, to the trauma of the world wars, the extent of the Second World War's horrors still coming into view while Goodman was writing; likely, however, he is also speaking to a specifically American set of socio-political concerns: the explosive suburbanization of culture, the beginning of the Cold War, and a commodity fetishism that Marx could not have fully anticipated. These historical trends lend some context to one of Creeley's most famous poetic lines of the 1950s: "the darkness sur- / rounds us" ("I Know a Man" [1955] 5–6). The line break bifurcating the word "surrounds" seems to emblematize simultaneously the feeling of being encompassed by binaric ideologies of East and West, Left and Right, Communism and Capitalism. The speaker of Olson's *The Maximus Poems* complains similarly:

> In the present go
> nor right nor left;
>   nor stay
> in the middle[.]   ("The Song and Dance of" [1953] *MP* 1:54)

Of course, Olson's declaration begs the question: go where, then? The issue of social organization persists throughout *Maximus*:

> the problem then is whether
>   a Federal organization
> or organization at all except as it comes

directly in the form of
the War of the World
is anything[.]   ("13 vessels" [1963] *MP* 2:198)

Olson's speaker echoes statements made by those as far afield as Eric
Hobsbawm and Jacques Derrida: not only were the democratic institutions of modernity at stake, but the very configuration of the political sphere as such. Suffice it to say, Goodman's proposed re-vision of
the avant-garde speaks to a set of collective concerns among the poets
and artists who congregated at Black Mountain: namely, can the avant-
garde still be relied upon to forge an alternative society? How might a
writing practice respond to this demand?

Several critics claim that BMC is an important predecessor of the counter-cultural movement, a nascent formation growing towards the subversive energies of the Beats, the San Francisco Renaissance, and the protest
poetics of the 1960s. But what is this nascence exactly, this designation of
an "almost but not quite" political status? That Denise Levertov and Robert Duncan adapt projectivist aesthetics to anti-war poetry would reaf-
firm this trajectory towards counter-cultural activities. The circumstance
to which Olson, Creeley, and others respond is more complicated still.
Those who worked at BMC during the early to mid-1950s did so during
a time in which the (inter-)national was being reconfigured: the establishment of the World Bank (1945) and the International Monetary Fund
(1944) inaugurated a new era of capital, the final revisions of the Geneva
Conventions (1949) sought to formalize the role of the United Nations,
and the convention designating a new "status of the refugee" (1951) was
introduced to respond to diasporas across the planet. Olson's theorization of "polis" in *The Maximus Poems* and Creeley's preoccupation with
friendship in *For Love* speak to an emergent politics related to these configurations. It would be more accurate to say of Black Mountain, I think,
that it exists in a historical moment "sur-rounded," as Creeley puts it,
not merely by conservative 1950s culture, but by a notion of totalizing
governmentality at national and international levels. Community, Olson
remarks, "needs now to be as wholly reconceived & newly created as
does the concept of Self (& whatever is coming as 'Society' – the present
Totalitarian State only a stage of passage)" ("West" 47). Olson's note affords greater optimism than in his poem cited above; it also clarifies the
historical and philosophical context for the literary-artistic experiments
at Black Mountain. The multi-authored development of field composition, the early writings that emerge from these developments in poetics,

in addition to the interdisciplinary experimentation undertaken at the college are consciously conceived within this milieu of a new collectivity responding to totality.

It is for this reason, and perhaps a bit ironic, that one should begin a study of Black Mountain with a reference to Paul Goodman. Goodman had written his essay on the renewed demand for advance-guard community shortly after teaching at Black Mountain College during the 1950 summer session. He had also just completed a book with his brother Percival entitled *Communitas* (1947), a study of American urban space, which endorses a "commune" model of social organization as an alternative to modern utopian city planning.[4] Reading the book in conjunction with his essay, it is clear that he considered experimental artists' enclaves as possible testing grounds for his vision of community; hence, there is good reason to suspect that he had hoped the place would be a concrete expression of the "communitas" he had theorized in his book on the subject. Although Black Mountain was by the standards of 1950s America a quite radically progressive institution, there were questions about Goodman's "ostentatious" bi-sexuality.[5] Olson's own attitude to homosexuality is not entirely certain, but Edward Halsey Foster records that the poet, in addition to being active in the anti-racism Common Council for American Unity during the 1940s, was also amenable to gay liberation, and forged friendships with gay teachers and writers like F.O. Matthiesen (*Understanding* 39). Ultimately, however, like many cultural and political movements of the 1960s, BMC members often combined radical critiques of capitalist society with predictably conservative attitudes to gender equality and sexual orientation.

It is along these lines that a schism separates criticism of Black Mountain, and, in particular, Olson's work. Scholars such as Don Byrd, Paul Christensen, Donald Allen, Stephen Fredman, Robert Von Hallberg, and Charles Altieri tend to read the Black Mountain poets as a crucial component of a counter-canonical trajectory of writers united in opposition to the New Critics. Versions of this literary history typically begin with Pound and Williams, Zukofsky and the Objectivists, and then on to the mid-century open form practices of the New York School, the Beats, and the San Francisco Renaissance. A broad tendency exists among these critics to highlight a correspondence between poetic process and cognitive, psychological processes. (Altieri, for instance, defines a neo-Romantic poetics of epiphanic disclosure in opposition to Eliot's "objective correlative.") If this approach to projective forms is at odds with the consciously social approach to the production of literature among the Black Mountain poets, then perhaps one should also ask why open form poetry should be understood as the lone subject's "true voice of feeling" when its principles were conceived to define "polis" in Olson's *Maximus*, to investigate friendship in Creeley's *For Love*, and as the platform for Levertov and Duncan's intensely dialogic anti-war writing? In recent years, critics such as Michael Davidson, Rachel Blau DuPlessis, and Libbie Rifkin have examined open form poetics in relation to heterosexist concepts of gender and the relationship between masculinity and the Cold War – indeed, Eve Sedgwick's critique of "homosociality" lends itself readily to such a project.

Certainly the women at Black Mountain recognized in its social structure what DuPlessis aptly observes in Olson's poetry: "a radical critique of humanist logos" expressing simultaneously a "subtext filled with conventional gender ideas" ("Manifests" 44). Assessments of the college by female artists, students, and staff persuasively challenge the sentimentalizing and celebratory recollections typical of their male counterparts. Hilda Morley describes mixed feelings about "Olson's boys," an apt phrase that would form the gendered exhortation in "Projective Verse": "go by it, boys" (240). Francine du Plessix Gray recounts that Olson and the milieu he cultivated at the college was at once "iconoclastic and dictatorial." Yet Olson's "militant" rebellion against traditional literary forms involved a demonstrably altered stance towards literary history in contrast with the early twentieth-century avant-gardes; she discerningly remarks, "he did not so much engage in Oedipal rebellion against contemporary fathers," but instead conveyed a "gigantic, archeological curiosity for all forms of 'immediate' discourse, past and present." Yet she too found herself deeply disappointed with the college's male bravado, finding "much redneck yahoo posturing in this Harvard-educated scholar" who routinely sermonized that one could not attain "freedom" until cleansed of all Western bias (302). Olson had undoubtedly influenced countless women writers of the past half-century. This is a point I will return to briefly in relation to Levertov, and then again in chapter 4; poets like Adrienne Rich, Audre Lorde, Robin Morgan, and Judy Grahn will appropriate open form technique, putting it to work for feminist aesthetics and politics. Yet we should say unequivocally – and not apologetically – that Black Mountain was both an advancement and a failure of egalitarian politics and art. Open form poetics signals a collectivist social project in opposition to the possessive individualism of 1950s consumer culture, while it failed to extend its principles of self-determination, local autonomy, and collective organization to women. Anticipating Morgan's probing criticism of the American New Left, poets of the Women's Liberation Movement will build upon this radical critique with the aim "to go further" (*Going Too Far* 61). Olson is fond of saying that the living and the writing are one. If indeed open form writing comes directly from a social theory of radical equality, then it will be necessary to document this connection with rigorous historical context, all the while carefully recognizing precisely where, along the way, these poets both succeed *and* fail to install this hypothesis into the writing and the living of community.

There is no question that the poets who worked at the college at mid-century found it a productive environment. By 1950, Olson and Creeley had already begun one of the most significant correspondences in American letters, an exchange that would ultimately bring Creeley to the college; and as I will argue in the next section of this chapter, the method of "field composition" detailed in Olson's famous "Projective Verse" essay emerged from these letters as a theory co-developed by both poets. It was at BMC that Olson composed the first twenty sections of *The Maximus Poems*, in addition to several of his most important early works collected in *Archaeologist of Morning*.[6] He also wrote a copious number of his most significant manifestos and essays, including his lectures entitled *The Special View of History*, "The Present Is Prologue," and the majority of essays compiled in *Human Universe*. For Creeley's part, between the time he first began writing to Olson and his eventual sojourn at BMC from 1954 to 1956, he would pen the majority of small volumes and chapbooks assembled in *For Love* – two of which involved collaborations with painters also working at the college (Dan Rice and Fielding Dawson). He also acted as editor of the *Black Mountain Review*, producing the first volumes from Mallorca, Spain, before arriving in North Carolina. Robert Duncan, too, engaged in fruitful correspondence with various members of the BMC community, arriving at the college first in 1955, and then again a year later to teach in the spring and fall terms. It was at this time that he worked on several poems later published in *Letters* and *The Opening of the Field*, two volumes whose titles reflect his growing interest in projectivist methods. Although scholars often make mention of Creeley's interest in abstract expressionism, other critical instances of interdisciplinary experimentation at BMC frequently go unnoticed. Olson's exposure to dancers like Katherine Litz and Merce Cunningham, and his participation in several theatrical productions, renewed his interest in these art forms. The intimacy of the college facilitated several important intermedial collaborations, including an early adaptation of Olson's poem "Glyphs" for a performance piece with Litz, Ben Shahn, and Lou Harrison. John Cage, however, organized the most significant example of intermedial performance; indeed, the first prototype of the Fluxus happening took place at the college, and Olson, along with the artist Robert Rauschenberg, pianist David Tudor, and a host of others, took part in its demonstration.

John Andrew Rice and several of his former colleagues founded the college in 1933, after Rice was dismissed from his position as Classics professor at Rollins College for unconventional teaching methods. From the beginning, the institution's opposition to mainstream pedagogy shaped its key principles of organization: there was no system of accreditation, no board of trustees, and the instructors themselves voted democratically on all issues pertaining to educational policies and procedures. A rector was elected among the faculty to administrate and lead meetings, but he received a single vote like all other members. In exchange for creative and pedagogical freedoms, however, there were severe monetary constraints, since the faculty received little compensation for their teaching, and students who attended the college did so with full knowledge that they would receive no degree for their work. During the era of the college in which Olson served as rector, the administrative structure that John Rice had envisioned at the height of the Great Depression was largely similar, yet Olson, Creeley, Duncan, and others increasingly conceived of the institution as an alternative to a condition of 1950s consumer culture and post-war nationalism. Just as the GI Bill had extended post-secondary education to working-class Americans, it had also swelled university enrolment to numbers that threatened to homogenize approaches to creative learning. Black Mountain thus sought to combine the accessibility of the post-war public institution with the intimate setting of a small arts community. Significantly, Olson had worked during the war as an Associate Chief in the Office of War Information (OWI) and then later accepted a potentially lucrative job in the Roosevelt administration. He resigned from the first position apparently in protest of the government's censorship of war reporting and abandoned the second after concluding that the artist could make no social impact in the modern democratic state. In a letter written to his former colleague at the OWI, the anthropologist Ruth Benedict, he admits, "I regret we are not city states here in this wide land. Differentiation, yes. But also the chance for a person like yourself or myself to be central to social action at the same time and because of one's own creative work" ("Letter to Ruth Benedict" n.p.).[7] It is enticing to interpret Olson's choice to become a poet commensurately with his retreat from the political sphere, but Olson refutes this notion of writing as being divorced from social action. In an early poem announcing his departure from government, he makes the point concisely: "[t]he affairs of men remain a chief concern" ("The K" [1945] 8). Elsewhere, in one of Olson's last poems, the speaker of *Maximus* echoes this project: "the initiation / of another kind of nation" ("I live underneath" [1969] *MP* 3:228). The proclamation here and Olson's letter to Benedict bears a striking resemblance to Goodman's concept of the avant-garde.

Because of the college's stated mandate, and certainly because of its exhausted financial resources as well, the school operated with a relatively small faculty and student body. During its twenty-three-year history, it enrolled approximately 1200 students (a figure that includes those who attended part-time) and graduated no more than fifty-five of those.[8] Yet the college attracted some of the most important poets, artists, dancers, composers, and architects of the 1940s and 1950s (most of whom were not yet recognized): among them, John Cage, Merce Cunningham, Robert Rauschenberg, Hilda Morley, Dan Rice, Josef Albers, Willem de Kooning, Ed Dorn, Buckminster Fuller, Michael Rumaker, Joel Oppenheimer, Jonathan Williams, Franz Kline, Robert Motherwell, Lou Harrison, Robert Creeley, David Tudor, Francine du Plessix Gray, Robert Duncan, Stefan Wolpe, and Paul Goodman.

During the 1950s, Black Mountain retained the basic structure of a college, but functioned more like an artists' colony. It was arguably most effective during its "summer sessions," when artists working in several fields congregated to engage in "short period[s] of intensive work and experimentation … in the setting of the Black Mountain community." The aim was to build a "co-operative work program" that expresses artistic exchange as a practice of living ("Black Mountain College Bulletin" 12; "Advertising Flyer" 1). In an open letter to the members of Black Mountain, Olson describes this project as "an assembly point of acts," stressing the convergences of ideas and heterogeneous artistic methods ("A Letter to the Faculty" 28).

Members of the Black Mountain community frequently characterize the college in terms of a changing collective identity. Just as Creeley remarks that "[p]eople were always drifting through, coming back, coming for the first time" (Creeley, "Interview" by Sinclair and Eichele 69), Ed Dorn proclaims that the "value of being at Black Mountain was that very able people and very alive people were there, back and forth and off and on and through it … I always thought of the place not as a school at all, but as a climate in which people work closely together and talk" (*The Sullen Art* 1–2).[9] Comparable sentiment comes from a diverse consortium of attendees at the college. It is compelling that John Cage, for one, believed the aims of BMC were commensurate with his anarchistic principles, citing the college as the most significant experiment in collaboration and experimental pedagogy he had ever encountered.[10]

A crucial element of the time spent at BMC, Olson tells one interviewer, involved "the struggles to define what is a society of this order" ("On Black Mountain (II)" 73). In fact, Olson makes no objection to the concept of literary and artistic community, just as long as one "put[s] the community as living," marked not by static sociological categories but as the changing "variation of all the people that were in it" (71, 74). In "Letter to the Faculty of Black Mountain College," he elaborates with an evocative analogy:

> The puzzle in general terms is one of *structure*. We understand a good deal about the *behavior* of electrons, neutrons and protons (for BMC, substitute, 'man'). But we have no *structure* for them (((Apply, here, BMC & 'MAN,' likewise)) …
>
> We are finding out, moreover, that what we are forced to call elementary particles retain *neither permanence* nor *identity*. That is to say, *they are always capable of change, one into the other.* ((DITTO, BMC, 'man' – right?))[.]
>
> ("A Letter to the Faculty" 29)

Anticipating a concern he will take up in *The Maximus Poems*, Olson is searching for a more adequate language in which to engage the collective subjectivity of communities – a language that neither a community of order (*gessellschaft*) nor a community of lived relations (*gemeinschaft*) can sufficiently describe. It is clear that Olson is consciously avoiding words like "individual" and "society" to denote the identities and institutions that structure human interaction, attempting instead to speak a language that captures the transformative aspect of collectivity:

we who throw down hierarchy,

...

do not fail to keep
a sort of company[.]   ("Maximus, at Tyre and at Boston" [1953] *MP* 1:94)

Yet what this "explanation / leaves out," the speaker insists, "... is / that chaos / is not our condition" ("Letter 22" [1953] *MP* 1:96). As I will argue later, "polis" is a concept worth holding on to for Olson because the city implies this metamorphosis: the construction, renovation, and demolition of buildings; streets that interconnect; the protean ethos of neighbourhoods that arise and disperse. By describing subjects as elementary particles that fuse and transform, Olson imagines community as having no fixed identity, no predetermined essence. Creeley's definition of friendship, Levertov's protest verse, and Duncan's notion of the poetic as a commune of words each employs a similar idea of an inclusive and changeable sociality.

Yet there is a danger in sentimentalizing the "open community" too greatly. If poets associated with Black Mountain celebrated the constantly shifting milieu of the college, its nomadic and protean quality, this is most certainly also because of the college's limited resources. The idea of a provisional community is also the consequence of needing to make do. This is an important yet often overlooked element of open form writing. Projectivism emphasizes immediacy, a writing that responds to a continuously changing environment in which the poet works with the resources available within her field of action. "Working in OPEN," as Olson calls it, does not refer to an infinite expanse, but a makeshift capacity to adapt to the immediate conditions that a given circumstance demands. Duncan derives from Olson: "[t]he poem is ... an area of composition where I work with whatever comes into it" ("Preface" *BB* vi). Open form is local.

Olson's pursuit of a community without recourse to a totalizing "structure" or permanent "identity" is a concern that permeates his theoretical prose in *Human Universe*, a collection of essays composed during his stay at BMC. In the title piece of that collection, the author outlines his objection to the "UNIVERSE of discourse," a concept he associates with the Greeks, and which he uses to describe the separation of knowledge from a world of experience: "[w]ith Aristotle, the two great means appear: logic and classification. And it is they that have so fastened themselves on habits of thought that action is interfered with" ("Human Universe" 4). The purpose of intellectual inquiry, for Olson, is not simply a matter of generating abstractions – not the "thing's 'class,' any hierarchy, of quality or quantity" – but rather to determine a thing's significance by virtue of its function. That is, "whatever it may mean to someone else, or whatever other *relations* it may have" (6; my italics). Olson elaborates on his concept of *relation* in other essays, particularly "The Gate and the Centre," where he remarks that the "problem now is not what things are so much as it is what happens BETWEEN things" (18). In opposition to the methodologies he associates with "discourse" (the rigid divisions of experience and phenomena into hierarchies), Olson imagines a poetics that investigates the *relationality* between the elements that compose any local social environment.[11]

Significantly, as early as 1949, Olson's call to investigate the relationship "between things" is a mantra he repeats several times in relation to social, institutional, and aesthetic activities at Black Mountain. Two documents aptly express the origins of Olson's thinking: the "Black Mountain Catalogue," a mission statement for the college (1949), and Olson's letter to W.H. Ferry,[12] outlining its interdisciplinary possibilities (1951):

> At the middle of the 20th century, the emphasis – in painting as well as in political theory – is on what happens between things, not on the things themselves. Today the area of exploration, the premise underlying systematic thinking, is that of function, process, change; of interaction and communication. The universe ... is seen, in microcosm and in macrocosm, as the continuously changing result of the influence that each of its parts exerts upon all the rest of its parts[.] ("Black Mountain Catalogue" qtd. in "Letter to W.H. Ferry" 11)

> What happens *between* things – what happens between *men* – what happens between guest faculty, students, regular faculty – and what happens *among* each as the result of each: for i do not think one can overstate – at this point of time, America, 1951 – the importance of workers in different fields of the arts and of knowledge working so closely together some of the time of the year that they find out, from each other, the ideas, forms, energies, and the whole series of kinetics and emotions now opening up, out of the quantitative world. ("Letter to W.H. Ferry" 11)[13]

There is continuity between these passages and Olson's "Projective Verse" essay, a document that similarly evokes the bicentenary ("Verse now, 1950") and a "stance toward reality" emphasizing a "kinetic" and non-hierarchical "kind of relation" among objects in the world (239). In fact, this emphasis placed on the changeable relations between things over the thing itself applies commensurately to field composition *and* to the organization of societies. Whether Olson is discussing Black Mountain College, his concept of "polis" in *Maximus*, interdisciplinary performance as a site of artistic interaction, or the elements that compose the field of a poem, he is interested precisely in how each assembles as a collectivity according to its respective ontological order. Just as the poets and artists at BMC are likened to atoms that amalgamate and transform, the field of the poem is a collectivity of objects that assembles as a social, material, and linguistic constellation. The "underlying systemic thinking" usually associated with open form poetry – "function," "process," "interaction," and "change" – is the premise upon which Olson conceived a much broader social vision. To put it plainly, a concept of community formation informs the development of projective aesthetics. The goal "at this point of time, America, 1951" was a writing that reflected a practice of community stressing the local, the collectively organized, and the autonomous.

We Are the Process: Towards a Theory of Field

Since its initial publication in *Poetry New York* in October 1950, Charles Olson's "Projective Verse" essay has become a veritable institution whose influence traverses a broad range of literary activities during the 1950s and 1960s, including the frequently overlapping projects of writers associated with Black Mountain, the Beats, the San Francisco Renaissance, the New York School, and TISH. Also referred to as "open form" or "composition by field," Olson's essay introduces some of the most central concerns now associated with mid-twentieth-century North American poetics: his principles of field composition, the function of the typewriter to score the voice on the page, and a stance towards reality that Olson calls objectism. The significant precursors are referenced explicitly: Pound, Williams, Ernest Fenollosa, and Louis Zukofsky.[14] This intertextual network of methods is adapted and extended further in the theoretical prose of Olson's contemporaries.[15] Olson's essay has since, unfortunately, become codified as an individual's principal declaration of open form poetics, as critics attempt to delineate linear traditions (and the discrete contributions to these traditions), usually in accordance with a counter-tradition from Pound to open form, yet field composition was a generative practice invented and transformed by a community of authors over several years. The practice emerged, not as a set of principles to be adhered to, but as a set of flexible strategies to be adapted.

At the beginning of Olson's essay, the poet makes an important – if easily overlooked – remark that composition by field (a practice of writing) is commensurate with what he calls an "objectist" stance (a practice of living). From the outset, Olson associates a system of prosody with the social theory he had been conceiving concurrently at Black Mountain. In one of Olson's early poems, "I, Mencius," the lines read

> that no line must sleep,
> that as the line goes so goes
> the Nation!   ("I, Mencius" [1954] 31–3)

The micropolitical line of the poem relates to a macropolitics of social organization. Yet such a forceful pronouncement by the speaker of "I, Mencius" begs a series of questions: how does Olson conceive of the line, how does the line operate within the poem, and how do poems relate to nation states, or any other social formation?

One might begin by stating that Olson's text defines the poetic in direct contrast to the New Critics' claim for the art object's autonomy; indeed, the aforementioned lines concisely express Anthony Easthope's contention that "just as poetry is always a specific poetic discourse, so line organization takes a specific historical form, and so is ideological" (*Poetry as Discourse* 24). In his landmark study of free verse, Charles O. Hartman claims that its dominant characteristic is the line: "*[v]erse*, he insists, *is a language in lines*. This distinguishes it from prose" (*Free Verse* 11). Although several critics – among them Marjorie Perloff, Robert Frank, Henry Sayre, and Mary Ann Caws – problematize this assertion in productive ways, one finds general agreement with Hartman's proclamation.[16] Frank and Sayre contend, for instance, that the "postmodern line" performs a defamiliarizing gesture, whereby "the project has become one of rescuing the line from the taming influence of popular practice, of literally freeing up the margin." "These poetries," they contend, "all share a sometimes aggressively disruptive character … disrupt[ing] their own practice even as they engage it" (*The Line in*

Postmodern Poetry xvii–xviii). The editors use the term "postmodern" liberally, citing examples such as Robert Lowell, Gary Snyder, Olson, and the Language Poets. Applying Easthope's analysis of poetic discourse to the contemporary moment, Frank and Sayre argue that "postmodern" practices articulate a subversive countercultural ideological formation – marked, as they are, by a "convention announcing unconventionality" (xvi). According to Frank and Sayre, postmodern free verse is to traditional forms as noise is to music. Despite the primacy given here to the poetic line, it might actually be more accurate to suggest that "postmodern" poetics privileges the line *break*. Apparently, such poetries define practice in terms of their refusal of tradition and authority, and in so doing, perform a countercultural politics – a poem like the hipster, outlaw, or hippy, living outside the grid of metrical pattern or predetermined forms.

One might debate the expansive lineage these editors construct, but just as significantly, Black Mountain poets such as Olson, Creeley, Levertov, and Duncan neither afford the line a position of centrality nor indicate that its principal function is only to disrupt. For these poets, the line exists among other elements in a *field* and the emphasis is on its relation with other variables; Olson explains in "Projective Verse" that "every element in an open poem (the syllable, the line, as well as the image, the sound, the sense)" act as "participants" within a social field of action (*PV* 243). Levertov similarly remarks: "writing is not a matter of one element supervising the others," but a mapping of the "interaction between the elements involved" ("Some Notes on Organic Form" 628). If a writer "works in OPEN," claims Olson, she must abdicate "inherited line, stanza [or] … form" (*PV* 239). Yet this does not mean that Olson disavows tradition or advocates a poetics of anti-convention for its own sake; rather, the poet cannot treat poetic form as the privileged "inheritance" of one's forebears, as one might expect to inherit land or title. The poem is deconstructive and reconstructive; it assembles in the moment of its composition, conditioned by the available elements and contexts that occasion it. Again, Levertov is close to Olson when she describes the act of composition as the *"build[ing of] unique contexts"* ("On the Function of the Line" 86). More will be said about the concept of field, but it suffices to note at this point that Olson, Levertov, Duncan, and Creeley use the term "field," and not "page." This is because the poem operates as a zone within larger social, political, and technological discursive fields. The task at hand, Olson remarks – both in reference to political organization and line organization – is to determine "what happens between things, not the things themselves" ("Letter to W.H. Ferry" 11). Contrary to the claim that the contemporary poetic line articulates a politics of pure confrontation through disruption and dissonance, the question is instead one of relation: how lines behave as "participants," indeed, how they collaborate, within a field of action. Open form poetics, its process and prosody, needs thus to be read in terms of the social vision that Black Mountain occasioned. It needs also to be read against the poetry that supposedly articulates this social vision.

"works in OPEN"

Early on in "Projective Verse," Olson advances three principles of open form writing:

1 The *kinetics*: "a poem is energy transferred from where the poet got it (he will have some several causations), by way of the poem itself to, all the way over to, the reader …. [T]he poem itself must, at all points, be a high energy-construct" (*PV* 240). The concept of "field" that Olson expounds borrows from a materialist-scientific model. The word "energy" is promptly followed by the word "construct" to refute any assumption that he has in mind a quasi-mystical understanding of creative production. This cautionary point aside, Olson's claim seems prosaic enough: that "several causations" imbue the poem with energy. But where does the poet get this creative force? Provided one accepts that Olson disputes the idea of the poem as a rarified, complete object, then the energy comes from an external source that animates language, only to be reanimated by another external force – the reader. Olson's contention that the pressure and duration of breathing can determine the length of the poetic line is often taken to express an organic model of aesthetics, whereby authority is located in voice and/or nature. But for Olson, like the speaker of "The Kingfishers," "[t]he factors are / in the animal and/or the machine" (90). Notably, Olson, Creeley, Levertov, Duncan, and others prefer the term "open form" to "voice-based"; that it is the typewriter which supplies the poet with the instrument to notate voice upon the page demonstrates the capacity to combine nature and culture as the social-technological-human assemblage that constructs any cultural artefact.[17] Meaning is not fixed to a text by an author; rather, poems are the nodal points that receive

meaning like electrical currents focalizing energy in a particular physical site. Olson reminds his readers that this "energy is peculiar to verse" insofar as the poem is a particular discursive arrangement of language, but its creation bears the necessary interrelationship between the "energy that propelled" it "in the first place" and the energy supplied in the act of reading (240). The "energy construct" that the poem ultimately comes to be combines material (language, typewritter), semiotic (meaning), and social (authors, traditions, readers) energies in its production.

2 The *principle*: "FORM IS NEVER MORE THAN AN EXTENSION OF CONTENT. (Or so it got phrased by one R. Creeley … [)]" (*PV* 240). This principle echoes what I have stated before about open form: that no predetermined form conditions the act of composition. One should clarify, however, that by "content" Olson and Creeley do not have in mind the sense of the poem as a discrete message or contained unity. The poem is an "energy-construct," and hence "content" refers to the nexus of external forces that bring the poem into being. The act of composition, being free of predetermined forms, is modular rather than formless, responding to the external world within which writing takes place. Olson cites Creeley's useful formulation, but it is the broader context within which the younger poet makes this assertion that is all the more telling.

The first draft of Olson's "Projective Verse" essay,[18] which he dutifully sent to Creeley, indicates that he was still grappling with a system of prosody to complement the social theory he had begun to conceptualize at Black Mountain. In response, Creeley offers an analogy to jazz: "Miles Davis's group being delighted with the SOUND of a French horn" (*Correspondence* 1:39). Creeley would coin his most quotable phrase, that "form is never more than an extension of content," in a letter nearly two weeks later, but the rudiments of this statement are already present in this earlier letter. That is, Creeley identifies in jazz a similar attempt to compose not according to a "form" that "extends" predictably from a predetermined metre, but rather a musical rhythm composed in "any given instance" (*Correspondence* 1:39). Creeley invites Olson to think of the participants within the field of the poem as being akin to the ensemble of instruments in a jazz performance. In both cases, spontaneity should not suggest a random production of sounds, but rather the negotiation between musical elements in the instant of composition. "The job," Creeley states paradoxically, "[is]… systematic disorganization" (1:39) – continuously re-organizing the elements of syntax, line, image, etc. – to reflect the conditions of the present moment.

3 The *process*: "ONE PERCEPTION MUST IMMEDIATELY AND DI-RECTLY LEAD TO A FURTHER PERCEPTION" (*PV* 240). The "process" may entice the critic to conclude that Olson's is a poet-ics of cognition, documenting the mental activity of a single con-sciousness. Rosemarie Waldrop rightly observes that the direction of movement is "outward and physical, toward perceptions rather than ideas" ("Charles Olson" 470). Olson remarks in *Human Uni-verse* that "man and external reality are so involved with one an-other that, for man's purposes, they had better be taken as one" ("Human Universe" 9). Perception marks not the continuous move-ment of interior thought but the continuous engagement with an external realm of experience – and hence, Olson carefully indicates that "one perception" leads directly to another, not "one's percep-tion." Levertov usefully extends this thinking in her concept of the "exploratory" line, likening open form poetries to ships that sail without need of charts "that traditional forms provide." "Risks are part of the adventure," she explains. "[A]s explorers travel they do make charts, and though each subsequent journey over the same stretch of ocean will be a separate adventure (weather and crew and passing birds and whales or monsters all being variables) neverthe-less rocks and shallows, good channels and useful islands will have been noted and this information can be used by other voyagers" ("Technique and Tune-up" 93). Once again, the movement is out-ward, not inward, traversing the field, negotiating the interaction between emergent variables.

The kinetic, the modular, and the processual combine as the method Olson calls "field composition." Below, I give Olson's most candid definition, but the reader should keep a couple of things in mind: the projective is frequently understood by way of social/communal analo-gies: jazz performance, navigation, etc. As I claim in the introduction to this book, the term "process" is applied very liberally in contemporary studies to denote poetries that refuse an autonomous status to the art object. Process in Olson's sense clearly does *not* mean a mapping of the interior thought process of a single speaker. It maps the relations and materials involved in the construction of poems:

It comes to this, this whole aspect of the newer problems. (We now enter, actually, the large area of the whole poem, into the FIELD, if you like, where all the syllables and all the lines must be managed in their *relations* to each other.) It is a matter, finally, of OBJECTS, what they are, what they are inside a poem, how they got there, and, once there, how they are to be used. This is something I want to get to in another way in Part II, but, for the moment, let me indicate this, that every element in an open poem (the syllable, the line, as well as the image, the sound, the sense) must be taken up as participants in the kinetic of the poem just as solidly as we are accustomed to take what we call the objects of reality; and that these elements are to be seen as creating the tensions of a poem just as totally as do those other objects create what we know as the world. (*PV* 243; my italics)

Critics such as Don Byrd suggest that Olson's concept of field is indebted to scientific models; in physics, "field" designates a space affected by an electromagnetic force. Waldrop speculates that Olson comes to the idea through Gestalt psychology, which had adapted the concept to designate "a kinetic model of mental states as balances of forces and vectors" ("Charles Olson" 468). But the language Olson employs clearly bears a strong affinity with his descriptions of community at Black Mountain, his statements on interdisciplinarity, his emerging process materialism, and the philosophy of relation that comes to unify these various concerns. The field being defined is also quite certainly a *social field* – not a psychological one. Olson applies his terms carefully. "Kinetic," a term repeated in the quotation, refers to the poem as a "high-energy construct," an assemblage of the material, semiotic, and social elements that constellate in and as the field of the poem: authors, readers, signs, a typewriter all participate, all labour, in its construction. The relationship between the poetic and the social is indicated by Olson's telling transition: field composition is "something" he "want[s] to get to in another way in Part II" when he discusses objectism. The elements of the poem manifest the same logic of relation "as do those other objects [that] create what we know as the world" (*PV* 243). The ontological order is specific to the poetic field, but it bears a logic of relation – an ontology of the "between things" – concurrent with a "stance toward reality" that brought it into being. Just as a nexus of "participants" organize relationally in the field of a poem, objectism denotes a commensurate experience of the subject within the field of reality he occupies and shares with a constellation of other objects: "'objectism [is] a word

to be taken to stand for the kind of relation of man to experience ...
the getting rid of the lyrical interference of the individual as ego" (*PV*
247). In an open form poem, any element that enters the field counts
equally. Every element is afforded an unqualified equality among all
others.

Olson tells his reader he favours the term "objectism" to "objectiv-
ism" if for no other reason than it evades the inevitable "quarrel" with
"subjectivism." More significantly, the term is used to evade the antagonistic logic that the subject/object distinction perpetuates by insisting
that a human being "is himself an object" (247). Olson affords the same
ontological status to any and all phenomena that populate the world.
Indeed, perhaps it is Alfred North Whitehead's useful phrase "community of actual things" (*Process and Reality* 214) that resonates most with
Olson, who in turn extends the concept of the social to include non-
human entities. His terminological revision has several implications,
not least of which for eco-criticism; for my purposes, I should emphasize that if "Projective Verse" is resituated within the nexus of correspondences and documents theorizing community at Black Mountain,
it becomes clear that Olson's interest in the ontological status of collectivities is related to his understanding of the poem as a communally
constructed artefact – indeed, the poem as a community of linguistic
elements.

Although it may seem challenging to prove that Olson, Levertov,
Creeley, and Duncan share stylistic similarities (for instance, the ex-
hortatory style of *Maximus* is not the tempered voice of Creeley's lyrics), no doubt their commitment to this most important consequence of
field composition is shared. Levertov's assertion that no one element
in composition should "supervise" the others insinuates a critique of
the emerging corporate culture of 1950s America, government bureaucracy, and the military industrial complex. Recalling a passage I cite towards the end of my introduction, Duncan is even more explicit in this
regard: since the advent of the Enlightenment, "in poetry as in government or religion, the goal is system or reason, motive or morality, some
set of rules and standards that will bring the troubling plenitude of experience 'within our power'" ("Ideas" 102–3). Excerpted from "Ideas
of the Meaning of Form," Duncan brings Olson's critique of Aristotle
to bear on poetic convention. Predetermined metres are governments
imposed on poetic writing. One may object that the form of state power
and the form of a poem are different enough in the consequences they
bring about to warrant a categorical distinction between them, but for
Duncan, it is not enough to locate the political among macropolitical

discourses of nationalism, geopolitics, justice, and representation; the political must be pursued locally among those practices that do not explicitly advertise their ideological orientations. Duncan's point is that any and all cultural activities manifest political choices. Whether one is talking of a "minuet, the game of tennis, [or] the heroic couplet, the concept of form as the imposing of rules and establishing of regularities, the theories of civilization, race, and progress, the performances in sciences and arts to rationalize the universe, to secure balance and class" – these practices may share a common logic ("Ideas" 102). The possibilities of projective verse were explicitly linked to an alternative concept of community, "a free association of living things – for my longing moves beyond governments to a co-operation" ("Ideas" 90). In a word, Olson, Creeley, Levertov, and Duncan understand that the form of a poem should reflect this axiom of autonomy and equality.

In this sense, they are getting at an idea of the poetic that foregrounds its own construction as a social artefact, that any institution, individual, or object manifests dynamics of power. The lines of poems are no exception. The following passage from "I, Mencius" is instructive:

> we are the process
> and our feet
>
> We do not march
> We still look
> And see
> what we see
>
> We do not see
> ballads
> other than our own.   ("I, Mencius" 75–83)

Words like "process," "look," (poetic) feet that "do not march," and the persistence of the social "we" signal the principles of field composition.[19] Olson disperses language across the field of the page by way of a "systematic disorganization" (Creeley's term) of the "march" of the metred line and the *four-by-four formation*[20] of the ballad stanza:

> Mao concluded:
> nous devons
> nous lever
> et agir!
>
> …

not accumulation but change, the feed-back proves, the feed-back is
the law

> Into the same river no man steps twice
> When fire dies air dies
> No one remains, nor is, one

Around an appearance, one common model, we grow up
many[.]   ("The Kingfishers" [1949] 50–3, 95–101)

The poem gives prominence to three concepts: Heraclitus's ontology of flux, Norbert Weiner's cybernetics, and Mao Zedong's communist directive. Some historical context is necessary to understand this
surprising amalgam of associations. The Heraclitian concept of flux
is evoked in the very first line of the poem: "what does not change /
is the will to change." Ralph Maud and George Butterick both argue
that Olson's famous line is likely not a direct translation of Heraclitus's
twenty-third fragment,[21] but the subsequent reference to the river apho-
rism clearly indicates that Olson was aware of the Greek philosopher's
crucial intervention into pre-Socratic theories of being and materialism.
Given that Olson would not read Whitehead until 1955, it is likely that
Heraclitus's concept of change, that objects are best understood as processes, lays the foundation for Olson's idea of the poem as energy field.
Regarding the second of these allusions, Olson learned of cybernetics
at Black Mountain College during a lecture given by Natasha Gold-
owski in 1949. The principle of feedback – by which some aspect of the
output generated by a system is passed back into the input – is used to
explain how systems account for modulation and change. Cybernetics seemed a plausible scientific explanation of Heraclitus's axiom: that
the only constant was change itself. As for the third reference, the significance of Mao is potentially more confusing. The phrase "nous devons / nous lever / et agir!" ("we must rise up and act") (51–3) came to
Olson by way of a friend, Jean Riboud. Olson retains the French partly
to recognize the debt to his friend and perhaps also to emphasize the
proliferation of Mao's message throughout the industrialized world.
The following passage is taken from Riboud's letter: "Voici l'ère histo-
rique dans laquelle le capitalisme mondial et l'impérialisme vout vers
leur condamnation, tandis que le socialisme mondiale et la démocra-
tie vout vers la victoire. La lumière de l'aurore est devant nous. Nous

devons nous lever et agir" ("Letter to Charles Olson" n.p).[22] Olson finished "The Kingfishers" in 1949. The Cultural Revolution and the Great Leap Forward are socio-economic plans yet to be conceived; it would be more than a decade and a half until the Black Panthers encountered Mao's "red book." At precisely the historical moment of Olson's reference, Mao represented to the West both the "red scare" of Soviet communism exported to the world and a generalized xenophobia towards an emergent Eastern-Orientalist threat. Ralph Maud observes that an affirmation of Mao in the poem would have indeed raised eyebrows (*What Does Not Change* 41). Several of Olson's friends had either been investigated or blacklisted by the FBI. Although Olson was never so explicitly involved in party politics after his departure from the Office of War Information, Black Mountain regularly received visits from the Bureau.[23] For Olson, like Riboud, Mao represented the possibility of a subversive energy in opposition to the totalizing projects of Western capitalism.

So here, then, are the three references that I have addressed separately, but field composition emphasizes that once an element appears in field, its relations with other elements will modify its meaning. Mao is not the communist leader in the poem; Mao is Mao in relation to cybernetic theory and Heraclitean ontology. As Olson puts it, objects do not simply "accumulate," they "change." Indeed, according to the cybernetic trope Olson advances, each concept might be thought to "feedback" into the others; each element reorients when encountered by another element. With this reflexive assertion in mind, it becomes apparent that all three allusions foreground multiplicity and change – in ontological, technological, and political arenas, respectively. Heraclitus theorizes the flow of material reality; cybernetics explains the interaction of physical systems; and Mao emphasizes the collective nature of political action. That Olson's poem blends natural, scientific, and human assemblages reinforces the premise of objectism; that is, Olson's text exhibits not the interaction between self and other selves (understood in liberal discourse as stable, autonomous, discrete entities) but instead how one is never separate from the social environments of which our subjectivity is an effect – that, indeed, subjects occupy a common world and "we grow up / many" (100–1).

The same could be said of the poetic line. Olson represents these concepts, or rather the relation between them, by amalgamating three variations of open form writing: a triadic line in the mould of W.C. Williams, a sprawling prose-poem line, and an indented verse paragraph. The triadic line, when used to express a phrase from Mao, breaks the directive into discrete actions, the fast-stepping movement of the lines echoing a call for an urgent pace. The continuous flow of the prose-poem line cleverly correlates to the cybernetic theory of feedback, generating the image of a typewriter carriage moving back in order for the composition to travel forward. And finally, the indented verse paragraph burrows Heraclitus into the fabric of this cybernetic allusion, insinuating a contemporary scientific discourse's reliance on an ancient philosophy of becoming.

Returning to the particular assemblage of concepts the poem constructs, the relation established between Heraclitus and Mao, in a certain sense, expresses what I have argued thus far about the role of community formation and the development of field composition. Olson suggests that the foundation for a political epistemology can be located in a materialist ontology. Expressed in less pretentious language, concrete political action must begin from a social vision emphasizing function, process, interaction, and change. Notably, his theoretical prose almost always names a particular time: "at this point of time, America, 1951," "Verse now, 1950, if it is to go ahead" ("Letter to W.H. Ferry" 11; *PV* 239). The very conception of open form poetics in the contemporary era is tied to these moments, to the calcification of communal relations into nuclear family, universal declaration (of war or of law), the corporation, the suburb – all producing socio-economic divisions, perpetuating the Aristotelian principles of hierarchy and classification. For Olson, Creeley, Levertov, and Duncan, the word "totalitarian" does not refer to America's enemies; it refers rather to any discourse that seeks to contain and paralyse political thought and creative activity.

It is upon this ground that Olson defines polis in *Maximus*, Creeley maps desire and the bonds between friends in *For Love*, and Duncan and Levertov develop a poetry of protest. It is also on this ground that one might begin to think of the "Black Mountain poets" as a group affiliated not by stylistic affinity per se (though similarities do exist), but instead by the mutual and transformative construction of a practice characterized by a reworking of the linguistic elements that bind poetic language and representation – that is, a poetics of relation that seeks to redefine the social. It is also precisely this desire that led Olson, John Cage, and other writers and artists to experiment with inter-artistic activities at the college.

To Join the Arts in Action: John Cage at the College

During the late 1940s, John Cage and Merce Cunningham had written to several colleges offering guest lectures in exchange for modest payment. Cage recalls that Black Mountain eagerly accepted their invitation but had no money to pay – a financial arrangement they accepted nonetheless.[24] Both Cage and Cunningham returned to the college to participate in the highly successful summer workshops during Olson's tenure as rector of the college. The faculty comprised an eclectic group of dancers, poets, composers, and visual artists; so many skilled individuals working across diverse fields of artistic practice created prime conditions for interdisciplinary experimentation. Many scholars note that abstract expressionism would influence Robert Creeley's work, but artists such as Josef and Anni Albers, Ilya Bolotowsky, Elaine and Willem de Kooning, Franz Kline, Kenneth Noland, and Robert Motherwell worked primarily at the college during the 1940s. (In fact, Creeley's first encounter with abstract art occurred at a Jackson Pollock exhibition in Paris during the early 1950s; he later collaborated with Dan Rice [*All that is Lovely in Men* (1955)] and Fielding Dawson [*If You* (1956)] at Black Mountain.) Some of these artists were still present by the time Olson arrived, but a regrouping had occurred: the college had come under the influence of artists and dancers like Cage, Cunningham, Ray Johnson, Robert Rauschenberg, David Tudor, and Katherine Litz. The arrival of Cage, in particular, had prompted increasing interest in intermedial experimentation.

In 1952 Cage invited members of the BMC community to participate in what has since been called a prototype of the Fluxus "happening" (although Allan Kaprow is credited with inventing this term).[25] Dada is clearly a precursor to Cage's activities – most notably the soirées at the Cabaret Voltaire and their simultaneous poem-events.[26] But whereas a critic like Richard Kostelanetz argues that the happening belongs to a tradition of "mixed-means theatre," Allan Kaprow and Michael Kirby link the practice to collage, assemblage, and environmental art.[27] Despite these debates about the artistic lineage of the happening, most critics generally agree that Cage's event at BMC constitutes the first known example. Cage recalls that the event "came about through circumstances of being at Black Mountain where there were a number of people present ... many people and many possibilities" (Kostelanetz, *Conversing* 110). Two of the most influential artistic practices to emerge at mid-century – projective verse and Cage's intermedial performance

– did so from a common context of collaborative artistic production. A former student at BMC, Francine du Plessix Gray recounts that Olson championed Cage's happenings "as one of the glories of the twentieth century" ("Black Mountain" 303). Yet the entangled history of these cultural activities remains largely unexplored. In the same letter to W.H. Ferry of 7 August 1951 cited earlier, Olson makes the following assertion: "PROJECTION, with all its social consequences, is the mark of forward art today." He continues, "it is one of the best ways we find out the kinetic secrets of projective art – the very way we do it – is to put art *in action*, to join the arts *in action*, to break down all stupid walls, even the wall of art as separate from society!" ("Letter to W.H. Ferry" 13). Cage would not stage his performance until a year after Olson wrote this letter, but clearly the poet had, by at least 1951, determined that if the projective was to have "social consequences," it should extend beyond the poem as such.

Notably, Cage's performance was not the first of its kind at Black Mountain. A significant interdisciplinary event at BMC precedes it – one involving Olson with the dancer Katherine Litz, the artist Ben Shahn, and the composer Lou Harrison. On 22 July 1951 Olson wrote to Creeley that Shahn had painted "A Glyph for Charles" in return for a poem he wrote for the artist also entitled "Glyphs." Five days later, Olson wrote again, describing "a GLYPH show, Shahn, Litz, & Harrison, taking up, somehow, and using, the little verse, on the Negro boy, and the auction show" (*Correspondence* 6:177, 211). The young African American in question, to whom the poem is dedicated, is the nephew of Malrey Few, one of two cooks at Black Mountain:

"Glyphs"
(*for Alvin,& the Shahns*)

Like a race, the Negro boy said
And I wasn't sure I heard, what
Race, he said it clear
                              gathering
into his attention the auction
inside, the room
too lit, the seats
theatre soft, his foot
the instant it crossed the threshold

(as his voice) drawing
the whites' eyes off
the silver set New Yorkers
passed along the rows for weight, feel
the weight, leading
Southern summer idling evening folk
to bid up, dollar by dollar, I

beside him in the door[.]   ("Glyphs" [1951] 1–17)

The poem depicts an outing to the nearby North Carolina township that borders BMC, where Olson and the young boy unintentionally stumble upon an auction in progress. Daniel Belgrad, in *The Culture of Spontaneity*, astutely observes that the poem begins with Alvin's rather innocent analogy of the auction to a foot race, yet the implications of "race" quickly intimate "a more sinister connection" to social Darwinism, Southern segregation, and echoes of slave auctions (92–3). Olson's formal cleverness further confirms Belgrad's analysis. Several phrases feature caesuras that disrupt the natural flow of the lines with unexpected pauses, imparting a sense of hesitancy as the pair walk into the auction. The slick and airy "silver set New Yorkers" alliteratively juxtaposes against the "weight[y]" procession of "Southern[ers]," their eyes striking the boy like a jury's. The following lines offer further evidence:

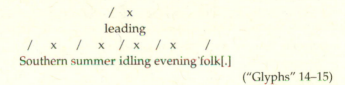

                                            ("Glyphs" 14–15)

Five consecutive trochaic feet, each ending with a suffix or gerund, slow the line to a slur, abruptly ended by a monosyllable (perhaps even an onomatopoeic pun on a racial slur). Yet the poem ends by disrupting such a concept of race. Belgrad insists, "Olson and Alvin establish a communion based on their resistance" (*The Culture of Spontaneity* 93) to the imagined community of Southern white nationalism: "I / beside him in the door" ("Glyphs" 16–17). Their companionship, Belgrad imparts, juxtaposes segregationist ideology with an altruistic conception of the "human race." Yet it is instructive to inquire further: how might this analysis apply to the collaboratively produced "Glyph Show," of which the poem was a single component?

The performance piece set around this text featured Ben Shahn's painting as a backdrop (see Figure 1), Litz performing a dance to a piece composed by Harrison, set to the words of Olson's poem. Thus, the event sought to represent a fluid conduit interlinking each genre. Olson's poem initiated Shahn's painting, which in turn inspired Litz's recital, and so on back to the poem itself. It clearly depicts a human body – likely a black body – whose skeletal and muscular features imitate the structure of a house. This may in turn function as another pun, mirroring the various connotations in Olson's poem: that is, Shahn juxtaposes the auction house (and its implications of a slave auction) with the body as one's own temple. Such a reading would reinforce Belgrad's interpretation of the poem, insofar as Olson's text solidifies a community of difference in opposition to white, Southern nationalism. The performance substitutes the exploitation of the slave economy with an economy of ethical exchange; interdisciplinary cooperation, in a sense, performs this exchange, as several "bodies" of work occupy a common space of action.

Olson's attitude towards the event is difficult to gauge. His celebratory claim "to break down all stupid walls" through inter-artistic collaboration aside, he confesses to Creeley regarding his first experience with the "Glyph show" that he did not "now know words' place in all this" (*Correspondence* 6:178). Between these extreme instances of exuberance and reticence, Olson offers a more reflective account:

> despite the wearing *closeness* of everything and everybody – the isolation and the common meals, the all-too-aesthetic compression … despite that (and a little *because* of it?), Shahn teaches Olson one hell of a lot about his verse, Kathy Litz picks up clues for pushing her own important advance in dance, Harrison makes music for Abby Shahn and others, Bernarda comes to listen to Olson when she can and shoots in shots of perception about the stuff he reads to the students which opens the eyes of sd students and lets them find out how to hear[.] ("Letter to W.H. Ferry" 9–10)

In chapter 5 I discuss the Four Horsemen, whose members make uncannily similar assertions about their performances: that once one demystifies the process of collaboration, refusing to sentimentalize

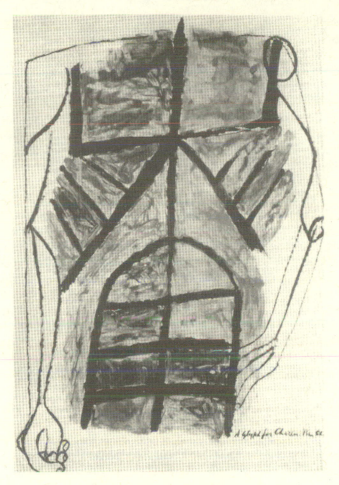

Fig. 1. Ben Shahn, "A Glyph for Charles," 1951, tempera on paper. Used with permission. Art © Estate of Ben Shahn/Licensed by VAGA, New York, NY.

a scenario of complete cooperation, collaborative activity can often generate productive conflicts, in which dispute, agreement, unity, and disruption are all part of a single arena of artistic exchange. The ad hoc collaboration between Olson, Shahn, and Litz, if nothing else, demonstrated to the BMC community the sort of intermedial opportunities available to a diverse range of artists and writers working closely together.

Cage's proto-happening took place during the summer session of 1952. Accounts of the performance differ considerably. This is, in part, due to the lack of documentation of performances such as these, but despite such problems, at least a few facts are likely. The performance took place in the dining hall and Cage chose a seating arrangement composed of four triangles, "with the apexes of the triangles merging towards the center, but not meeting" (Cage, "Interview" by Kirby and Schechner 52). Cage had sought to undermine the logic of the proscenium stage – the idea that all audience members should look in the same direction, at the exact same action: "[O]ur experience nowadays," he asserts, "is not so focused at one point. We live in, and are more and more aware of living in, the space around us." Cage acknowledges the theatre in the round, claiming that it is likely to "produce more interesting conversation afterwards or during intermission because people didn't see the same side" ("Interview" 52), but complains that it never adequately subverts the perceptual function of the proscenium stage, since it similarly fixates attention on a central set of actions, differing only by the angle one perceives an event. The triangle structure of Cage's stage creates an intersection of traffic that integrates audience and performer. Like the theatre in the round, audience members are visible to one another, but unlike its predecessor, the main action of the performance takes place outside the central space of the stage, making it unlikely that any two audience members will have an identical experience of the performance.

That Cage had chosen the dining hall as his location for the mixed-media event is not without significance. The room had social import for faculty and students at the college as a meeting ground for artistic exchange, and Cage himself had befriended several students who regularly met with him in the hall: "[w]hat I think was so important at Black Mountain was that we all ate our meals together … I would sit at a table three times a day (laughs) and there would be conversations. And those meals were the classes. And ideas would come out, what McLuhan called the 'brushing of information.' Just conversation" (Held Jr qtd. in Kostelanetz, *Conversing* 266).[28] Cage managed to integrate this aspect of Black Mountain's communal culture into the performance: empty styrofoam cups were placed on each seat and it is recorded by him and others that coffee was served (although some chose to use the cups as ashtrays). Cage claims to be indifferent about the significance of this gesture; he merely notes that no explanation was given as to its import, only that "the performance was concluded by a kind of ritual,

pouring coffee into each cup" (Cage, "Interview" by Kirby and Schechner 53). Given his meticulous attention to context and his emphasis
on the dining hall as a communal space (and elsewhere his interest in
mushrooms), it is fair to argue the stimulant serves as a catalyst – encouraging audience members to "wake up." But, more importantly,
coffee's "ritual" function serves to encourage *conversation*. Indeed, one
of the central functions of stage organization and the larger context of a
performance, Cage remarks, is to elicit "conversation afterwards" (52).

If the historical accuracy of the stage structure and space of the
performance is relatively dependable, the number of participants involved in the piece and their individual contributions is somewhat
less certain.[29] Based on numerous interviews and memoirs provided
by participants and audience members, it is likely that the performance included the following: (1) John Cage read from his Juilliard
lecture; (2) Robert Rauschenberg's "white paintings" were suspended
from the ceiling above the audience; (3) he also played records on
a gramophone during the performance; (4) Charles Olson and M.C.
Richards read their poetry from a ladder; (5) David Tudor played a
prepared piece on the piano; (6) Merce Cunningham and an undis-
closed number of his troupe danced in the aisles; and (7) a film played
against one of the walls of the dining hall. In addition to these seven
components, a dog in attendance decided to participate in the festivities, barking and chasing Cunningham as he danced. All accounts
suggest that the audience members enjoyed themselves, except for
the composer Stefan Wolpe, who left mid-performance in protest. The
most remarkable aspect of the various accounts of the event is a tendency to recall form but not content. Every record of the performance
cites Olson's reading from a ladder but no one is exactly sure which
poem he read. Several attendees mention the gramophone, yet there
is disagreement about the music played. For instance, Francine du
Plessix Gray was confident that Edith Piaf records were played at increased speed, while David Weinrib insists that they were popular records from the 1920s and 1930s. Audience members tend to fixate on
the intersection of multiple registers of data, rather than the content
of information conveyed. The simultaneity of these different actions,
coupled with a stage set-up that both utilizes multiple surfaces of the
room and integrates performers and audience members, resists a totalizing impression of the event. Instead, the audience must fixate on
partial elements of the performance, which might include focusing on
the verbal-visual-tactile aspect of one element or a cluster of elements.

To use Cage's apt phrase, a given artistic form "brushes" against another, generating unexpected points of connection.

Cage's performances, and subsequent happenings by artists such as Allan Kaprow and Claes Oldenburg, often elicit the misinterpretation that such events lack structure. Although the raucous dog seems emblematic of the seemingly chaotic show, Cage devised a series of overlapping "time brackets" within which individual contributors were permitted to perform. He generated these "brackets" aleatorically, and then assigned each discrete practice a number of segments during the event when the performer was free to play. Cage likens this framing structure to "a green light in traffic," creating indeterminate connections between artists within relatively broad and flexible limitations (Cage, "Interview" by Kirby and Schechner 53). Martin Duberman criticizes this decision, suggesting that such constraints compromise the total spontaneity that happenings ostensibly seek to achieve, but Cage and other practitioners of Fluxus events insist that the happening never promises total freedom, if what is meant by this notion is the complete absence of structure. Instead, Cage seeks to eliminate any model of organization that arranges the elements of composition into a complete, unified work; the aleatorically generated time brackets create zones within the happening in which a given combination of objects, agents, and instruments might produce unexpected inter-artistic results.

Cage, therefore, jettisons the typical conventions of traditional theatre such as linear progression or narrative closure.[30] That is, the BMC performance presents a nexus of simultaneous practices with no predetermined relationship to one another, nor a unifying framework to which they are subordinate. The "composition" of a happening, Kaprow remarks, involves a "collage of events in certain spans of time and in certain spaces"; "The field" of a happening "is created as one goes along" (*Assemblage, Environments, & Happenings* 198, 159). Its materials may be pre-chosen, but no formal organization that would predetermine the relationship between these elements should be employed. It is better, remarks Kaprow, "to let the form emerge from what the materials can do" (202). The audience member, therefore, is free to generate connections between the various events, objects, and tasks that populate the space of action.

Despite agreement among critics as to the origins of the happening at Black Mountain, debates regarding the definition of the practice and its historical formation tend to ignore the role of the BMC community – despite Cage's own claim that the happening was a consequence of

Black Mountain itself: an aesthetic materialization of the community's resources, as it were. Kaprow studied with Cage at the New School for Social Research in New York during the late 1950s; his practice and theorization of the happening overlaps significantly with Cage's work and teachings. It is for this reason that Kaprow's use of the word "field" to describe the interaction of elements in the happening deserves pause. There is no evidence that Kaprow borrows this term directly from Olson, and of course, there are striking differences between Olson's and Cage/Kaprow's aesthetics. For instance, although Olson advocates a radical collapse of disciplinary boundaries in his letter to W.H. Ferry, in the "Projective Verse" essay, he maintains that the field of the poem and the field of reality are homologous but ultimately separate ontological orders. Thus, he never attempts the radical conflation of art and life that Cage does in a piece like 4'33" (1952). Moreover, Olson is suspicious of Cage's mode of aleatoric composition, which, although it seemingly reflects Olson's call for a non-egoistic poetics, requires an abnegation of authorial control that Olson is not prepared to relinquish.

Yet if one accepts my claim that open form's principal function is social, and if Olson's expressed desire for projection to join the arts in action is to be believed, then similarities between these cultural practices seem more plausible. In fact, Olson's operative concepts of process, interaction, and change are also the ideas that guide the happening, its refusal of hierarchy, unity, and completion. Field composition is a practice that explores the kinetic relationship *between things*, between the "participants" that compose the area of the poem as a field of forces: "every element in an open poem … must be managed in their relations to each other" (*PV* 243). "Work[ing] in OPEN," as Olson calls it, refers to the makeshift capacity to adapt to the immediate, continuously changing conditions that a given circumstance demands. Levertov's assertion that no single element in the process of composition should supervise the others and Duncan's claim that the poem's area of composition determines its elements cohere with Kaprow's description of the happening as a "field" whose parts assemble in the process of a work's unfolding. The poem/happening is an "energy construct" of material, semiotic, and social flows, whose intelligibility, recalling Latour's assertion, the reader/viewer must discern by tracing the "associations between heterogeneous elements" (*Reassembling* 5). Cage's final sentence in his Julliard lecture, read as part of the BMC happening, is telling: "a piece of string, and a sunset, possessing neither, each acts" ("Julliard Lecture" 111). Not only does the happening jettison any totalizing structure, it permits dissimilar objects, agents, materials, and modes of signifying to occupy and interact within a common zone of action. Both cultural practices emerge within a common milieu at Black Mountain, where poets and artists were attempting to conceive a politics of open affiliation in opposition to the dominant communal paradigms of capitalism and nationalism. Both art forms underscore a makeshift, local community of things that Olson states must be forged "inside totality."

Polis and Totality in *The Maximus Poems*

[F]irst I tell you their names and places, to indicate how I am of the heterogeneous present and not of the old homogeneity of the Founders, and the West.

– Charles Olson[31]

In 1959 the poet and editor David Ignatow wrote to Charles Olson soliciting a poem for inclusion in a special issue of *Chelsea*. The purpose of the issue: to bring "together the best political poetry being written today" and thus resume the "prominence" given to political themes "in the early 20s & 30s" ("Letter" n.p.).[32] The context for such a statement is not difficult to decipher. A vast industry of anecdotal lyricism had dominated the poetic landscape for the better part of a decade. Presumably, Ignatow would have expected a like-minded statement from the writer who admonished "the-private-soul-at-any-public-wall" (*PV* 239). Yet his request elicited the following response by Olson:

> Right off the top don't quite get what you propose as 'political' … [A]re [you] talking abt. the drop, since the '30s, of the social subject – like the old 'Left' … I lead to you, simply that both Duncan and myself, say, have been for years doing nothing but poems almost of – in his case, *polity*, in my own *polis* (the Maximus, now coming out as Volume 3 in March etc) … I see no reason not to think that exactly the 'political' is what is … conspicuously corrupt as in present existence (both scale-wise: bipartisanism; world-wise: universalism[.] (*Selected Letters* 267–8)

Olson adds the following marginal note in longhand: "the conception & the creation of a society is the act of politics, is it not?" (267). This objection cuts to the core of Olson's understanding of writing, both as a method of composition and as the construction of a social theory: in order to imagine a different configuration of the political, one would have to reconfigure the social formations through and in which politics is practiced. For Olson, the question of politics is inexorably bound to issues of subjectivity and collectivity.

The first twenty sections of Olson's long poem were first published in two runs by Jonathan Williams's Jargon press: *The Maximus Poems / 1 – 10* in October 1953 and *The Maximus Poems / 11 – 22* in the fall of 1956. The first four poems were written between May 1950 and January 1953, either at his Washington residence or at Black Mountain, and would undergo more substantial revision than most of the subsequent poems, while sections five through twenty-two were mainly written between the period of March and May 1953 at the college. Composed mainly as "letters," Olson would read the first twenty-two poems at BMC in August of that year. The remaining fifteen poems, which together make up the first volume of *The Maximus Poems*, were written during the last years of the decade in Gloucester, Massachusetts, the setting for Olson's verse epic.

The first and all subsequent editions of the text feature a dedication and an epigraph on a single page at the beginning of the volume:

for ROBERT CREELEY
    – the Figure of Outward

All my life I've heard
one makes many[.]

The dedication to Olson's friend excerpts an unpublished poem entitled "For R.C.," while the second epigraph is yet more cryptic. Olson appropriates the phrase from Cornelia Williams, one of the cooks at Black Mountain. He describes the following scenario to Creeley in a letter dated 1 June 1953:

        (this bright Cornelia, the cook,
says today:
    all my life I've heard, "One
    makes many"
        and it sounded
    like the epigraph fit to go with the
    Figure
        Or to be
    IT! ...[.]   ("Letter to Robert Creeley" 4)

George Butterick notes that Olson would repeat this phrase in several other contexts. In his copy of Whitehead's *Process and Reality*, he highlights the following statement: "the term 'many' presupposes the term 'one,' and the term 'one' presupposes the term 'many,'" adding in the margin: "*exactly* Cornelia Wms, Black Mt kitchen, 1953." Elsewhere in his notebook, Olson calls the epigraph "'the dominating paradox on which *Max* complete ought to stand'" (qtd. in Butterick, *A Guide* 4–5). Butterick thus concludes that Williams's statement was for Olson a quintessential expression of "the fundamental problems of thought and politics, the problem of 'the One and the Many'" (4). In Williams's dictum and the passage that Olson underlines in his copy of *Process and Reality*, however, it is not simply a matter of the relationship of the One *to* the Many but that the One *makes* Many. The relationship between subject and other is co-dependent, and thus irreducible to stable categories of either the individual or society.

As I have argued, Olson was far more engaged with issues of community during the early 1950s than is typically acknowledged. His collaborative approach to poetic method, his writings about Black Mountain as an institution, and his interdisciplinary practice all suggest that issues of social collectivism preoccupied the poet. The early poems that make up the first volume of *The Maximus Poems*, which were largely composed at BMC, indicate a similar point of focus. A cursory glance at the text confirms this: Olson advances his concept of the "polis" in the form of a sequence of letters addressed to the citizens of Gloucester. That said, although Olson's reference to a statement made by the cook at BMC and his anticipation of Creeley's arrival at the college frame the first volume of Olson's long poem, it would be an error to read this text biographically. Rather, the epigraph and dedication both suggest that *The Maximus Poems* emerge amid a growing debate about the nature of community, and it is within this context that one should assess the text.

As early as 1945, Olson indicates in various notebooks that he wished to write a long poem on the subject of the West. In its earliest manifestations, this was a poem that would encapsulate an expansive and detailed survey of civilizations from the "earliest man in Am[erica]" to his own epoch.[33] Olson gradually abandoned this project; increasingly, he would question whether such a poem was even feasible, or whether "American experience [is] too stiff, historical, unfabled for use?" ("The Long Poem" 38). Between 1948, when Olson first records these concerns in his notebook, and 1953, at which point the first volume of *Maximus* evolves into a poem with a recognizable structure, Olson's approach to the long poem would undergo a radical transformation: towards a notion of the epic as local and a genealogical method intended to demystify history. In so doing, Olson modifies a significant convention of the epic by adapting a genre usually reserved for proclamations on the nation or the genesis of a civilization to an experience of immediate and tactile community.[34] Hence, the majority of the first twenty sections of *Maximus* are "letters" addressed from Maximus to the city. As an extension of localism, the epistolary genre conflates the private and public, using a personal form for a public address. Readers of *The Maximus Poems* observe that by 1948 the author's consternation with the yet "unfabled" history of America indicates that he still conceived of his planned epic in mythological terms. Just as Olson reframes his epic as an examination of the local, by 1953, in notes entitled "West" and "Post-West," Olson's distrust of abstraction leads him to reject a poetic economy of "Symbols": "not even the Virgin … [is] more than a wooden statue" ("Post-West" 54). In *Maximus*, the speaker echoes this sentiment:

Venus

does not arise from

these waters. Fish

do.   ("The Song and Dance of" *MP* 1:57–8)

The poet must proceed by "precise FACTS … thus, flatly, 'historical,' the flattest, literal substances, persons, names, places, things, dates" ("Post-West" 54). Symbolism functions like "Money," insofar as symbols "stand in the place of" and thus obfuscate the material labour that brings a society into being ("West" 47). To write a history of Gloucester – indeed, to record the formation of any community – one must proceed by presenting such a process as the collective, material production of its citizenry. Against the depth of metaphor, Olson's technique involves the "flatness" of metonymy. Complementing the practice of field composition, *Maximus* traces a nexus of connections among the constellation of persons, places, and things that compose its relations.

Just as field composition is meant to express a particular stance towards reality, Olson's changing approach to methodology and genre reflects his philosophy of collective being. The following passage is taken from his notebooks in preparation for *Maximus*: "[t]hus the personal (which is intimate, & where desire moves personal over to another … one must speak of a third place, force, engagement to the modern dualism of Individual & Society." This "3rd being," he tells us, "what used to be called Family, previously was Gen[eration]s (?), and needs now to be as wholly reconceived & newly created as does the concept of Self (& whatever is coming as 'Society' – the present Totalitarian State only a stage of passage)" ("West" 47). Echoing the epigraph he borrows from Cornelia Williams, the poet's task is not simply to elucidate the relationship between the one (individual) and the many (society), but rather to overhaul these categories by contesting their antithetical foundations. In *The Special View of History*, Olson complains that "it is a lie of discourse" to generate this distinction (25). The "personal," in Olson's lexicon, should not be confused with an inward-turning narcissism. Quite the opposite in fact: the problem, he states, is that the "personal" – the desire to move "over to," to connect with others – is enclosed and contained within rigid unities such as the "Family" or "Generation." Like Creeley, Olson rarely addresses war explicitly, but his reference to totalitarianism suggests that he was painstakingly aware of the dangers of nationalism. Olson resists equally narcissistic declarations of individualism and homogenizing ideologies of nationhood. The project of *The Maximus Poems*, then, is to present the "personal" energies of Gloucester – that is, to investigate how a particular social space, a community, comes to be the social formation of geography and individuals, institutions and discourses that it is. But against the tendency to abstract a unity from such an investigation, and thus present a static vision of community, Olson endeavours to preserve the multiplicity of affiliations that emerge.

His refusal to impose static sociological categories on the citizens of Gloucester bears an uncanny similarity to his discussion of Black Mountain as a permeable, social environment. Of course, Gloucester is not Black Mountain, and the social space of the college is not the textual space of Olson's poem. Rather, Olson argues that the discursive field of the text can also function as a site of social exchange. The response by the speaker of *Maximus* to Vincent Ferrini regarding the social function of the little magazine demonstrates the point:

A magazine does have this 'life' to it (proper to it), does have streets,
can show lights, movie houses, bars, and, occasionally,

for those of us who do live our life quite properly in print

as properly, say, as Gloucester people live in Gloucester

you do meet someone[.]   ("Letter 5" [1953] *MP* 1:24)

The little magazine and Gloucester each consists of an ontology quite *"proper* to it"; that is, each functions as a distinct social field of action. Olson means by "polis" a "meeting place" – a site of communal exchange that can take place in a correspondence, a geographical location, a little magazine, or a poem. Polis, then, is mobile and can adapt to the changing conditions of contemporary life.

The poet's most candid definition of his term appears in an essay entitled "Definitions by Undoings." Referring to the ancient Greek notion of the ideal city, in its baldest sense, Olson uses it to denote "the community or body of citizens, ... [their] being as group with will" (11). Elsewhere in an essay written in 1952 he elaborates that the "State," "The System" was beginning to envelope "the very whole world," threatening total homogeneity and concentration of power. The stated function of "polis" is "to invert totality – to oppose it" (qtd. in Butterick, *A Guide* 25). If one recalls Olson's preferred metaphors for articulating the constitution of a social subject – the amalgamation of atoms, the intersection of city streets, or the rhizomatic character of weeds – the emphasis has been on a protean collective irreducible to the static opposition of the One and the Many. The possibilities of a social theory emphasizing process and change, for Olson, is a community evading totality – but, importantly, this is both the totality of "Society" and the totality of the "Self."

In the early poems collected in *Maximus*, Olson promptly introduces two alternative models of collectivism: "polis" and "pejorocracy." The latter term is borrowed from Pound's *Pisan Cantos* (LXXIX); derived from Latin, it loosely means "worse-rule." First appearing in "The Kingfishers," the speaker of the poem hints at the socio-economic policy of post-war America: "with what violence benevolence is bought / what cost in gesture justice brings" ("The Kingfishers" 162–3). In *The Maximus Poems* Olson elaborates, describing pejorocracy as the discourse of all financial and political exploitation: "the trick / of corporations, newspapers, slick magazines, movie houses" – what Olson refers to as the "musicracket of all ownership" ("Letter 3" [1952], "The Songs" [1953] *MP* 1:10, 14). Although this list of offenders initially seems like a somewhat vague denunciation of all capitalist motives, Olson is specifically concerned with the role of language in strategies of capitalist-state control. Olson's poetry is rarely topical, but it is indeed political, particularly when government or corporate coercion infiltrates the practice of everyday life. For instance, the first mention of "pejorocracy" is in reference to the "twitter" of the streetcars in Oregon; contemporary readers would have identified this allusion to the music piped into public transit to pacify commuters ("I, Maximus" [1950] *MP* 1:3). The "mu-sick, mu-sick, mu-sick" (1:3) of government seeks to produce "docile bodies," as Foucault would suggest, achieved through a "gentle way of punishment" (*Discipline and Punish* 104). The discourse of worse-rule is a function of a state whose incipient strategies are to train habitual compliance among its citizenry.

"Mu-sick" is thus the language of a community dispossessed of the right to govern itself. Although commentators such as Michael Bernstein question the capacity of such "code-words to carry … [the] weight of concrete analysis and emotional conviction" (*The Tale of the Tribe* 260), the concept elsewhere yields more awareness of the erosion of civic politics by the amalgamation of state and corporate power. The following passage from "Letter 15" provides an example of Olson's mode of investigation:

> The American epos, 19-
>
> 02 (or when did Barton Barton Barton Barton and Barton?
>
>   To celebrate
>
>   how it can be, it is
>
>   padded or uncomforted, your lost, you
>
>   found, your
>
>   sneakers
>
>   (o Statue,
> o Republic, o
>   Tell-A-Vision …[.]   ("Letter 15" [1953] *MP* 1:71)

An "American epos, 19- / 02" likely refers to Brooks Adams's study, *The New Empire*, which offers 1902 as the inaugural year of America's emergence as a world power. Olson thought enough of the book to review it in the summer 1954 issue of the *Black Mountain Review*, where he summarizes its thesis: "in civilization nothing is at rest, the movement is trade, the necessity is metal and the consequent centralization of power also moves" ("Rev. of *The New Empire*" 63). The humorous repetition of

"Barton" in the next line refers to a founding member of Batten, Barton, Durnstine, and Osborne, one of the largest advertising companies in the United States during the first half of the twentieth century. Olson makes no causal connection between these allusions, but instead arranges a nexus of names and objects paratactically across the field of the poem. The reader is invited to investigate the associations between American imperialism and the emergence of advertising, while the "Statue" and the "Tell-A-Vision" enjoy an equivalent status as artefacts that advance a nationalist ideology. The indented column of text bears the trace of a more cryptic allusion. An earlier version of the poem reads: "your lost, your / found, you / seekers," which, given the following reference to a statue, is likely an allusion to the famous poetic inscription at the base of the Statue of Liberty: "Give me your tired, your poor, / Your huddled masses yearning to breath free."[35] Not unlike Hobbes's *Leviathan*, the Statue of Liberty homologizes the social body of the nation, while its inscription gives voice to that collective body that promises a place for the disenfranchised. America as an assembly of the lost undergoes a cynical revision, becoming a "lost and found" where one goes to retrieve misplaced valuables. Olson concludes this section of "Letter 15" with a mangled jingle for Coca-Cola: "is for Cokes by Cokes out of / Pause."

Butterick observes that Olson's syntactically odd phrase may parody typical slogans from the time period. Compare the line again with these examples:

"Busy people pause for Coke.
The Pause that Refreshes."   (qtd. in Butterick, *A Guide* 108)[36]

The first example reads as a four-beat line, with the slight chance of a minor variant in emphasis:

/ x   / x   /   x   /
Busy | people | pause for | Coke.

/ x   / x   /   x   /
Busy | people | pause | for Coke.

Either the line reads as three trochees in succession with a final stress on the monosyllabic noun, or, alternatively, the reader could pause on the word "pause," making the final foot an iamb. In each case, the apparent sing-song quality of the line is precisely what Olson wishes to disrupt:

```
x x   /   x   /   x   x
is for Cokes by Cokes out of

  /
Pause[.]
```
                                                      ("Letter 15" *MP* 1:71)

Indeed, the speaker of the poem deliberately convolutes any assignable rhythm to the line. Isolation of the word "Pause" should encourage the reader to interpret the term in its poetic context. A pause in metre can organize and regulate rhythm, but it can also disrupt it. In the example of the Coke jingle above, uniform pauses divide poetic feet and regiment the duration of speech; in Olson's parodic culture jam, a line break upsets an expected metre, causing one to pause at the word "pause" – hence, Olson teases out yet another of the word's connotations as a contemplative act, a self-reflexive gesture that invites the reader to interrogate the implications of sound in the production of sense. The phrase "Cokes out of" puns on "coax," reinforcing a reading of the poem as a disruption of rhythm and what Olson perceives as the function of the jingle to lull the community into a habitual pattern of control. When Olson elsewhere proclaims that "as the line goes so goes / the Nation" he has in mind a relationship between the syntax of a language, the organization of words into larger units of meaning, and community, the mode of social organization by which human beings structure human interaction. It is this relationship between discourse and action that frames the underlying dilemma announced at the beginning of the text: how does one proceed by "the / ear" and "where shall you listen / when all is become billboards" ("I, Maximus" *MP* 1:2)? Ultimately, Olson's point is that any resistance to the coercive rhetoric of government and corporate power requires that one be able to "listen," to read the rhythms of nationalism and fiscal exploitation as those "who use words cheap."

In opposition to the community of worse-rule, Olson offers his concept of the "polis" or "ideal city." Clearly it is not Olson's contention that Gloucester has achieved such a status, but rather he imparts that laid buried in any city is the capacity for polis to exist. Assertions like these risk accusations of utopianism, but the concept of community advanced in *Maximus* is, in fact, decidedly anti-utopian, if what one means by this notion is a pre-conceived definition of the perfect society. After Olson left the Roosevelt administration, he refused any allegiance to a political party. As I cite at the beginning of the chapter, Olson advises that one accept neither the Left nor the Right of political discourse, nor "stay / in the middle, where they'll get you, the 'Germans' / will" ("The Song and

Dance of" *MP* 1:54). Olson refers in his Berkeley lecture to the Cold War politics of "America and Russia," and the rise of the military industrial complex during the 1950s, as that "Great Business Conspiracy" (*Reading at Berkeley* 14) whose polarizing strategies merely recapitulate strict adherence to a pathological xenophobia. Michael Bernstein observes that Olson is "equally dismissive of monopoly capitalism and state socialism," and hence the impracticality of Olson's polis, which, according to Bernstein, is therefore a "utopian dream" (*The Tale of the Tribe* 263). Bernstein's frustration is understandable, but if the complaint is that Olson does not supply the prescriptive political program to replace monopoly capitalism and/or statist socialism, then perhaps this is too much to ask of the poet. Olson's quite prescient suspicion of an emergent world order of government and corporate collusion aptly characterizes the late twentieth century. But Bernstein's criticism also reveals a more endemic problem of representation: if Olson were to circumscribe a concrete vision of an ideal society then he will generate precisely the sort of rigid truths that utopianism engenders. One should keep in mind that the eradication of "non-Germans" and the erection of an Aryan state were conceived by its proponents as a utopian project. That Olson's renunciation of the left/right political opposition occupies the field of the poem with an allusion to Nazism invites the reader to identify the polarizing ideological manoeuvres common to each historical moment and political circumstance. It is Olson's contention that both advance notions of community predicated on foundational myths of ethnic purity or national superiority. Marxist critics like Terry Eagleton and Raymond Williams make this point: "we can, after all, describe the future only in terms drawn from the past or present; and a future which broke radically with the present would have us straining at the limits of our language" (Eagleton, *Why Marx Was Right* 74); ultimately, our actions can only be guided by an axiomatic commitment to unqualified equality, a commitment "to ensure the means of life, and the means of community. But what will then, by these means, be lived, we cannot know or say." (Williams, *Culture and Society* 321). In chapter 4 we encounter a feminist poetics that revives a prescriptive, even universal conception of the political (albeit one very different from a liberal-humanist notion of universalism). For Olson and his collaborators, their project is to identify the conditions that would bring a community of equals into being. That every element counts, that every element bears an equal status in relation to any other, applies equally to the textual field of the poem and the political field of social life. It is in this sense that the epigraph to *Maximus* is most instructive because it imagines a community that is irreducible either to the "One" of atomistic selfhood (i.e., I am the only one that counts) or the Many of homogenous nationalism (the Many that makes itself a One).

In "Letter 3" of *Maximus*, the poet comments: "As the people of the earth are now, Gloucester / is heterogeneous, and so can know polis" (1:10). In "The Present Is Prologue" he contrasts the "heterogeneous present" to the "old homogeneity of the Founders, and the West" (39). Olson's statement in this essay precedes an autobiographical note about his mixed Swedish-Hungarian parentage, but in light of the evolution of his long poem – his rejection of the West as a model for an epic – it is clear that Olson is increasingly suspicious of any notion of community that begins from homogenous foundations (the nation, the volk, the party, etc.). As a prerequisite for polis to occur, "heterogeneity" disrupts originary myths of racial supremacy or geographical entitlement by insisting that the "group with will" is from the beginning always already a multiplicity. Maximus's address to his city in the same letter illustrates this point: "o tansy city, root city / let them not make you / as the nation is" ("Letter 3" *MP* 1:11). It is enticing to read the first line of this passage as a nostalgic vision of a pre-industrial "city of nature," but further consideration of the allusion suggests otherwise. Tansy is a rhizomatous herb, which Olson recounts "'was brought on the bottom of bags in cargoes'" by early settlers of Gloucester (qtd. in Butterick, *A Guide* 22). Hence, the plant's proliferation bears testimony to patterns of migration. Olson will make this assertion explicitly later in *Maximus*: "we who throw down hierarchy, / who say the history of weeds / is a history of man" ("Maximus, at Tyre and at Boston" *MP* 1:94). Significantly, this phrase is appropriated from botanist Edgar Anderson's study, *Plants, Man and Life*. The original context of Anderson's assertion is instructive:

> Fennel, radish, wild oat, all of these plants are Mediterraneans. In those countries they mostly grow pretty as they do in California, at the edges of towns, on modern dumps and ancient ruins, around Greek temples and in the barbed-wire enclosures of concentration camps. Where did they come from? They have been with man too long for any quick answer. They were old when Troy was new. Some of them are certainly Asiatic, some African, many of them are mongrels in the strictest technical sense. Theirs is a long and complicated story, a story just now beginning to be unraveled but about which we already know enough to state, without fear of successful contradiction, that *the history of weeds is the history of man*. (15; my italics)

By virtue of their common lineage, Anderson contends, a given weed might reveal the origin and development of human societies. But perhaps as well, Olson would have taken notice that most weeds are hybrids, their material bodies heterogeneous "mongrels" of multiple plant forms, having the capacity to adapt to diverse ecological environments. Applied to the "history of man," the passage aptly characterizes Olson's genealogical method in tracing the "tangled history" (16) of Gloucester as a rhizomatous assemblage of individuals and events, social formations and migratory routes.

Localism for Olson is hence not antithetical to cosmopolitanism exactly. It is not, to use Creeley's predilection for deictic elements, the xenophobic preservation of a *here* and *now* from external factors threatening its present constitution. The "heterogeneous present" marks a collective will to know its own mongrel history, a function of polis that demystifies myths of cultural purity; but it also marks an economy of use – not unlike the way I have argued "working in OPEN" involves a localist capacity to adapt to the immediate conditions that a given environment demands. In *Maximus*, the "tansy city" is a collectively organized, self-managed community in contrast to the state's top-down rule of law. The nation is that multiplicity forfeiting its "heterogeneity," becoming a singular, reducible entity:

> I speak to any of you, not to you all, to no group, not to you as citizens …
> 　　　　… Polis now
> is a few, is a coherence not even yet new (the island of this city
> is a mainland now of who? who can say who are
> citizens?　　　　　　　　　　　　　　　　　　　　　(1:11)

The word "few" typically designates an immediate and intimate group of individuals. But Olson fixates on the term as a numerical quantity. Frequently assigned an indefinite article, "a few" is not a fixed number. It names an intimate yet unquantifiable sum that resists atomized selfhood and the totalizing "you all" of nationhood. It is a newly formed "coherence" or provisional unity and its citizens possess no fixed properties: "who can say who are citizens?" (1:11).

Yet this is a selective reading, one that certainly gives Olson the benefit of all doubts. The women of Black Mountain routinely asked who counts as a citizen. It was said previously that a patently gendered call to arms features prominently in Olson's "Projective Verse": "there it is, brothers ... go by it, boys." More insidiously, however, the title's militaristic evocations signal an often aggressive and exclusionary masculine posture. Rachel Blau DuPlessis acutely observes that the projective suggests both a violent and a phallic thrust of "(projectile (percussive (projective" movements, penetrating the space of the page by way of a ballistic image. "These words," she explains, "(re)claim poetry for masculine discourse, making poetry safe for men to enter, making poetry a serious discourse of assertive, exploratory, and sometimes aggressive manhood" ("Manifests" 45). Consider as well that the metaphor of the missile – its planned launch and predetermined descent towards a selected target – grossly contradicts the purpose of projective verse as a content determined in the act of composition.

One finds this compromised vision of an open form community elsewhere in Black Mountain's cultural work. Olson's speaker insists adamantly in *Maximus* that a magazine, like Gloucester, can have polis, yet Olson's overbearing personality could sometimes undermine his commitment to co-operative publishing. The founding of *Origin* is instructive in this regard. At approximately the same time "Projective Verse" first appeared in 1950, Olson and Creeley had each begun an important correspondence with an upstart editor by the name of Cid Corman. Creeley had tried and failed months earlier to start his own magazine called *The Lititz Review*; although he was forced to abandon the venture, he had solicited a substantial number of poems, many of which Corman would later use to launch the first volume of *Origin*. In turn, Corman's magazine would act as a central meeting place for a network of poets who later contributed to the *Black Mountain Review*. A triadic relationship evolved between the three men, since Olson sent many of Corman's letters to Creeley with his comments. The three men planned a collaborative special issue that would introduce Olson's theories of open form writing. Corman, for his part, was adamant that although the magazine would provide an alternative to the post-war lyric endorsed by the New Critics, it would not advance a dogmatic agenda. His letters indicate that he was wary of Olson's dismissive attitude to mainstream publications like the *Hudson Review*, insisting that his "program ... will be a positive one," foregoing the usual "vindictive attacks" (29).[37] A little magazine, he insists, should function "[n]ot as competition, but as community," establishing "the continuity and relation of writers" (244–5).

A sense of proprietorship on Olson's part invariably infiltrated what had begun in earnest as an attempt to document the gradual emergence of a literary network. Recalling Francine du Plessix Gray's deft assessment, Olson seemed always both more "iconoclastic and dictatorial" than his collaborators. For instance, at Corman's suggestion of a forty-page section in the magazine devoted to Olson alone, he has this to say:

> what would be much better than this one man (what could almost be anonymous, the work issuing in its course, and, by that work alone the men be known) is this hot:
>
> 50 pages to be a movement, a composing fr the shifting correspondence of two writers, poems and stories coming up in the progress of that correspondence, the nature of it also representing examinations of what key points on the whole front of life & work today that correspondence get to[.] (58)

Such an assertion testifies not only to Olson's emphasis on process, but also the degree to which field composition should be understood as a co-production between Creeley and himself. Any attempt at simulating the evolution of Olson's poetics would be more accurately represented by a synthesis of he and Creeley's work, by "50 pages of woven stuff from the heads & hands of two men" (60). Elsewhere in a letter composed on 3 May 1951, Olson expands on this notion of the magazine as a nexus of communal expression:

> … any given issue of ORIGIN will have maximum force as it is conceived by its editor as a FIELD OF FORCE …
>
> that is, that, as agent of this collective (which ORIGIN is going to be) the question is larger than, yr taste, alone: it is the same sort of confrontation as – in any given poem – a man faces: how much energy has he got in, to make the thing stand on its own feet as, a force, in, the fields of force which surround everyone of us, of which we, too, are forces: to stand FORTH. (139, 141)

Olson conceives of the little magazine in projectivist terms, wherein editorial collectivism eschews the "individual ego" and positions the selections within an issue as "participants" in a field of force relations. Between the subjective (egoistic) program of a single editor's personal taste and the flimsy eclecticism of magazines that claim non-partisanship is a possible conception of the magazine volume as a unit of composition born from an objectist stance towards reality, in which "units are juxtaposed" to "declare" a communal aesthetics (141).

Olson advances an exciting idea, but the focus on him and Creeley alone indicates a desire for control on Olson's part that understandably prompted Corman's suspicion.[38] Indeed, if Olson's suggestion that their work remain anonymous seems half-hearted, the word "movement" seems to slip from its emphasis on the fluid aesthetic interchange between two writers into a more programmatic "movement" as an advance-guard ideology. By the end of this passage in Olson's letter, he reminds the young editor that such an approach is merited by the implicit assumption he attributes to Corman: "that, the two of us, are central to, your conception of, the MAG" (59). The first issue of *Origin: A Quarterly for the Creative* appeared in April 1951. Given the range of its contents, it would seem Corman agreed with Olson that a magazine should include letters, essays, and other supporting materials that contextualize the poetry and chronicle the development of a literary community. He opted, however, for the initial plan of forty pages devoted to the work of Olson, with a similar feature section in the second issue allotted for Creeley. Corman jettisons Olson's plan for a magazine that charts the integrated poetics of two writers; he chose instead to expand this community of correspondents.

The decisions of Olson and Corman each have their benefits and limitations. Had Corman documented the emergence of open form as a *practice* developed between Olson and Creeley, as the former encouraged him to do so, then from the outset field composition's social function might have been better understood. Yet, by playing Amy Lowell to Olson's Pound, Corman rightly made a democratic "beer garden" of a poetic practice that would no doubt have come under Olson's sometimes possessive authority. Which, in the final analysis, aptly analogizes both the impressive contribution and the ultimate limitation of Olson's cultural poetics. He insisted that poetry should embody an emancipatory vision, that indeed literature can propose to politics a different configuration of its space. The poem, he insists, is a "polis" awaiting enactment. Yet his poetry and his cultural work at BMC fulfil this project only partially. No doubt this makes him human, but one should not apologize for the sexism and occasional elitism that pervades both the poetry of *Maximus* and the political project of Black Mountain. In a sense, what remains of this chapter, and then taken up again in the fourth one, pursues this tension between field composition as a masculine discourse and as a poetics "woven" by a litany of hands. That is, how open form poetry originates is only part of the story; how others adapt and transform it is another.

For Love Revisited: Robert Creeley and the Politics of Friendship

In an undated poem likely written some years after Robert Creeley's tenure at Black Mountain, the poet reflects on his experience at the college:

"An Ode"

    (for Black Mt. College)

There is this side of it.

…

And why not. One is much too
repentant. The secrets are
to be shared.

Why go to college. Or, as a man said, it
is too far away.

Why go.   ("An Ode" 1, 6–11)[39]

The question "[w]hy go" has several connotations. Creeley had attended Harvard during the early 1940s, opting to leave the university before completing an undergraduate degree.[40] Moreover, he had visited Black Mountain before accepting a teaching position at the college. Creeley travelled there during the mid-1940s to visit his partner and eventual first wife, Ann, who had enrolled at BMC to study art and music. Apparently, he disliked the college and its students, later complaining to Olson in a letter dated 28 September 1950 that "there was no quiet, or no root in any of it" (Buttrick, *Correspondence* 3:43). The additional reference to an unnamed "man" provides another possible explanation. Creeley had said famously about Olson that their friendship was "a practical college of information and stimulus" (Creeley, "Interview" by Ossman 7). To "go to college" would mean Creeley's first physical encounter with a friend with whom he had corresponded for the better part of five years.

Biographer Ekbert Faas notes the "constantly regrouping friendships and literary allegiances" (*Robert Creeley* 156) that dominated the poet's social life during the early to mid-1950s, yet this is an observation one might also extend, more properly speaking, to his literary practice. The years Creeley spent composing the several volumes collected in *For Love* were marked by intensive literary, editorial, and artistic collaboration. By the time he arrived at Black Mountain in 1954, he had already begun invaluable correspondences with several writers, including Olson, with whom he elaborated the purpose and possibility of projectivist poetics. He established the Divers Press while living in Mallorca a few years earlier, and later became the editor of the *Black Mountain Review*, publishing the first of seven issues in 1954. And although the relationship between abstract expressionism and Creeley's evolving poetics is well documented,[41] few consider that three of the books collected in *For Love* originally featured intermedial collaborations with artists René Laubiès, Dan Rice, and Fielding Dawson. Citing Pound's dictum that "whenever a group of people begin to communicate with one another, something happens," for Creeley, Black Mountain was "as viable and as momentary and as moving as the fact that people moved around in their lives ... [P]eople were always drifting through, coming back, coming for the first time" (Creeley, "Interview" by Ossman 7; "Interview" by Sinclair and Eichele 69). His impression of the college had not changed since his initial visit. There was still no "root in any of it," but such a sentiment was now understood affirmatively.

The relationship between *For Love* and Creeley's various collective endeavours is intriguing if, for no other reason, themes related to failed romantic love and alienation have come to dominate the critical reception of Creeley's early poetry. One contemporary reviewer of *For Love* observes that "the best of [Creeley's] poems are those dealing with the intricacies that exist between men and women" (Davison, "The New Poetry" 85). Taking issue with several reviewers' tendencies to ignore formal innovation in Creeley's work, a critic such as Arthur L. Ford seeks to demonstrate how desire operates at the level of form, but retains a focus on heteronormative desire. Charles Bernstein, on the other hand, makes no excuses for Creeley's sexism; he is rightly "put off by ... the oppressiveness of sexual role stereotyping ... in his talk of 'fair ladies,' of the pervasive image of women as set apart, objectified" ("Hearing 'Here'" 91):[42]

Were I myself more blithe ...

I would marry a very rich woman
who had no use for stoves,
and send my present wife
all her old clothes.   ("Song" 1, 9–12)

Praise god in women.
Give thanks to love in homes.
Without them all men
would starve to the bone.   ("The Wind" 5–8)

Like a river she was,
huge roily mass of water
carrying tree trunks
and divers drunks.

Like a Priscilla, a feminine Benjamin,
a whore gone right over
the falls,
she was.   ("The Memory" 1–8)

A quick assessment of *For Love* uncovers predictable instances of cli-
chéd complaints by a jilted male lover and the sort of gendered ex-
hortations found in Olson's *Maximus* – a machismo element at Black
Mountain documented by writers like Francine du Plessix Gray
and Hilda Morley. Noting Creeley's developing relationships with
Michael Rumaker, Ed Dorn, Jonathan Williams, and John Wieners
while he taught at BMC, historian Martin Duberman observes that
his friendship and artistic collaboration with Dan Rice was decidedly
more "complex":

> Not only did Creeley and Rice fall in love with the same student, and the
> three of them pull each other apart in an agony of shared concern and con-
> fusion, but also he and Dan all but interchanged identities, mixing their
> emotions and intelligence to the point where some thought the only way
> to describe these two *wholly heterosexual men*, was as 'lovers.' (*Black Moun-
> tain* 394; my italics)

Readers should take note of Duberman's qualification of Creeley and
Rice as "wholly heterosexual men" and the accompanying citation,
tucked away in the book's notes, indicating that the details he obtained
regarding their friendship comes from a "variety of sources, which
must go uncited" (491n.23). Amid so many regrouping allegiances, in-
terchanging identities, mixed emotions, mutual confusion, and shared
concern, the temptation to separate out – like a good Aristotelian category – the wholly heterosexual men of Black Mountain *should not go
uncited*.

A comparable erotic mixture can be found in *For Love*, in which misogynistic lyrics like the ones excerpted above appear alongside odes to male friends, family members, and an intertextual network of writers and artists associated with Black Mountain – indeed, a test case for Eve Sedgwick's homosocial critique. Preoccupations with friendship, hospitality, and erotic love are found at every turn in a collection whose interplay of pronouns, *mêlée* of bodies and names, connections and disconnections, create a frenzy of potentially misplaced sexual identifications. As a variety of passages below will indicate, many of the poems in *For Love* adopt what Christopher Nealon calls a "camp-posture toward the 'damage' of late capitalism" ("Camp Messianism" 579). Let me say here unequivocally that any queering of Creeley's work *is done against the grain of intention*; it would be wrong to attempt the sort of reading that sets out to "redeem" Creeley in light of the gender stereotypes his poems sometimes perpetuate, or the homophobia implied by Duberman's account of Creeley's relationship to Dan Rice. Better, I think, to recognize the poet's shortcomings in this respect, observing, in turn, that if open form writing purportedly advances a radical equality *"between things"* in the poem, then Creeley, like Olson, will require the Women's Liberation Movement's discerning intervention. With this important caveat in mind, the Marxist-inflected definition of camp that Nealon dutifully borrows from Andrew Ross gives pause: "camp 'is the re-creation of surplus value from forgotten forms of labor,' … a polemical affection for waste, which animates not just camp in its queer subcultural matrix but also in its migrations beyond subcultural boundaries" (580). Nealon locates this tendency in late twentieth-century poetry, yet this polemical revivification of the "obsolete, misguided or trivial" from an immanent position within capital is undoubtedly much on the minds of Olson and Creeley as well. The latter finds in the disused language of forgotten forms, the throwaway lines of a friend's letters, or the repurposing of poems in artistic collaborations just this sort of erotics of friendship.

The following excerpts from a poem entitled "Hart Crane" (1952) provide a useful point of departure:

He had been stuttering, by the edge
of the street, one foot still
on the sidewalk, and the other
in the gutter …

...

The words, several, and for each, several
senses.
        'It is very difficult to sum up
briefly ...'
            It always was.

(Slater, let me come home.
The letters have proved insufficient.
The mind cannot hang to them as it could
to the words.

...

He slowed
        (without those friends to keep going, to
keep up), stopped
            dead and the head could not
go further
        without those friends

... And so it was I entered the broken world
Hart Crane.
        Hart[.]   (1–4, 7–15, 39–47)

The poem is dedicated to Crane's close friend, Slater Brown, who, by the time of composition, had become an intimate of Creeley's. The text is a woven amalgam of Brown's recollections of Crane, Creeley's parenthetical observations, and quotations taken from Crane's own poetry. Creeley's method involves a movement in and out of the (inter-)textual space of the poem into a social space of kinship; the paratextual epigraph, in effect, enters the field of the text to participate in the construction of a collective portrait. The conclusion of the poem suggests that Crane's dissolution is augmented if not caused by abandonment, ending with an italicized line quoted verbatim from Crane's last poem, "The Broken Tower." Taken independently, Creeley/Crane's line seems a typical expression of modernist isolation, yet this is not the case when viewed in its original context: *"and so it was I entered the broken world /* to trace the visionary company of love" (17–18). The following passage appears at the end of the last poem in Creeley's *For Love*, for which the collection is titled: "that face gone, now. / Into the *company of love* / it all returns" ("For Love" [1962] 61–4; my italics).[43] Crane's lines frame, indeed erotically envelope, Creeley's text. The speaker of *For Love* may "enter the broken world," but it is to trace a populous "company of love." Though it may initially seem inexplicable, "Hart Crane" was originally titled "Otto Rank and Others";[44] Butterick points to a letter Creeley sent to Jacob Leed on 21 June 1948, in which Creeley endorses the psychologist's "'rejection of Freud's idea of the artist as a thwarted neurotic whose basis of creativity depends on the sexual'" (qtd. in Butterick, "Tradition" 122–3). A reading of Creeley's essay on Crane confirms Butterick's astute observation that the title is meant to refute reductive biographical assessments of Crane's homosexuality.[45] In any event, Creeley recreates Crane's poem, such that the "friend" may "go further"; the company of love is thus theme and formal technique.

Creeley is most suspicious of those institutions that impose ethical generalities and regulate social bonds. His objections to marriage, organized religion, and consumer culture are hardly cryptic: "The church," the poet states, "is a business, and the rich / are the business men" ("After Lorca" [1953] 1–2). The concluding remarks of "I Know a Man" (1955) – "shall we & / why not, buy a goddamn big car" (8–9) – ably portends a practice of community formation through conspicuous consumption and brand loyalty that would come to dominate American culture in the years after the Second World War. Yet it would be incorrect to suggest that Creeley opts instead for solipsistic isolation – for, "if you never do anything for anyone else / you are spared the tragedy of human relation- / ships" ("The Immoral Proposition" [1953] 1–3). In *For Love*, the diverse and malleable forms that friendships take afford alternatives to the preconditioned bonds that such institutions impose. This is an assertion applicable to the poems in Creeley's collection and the condition of its publication.

Indeed, the publication history of Creeley's early poetry provides a significant – if frequently ignored – context for the author's work. First published in 1962, *For Love* assembles seven prior books published between 1952 and 1959: *Le Fou* (1952), *The Kind of Act of* (1953), *The Immoral Proposition* (1953), *All That Is Lovely in Men* (1955), *If You* (1956), *The Whip* (1957), and *A Form of Women* (1959).[46] The last two collections republish a substantial number of poems from the other five, and several of the poems were first published in little magazines such as *Origin*, *Fragmente*, and the *Black Mountain Review*. Creeley ultimately decided to organize

For Love chronologically, dividing the anthology into three sections according to the time of composition: 1950–5, 1956–8, and 1959–60. The effect of this decision, according to Arthur L. Ford, allows the reader to document key psychological shifts in Creeley's work (*Robert Creeley* 73–6), but it also potentially obfuscates critical information about the original conditions of publication.

Most notably, three of these smaller volumes feature collaborations with visual artists, two of whom were affiliated with Black Mountain College. René Laubiès provided drawings for *The Immoral Proposition* and Dan Rice illustrated *All That Is Lovely in Men*, while *If You* contains linocuts designed by Fielding Dawson. Creeley's collaborations with artists total more than forty projects, spanning every decade of the poet's life. In addition to the artists who contributed to his early books collected in *For Love*, some of Creeley's most significant work would bear the mark of such artists as Robert Indiana (*Numbers*, 1968), Arthur Okamura (*1°2°3°4°5°6°7°8°9°*, 1971), Martha Visser't Hooft (*Window*, 1988), and Cletus Johnson (*Theaters*, 1993).[47] The art includes a broad range of media: sculpture, photography, lithography, linocuts, screen-prints, photogravures, and Xeroxes. Art historian Elizabeth Licata astutely comments that although Creeley's early work certainly features the influence of abstract expressionism, his long and complex career "has since performed successive mutations, creating a continuum of relationships with artists that is uniquely transformational … always com[ing] from the symbiosis between poet and painter" ("Robert Creeley's Collaborations" 11). Collaboration itself is of course a social gesture that bears testimony to the importance of artistic community. And if the volumes collected in *For Love* exclusively depict an isolated, dejected lover – as some critics insist – then Creeley's mode of publication suggests a contrary scene of social interaction.

Creeley's first three collaborations mark his initial exposure to abstract expressionism. *The Immodest Proposal* was begun in 1953, just after Creeley had encountered the work of Jackson Pollock at the Fachetti Gallery in Paris (the same gallery that featured Laubiès's work). The next two were prepared at BMC, during Creeley's tenure as a faculty member at the college and as editor of the *Black Mountain Review*. In each case, the nature of the collaboration is similar, although there is evidence of a growing interest in the sequential order of the poems and artwork. In *The Immodest Proposal* and in *All That Is Lovely in Men*, poems and drawings appear alternately on facing pages, so that the reader encounters image and text simultaneously. In the tradition of the *livre d'artiste*, both volumes contain poems and drawings that were conceived independently, and then subsequently arranged to elicit certain connections between them. Interestingly, the title of the second volume, *All That Is Lovely in Men*, appears as the title of the last poem in the collection, and features an ironic and embittered declaration of love's failure, yet given Creeley and Rice's intense personal relatonship, it aptly describes the literary-artistic partnership in entirely different terms. Wayne Koestenbaum's assertion in *Double Talk: The Erotics of Male Literary Collaboration* that "collaboration is always a sublimation of erotic entanglements" (4) is equally applicable to interdisciplinary partnerships as well, and the infatuation both men had with the same woman might arguably be read as displaced desire for one another. In any case, within the larger context of Creeley's publishing ventures during the 1950s, it is intriguing that poems devoted ostensibly to heteronormative relationships should involve collaborations with male artists, each attempting an intimate union of text and art.

As early as 1956, while working at BMC, Creeley was beginning to think seriously about the function of collaboration as an integral part of his poetic practice. Olson's remark to W.H. Ferry that "the emphasis" at the college "is on what happens *between things*" is equally applicable in Creeley's case. Nor would it have been lost on Creeley that interdisciplinarity and collaboration challenge the New Critical conception of the poem as an autonomous artefact. What is more, these activities problematize Altieri's contention that Creeley's poetics "is a matter of individual not collective experience" (*Enlarging the Temple* 44). Collaboration involves an artistic process that mixes the subjectivities of its participants, disrupting the mythic autonomy and stability of the author as a solitary figure. Practical concerns involved in the publication of *For Love* would have prevented Creeley from including these collaborations, but since his subsequent participation in several intermedial projects suggests that this was not merely a passing curiosity, there is no reason to downplay their importance to the reception of these three smaller volumes. In regards to the art itself, these texts in particular – and his exposure to abstract expressionism more generally – introduced Creeley to a non-referential practice that would gradually influence his own writing. Upon seeing the work of Jackson Pollock, Creeley recalls that he "was attracted to the fact that this painting was not verbal, that it's a whole way of apprehending or stating the so-called world without using words as an initiation … a way of stating what one feels without describing it" (Licata, "Robert Creeley's Collaborations" 11).

With reference to *For Love*, there appears to be an irreconcilable contradiction: the collaborations Creeley undertook with artists at Black Mountain complement the central themes of friendship and community in the poems, yet his formal technique indicates a shift away from biographical documentation and referential writing. Notably, it is Charles Olson who first comments on this nascent tactic in Creeley's work. In response to "For Rainer Gerhardt" (1952), Olson remarks that Creeley has developed a poetic approach that advances by way of the "conjectural as its hidden methodology" (Butterick, *Correspondence* 9:68), one that gradually vacates the poem of imagistic content. But what is more, Olson is clearly aware of the paradox involved in such a procedure: it is, as he states, by absenting "image and drama" from verse that Creeley more forcefully engages a "sense of the physical world" (9:67–8). Despite Creeley's experiments with unconventional modes of representation, none of his collections attempt the radical semantic indeterminacy of the Language poets. Perloff makes this point succinctly: "Creeley's poetics is not quite that of *In the American Tree*. What Bruce Andrews has called deprecatingly 'the arrow of reference' is still operative in Creeley's lyric, his collocations of words and morphemes are never as non-semantic or disjunctive as those of later Language poets."[48] Perloff's "not quite" arrives at a significant problem with the reception of *For Love*. Many of the collection's poems occupy an interstitial zone between anecdotal reference and resistance to referential writing, combining a mode of description that constructs relationships between subjects and a technique of abstraction that resists the fixture of meaning. Why is it, for instance, that Creeley oscillates between poems such as "Hart Crane," which evoke an intertextual and paratextual network of quotations, epigrams, and proper names, and texts like "The Names" (1959) and "The Place" (1959), which feature Creeley's signature combination of abstract noun and deictic speech act? It is enticing to characterize this development as a shift towards an increasingly non-referential practice, yet both formal strategies persist throughout Creeley's later collections of verse.

Instead of taking the lyric to be a discursive mode, the purpose of which is the construction of one's singular, autonomous identity, Creeley uses it to map relations between a multiplicity of singular beings. By foregrounding relationships, the permutations of these relations, and the provisional nature of their connection, what is being "conjectured" or "defined" is an emergent bond between singularities – the ways in which they encounter, entangle, and disperse. Everywhere in the collection pronouns collide in a "gro- / tesquerie" of "form": "I to love / you to love: syntactic accident" ("The Place" 1–2, 23–4). By way of conjecture and subsequent explication, Creeley sets out to define the formation of social bonds:

> You send me your poems,
> I'll send you mine.
>
> Things tend to awaken
> even through random communication.
>
> Let us suddenly
> proclaim spring. And jeer
>
> at the others,
> all the others.
>
> I will send a picture too
> if you will send me one of you.   ("The Conspiracy" [1954] 1–10)

The poem was first published in a small volume of occasional pieces entitled *A Snarling Garland of Xmas Verses* in 1954, approximately seven months after arriving at BMC. The "wallet pocket-book" contains only five poems and was published anonymously by the author. According to the editorial note supplied by Creeley's bibliographer, Mary Novik, it is likely that Creeley arranged the volume "mainly for friends," given the relatively few number of copies published (approximately one hundred) (*An Inventory* 5).[49] But then, why would Creeley choose to publish the volume anonymously if it were intended for close friends? "The Conspiracy" is an occasional poem that marks no specific occasion, an anecdotal lyric that evades biographical certainty. Forgive the anachronism, but Creeley here rewrites O'Hara's person-ist "Lunch with LeRoi" without particular reference to place or person. Formally, the five-stanza, ten-line poem with its final couplet and period create a sense of closure. Thematically, too, the poem advances the sort of agonistic closure indicative of avant-garde manifestos. The evidence of an "us" in opposition to "all the others" ("The Conspiracy" 5, 7) chimes with numerous declarations resounding with similar calls "to stand on the rock of the word 'we' amidst the sea of boos and outrage" (Burliuk et al., *A Slap in the Face* 223). Yet the tone and rhyme scheme's playful flirtatiousness undercuts the seriousness of such proclamations. The poem announces an "awakening" reinforced by the image of spring, but Creeley's concept of innovation as the hallmark of their clandestine encounter is prompted by "random communication" ("The Conspiracy" 4). Indeed, the speaker declares: "Let us suddenly / proclaim spring" as though the sequence of seasons did not matter (5–6). This is not the programmatic aesthetic of a movement but instead the spontaneous possibility of an intimate encounter and the eruption of unforeseen possibilities that such moments can generate. And though the poem seems to "close" unequivocally, the word "you" is both the first and final word of the text, creating not so much an end point in time as a network of return. The poem also begins with a contemplation of writing that ends with the promise of a physical encounter. Since the poem lacks a dedicatory epigram (a device Creeley uses frequently), it is enticing but ultimately problematic to read the poem as a commentary on the correspondence he shared with Olson, in particular, his stated desire for their correspondence to result in a meeting between the two (Butterick, *Correspondence* 1:118).[50] The photograph ironically promises a visual representation of author and recipient, yet the poem remains indeterminate. By refusing a precise reference to the external world, the reader is left with something like a map or blueprint of an emergent correspondence; echoing Pound's dictum that "whenever a group of people begin to communicate with one another, something happens," the poem inaugurates a poetic based on networks of exchange.

Even in texts that reference the proper name of the friend, the intent is never to essentialize an identity but to map a relation between singularities. "For Rainer Gerhardt" (1952) is likely the first of Creeley's poems to employ a logical structure in which the poem "define[s]" its initial conjecture, in this case, the "conditions / of friendship" with the German writer to whom the poem is dedicated. Yet from the outset the poem announces the impossibility of its own intention:

Impossible, rightly, to define these
conditions of
friendship, the wandering & inexhaustible wish to
be of use, somehow
to be helpful

when it isn't simple, – wish
otherwise, convulsed, and leading
nowhere I can go.

What one knows, then, not
simple, convulsed, and feeling
(this night)
petulance of all conditions, not
wondered, not even
felt.

I have felt nothing, I have
felt that if it were simpler, and
being so, it were a matter only of
an incredible indifference
(to us)
they might say it all –

but not friends, the
acquaintances, but you,
Rainer. And likely there is
petulance in us
kept apart.   ("For Rainer Gerhardt" 1–25)

Friendship, for Creeley, is determined by a tension between the "in-exhaustible wish to / be of use" and the unavoidable "conditions" that establish the limits of one's hospitality (3–4, 2). It was Pound who first instigated a correspondence between the two poets, after which Gerhardt invited Creeley to join the editorial board of his magazine *Fragmente*. It was Gerhardt's magazine that had exposed Creeley to a cultural project for writing that surpassed what he felt were the my-opic agendas of magazines he had encountered in the United States. Together with his wife Renate, the poet and editor had undertaken the daunting project of publishing German literature and other West-ern literary traditions after years of Nazi rule and economic turmoil.[51] Creeley grasped the importance of their work: "[t]heir conception of what such a magazine *might* accomplish was a deep lesson to me. They saw the possibility of *changing* the context of writing" at a moment in which the political left in Germany found itself in profound despair ("On *Black Mountain Review*" 254).[52] Towards the end of August 1951, while Creeley and his wife Ann were living in Mallorca, he decided to make the trip to Freiburg, Germany, to visit his friend.[53] Creeley recalls the experience:

I felt very close to this man – selfishly, because he gave me knowledge of a world I had otherwise no means of knowing. We were of the same age, but the life he had been given was far from that I knew. When he spoke of growing up in the Hitler *Jugend*, of the final chaos of his feelings and sense of possibility after he had been drafted into the army – of his desertion, then, to Tito's forces in Yugoslavia – finally, of all the world of chaos after the war, of his marriage and his two young sons who had to go daily through the streets of collapsed buildings[.] ("Rainer Gerhardt: A Note" 221)

Creeley was understandably shaken by what he saw during his visit to post-war Germany. To be sure, Gerhardt's most crucial lesson was not lost on him: "[h]e spoke to me of what he felt to be the community, the complex of people any city or town describes. He felt that a writer was not distinct from such a unity, but rather helped very literally in its definition" (222). For the speaker of Creeley's poem, to "be of use, somehow / to be helpful" indicates not only a personal wish to be hospitable to his friend, but also his dissatisfaction with the political circumstances that conditions such a friendship. Though the poem appears to chronicle the disintegration of a personal bond between friends, Creeley's precise phrasing is meaningful: it is the "petulance of all conditions" that compromises their friendship. The inevitable sanctions binding an "inexhaustible wish" foreground an aporia framing the speaker's unconditional desire to be available to the other, and, for survival's sake, the conditional necessity to organize one's hospitality and to quantify one's responsibilities to the friend.

Of course, none of this historical contextualization or Creeley's quite candid recollections of his friend can be found in the poem beyond the evocation of a proper name. Gerhardt is indeed a German friend, an editorial colleague, and a like-minded writer. They are bound by approaches to verse, literary institutions, and subject to the laws of nation states – the sort that give conditional permission for an American to visit Germany. Yet the poem bears no reference at all to nationhood or to citizenry. There is none of the filial relation or gendered proclamation of brotherhood found elsewhere in the collection – instead, only a bond between singularities, before those principal marks of the politicized other. When the speaker of Creeley's poem insists that it is "impossible" to "define these / conditions of / friendship" ("For Rainer Gerhardt" 1–3), one possible meaning of this assertion is the impossibility to contain one's friend within the conditioned parameters of identities

or territories, and, therefore, to unbind one from these bonds, while simultaneity prescribing a radical equality for all.

The "wish to / be of use," as Creeley puts it, disperses like a meme
at mid-century. Olson's exhortation in "Projective Verse," "USE USE
USE the process … its excuse, its usableness, in practice" (240–1), comes
on the heels of his own appropriation of Creeley's methods. As for the
common field they were jointly building, Creeley would reflect in an
interview on his relationship with Olson and his experiences at Black
Mountain College during the mid-1950s: "I believe in handing everything over. If I find anything of *use*, I try to get it as quickly as possible
to whomever I consider might *use* it" (Creeley, "Interview" by Ossman
7–8; my italics). Elsewhere, Creeley remarks similarly: "I am pleased by
that poem which makes *use* of myself and my intelligence, as a partner
to its declaration. It does not matter what I am told – it matters, very
much, how I am there *used*" ("A Note" 33). This is a radical gesture
imperfectly executed, since women were not included in the company
of love more fully; we should look back on Black Mountain with a degree of disappointment for this reason, but we should also recognize
the prescience of Creeley's comments nonetheless. Let us call it open
form's gift economy, its "usableness" installed as the principal axiom of
the post-war era's first great poetic vision. Looking forward, members
of the Toronto Research Group, Fluxus, and Language writing would
likely herald this "We-full, not I-less" (McCaffery and Nichol's term)
model of writing, materializing as the "woven stuff" of many "heads
and hands." How open form gets used in the protest verse of the 1960s
is the stuff of the next section.

"Public Parks" and "Poetic Communes": Denise Levertov and Robert Duncan's Open Form Protest

In the preceding sections, I have argued that open form poetries were
conceived in opposition to centralized political institutions in the
United States at mid-century. If the concrete ramifications of Olson
and Creeley's work were not immediately clear, this is because Olson
determined that political change would first require a fundamental
transformation of one's perception of reality and language. For Creeley, friendship was that type of communal relation that problematized
the macro-categories shaping political discourse: religion, marriage,
nationalism, etc. In the years after the formative work conducted at

Black Mountain College, open form poetics would rhizomatically disperse, perhaps like no other poetic practice of the twentieth century, inspiring Allen Ginsberg, Jack Kerouac, and members of the Beat group, Frank O'Hara and the New York School, the San Francisco Renaissance, TISH, Amiri Baraka's Black Arts aesthetics, the feminist writing of Adrienne Rich, the eco-poetic tradition of Gary Snyder, and a diverse group of authors associated with the St Mark's Poetry Project in New York. Field composition spreads and adapts within the tumultuous social climate of the 1960s: protest of the Vietnam War and the countercultural movement give open form poetics a more explicitly political task. I have argued that projectivism is closely bound to several experiments in collaboration; developed in conjunction amid a network of physical encounters and correspondences, open form is linked to debates about community at Black Mountain, to interdisciplinarity, and to themes of polity and friendship. Duncan and Levertov will further expand this concept of field composition, exploring it through formal and theoretical investigations of activism and public space. In *To Stay Alive* (1971), Levertov conceives of the page as a site of multiple inscriptions, using strategies of appropriation and collage to write the anti-war protest into her text – in a sense, reimagining the projectivist field as a "public park." Olson had speculated on the role of the projective in other artistic disciplines and Creeley pursued the possibilities of inter-artistic experimentation as an integral component of an open form practice, but it is Levertov who experiments more fully with the terrain of the page as a site of many converging voices. For Duncan's part, he had famously called himself a "derivative" poet.[54] In clear opposition to the proprietary basis upon which the "anxiety of influence" operates according to Harold Bloom, Duncan freely and openly appropriates techniques from many writers, including Gertrude Stein, Paul Verlaine, H.D., Walt Whitman, and Olson. As he would state years later: "[t]he goods of the intellect are communal" ("The HD Book" [1983] 63).[55] To be "derivative" is to understand language as the material of a literary commons: "[t]here is no / good a man has in his own things except / it be in the community of every thing" ("Orders" [1968] 65–7). *The Opening of the Field* (1960) is often referred to as the beginning of Duncan's "mature" verse, but it is also clearly an explicit reference to field composition, and thus signals both a dependence on a community of authors and open form's possible expansion as a practice.

Common and Divergent Fields

The question of how a protest poetry should be written would come to dominate a considerable aspect of Denise Levertov and Robert Duncan's correspondence.[56] Duncan was drafted for service in the Second World War in 1940 but was later discharged; Levertov worked as a civilian nurse in London from 1943 to 1944. They lived through the Korean War, the Cold War, and the Vietnam War. Not until the onset of Vietnam, however, did a more explicit politics emerge in the verse of both poets, after a decade in which both had focused primarily on personal themes. Yet Vietnam would also generate divergent routes towards a poetics of protest. During the 1960s, Levertov became increasingly involved in the peace movement, helping to promote RESIST, a group which supported draft dodgers during the war; as the decade progressed, she frequently read at political rallies, integrating her activism and her poetry.[57] Duncan, on the other hand, refused to participate in organized political resistance. His commentary on an interview Levertov gives to the Public Broadcast Lab[58] at the Rankin Brigade Washington protest helps to clarify his objection:

> The person that the *demos*, the *citoyen*-mass of an aroused party, awakes is so different from the individual person … [A]s always in the demotic urgency, [one observes] the arousal of the group against an enemy – here the enemy clearly being the whole state structure against our *humanity* … In the PBL view of you, Denny, you are splendid but it is a force that, coming on *strong*, sweeps away all the vital weaknesses of the living identity; the *soul* is sacrificed to the demotic personal that fires itself from spirit. (Berholf and Gelpi, *The Letters* 607)

Duncan's accusation is clear: Levertov had allegedly succumbed to the glorification of the individual "personality," the one claiming to speak for the many. But more importantly, she had, in poems like "Staying Alive," subordinated poetry to propaganda. Just as the body of the speaking subject fuses leviathan-like in and as the body politic, the poem becomes undifferentiated from the political dogma of a given group. Duncan claims to reject the "us/them" dichotomy that political factionizing engenders. By "tak[ing] up arms against the war," revolution perpetuates the logic of violent opposition. Instead, Duncan advocates what might be called a politics of non-cooperation with agencies of power and domination. In the same letter to Levertov, he encourages war refusers to "go underground, evade or escape the conscription. As in South Vietnam, it is not the Liberationists that I identify with but the people of the land who are not fighting to seize political power but are fighting to remain in their daily human lives" (Bertholf and Gelpi, *The Letters* 608). The role of poetry, then, is not active participation in the construction of a "new politics," but rather its purpose is to expose the discursive apparatus of power, and to determine how the individual may withdraw from it.

It is significant, however, that Duncan's commentary focuses on Levertov's appearance rather than her message. Partly this is his point: that the visual spectacle of the rally overpowers the political message; yet, nonetheless, Levertov's speech problematizes Duncan's objection: "Mothers, don't let your sons learn to kill and be killed. Teachers, don't let your students learn to kill and be killed. Wives and sweethearts, don't let your lovers learn to kill and be killed. Aid, abet, and counsel young men to resist the draft!" (Bertholf and Gelpi, *The Letters* 677). Levertov's "war against the state" constitutes a non-violent form of opposition, if not an alternative form of citizenry – a position not altogether different from Duncan's. She contends, however, that it is precisely those institutions within the state – the family, the school – that have the capacity to participate in the protest rather than collude with government ideology. Levertov insists that collective agency can take place within these official mechanisms of power.

The "People's Park"

The debate between Levertov and Duncan has led some critics to draw a connection between the former's political pragmatism and a lyric poetry of witness. Robin Riley Fast insists that Levertov foregrounds a "recognition of the political nature of individual experience" ("She Is The One" 107); Anne Dewey observes that she "subordinates poetic plot to history in her diary/documentary 'Staying Alive,'" portraying the "individual as increasingly overwhelmed by history's turbulent floodwaters" ("Poetic Authority" 118). It is precisely this fusion of poetic lyricism and political declaration that Duncan criticizes as the permission to propagandize under the protection of poetic licence. Yet this emphasis on the anecdotal lyric-cum-political documentary obfuscates the most interesting formal experiments of her protest verse.

Levertov is suspicious of the confessional mode. In an interview with Michael Andre, she observes that it often "exploit[s] the private life":

"I think the first poem in which I was largely autobiographical was in a group called 'The Olga Poems' about my sister and that will be reprinted in my new book. It seems to be a prelude to some of the later stuff and I want to get it all into one book" ("Denise Levertov: An Interview" 65). The volume she is referring to is *To Stay Alive*; in an introductory note to this work, Levertov expresses her decision to reposition "The Olga Poems" in this collection: "it assembles separated parts of a whole. And I am given courage to do so by the hope that the whole will be seen as having some value not as mere confessional autobiography but as a document of some historical value" (*To Stay Alive* ix). Levertov's concern with poetic sequence resonates with an aesthetic shift in her writing towards techniques of appropriation and verbal collage. If "The Olga Poems" are indeed a "prelude" to something, it is the lyric "I" exposed to a multiplicity of poetic and non-poetic forms. In *To Stay Alive*, the author "assembles" autobiographical lyric with narrative modes, visual signs, and an intertextual network of quotations from friends, poets, and members of revolutionary collectives. Her long poem in the collection, "Staying Alive," interweaves personal anecdote with excerpted manifestos, prose passages, and war reportage. The text features mimeographs, transistor radios, cassette recordings, and PA systems belting out a multiplicity of voices (*SA* 42, 47, 78).

At the centre of "Staying Alive" is a description of the "People's Park," a reference to the activist communities at Berkeley during the late 1960s. Yet the park also provides Levertov with an organizing metaphor for the text under construction. In a sense, the "field" of projective writing undergoes a subtle but important terminological adaptation. What is the difference between a field and a park? Both are suggestive of social interaction and play, but the park tends to emphasize festivity, and hence is the preferred site of picnics, festivals, rallies, carnivals, and protests. It is, indeed, more likely to evoke a public space of celebration. The etymological evolution of the word is instructive: initially referring to lands held by royal grant, the word in modern usage came to denote a site of "public recreation" (*OED*). One might understand Levertov's adaptation of field composition and its operative social metaphor as an intensification of its capacity to accommodate a multiplicity of forms and expressions. Levertov describes the park:

May 14th, 1969 – Berkeley
Went with some of my students to work in the People's Park. There seemed to be plenty of digging and gardening help so we decided, as Jeff had his

truck available, to shovel up the garbage that had been thrown into the west part of the lot and take it out to the city dump.

...

> – scooping up garbage together
> poets and dreamers studying
> joy together, clearing
> refuse off the neglected, newly recognized,
> humbly waiting ground, place, locus, of what could be our New World
> even now, our revolution, one and one and one and one together[.]

(*SA* 43–4)

There is no question that Levertov's description romanticizes the social network at the park, but arguably the reference to the work undertaken to rebuild the site also unworks this mythologization by emphasizing a mixture of communal labour and celebration. In May of 1969 students and community activists at Berkeley expropriated unused university parklands for the creation of a space for demonstrations and communal gatherings. School administrators were largely tolerant of the actions taken by the students, which earned Berkeley the reputation of being "a haven for communist sympathizers, protesters and sex deviants"[59] – at least, this was the belief of the then-governor of California, Ronald Reagan. Believing the appropriation of the park to be an illegal seizure of university property, and without the university chancellor's consultation, on 15 May 1969 Reagan ordered 250 Berkeley police and California Highway Patrol officers into the People's Park, erecting a fence around its perimeter. By noon some three thousand protesters had arrived at nearby Sproul Plaza for a rally and subsequent march towards the park. Levertov records the following conflict between students and police:

Thursday, May 15th
At 6 a.m. the ominous zooming, war-sound, of helicopters breaks into our sleep.

To the Park:
ringed with police.
Bulldozers have moved in.

...

The fence goes up, twice a man's height.
Everyone knows (yet no one yet
believes it) what all shall know
this day, and the days that follow:
now, the clubs, the gas,
bayonets, bullets. The War
comes home to us[.]   (*SA* 44–5)

By the end of the conflict, police had killed one person, while another
was blinded and several were injured. The incident at the People's Park
instigated similar confrontations between Leftist organizations and
government officials over control of public land and freedom of assembly rights.

The concept of the "Park" comes to constitute a set of formal practices in the text. Part 2 of the poem features a mimeographed leaflet of
A.J. Muste's message of peace, followed promptly by the appropriated
speech of a young protester, Chuck Matthei, who declares that "[n]o
one man can bring about a social change" (*SA* 42). Levertov applies a
comparable logic to the poem itself, interweaving the text of a manifesto
published in *The Instant News*, a publication affiliated with the Berkeley student protests, and the reproduced message from a Black Panther
support button.[60] The first provision of the Berkeley manifesto – "[b]e
in the streets – they're ours!" – aptly describes the public space of language she creates in the poem. The poet carefully assembles discourses
of the war-resister movement, the Berkeley student movement, and the
Black Panther Party. Levertov's poetry of reportage chronicles these
events, but just as important, the formal politics of her poem operates
by converting the page into a site of public assembly, converting the poetic field into a park, and thus opposing the property relations that restrict the function of a university campus or a written text. Rather than
conflate all of these communities into a singular identity expressed
through a lone lyric voice, she employs collage in order to preserve
their heterogeneity, generating a "chain of equivalence" (Mouffe and
Laclau's term) between collective entities in opposition to the Vietnam
War and the U.S. government's suppression of civil rights.

With her strategies of appropriation and collage in mind, it is instructive to recall that which Levertov emphasizes about projectivism:
"writing is not a matter of one element supervising the others" but a
mapping of the "interaction between the elements involved" ("Some

Notes on Organic Form" 628). Collage functions by intersecting, over-lapping, and juxtaposing formal elements, none of which receives primacy, nor does the amalgam created produce a homogeneous or au-tonomous entity. Levertov equates this practice with a model of social action, one that neither privileges the community by subordinating the individual to the state, nor a model that understands society as the ag-gregate of discreet selves. Collage assembles elements so that each is recognizable but only meaningful in relation to the assemblage within which it participates. Levertov asks of us to conceive of subjectivity in commensurate terms.

The "Commune of Poetry"

Despite Duncan's suspicion of the war resistance, he was not opposed either to literary or political group action. He was a central figure in the Black Mountain and San Francisco scenes during the 1950s and 60s, and a vocal opponent of war. Moreover, anarchist theories of com-munity had shaped the poet's political orientation from the 1940s on-ward.[61] Duncan's refutation of the anti-war movement had to do with the form of rebellion it took, believing that such movements often end up mirroring the systems of power they seek to overthrow.

Duncan claims that poetry must refuse didacticism, if it is not merely to recapitulate party propaganda. The poem cannot instruct the reader to act; simply, it should expose and make evident the systems of co-ercion that organize and oppress communities. The system of power under scrutiny in Duncan's 1960s verse is the "military-industrial com-plex" of which Eisenhower warns in his 1961 farewell address to the nation. In *Bending the Bow* (1968), Duncan identifies

not men   but heads of the hydra

   his false faces in which
     authority lies

hired minds of private interests[.]   ("The Multiversity" *BB* 1–4)

These "faces," the reader learns, are the "heads of the Bank of Amer-ica," "heads of usury," "heads of war" (6, 8). President Johnson, too, is only a figurehead, joining the "great simulacra of men, / Hitler and

Stalin" ("Up Rising" *BB* 1–2). Like the image of the hydra, the "simulacra of men" suggests that the appearance of plurality masks a singular source of power. For Duncan, this power is not any individual but instead the "business of war," a system to which the heads of state (government), the heads of war (military), and the heads of usury (industry) ultimately submit.

Duncan's blending of the mythological and the topical constitutes an attempt to abstract this system of power relationships from the lived experience of events:

> The monstrous factories thrive upon the markets of the war,
> and, as never before, the workers in armaments, poisond
> > gasses and engines of destruction, ride
> high on the wave of wages and benefits. Over all,
> the monopolists of labor and the masters of the swollen
> > ladders of interest and profit survive.
>
> The first Evil is that which has power over you.
>
> > Coercion, that is Ahriman.
>
> In the endless Dark   the T. V. screen,
> > the lying speech and pictures   selling its time and produce,
> corpses of its victims burnd black by napalm
>
> – Ahriman, the inner need for the salesman's pitch – [.]
> > > > ("The Soldiers" *BB* 82–93)

"Ahriman," a concept borrowed from Zoroastrian theology, signifies "destructive spirit." For Duncan, Ahriman is not a personification but a force embodying subjects and systems in the greater processes of history. In a contemporary American context, the forces of coercion emerge and re-emerge in the "speech[es] and pictures" of political pundits and the "salesman's pitch" of war profiteers. President Johnson's advocacy for war is a pre-packaged formula: "Johnson now, no inspired poet but making it badly, / amassing his own history in murder and sacrifice / without talent / ... the bloody verse America writes over Asia" ("The Soldiers" *BB* 32–4, 37). Duncan's tactic is akin to Olson's critique of "Mu-sick" – the role of the political poet is to expose those "who use words cheap" ("Letter 3" *MP* 1:9). To follow the lines of power, one must pursue not only the war of flesh, but also the war of industry, information, technology, the war of markets. Topical writing alone is myopic, according to Duncan. If war is the ultimate instrument of a given system to discipline and dominate populations, then a poetry of witness is misguided, since what needs to be witnessed is precisely the modes of power that underscore acts of oppression.

According to Duncan's letters to Levertov, he would have his readers believe that the descriptive exposition of power's techniques is the arena of the poet, and not the prescriptive formula of an organized rebellion against it. Yet the reader of texts like *Bending the Bow* cannot help but notice the frequency with which Duncan evokes the "hidden community" and the "commune of Poetry," beset on all sides by capitalism's "terror and hatred of all communal things, of communion, of communism" ("Up Rising" 32–3; "Preface" vi; "Multiversity" 62). Duncan's letters indicate his familiarity with the work of anarchist thinkers such as Peter Kropotkin and, especially, Bartolomeo Vanzetti, whose concept of the "volitional politic" he cites frequently (*The Letters* 542, 568, 629ff). In Vanzetti's letters, the anarchist thinker emphasizes the necessity of human agency, "but I wholly share of your confidence in co-operatives, and, what is more, in real co-operatives, free initiative, both individual and collective. Mutual aid and co-operation … shall be the very base of a completely new social system, or else, nothing is accomplished" (Frankfurter, Denman, and Jackson, *The Letters of Sacco and Vanzetti* 143). Duncan repeats a version of this pronouncement in *Bending the Bow*:

> Where there is no commune,
> the individual volition has no ground.
> Where there is no individual freedom,   the commune
> is falsified.   ("The Multiversity" *BB* 32–5)

Vanzetti's letters suggest a practice of community that synthesizes individualism with social anarchistic principles of "mutual aid" and "cooperation." For Duncan, community and individualism are not antithetical but codependent; his "longing" for a community that "moves beyond governments to a co-operation" must be founded on the "free association of living things" ("Ideas" 90). Poetic propaganda establishes a false community because it robs the individual of the volition to formulate her own position, and thus the voluntary commitment to a communal ideal.[62]

Recalling Olson's premise that a poetics must express a "stance toward reality," Duncan remarks similarly in "Ideas of the Meaning of Form" that freedom – the "free association of living things" – "may have seeds of being in free verse" (90). The possibility of "variable forms[,] … when they are most meaningful," possess "the same volition of reality that Vanzetti means in his voluntarism" (*The Letters* 568). For Duncan, the commune not only represented a way of life, it served as the foundation of his practice of writing: projectivist writing, he insists, has the capacity to manifest anarchist notions of communal life at the level of poetic form.

Towards the end of the 1960s and with the publication of *Bending the Bow*, Duncan's approach to serial composition had also undergone radical changes. Like Levertov, Duncan experimented with serial arrangements, often repositioning texts in subsequent volumes. The sequence of poems he calls "Passages" weave through *Bending the Bow*, *Tribunals*, and *Ground Work: Before the War*, while certain sequences, such as the "War" passages, were additionally published as separate volumes. Duncan subverts the linear arrangement of his collections in order to generate a "new process of response": each text is "conceived as a member of every other part, having, as in a mobile, an interchange of roles" ("Preface" *BB* ix). The principal images in *Bending the Bow* – fields, mobiles, communes, and constellations – echo this design. Again, not unlike Levertov's use of verbal collage, Duncan stresses systems and social configurations of interdependence: each text is partially autonomous and partially connected, conveying Duncan's assertion that community requires both individual volition and mutual aid.

I mention earlier that Duncan, like Levertov, Olson, and Creeley, understood poetic convention to be akin to a "government" imposing order on a community of words: "some set of rules and standards that will bring the troubling plenitude of experience 'within our power'" ("Ideas" 103). Duncan sought a poetry capable of representing a more flexible arrangement of poetic elements. Indeed, if the poem is a "free association," then its design must imitate open collectivities:

> The design of a poem
> constantly
> under reconstruction,
> changing, pusht forward;

alternations of sound, sensations;
    the mind dance
wherein thot shows its pattern:
    a proposition
    in movement.

    The design
not in the sense of a treachery or
    deception
but of a conception betrayd,
    without a plan,

...

reveald in its pulse and
    durations[.]   ("An Essay at War" [1951] 1–14, 18–19)

With Duncan's understanding of the politics of form in mind, the "design of the poem" expresses the principles of the "commune": community's open definition, a "proposition" continuously changing, "without" a predetermined "plan." The most often quoted principle of projective writing, that a content should determine its form, articulates a practice of living.

In describing the projects of these writers, it is enticing to sentimentalize about a poetry of protest in opposition to state and corporate power. It is clear from both writers that community is something continuously fought for and under threat. Levertov speaks of a "momentary community" (*SA* 77); she finds it emerging among a group of young war resisters (21–8), again among Sudanese activists in Rijeka (68, 77), and once more in the clandestine conversations of protestors at the Juche Revolutionary Bookstore (77). Like Creeley's "conditions" of ethical obligation to the friend, there is the "inexhaustible wish" for an infinite openness to the other that violently collides with the restrictions that delimit such a desire. These pronouncements retain a degree of preciousness if they are not tested within concrete circumstances – a town such as Gloucester, the formation of friendships amid the ravages of war, or a protest besieged by the state.

What, then, shall we say is the meaning of Black Mountain? A reductive question to be sure, but we should hazard an answer. Its import, I believe, can be found in open form writing as a cultural poetics fusing localism and freedom. For Olson, Creeley, Levertov, and Duncan any element that enters the field of the poem must count equally.

Every element is afforded an unqualified equality among all others. This is taken up as a poetic practice and a political project, insofar as poetic discourse is meant to reconfigure the space of social experience. If these poets explore the idea of a mobile, permeable community, it is unqualified equality that allows such a political configuration to come into being. To this end, the Black Mountain poets give the mobile community another meaning. To say that community is "provisional" is to acknowledge that it is often makeshift, limited to a finite set of resources, under pressure, and often only partially successful. The title of Levertov's collection, *To Stay Alive*, speaks at once to a community both as ideal and as pragmatic solution. It is within these terms that critics should understand the politics of projective verse. Open form does not imply a poetry without rules, or that the poet works with unlimited freedoms; rather, field composition responds to the demands of a concrete historical moment. To "work in OPEN" means to forge a poetic writing within an immediate context, using whatever resources are locally available, using whatever ideas, images, technologies, and collaborators present themselves within a field of action for use. A great body of criticism has been written dealing with Black Mountain's influence on a truly daunting array of poets and literary scenes during the 1950s, 1960s, and 1970s. Poets affiliated with the Beats, the San Francisco Renaissance, the New York School, Black Arts, and the poets of Women's Liberation all cite its important contributions. And although the mechanics of open form is said to link these practices, more specifically it is the fusion of field composition with an explicitly socio-political objective that connects these poets: Baraka's Black militancy; O'Hara's cosmopolitan camp; the anti-war writings of Ginsberg; and the feminist poetics of Rich, Grahn, Morgan, and others, who, in bidding farewell to the New Left, take open form writing with them.

We will return to this crucial act of appropriation in chapter 4, but first let us address the Cold War's consequences for communities beyond the borders of the United States. Turning now to the Caribbean Artists Movement, the reader will find no conscious influence or explicit intertextual link between the poets discussed in the chapter just completed and the one now to commence (Brathwaite wrote with no knowledge of Black Mountain). In a sense, the book begins again from a different geographic and social location. From the local environs of a small college in North Carolina we move to the cosmopolitan milieu of London, England; from a group composed largely of white American writers negotiating Cold War containment within the world's most powerful empire to a group of mainly Black Caribbean poets displaced (some voluntarily, some involuntarily) to the United Kingdom. One should remember that Cold War ideology – like the Bush doctrine in the wake of the September 11th attacks – influenced the immigration policy of innumerable countries, patterns of migration, and global policies defining the status of the refugee. If the Cold War's reach is global, then we will need to move from Creeley's surrounding "darkness" to the walls erected to keep Brathwaite's "arrivants" out.

3   The Caribbean Artists Movement: A Poetic of Cultural Activism

'[A]rticulation' … the term has a nice double meaning because 'articulate' means to utter, to speak forth, to be articulate. It carries that sense of language-ing, of expressing, etc. But we also speak of an 'articulated' lorry (truck): a lorry where the front (cab) and back (trailer) can, but need not necessarily, be connected to one another. The two parts are connected to each other, but through a specific linkage, that can be broken. An articulation is thus the form of the connection that *can* make a unity of two different elements, under certain conditions. It is a linkage which is not necessary, determined, absolute and essential for all time. You have to ask, under what circumstances *can* a connection be forged or made?

– Stuart Hall[1]

CAM [the Caribbean Artists Movement] was part of how I was conceiving of the world. I mean, the poetry was saying the same thing that CAM was doing, that is, that we must have a community … that we should all submerge ourselves … and that Caribbean people, since we are submerged, Third World, that we needed to become Renaissance.

– Kamau Brathwaite[2]

Link-up: A Poetic of Articulation

The objective of this chapter might be summarized as an inquiry into Brathwaite's contention that his "poetry was saying the same thing that CAM was doing." How did the Caribbean Artists Movement (CAM) operate as an organization that enabled the cultural production of Caribbean exiles living in London, England, and what specifically was the relationship between the group and a practice of writing? Readers of Brathwaite will no doubt observe some intriguing terminological consistencies between this passage and statements elsewhere in his poetics and cultural research. "Submergence" is a term he uses to define a notion of writing called "nation language," or as he and his frequent collaborators John La Rose and Andrew Salkey put it, a "submerged language," an "underground language" (Brathwaite, *History of the Voice* 7), operating under the radar to challenge and transform the dominant discourse.[3] In a letter to La Rose dated 19 September 1967, Brathwaite laments the lack of community among Caribbean authors in London; exclusion from mainstream English institutions meant they needed to connect with one another by "tunneling under the established structures" (CAM Papers 3/190 [1]). Notably, Brathwaite's poetry is acutely attentive to the semantic relation between phonemes in a single sign;[4] the suggestive relation between prefix and verb in a word like "submerge," a double movement below (sub-) and across (-merge), constitutes precisely the sort of punning he frequently employs. The word's various significations imply marginalization (subordinate, subaltern) but also a system of connection (convergence, fusion). To be submerged evokes an image of the diaspora, and hence a condition of displacement, but it also intimates the stability that a submarine network of like-minded collaborators can build together.

For Brathwaite, questions of language and questions of social formation are inexorably linked within the same project of aesthetic and political activism. His cross-cultural poetics draws connections among African, Caribbean, African American, and subversive Western traditions of social activism and literary practice. Granted, he contends that language alone cannot serve as the domain of revolt. Whether one is referring to the French or Haitian revolutions, "it was not simply that people were hacking down or destroying the Bastille of words, but they were also destroying physical and ideological Bastilles as well" (Brathwaite, "Interview" by Mackey 17). The role of the poet involves a self-conscious critique of the way language functions and participates within social and ideological formations, including the way language can operate to oppress or enable resistance. The "world-maker" is necessarily a "word-breaker" ("Ananse" [1969] *A* 64); communities assemble, in part, in language where the poet works – in the ways one modifies, adapts, and shares language in order to produce new modalities of social existence.

The Caribbean Artists Movement refers to an organization of poets, artists, academics, and activists living and working in London during the late 1960s. Its founding members were Kamau Brathwaite, John La Rose, and Andrew Salkey, and during its approximate six-year history (1966–72), it attracted the likes of Orlando Patterson, Aubrey Williams, Wilson Harris, Anne Walmsley, Stuart Hall, Sarah White, Louis James, Gordon Rohlehr, and Kenneth Ramchand, among others.[5] Their activities were well organized: a combination of private sessions, public meetings, three conferences, a newsletter that ran consistently for half a decade, and a little review called *Savacou*. They held their public meetings and performances at the West Indian Student Centre, encouraging productive connections among the arts community, members of the Afro-Caribbean general public, and white British leftists. CAM was a recuperative project, both in the sense that it sought to establish a community of exiles in London and to historicize a pan-Caribbean culture threatened by colonization and displacement. That said, to call this group of writers "exiles" is somewhat misleading. While a writer such as Kamau Brathwaite was studying in London and had intentions of returning to Jamaica to resume a teaching position at the University of the West Indies, many in the community, including its two other founding members, John La Rose and Andrew Salkey, had decided to stay in Britain. Their relationship to the host nation was not a temporary but a permanent one. CAM was equally devoted to forging a British Afro-Caribbean community in London, whose chief aim was to improve conditions for minorities. The New Beacon bookstore and publishing house, the West Indian Student Centre (WISC), Bogle L'Overture, the Negro Theatre Workshop and the Caribbean Students Performing Group, the Campaign Against Racial Discrimination (CARD), the Caribbean Education and Community Workers Association (CECWA), the Black Parents Movement and Black Youth Movement, and the George Padmore Supplementary School afford but a shortlist of activities either established by CAM members or closely aligned with its political efforts.

The literary activity during this period was sizeable. Brathwaite was at work on the books composing his first trilogy: *The Arrivants* (*Rights of Passage* [1967], *Masks* [1968], and *Islands* [1969]). John La Rose, often better known as a publisher and education activist, had published a book of poems called *Foundations* (1966), while Andrew Salkey had become well known as a novelist, having published several well-received books, including *A Quality of Violence* (1959) and *Escape to an Autumn Pavement* (1960), in addition to a series of "postcard" poems closely aligned with his *Havana Journal* (1971) and *Georgetown Journal* (1972). While little has been written about Salkey or La Rose's poetry, the sizeable critical attention to Brathwaite's body of work typically reads his poetics within an exclusively Caribbean rather than a Black British context. This, of course, is a perfectly reasonable approach, but much of *Arrivants* was completed during Brathwaite's tenure in London, and read to an activist community that included his closest collaborators and most important influences. If the poetry was doing the same thing CAM was, then we should take seriously the connection between Brathwaite's writings of the late 1960s and the immigrant activism underway in the English capital.

Due to the post-war labour shortage in Great Britain, approximately one hundred thousand Caribbean-born immigrants were encouraged to settle in England between 1948 and 1962.[6] Prior to the implementation of the Commonwealth Immigrants Act (1962), all citizens of the Commonwealth could settle in England without restriction. The demographics of West Indies migrants included a socio-economically diverse group of the working and middle class from several nations, along with a large number of students who were enrolling in post-secondary studies. Towards the end of the 1950s, an estimated twenty thousand immigrants from the Caribbean were arriving per year, along with thousands more from other former British possessions. The government thought it prudent to end the practice of common citizenship, an irony foretold by the renowned Jamaican poet Louise Bennett in "Colonization in Reverse" (1957):

> What a joyful news, miss Mattie;
> Ah feel like me heart gwine burs –
> Jamaica people colonizin
> Englan in reverse.
>
> By de hundred, by de tousan,
> From country an from town,
> By de ship-load, by de plane-load,
> Jamaica is Englan boun.   (1–8)

The poem predates the Immigration Act by half a decade, but the dramatic rise in migrant workers pouring into the "motherlan" during the late 1950s was already perceived by many in London's white community as a threat to employment opportunity and to the "purity" of

English culture. In the late summer of 1958, a marked increase in violent hostility directed against minorities living in London culminated in a riot orchestrated by approximately three hundred to four hundred white youths (variously affiliated with fascist groups) who attacked minorities and vandalized the homes of the Caribbean community in the Notting Hill neighbourhood.[7] Although measures were taken against the offenders, in the years that followed, the Conservative Party capitalized on white working-class disaffection and xenophobia, restricting migration to those with government-issued employment documents and students studying abroad.[8]

The founders of the Caribbean Artists Movement, and many of those who regularly attended its meetings and events, either emigrated before the act was implemented or were admitted into the country as students with temporary visas. Born in Barbados, Kamau Brathwaite first came to England in 1950 to study history and education at Cambridge. He later travelled to Africa, where he took a job in the Ministry of Education in Ghana, working in the Textbooks and Syllabus division. Brathwaite returned to England in 1966 to undertake postgraduate work after a two-year stint at the University of West Indies (UWI) at Mona, Jamaica.[9] As historian Anne Walmsley rightly observes, his experiences in Ghana were life changing. He witnessed the country's successful independence in 1957 from British colonial rule, and became immersed in a West African culture whose traditions and practices he began to recognize in the slave trade descendants of the Caribbean.[10] In 1962 he settled in St Lucia in order to take up a position as the country's resident tutor for the UWI Extra-Mural Department. Brathwaite worked with a range of artists, writers, playwrights, and actors, and even brought the arts program live to air on Windward Islands Radio.[11] A year later he took a position at the UWI, where he would encounter eventual CAM members Louis James and Gordon Rohlehr, as well as writers Derek Walcott, Errol Hill, and C.L.R James. Bridget Jones astutely observes that Brathwaite's travels during this period helped to cultivate a pan–Afro-Caribbean consciousness,[12] but perhaps no less important were the crucial skills he accrued working in arts programming, education, and academic environments, developing the necessary organizational know-how that would prove invaluable in the context of CAM.

John La Rose was born in Arima, Trinidad; from his late teenage years he had become seriously involved in Marxist struggles. In the late 1940s he became the General Secretary of the Workers Freedom

Movement (WFM), forging alliances with the Federated Workers Trade Union (FWTU). Along with other anticolonial trade unionists, La Rose organized communities in the oil-rich southern regions of the country with the express intent of bringing independence to Trinidad and nationalizing its natural resources. The WFM and the FWTU amalgamated in 1952, becoming the West Indian Independence Party (WIIP), promoting national independence under a democratic-socialist platform. After travelling to Eastern Europe as a delegate for the World Federation of Trade Unions Congress, La Rose was blacklisted back in Trinidad and branded a subversive radical by the colonial powers (Alleyne 122–5). Importantly, La Rose never separated his political and literary ambitions. At the same time he took a position in the WFM, he forged organizational alliances with the Trinidad and Tobago Youth Council (TTYC) and the Trinidad All Steel Percussion Orchestra (TASPO). Like Brathwaite, La Rose directed a radio show, *Voice of Youth*, programming discussions on literature and calypso alongside lectures promoting socialism in the Caribbean. Years later La Rose studied Spanish and French literature in Port of Spain and was introduced to the work of Venezuelan, Cuban, Haitian, Puerto Rican, and Martinique poets – most notably Aimé Césaire.

By contrast, Andrew Salkey brought a slightly different set of skills to the organization. He worked primarily as a freelancer for the BBC, reporting for the Pacific, the African, and the World Services. Born in Jamaica, he arrived in Britain in 1952; a variety of freelance writing jobs enabled him to enrol at the University of London. Having come earlier to the city than either Brathwaite or La Rose, Salkey had been present during the mid-1950s, at which time the likes of George Lamming, Sam Selvon, and the BBC program Caribbean Voices had begun to showcase work by Caribbean writers. Salkey contributed to the program and met many editors, writers, and community organizers in the city. Brathwaite recalls that "thanks to Andrew, we started making a lot of important connections. Not only with writers – because he knew where to find everyone instantly – but with people in the English establishment, people who he felt would help us. And so the three of us together started a kind of combination" (CAM Papers 6/9 [3]). Like La Rose, Salkey had read extensively in Marxist theory. He became involved with the League of Coloured Peoples (LCP) and the Movement for Colonial Freedom (MCF), and like La Rose, joined the Campaign Against Racial Discrimination (CARD), a movement formed after Martin Luther King Jr's historic visit in 1964.[13]

These brief personal histories disclose some important facts. The first regards social location: CAM members faced the same systemic racism encountered by all Black British individuals attempting to live and work in the UK; they were, however, well-educated men, giving them comparatively greater access to positions of power than either women or working-class minorities. Brathwaite, La Rose, and Salkey each came from middle-class backgrounds, receiving British education in St Lucia, Trinidad, and Jamaica, respectively. It is fair to conclude that CAM's founding members were among the most privileged of a dispossessed class, which, in turn, comprised so many ethnic and cultural distinctions (e.g., the Jamaican, the St Lucian, and the Trinidadian experience differed greatly in some respects, not to mention, say, the Haitian, the Guyanese, and the Cuban traditions from which CAM routinely draws). In this regard, CAM affords an instructive comparison with the Black Mountain poets. Both were predominantly male communities with relatively high levels of education, but arguably, while Olson and Creeley routinely agonized over the state of the American polis, their right to assert a sense of place and belonging – in Olson's concise phrasing, "this point of time, America, 1951" – is never consciously questioned nor violently contested.

Second, the biographies of CAM's founding members reveal that each had extensive experience as social activists and arts programmers. Given the convergence of artistic and political organizing among Black British immigrants during the 1960s, this was a valuable set of skills. In the late months of 1966, Brathwaite sent a letter outlining the objectives for an artistic movement to several people whom he thought might take interest. The following is an excerpt from the letter he sent to Bryan King, chair of the West Indian Student Centre:

The more I stay here in England, the more it seems to me that our writers and artists are missing a wonderful opportunity to communicate with themselves and with British and Commonwealth artists around them. What I'd like to start going (and it has no doubt been attempted before) is some sort of WI artists' and writers' group concerned with discussing WI art and literature ... not only by established artists, but by students and others who feel they have something to say. I would not, however, like to see this confined to West Indians. There should be a link-up with C'wealth and British writers and artists[.] (CAM Papers 3/1 [1])

Brathwaite continues in the letter to expand the number of participants to include the work of French and Spanish Caribbean authors, and to invite "publishers, BBC types and British critics." From the beginning, both he, La Rose, and Salkey imagine a populist, interdisciplinary, polylingual, and international movement, one that includes artists and non-artists, immigrants and British-born members, those marginalized in Britain and those with access to the institutions that promote and define British culture. Brathwaite and other CAM members are prepared to name a "common enemy" as the racial oppression of minorities in London, but rather than adamantly refuse the participation of British institutions, he asserts that "we needed to make contact with the British establishment," that only by confronting these sources of institutional power could equality occur (CAM Papers 6/9 [7, 19]). In comparison with BMC members, who sought to forge a local community outside the jurisdiction of state authority, immigrant communities in London witnessed the end of common citizenship. CAM could not simply ignore a state whose powers now included the legal deportation of "foreign-born" subversives.

The open egalitarianism of Brathwaite's planned community ultimately took a slightly different form. A series of preliminary private meetings were held, attended by La Rose, Salkey, Brathwaite, White, Gordon Rohlehr, Louis James, Orlando Patterson, and Aubrey Williams. Over the course of these preliminary sessions a basic structure gradually developed. Public meetings took place monthly and anyone could attend, yet the semi-private sessions continued, often in the evening after a public event. As Walmsley remarks, the public meetings were the "backbone" of the movement, where talks, symposia, and performances went on, while at the smaller gatherings, which members had taken to calling "warishi nights," a "much freer interchange" took place, fostering an environment for post-meeting reflection and an opportunity to give direction to their public activities (CAM Papers 3/247 [1]).

The letter Brathwaite sent to Bryan King also contained the request that CAM meetings be held at the West Indian Student Centre. Brathwaite received immediate permission and full encouragement. Opened in 1955, the centre had been associated with the West Indian Student Union. Walmsley notes that until the centre's formation, students typically congregated at the British Council buildings in Hans Crescent, while non-students looking to organize political and artistic events could only find suitable venues in church halls and the like.[14] The centre dissolved this distinction, creating a space in which students, artists, activists, and members of the West Indian community could come together. In addition to CAM, organizations such as the Commission for Racial Equality, the West Indian Standing Conference, and the Caribbean Students Performing Group called the centre home, creating the sort of artistic, social, and political rhizomes of activity that contextualize CAM's poetic practice. Their activities are well documented in part because group members recognized the value of giving some posterity to their collaborations; Brathwaite insisted on tape-recording CAM meetings, partly because the tapes would allow members unable to attend the opportunity to hear the proceedings, and because, as a historian of the diaspora, he knew full well that cultural history can be easily lost or destroyed. CAM meetings were transcribed and reproduced in synopsis as a cyclostyled newsletter, which also contained lists of recent publications, planned exhibitions, readings, lectures, and a section entitled "News from the Caribbean" that kept London exiles apprised of literary activities back home.

Three conferences were held in successive years: 1967, 1968, and 1969. The first two took place at the University of Kent, while the third was held at the West Indian Student Centre. The conferences were intended to bring together the students and artists who had been regularly attending the public meetings with academics and members of the British Establishment. Brathwaite personally invited representatives of the BBC, several newspapers and periodicals, and members of the British Council and the Arts Council. The event attracted several mainstream British publishers, but few journalists or government council officials. Walmsley, who attended on behalf of Longman publishers, confirmed the diversity of attendees, including writers, artists, actors, critics, university and high school teachers, librarians, several housewives, and other interested members of the Caribbean community. An important alliance was formed between Caribbean authors and British publishers. In addition to La Rose's New Beacon Books, Salkey, Brathwaite, and other notable poets and authors would find support from British publishers, in particular, Oxford University Press, under the direction of Jon Stallworthy.

The few historical accounts of CAM events tend to describe an "informal structure ... an autonomous organization outside the constraints

of academic or governmental institutions" ("A Sense" 102–3).[15] Walmsley's comments echo those sometimes made by Brathwaite himself,
who values the flexible constitution of their activities: "all three of us
– the founding members – were anti any kind of formality, any kind
of bureaucracy, any kind of rigid structure" (CAM Papers 6/9 [17]).
At one point, he even refers to CAM as a "creative commune" (19).
Interaction between CAM members might have been relatively informal, but compared with the activities of the Black Mountain poets,
the Toronto Research Group, or a community of artists such as Fluxus,
CAM was very organized. The communal structures and conceptual
frameworks that CAM built – sessions, meetings, conferences, movements, and student centres – not only bear to some extent the mark
of Western institutions, but they also indicate the need for stability in
order to facilitate and to develop their work. For this reason, CAM
presents a problem for critics in North America deriding the "institutionalization" or "professionalization" of poetry, that apparent anathema to creativity and innovation. These arguments beg the question:
what about writers so violently or systematically displaced because of
colonialism and political exile that such social and educational institutions become necessary frameworks through which writers might
come together, recuperate their histories, and challenge racist ideologies? CAM's specific goals involved coordinated efforts with organizations tasked with challenging the UK publishing industry, its
education system, and its legal apparatus.

While simultaneously helping to forge CAM, La Rose and Sarah
White opened New Beacon in 1966 at their apartment in Hornsey,
North London.[16] A publishing house, a book service, and shop, New
Beacon anchored much of CAM's activities by putting its members
in touch with several Marxist and anticolonial intellectual traditions
drawn from the Caribbean, Africa, and North America. (The source
of La Rose's chosen name for their book-publishing venture is *The
Beacon*, a journal launched by a group of intellectuals in La Rose's
native Trinidad, among whom C.L.R. James was a member.) Adolph
Edwards's *Marcus Garvey, 1887–1940* (1967), Wilson Harris's *Tradition, The Writer, and Society* (1967), John Jacob Thomas's *The Theory
and Practice of Creole Grammar* (1969 [1869]), and La Rose's own volume of poems, *Foundations* (1966), form a selection of New Beacon's
early publications, juxtaposing new titles by CAM members with historically important texts ignored by the predominantly white British

literary establishment. Notably, Thomas's study of creole grammar, along with *Fraudicity* (also republished by New Beacon in 1969), affords an invaluable historical antecedent for Brathwaite's conception of "nation language." Thomas, a Black schoolteacher and tireless activist, wrote his tract as a retort to the Oxford historian James Anthony Froude's *The English in the West Indies* (1888), an obtuse defence of English colonialism masquerading as a largely inaccurate account of Caribbean English. New Beacon's publishing list indicates that CAM and its collaborators sought to bring diverse legacies of Black struggle to bear on the immediate activities of Black British activists.

Moreover, CAM members spent considerable energy on education reform. The Black Parents Movement (BPM) and Black Youth Movement (BYM) were tandem organizations established in 1975 following a police assault on Cliff McDaniel, a personal friend of John La Rose's children, Michael and Keith. The BPM's formal structure mirrored CAM's in several ways (the group held regular meetings, conferences, and distributed a periodical called *Front*), but its specific mandate was youth focused: challenging racism in the classroom, establishing legal defences for young minorities, and protesting anti-deportation laws. La Rose had long participated in such actions. The BPM followed considerable work on the part of education activists during the 1960s, in particular, the Caribbean Education and Community Workers Association (CECWA), which formed in 1969 after La Rose and other parents learned that minority children were routinely relegated to Educationally Sub Normal (ESN) streams in British schools. New Beacon published an important document authored by Bernard Coard, *How the West Indian Child Is Made Educationally Sub-normal in the British School System* (1971). The BYM complemented these activities with events organized by Michael and Keith La Rose, along with other inner-city Black youths. Recreational sports programs, music shows, and carnival festivities were designed for poor and alienated minorities particularly vulnerable to police brutality and the lure of criminal activity. That same year La Rose, together with his former wife Irma and other Black parents, established the George Padmore Supplementary School (GPSS). It differed significantly from private, charter, and home-schooling movements found elsewhere in Britain and throughout the West. The school's founders never entertained the prospect of a permanently separate Black-only system. The supplementary school was precisely that – a provisional but necessary addition designed, ultimately, to complement broader struggles to transform a British system that was alienating Black students. The GPSS offered classes in primary topics – English, math, and science – but it also stressed world geography and study of African and Caribbean cultural history. La Rose insists, however, they did not "neglect" European history; "after all," he points out, "the kids were growing up here." The objective was to generate awareness of cultural practices and social struggles beyond the borders of the British nation state.[17]

Several subsequent developments during the 1970s and 1980s, such as the *Race Today* Collective, the Creation for Liberation, the International Book Fair of Radical Black and Third World Books, Peoples War Sound System, and Carnival Band, were indebted to the pioneering work of CAM. Nor did these group affiliations stop at the edge of London: CAM members published in *Bim*, Frank Collymore's Barbadian magazine, and kept in contact with other Caribbean arts organizations, such as Yard, the Barbados Writers Workshop, the Arts Guild in St Lucia, and a network of Cuban writers and artists. La Rose and Salkey travelled to Cuba in 1968 to participate in the Havana Congress of Third World Intellectuals – an event that had great significance for the political and literary commitments of both writers. Brathwaite recollects in an interview that the group participated in a "spider's web" of activities that opened up "new directions … [and] more organizations" (CAM Papers 6/9 [17]). Speaking of CAM with this range of concerns in mind, La Rose proclaims: "I have always found that when you start by discussing culture, as distinct from when you start discussing politics, the area of centers is much wider." He elaborates that a "cultural point of view means you are discussing society, history, politics – all kinds of social movements and individuals" (CAM Papers 6/44 [6]). It bears stating explicitly: La Rose would never have reduced politics to identity let alone fashion. His "cultural point of view" is conjunctional, bringing poetry, calypso, and carnival in step with education reform, publishing, and poverty activism.

Given the heterogeneous identities of Caribbean communities making up London's literary circles, it was clear from the outset that an essentialist notion of collective identity (a philosophy of Black nationalism and Black consciousness) offered an inadequate model for the movement. "This was always," Brathwaite remarks,

part of our thing, to keep opening up, opening up, because the Caribbean by definition is not only a European ancestral element, but it is also a pan-Caribbean context – which John La Rose was helping us with; it also has

an Amerindian context, which Aubrey and Wilson Harris were helping
us with; and it also has an African and a Black American context. And in
London there were exiles who were from Black America and from Africa.
(CAM Papers 6/9 [14])

It is additionally important that progressive, left-oriented white British members such as Sarah White and Anne Walmsley helped to create
the movement. To be clear, CAM rejected two potential forms of community, *ethnic* and *cultural* nationalism: community defined by a fixed,
essential identity and community defined by the uniqueness and autonomy of a cultural tradition.

The group's objection to the former was more obvious. No doubt
the African American struggle had its influence on Britain. Martin Luther King Jr, Malcolm X, and Stokely Carmichael all made visits to
London between 1964 and 1967. These events, along with CARD's
failed attempt to repeal the 1962 ban on Commonwealth privilege,
galvanized a diverse Afro-Caribbean community and dramatically influenced black intellectuals and activists in Britain (particularly CAM
member Locksley Comrie, who had encountered Carmichael during
the latter's visit to London in 1967). Still, the Black British experience
of 1960s London was demonstrably different than the African American experience in significant ways. Paul Gilroy observes in African
American letters the presence of "absolutist conceptions of cultural
difference allied to a culturalist understanding of 'race'" (*The Black
Atlantic* 15). Amiri Baraka's call for an authentically "Black Art" – a
"black poem ... And a / Black World," "Black as Bessie Smith or Billie Holiday" – made less sense in the ethnically, nationally, and even
geographically diverse Caribbean context that Brathwaite describes
("Black Art" 50–1; "The Black Arts Movement" 502). Stuart Hall, Gilroy, and Homi Bhabha, along with a litany of post-colonial critics,
have theorized what Hall calls a shift in Black British cultural representation and the construction of "new ethnicities," "mark[ing] ...
the end of the innocent notion of the essential black subject" and an
emergent "recognition of the extraordinary diversity of subjective positions, social experiences and cultural identities which compose the
category 'black'" ("New Ethnicities" 442).[18] Hall conjectures that this
historical development may indicate "a new phase," but he is resis-
tant to name a radical political break, since such language erroneously
evokes the "substitution" of one politics for another. Nevertheless,

Hall is writing in 1989 about recent Black British cinema. There is no doubt that CAM is the forerunner to this "construction of new ethnicities," refusing tellurian and autochthonal bonds through which to forge a collective.

Just as emphatically, the group thought a project of cultural autonomy to be equally misdirected. CAM's national and artistic heterogeneity led its members to reject what Gilroy calls the inevitable "insiderism" of cultural *autonomy*. The principle of cultural difference taken to "its extreme conclusion," Brathwaite argues, "would prevent Trinidadians from playing in steelbands, since the steel from which the instruments are made comes from iron ores which are not found in Trinidad" (*Contradictory Omens* 55–6). Humour aside, members of CAM – particularly La Rose – had witnessed first-hand the work of socialist movements from the Caribbean to Eastern Europe. Attempts to regulate, purify, and police cultural syncretism seemed oppressive if not fruitless. The Maoist agenda to cleanse Chinese culture of Western influence was intolerable, according to La Rose, since such models of cultural nationalism invariably replicate supremacist ideologies.

Caribbean literature has recently been theorized under the names of rhizomatics, nomadism, hybridity, and relationality. These concepts are most evocative when read against that which is arguably its most powerful (and prevalent) symbol: *the ship*. Indeed, for critics such as Paul Gilroy and Édouard Glissant, the slave trade and racial terror, the middle passage and colonial expansion, industrialization and modernity all converge within its signifying power. And while the symbol nicely conveys a mobile, interstitial, and diasporic condition, Gilroy aptly observes "something more – a means to conduct political dissent and possibly a different mode of cultural production." "The ship," he insists, "provides a chance to explore the articulations between the discontinuous histories of England's ports, its interfaces with the wider world" (*The Black Atlantic* 17). Glissant's rhetoric is yet more celebratory. Informed by the work of Gilles Deleuze and Félix Guattari, he details the "nomadic" features of francophone Caribbean poetics: to replace the nation as "the entrenched [*enracinée*] necessity of relation to the world"; a "wandering [*errance*] emerges silently from the destructuring of national compacities, which only yesterday remained triumphant" (*L'Intention Poétique* 72; *Poétique de la Relation* 30). Glissant valorizes the nomadic traveller: "exhaust[ing] no territory,

he is rooted only in the sacredness of air and evaporation" (224).[19]
The work of CAM reveals greater caution. Its members state unequivocally that the diaspora had generated as many disconnections
as possible new transnational configurations; deracination was not a
condition to be celebrated but a source of dispossession. Anticipating radical feminist Jo Freeman's refutation of "structurelessness" as
an end in itself, the goal should be the formation of communities that
facilitate radical emancipation, such that an absence of organization
was not productive to this end. After all, it is precisely this lack of
structure that occasioned CAM in the first place:

is de dark o' de dead
o' de desert an' all dem
travellin' years: tramp

o' foot, stamp
o' cotton, an' we root-
less, waterless years.

But we want to stop
as others have stop
want to stan'

as other have stood;
want to rest, want to build …[.]   ("Cane" A 49–59)

And elsewhere in the volume:

it is not
it is not enough
to be pause, to be hole
to be void, to be silent
to be semicolon, to be semicolony;

…

So on this ground,
write[.]   ("Negus" A 73–7; "Vèvè" A 51–2)

The author of *Arrivants* would have would have no doubt known that
the verb "arrive" takes its own voyage from the Latin through French

and on into English, originally meaning "to touch the shore," "to reach the end of a journey by sea." It is certain that Brathwaite rebukes the nostalgic idea of a fixed, unchanging origin, but "this ground" needs at least to be a semi-permanent ground on which to stand, to organize, and to write.

The sort of community that CAM ultimately envisions has more to do with membership than with subjectivity. That is, for Brathwaite, La Rose, and Salkey, it was not a matter of defining a unified Black identity, but instead a question of creating collectives in which artistic and political groups of any ethnic background committed to an emancipatory politics could collaborate together in opposition to racism and class oppression. If CAM rejected the Black Power model, it most certainly does not substitute ethnic nationalism with a Caribbean variant of liberal pluralism. Brathwaite, like La Rose, explicitly rejects the "Out of Many, One People" model, whether applied to the Caribbean or to cosmopolitan London. "What we have to ask ourselves to do," Brathwaite remarks, is to find "a way that starts us talking about sharing/using common symbols; or, using them as *frisson* (match: spark: creative fire) to intensify our sense of ... a meaningful federation of cultures" (*Contradictory Omens* 55). (In the next chapter devoted to the poetry of the Women's Liberation Movement, we will encounter an expanded theory and practice of the "common.") Brathwaite is often cited for the distinction he makes between *accultural* and *intercultural* modes of creolization: the former indicating a "process of absorption," while the latter refers "to a more reciprocal activity, a process of intermixture and enrichment, each to each" (*Contradictory Omens* 11). Critics such as Gayatri Spivak, Fernando Ortiz, Stuart Hall, bell hooks, and Mary Louise Pratt rightly observe that theories of cultural hybridity and creolization risk sidestepping the asymmetrical power relations that inform how hybridization unfolds historically.[20] In a sense, interculturation attempts to forge a model of collective action and cultural appropriation that elides the totalizing ideologies of a "One People" model and the political quietism of "The Many" celebrated for its own sake. Brathwaite rejects the idea that a community needs to define itself as totally separate from other identities, but nor does the "intercultural," as it manifests itself in "nation language," mean simply a celebration of linguistic diversity in English. CAM's approach to cultural synthesis is altogether more radical: whether an appropriation of white institutions (the university), its subversive traditions (Marxism), or its language ("nation language"),

CAM not only asserts its own identity, but rather deprives the white majority of its total control over British language and culture.

The collage of synthetic communal models CAM actually develops is telling. Brathwaite emphasizes an African and a Caribbean connection: speaking on the intent of the movement as a creative "community," he asserts that "individuals ... should be prepared to submerge themselves ... give up some of your own primadonna thing for the group, right. And that came from Africa. I then returned to the Caribbean, and I think the year in St Lucia as a Extra-Mural tutor must have given me a lot of ideas of how people could be brought together" (CAM Papers 6/9 [34]). Artist and CAM member Aubrey Williams likens these semi-private gatherings to the "warishi nights" he experienced in Guyana, an Amerindian word he translates to mean a collective "unburdening." The word *warishi* also refers to the traditional "woven baskets" made from tibisiri vine, used by indigenous communities for carrying heavy loads. Thus the "nights" seem to suggest the celebrations following a period of labour. The type of celebration Williams describes likely shares an origin with the *mashramani*, a term that has since been used to signify the national festival commemorating the formation of the Co-operative Republic of Guyana in 1970. Prior to this usage, however, the Amerindian word *mashramani* designated any "voluntary work done co-operatively ... followed by a spree" (*Dictionary of Caribbean English Usage* 374). Compounding the complexity of cultural and linguistic connotations of the "warishi night," the term "spree" has rich implications for Caribbean speakers. Like British and North American English, "spree" can insinuate a flourish of violence (e.g., a "crime spree"), but it can signify joyous revelry, extravagance, and flirtatiousness as well, bearing some similarity to the French word *mêlée* (in the sense expressed by Jean-Luc Nancy).[21] Returning to the meaning privileged by Williams, the warishi night was a collective unburdening ("un-loading"), a cathartic experience of communal interaction after labour collectively undertaken for the good of the community. In response to Brathwaite's essay "West Indian Poetry: An Area of Experience," delivered at a CAM meeting in December of 1967, John La Rose explains that the group is "involved in what I have called at one of our 'warishi nights' a theory of unmaking" (*Foundations of a Movement* 170).

Yet these etymological and anthropological investigations into the African and Caribbean cultural practices that inform CAM's social organization constitute only part of the story. What about terms like "movement," "meeting," "conference," and "student centre"?

Brathwaite's attitude towards the role of the university may be gleamed from his assessment of the Creative Arts Centre (CAC), an institution created in 1968 at the UWI, Mona. In an article published in the CAM newsletter, Brathwaite praises the centre, but cautions that a creative arts program "based on the university" alone would not interpret "community" widely enough. He urges its organizers to include writers affiliated with the UWI and those found among the "wider community," such as Louise Bennett, Elaine Perkins, Norma Fay Hamilton, and Rastafarian writers. He further suggests that the centre should be a site of pan-Caribbean rather than only Jamaican concerns, and that it include French and Spanish work by writers and artists such as Aimé Césaire and Haitian painters ("Caribbean Report, January/March, 1968" 2–5). Brathwaite does not object to an alliance between artists and the university; instead, he prefers a model such as a community centre, since academics, artists, activists, and members of the general public might find opportunities for collaboration within such a space.

Brathwaite, Salkey, and La Rose are academics and activists; the models of social interaction they create are equally indebted to an educational system emerging from what Habermas calls the "bourgeois public sphere" as well as Marxist-informed extra-parliamentary tactics of grass-roots organization. I would not want to suggest that the "movement" as a form of collective action is solely a Western invention, but La Rose and Salkey's Marxist training and, in particular, the former's attempted implementation of a socialist regime in Trinidad, suggest this as an important model for CAM. As a group undisturbed by the legacy of early twentieth-century avant-gardism in Europe (more to the point, its allegiances to fascism), for Brathwaite, Salkey, and La Rose, the term "movement" was understood in its political and cultural sense divorced from the concerns that preoccupied the Black Mountain poets, the New York School, the Toronto Research Group, or the Language poets. CAM never worried about rescuing a concept of literary community from its associations with the militarist rhetoric of Futurism and Vorticism.

La Rose's definition of cultural action bears some resemblance to the New Left and New Social Movements, both of which stressed that class struggle would need to make room for marginalized identities and human rights (rather than labour focused) issues. CAM no doubt finds common cause with collectives such as the peace movement, the student movement, like-minded minority rights groups, environmental activists, and so on. The conflict had grown more complex. The Left would need to learn how to build alliances between numerous subjects with goals that at times overlapped and at other times diverged. But notably this condition of political and social multiplicity was already the condition of Caribbean people at home and abroad. The question for La Rose and his collaborators is how any ensemble of actors might come together to form a militant subject. Brathwaite will call this "possession": "in the moment of possession, the ... charge becomes grounded" so that the ground beneath our feet and those who stand upon this common ground share in a "special significance" ("Glossary" A 271).

CAM saw a possible link between Caribbean and West African notions of collectivity and the new social movements that emerged in the West during the 1960s. The activist model of the student centre might be thought of as a political reversal, turning the supposedly egalitarian structures of European invention back towards itself. Drawing comparison to the Third International, one might conceive of their use of the meeting, conference, and student centre as a *détournement* of the bourgeois public sphere, appropriating the organs of academic culture and the civic space of the community centre in order to launch an anti-racism campaign in the English capital and abroad. Needless to say, this creolization of British social institutions intersects with the formation of "nation language" as an aesthetic practice.

Underground Language

[T]he dialect is directly connected with the Standard English because, you see, the dialect is within both. I think it is a continuous form of West Indian speech, both things are closely combined. I attempt therefore to combine both things simultaneously.

– John La Rose[22]

So, how did the activities of the Caribbean Artists Movement relate to their poetry? Certainly Brathwaite and others did not invent what he calls "nation language." Both he and CAM member Gordon Rohlehr trace its development to early slave songs, calypso music, and folklore. Its possibilities are further developed among poets and musicians associated with CAM, Rastafarianism, dub, and reggae – performers as diverse as the Mighty Sparrow, Louise Bennett, George Campbell, Frank Collymore, Derek Walcott, John Figuero, Bob Marley, Bongo Jerry, Michael Smith, Jane Breeze, Mutabaraka, and Linton Kwesi Johnson. The term, in its specific sense, refers to Caribbean writing, but in Brathwaite's now-canonical *History of the Voice*, he cites a motley consortium of non-Caribbean predecessors: Dante Alighieri (the poet's use of his own Tuscan vernacular), Basque and Gaelic as languages that challenged European colonial rule, and even T.S. Eliot, whose voice, for Brathwaite, delivers the "riddims of St. Louis" (30–1n41). The inclusion of European examples emphasizes a non-essentialist relationship between language and its community of users. The Caribbean Artists Movement, then, is not the originator of a creole poetics, but rather one site of its production and *articulation*, that is, in the proper sense that Hall gives to this word as a "linkage" between "languaging" subjects. The aesthetic and political possibilities of creole are identified and theorized within this context, mapping associations between Afro-Caribbean writers and traditions, and fostering directions for further experimentation.

On 6 January 1967 the second of two early meetings that led to the official launch of CAM took place at the novelist Orlando Patterson's flat in London. He delivered what would turn out to be a controversial talk entitled "Is There a West Indian Aesthetic?" The radical plurality and displacement that characterizes the Caribbean led the author to surmise that "West Indian society … is in many ways traditionless." Hence, he concludes, "[o]ne doesn't have a basis for retaliation against the colonial experience in an indigenous culture as occurs in the case of the African or Asian" (1). Patterson had become a celebrated novelist with the publication of *Children of Sisyphus* (1964), a work of social realist fiction narrating the lives of Rastafarian youths living in the poorest regions of Kingston, Jamaica. He claims that the writer must work as a sociologist; Caribbean artists should not retreat to a suppressed indigenous culture, but rather they must address contemporary issues, "arousing [a] national, social and cultural consciousness" (2). Patterson's argument elicited enthusiastic discussion, and in many ways it frames one of the key directives of the movement: to name and historicize a Caribbean aesthetics. Attendees at the meeting took no particular issue with Patterson's sociological focus on West Indian writing, but they objected to the claim that the Caribbean lacked tradition. Brathwaite and Gordon Rohlehr were especially vocal. Neither wanted to accept Patterson's claim, but nor did they wish to assert that the Caribbean had a unified, singular culture.

On 7 April 1967 Rohlehr delivered a talk entitled "Sparrow and the Language of the Calypso" at the second of CAM's public meetings at the West Indian Student Centre. Rohlehr wished to disprove Patterson's argument by presenting evidence of the Trinidadian musical form as a positive example of Caribbean cultural history and practice. The critic had initially planned a talk addressing Sparrow's music, Louise Bennett's creole verse, and Sam Selvon's novel *The Lonely Londoners*, but lacked sufficient time to prepare this more ambitious project. His more focused lecture had broad implications nonetheless: to make a case for the aesthetic value of popular culture. Calypso is associated with the "masses of Trinidad" ("Sparrow" 87). One of the most famous calypsonians, the Mighty Sparrow, traces the musical form to the slave song:

> We had to chant and sing to express our feelings
> To that wicked and cruel man
> That was the only medicine to get them to listen
> And it's so calypso began.   ("The Slave" [1954] 1–4)

To include discussion of this practice alongside debates about the contemporary Caribbean novel and established poetic traditions was a landmark moment in Caribbean cultural studies. In the speech delivered to members of CAM, Rohlehr contends that calypso affords a set of techniques "which our poets have not yet discovered": "[i]t may help the West Indian poet to realize the rhythmic potential of his ordinary use of English" (99). In the fourth CAM newsletter, Brathwaite published a brief response to Rohlehr's talk, in which he rejects Rohlehr's implied distinction between the calypsonian and the poet, "the preconception that an artist like Sparrow is in some way an entirely different being from an artist, say, like myself" (CAM Papers 1/4 [8]). He mentions Derek Walcott, Lorrimer Alexander, and Wordsworth McAndrew as poets who have successfully employed such "speech rhythms" in their verse.

In the opening pages of *History of the Voice*, a lecture he delivered at Harvard University in 1979, Kamau Brathwaite makes a casual but telling remark regarding an earlier talk given by the South African poet and activist Dennis Brutus: "he was speaking about the structural condition of South Africa ... [b]ut instinctively people recognized that the structural condition described by Dennis had very much to do with language ...[,] the relationship between language and culture, language and structure" (5). When Brathwaite – and this is equally true of La Rose and Salkey – discusses language, poetic and otherwise, he is specifically interested in the consequences of language change for a community's sense of itself. Like Robert Duncan, Brathwaite insists that the form of language maps social structures. The term "nation language" already suggests this, but the emphasis on nationalism is misleading. Although Brathwaite retains the word "nation," he actually means to problematize its associations.

Caribbean language is defined by a radical plurality. Brathwaite offers a taxonomy that I here condense for purposes of concision: (1) imperial English ("the imposed language"); (2) Creole ("a mixture of English and an adaptation that English took in the new environment"); (3) nation language ("the language of slaves and laborers, the servants who were brought in by the conquistadors" – consisting largely of the West African languages Ashanti, Congo, and Yoruba); and (4) ancestral languages (the largely dissipated languages of the Amerindians). This "prism" of speech, as Brathwaite calls it, is further complicated by the introduction of French, Spanish, and Dutch. One should also bear in mind the South Asian and Chinese influences in the region, and thus the remnants of South and East Asian languages as well. The European colonization of the Caribbean, the decimation of the Amerindian population, and the importation of African slaves to the region would contribute to this radical linguistic heterogeneity.

Imperial powers perceived this linguistic diversity as a threat, and sought to eliminate it. The school system became the locus of an assimilationist project to institutionalize European languages on the island. Like the pervasive ideological projects to erase indigenous and minoritarian languages in South Africa and the residential schools of Canada, Brathwaite

... was told their tales

were wrong; saw those who taught
him songs of what he ought to, what he ought
not do, take off their hats to the white

inspector's car. learn your books good,
lookin
good like him. ponds beauty cream

will lighten the skin and the black night longs for the moon
an old cracked face looks up from the well
and the dish run away with the spoon[.]   ("Journeys" [1975] 19–28)

The appropriation of children's rhymes and racialized advertisements echo Charles Olson's critique of "mu-sick," whereby the rhythms of language seek to lull the subject into complacency and acceptance. In what was an object lesson in Foucauldian modes of institutional discipline, children were obligated to memorize poetic sequences such as "the snow was falling on the canefields," a derivative adaptation of the line, "the snow was falling on the playing fields of Shropshire" (*Voice* 9). The imposition of a British image onto the social experience of the Caribbean is clearly absurd. Brathwaite notes that until quite recently Caribbean children were required to create drawings of such images, of "white snowfields and the corn-haired people who inhabited such a landscape" (9). But such a line – as prosaic as it may sound – perfectly articulates Brathwaite's distinction between acculturation as a process of absorption and interculturation, which generates the frisson of a deliberate synthesis commenting on the process of creolization itself. Nation language constitutes a response to this moment of creolization, not by refusing cultural syncretism (since colonization and migration make syncretism inevitable), but rather by deliberately exposing the power relations of this encounter, by establishing the page as an arena of agonistic pluralism (to use Mouffe's phrase) between the linguistic communities that represent through language.

What interests Brathwaite most of all is the slippage, the trace of a heterogeneous language that evades the systems of power seeking to regulate and police linguistic, and thus communal, expression: "[w]hat these languages had to do, however, was to submerge themselves, because officially the conquering peoples – the Spaniards, the English, the French, and the Dutch – insisted that the language of public discourse" remain these "official, standard" languages (5–6). But as is often the case, attempts to restrict and police linguistic syncretism fail:

this very submergence served an interesting interculturative purpose, because although people continued to speak English as it was spoken in Elizabethan times and on through the Romantic and Victorian ages, that English was, nonetheless, still being influenced by the underground language, the submerged language that the slaves had brought. And that underground language was constantly transforming itself into new forms. (*Voice* 7–8)

As I noted above, terms such as "submerge" combine notions of convergence and interaction. One finds the same complex of meanings in "underground," particularly in the African American context that Brathwaite is likely drawing upon. Below the surface of oppressive rule is a system of connection:

> & learn-
> in prospero ling
> age & ting
>
> not fe dem/not fe dem
>
> ...
>
> but fe we
> fe a-we
>
> ("X/Self xth letter" 143–6, 149–50)

This later poem from Brathwaite, written during the 1980s, concisely illustrates a formal procedure he begins to develop during the mid-1960s (a practice I will discuss more fully in the next section of the chapter). By placing a line break to separate the phonemes of "learn- / in," the first line becomes a grammatical directive, a lesson imposed upon a student by a master. The second line, "in prospero ling," treats language as a social environment one enters and occupies. By placing a second line break separating phonemes in the word "ling / age" (language), he creates the line "age & ting" (things), further insisting that language is situated within a time and a place. "Prospero ling" is the colonial language within which the Afro-Caribbean subject is "imprisoned by his master," as Caliban will attest. Yet Brathwaite's line breaks in stanza one anticipate the liberating rupture of the second stanza, the possibility of creative misunderstanding and playful reversal akin to Henry Louis Gates Jr's concept of "signifyin(g),"[23] and the tradition of the trickster figure he cites. Brathwaite's contention, however, emphasizes the communal nature of this appropriation and adaptation of Standard English, by insisting that this process articulates and defines "a-we." A "we" is constructed in opposition to a "them," but the position of the indefinite article resists closure, essence, and finitude.

Some critics wonder why CAM members did not write exclusively in nation language. The reader of Brathwaite's *Arrivants*, for instance, encounters passages of British English (both standard and cockney), African and Southern U.S. idioms, nation language, and West African signifiers. La Rose's *Foundations* (1966) likewise integrates political speech with art, calypso rhythms with decidedly abstract poetic modes, macrohistorical analysis with anecdotal lyricism, the language of academic conferences and the polyphony of the carnival. Some stanzas culled from "Fantasy in Space" (1966) give an illustration:

> The space machine taunts
>   The man-animal
> Hurtling impatiently through
>   Haunted skyscape
> Toward one future's flimsy.
> …
>
>   Iscariot's successors
>   Succumbed
>   Eternal imprudence.
> …
>
> She eh come yet
> But she comin'.
> Dey eh done yet
> Buh dey dancin'.
> Dey shakin'
> An dey winin'
>   Oh God
>   Oh God
>   It comin'.
>
> Back to the grinding
>   Poverty,
> Back to the bitter
>   North wind,
> Back to the lonely acres
>   Of Green,
> Back to an aeon
> Among bulging stone[.]   (1–5, 10–12, 27–43)

In La Rose's poem of diasporic shifts and displacements, images of modern technology collide with the carnival. One encounters the ana-phoristic quality common to poetic and political/sermonic discourse, while the first of these stanzas exhibits aspects of modernist abstraction and compression. La Rose often employs this method to describe phys-ical and existential displacement: "The lineal connection / Between space and time / Tangles like ship's rope" ("Connecting Link" [1966] 1–3). One recalls that Brathwaite had objected to the children's verse on mimetic grounds, since it did not sufficiently represent Caribbean social experience. Yet the British context was a cosmopolitan one with which Brathwaite and La Rose had to negotiate and to transform.

The collective articulation of "a we" in language is always already situated within a perpetually creolizing federation of "we's." As one turns to the poetry of Brathwaite, La Rose, and Salkey, the operative metaphor is one of linkage. Like the fusion of African communitarian models and Marxism used to build the Caribbean Artists Movement's institutional structure, the composition of their poetry features an iden-tical approach of interculturation: that is, a *deliberately selective* linkage of groups, metaphors, and associations that participate in a common project of emancipation and radical equality.

"Eating the Dead": Kamau Brathwaite's *Arrivants* in London

The basic point about African gods and the Caribbean gods that derive from them is that they can 'possess' and be possessed by the ordinary, believing, participating, individual worshipper ... The celebrant's body acts as a kind of lightning conductor for the god. In the moment of possession, the divine elec-trical charge becomes *grounded* ... Even in the Caribbean, these African-derived religions are looked upon as the province only of the underprivileged and de-prived masses of the population.

– Kamau Brathwaite[24]

The first of CAM's public readings was presented by the London Tra-verse Theatre Company in association with La Rose's New Beacon Press at the Jeanette Cochrane Theatre on 3 March 1967. Kamau Brath-waite read the entirety of *Rights of Passage*, the first text in his *Arriv-ants* trilogy. On 27 September 1967 he read *Masks* at a gathering at his home, and almost two years later to the day, on 29 September 1969, he read *Islands* at the West Indian Student Centre. Pearl Connor, the director of the Negro Theatre Company, present for the first of these readings, observed that "we hadn't presented any one of our writers, in the sense of poet, in that way before" (CAM Papers 6/14 [1]). The "way" of reading to which Connor refers is a tradition of orality and musicality more suited to a calypso concert. There was a populist element to the reading, and a sense that students, activists, and members of the broader Caribbean British community could partake. Brathwaite's trilogy combines nation language, British English, and West African languages; his work connects the migratory histories and cultural traditions of Africa, Europe, the Caribbean, and the Americas. From U.S. jazz and blues to Ghanaian and Jamaican folk cultures, from calypso and carnival to Haitian Vodou, from subversive appropriations of European literatures to the celebration of Caribbean social revolutionaries, Brathwaite's practice might be understood through one of his operative metaphors: "driftwords." The image resonates with his concepts of submergence and connectivity, both as a migratory transference from place to place and as the drift of information shared among communities. "Driftword" is also a pun relating to the discarded material of wreckage and waste. Yet unlike Eliot, the fragment need not signify a wasteland; instead, Brathwaite indicates that he was "constantly trying to create integration" (Barthwaite, "Interview" by Mackey 18):

> ... how will new maps be drafted?
> Who will suggest a new tentative frontier?
>
> ...

> making
> with their
>
> rhythms some-
> thing torn
>
> and new[.]
>   ("The Cracked Mother" [1969] *A* 118–19; "Jou'vert" [1969] *A* 72–6)

His aim is to recover from the "driftwords" of past traditions an aggregate of social and linguistic structures upon which to assemble "our common ground" ("Unrighteousness of Mammon" [1967] *A* 18). Brathwaite is committed to this project of "integration" as a poet, critic, historian, and community organizer.

Unlike La Rose and Salkey, whose activism and journalism inform a more explicitly political poetics, Brathwaite's *Arrivants* trilogy expresses a poetry of resistance in more broadly historical, even cosmological, terms. How did this trilogy of texts inform the social activism of the Caribbean Artists Movement, particularly since Brathwaite himself saw these as commensurate projects? Another way of formulating this question might be to imagine: how was the poem relevant to the community of organizers, activists, and artists who attended the reading that day in 1967? Several critics analyse Brathwaite's *Arrivants* trilogy for its complex weave of history, its intertexts, its critique of colonialism, and its aesthetic mastery of the epic form, yet through its religious and historical system of associations, the text also assembles a template for social activism.[25] The reader of *Arrivants* encounters a synthesis of three orders: (1) the *mythological*: a makeshift pantheon of West African, Haitian, and Christian gods and ritualistic practices; (2) the *historical/revolutionary*: figures of Afro-Caribbean and American revolt, from Tacky's rebellion and Toussaint L'Ouverture to Che Guevara and Martin Luther King Jr; and (3) the *linguistic*: a blend of West African, Amerindian, and minoritarian European "ling / age." Brathwaite invites his readers to pursue this specific linkage between a pluralistic pantheon of gods, a history of Third World liberators, and a poetic practice formed from nation language. Indeed, Brathwaite's claim that "the poetry was saying the same thing that CAM was doing" may offer a yet unrevealed poetics of protest. Just as CAM was integrating Marxist practices of organization with Afro-Caribbean communitarian models, Brathwaite was building a syncretic "common ground" in *Arrivants*, understood as an emancipatory practice of writing linked with the struggles of London's immigrant communities.

From Myth to Social Action: The Cosmological "Ground"

A brief glance at Brathwaite's large corpus of poetic works reveals two commensurate and interconnected projects: a continuous long poem and a series of collections largely comprising odes, elegies, and occasional poems. Brathwaite wrote his major trilogies – *Arrivants* (*Rights of Passage* [1967], *Masks* [1968], *Islands* [1969]) and *Ancestors* (*Mother Poem* [1977], *Sun Poem* [1982], *X/Self* [1987]) – alongside collections such as *Other Exiles* (1975), *Black + Blues* (1976), *Third World Poems* (1983), and *Jah Music* (1986), which counterpoint long poems investigating colonialism, the diaspora, and community formation with occasional pieces devoted to figures of social protest and cultural influence. In a sense, a macro- and a micropolitical thread runs alongside one another. The author, however, had the habit of republishing individual poems from his epic sequences within these smaller volumes, so that texts from his *Arrivants* trilogy like "Jah" reappear in a collection such as *Jah Music* next to poems about activists, poets, and musicians. The effect is that of weaving religious, literary and political concerns into the serial organization of his collections.

A comparable development occurs at the poetic level as well. From the early poems of *Masks* in *The Arrivants* trilogy to the poems of *X/Self* in *Ancestors*, Brathwaite establishes a link between mythological figures and social revolutionaries. Separate poems honouring the African Vodun gods Jah, Ananse, Legba, and Ogun are found alongside poems referencing social revolutionaries like Toussaint, Bussa, Tacky, and Che. By *X/Self*, one finds them sharing lines of the same stanza:

> daaga. yegon. toussaint legba
>   bussa. fidel. sister stark
>
> …
>
>   nanny fanon accompong
> keepers of the word shall come
>   Mandela Malcolm cir
>
> …
>
> give me vengeance w/thy word[.]   ("Dies Irie" 7–8, 26–8, 72)

The gradual omission of punctuation encourages the reader to blend one name into the next, whereby they link, even embody one another. To "embody" is "to give a concrete form to … principles, thoughts, intentions," to render such ideals "in an institution, work of art, action, [or] definite form of words" (*OED*). To embody is to hold together a "system or complex unity" of elements. Elsewhere Brathwaite describes this strategy as an event collage that brings historical moments "together in the same space, even if they come from two different time centres" (Brathwaite, "Interview" by Mackey 22). For Brathwaite, history is accumulative rather than sequential – "It was December second, nineteen fifty-six. / It was the first of August eighteen thirty-eight.

/ It was the twelfth October fourteen ninety-two" ("Caliban" [1969] *A* 29–31) – historical traumas that still reverberate on the bodies of contemporary subjects. What is more, Brathwaite seeks to mobilize those "time centres" of agency into an assemblage, an embodiment, of a revolutionary ideal. Columbus is one time centre, but so is Bussa, the early nineteenth-century leader of a mass slave rebellion:[26]

... wid nev-

er a scare dat de gov-
ernor come-

in an de white
people vex

dat we fight-
in instead a flight-

in from dem jess be-
cause a dis man

who couldn't care less
bout defeat ...[.]   ("Portrait of Bussa" [1983] 113–23)

If Columbus is still very much present in the contemporary moment, then so can Legba and Bussa, Ananse and Toussaint, Ogun and Che come to constitute a platform upon which to ground collective resistance.

This chapter is not the place for a detailed study of West African Vodun, Haitian Vodou, santería, Rastafarianism, and the syncretic influences of Catholicism,[27] nor is there room for a comprehensive discussion of the complex and unique interweaving of these traditions in various Caribbean nations over several hundred years of practice. Yet one can ask the comparatively less onerous question: why, amid the complex mythologies of West Africa and their various adaptations in a Caribbean context, does Brathwaite select this particular assemblage of gods, and what are their roles in *Arrivants*?

In a section of the third volume in Brathwaite's trilogy, entitled "New World," the speaker introduces the principal archetypes that preside over the text: Jah, Ananse, Legba, and Ogun. These names reference traditions of a West African past, but now as "driftwords," await reconstitution in a new configuration: the pantheon of gods must change, must

mutate into a different federation, to meet the needs and historical circumstances of the moment. Depending on the cultural context Jah has
significance for Christian, Jewish, and Rastafarian religions. Ananse,
Legba, and Ogun had their origins in the West African mythologies of
Yoruba, Akans, and Ashanti cultures, and came to occupy important
roles in Haitian Vodou and African American folk traditions.[28] I will
examine these archetypes momentarily, but for now, suffice it to say
that all four are creator figures to varying degrees, and all possess poly-
morphic characteristics. The role and significance of individual gods
change depending on geography, group, and practice of worship. That
is, a particular configuration of archetypes drawn from the larger West
African-Caribbean pantheon is always a unique mutation – something
"torn / and new" – and it is precisely this migratory and combinatory
quality that Brathwaite privileges from the poem's outset.

Jah, associated with the Hebrew abbreviation for Jehovah, figures prominently in Rastafarianism as Jah Jah. Rohlehr argues that Brathwaite's use
of "Jah" refers neither to the Rastafarian nor the Hebrew deity, but instead symbolizes an "Anglo-Saxon Protestant perversion of the Christian
message." Jah, he argues, "is the colonizer's God; or, he is the colonizer
as god," the capitalist system exploiting African and Caribbean societies
(*Pathfinder* 166). In the poem, "Columbus rides out of the Jungle's den,"
while the United Fruit Company is found "eating the dark men,"

> … here God looks out over the river
> yellow mix of the neon lights
> high up over the crouching cotton-wool green
> and we float, high up over the sighs of the city,
> like fish in a gold water world[.]   ("Jah" [1969] *A* 15, 10, 40–4)

Figures of imperialist exploitation (Columbus) mingle conspicuously
with references to mid-century neoliberal economic expansion (United
Fruit, Barry Goldwater). Given Brathwaite's propensity for linguistic
and symbolic polysemia and reversal, there is reason to believe that
several meanings imbue the sign of the deity. Indeed, Brathwaite's
claim for culture as a common resource suggests that the figure of Jah
(its significance for Judaism, Haitian Vodou, and Rastafarianism) explodes and multiplies its economy of meaning, purpose, and status
from any singular, unified religion. The sign of "Jah" playfully subverts
monotheism as such. Just as United Fruit can "eat the dark men," a reversal is possible. The poem begins:

Nairobi's male elephants uncurl
their trumpets to heaven
Toot-Toot takes it up
in Havana
in Harlem[.]   (1–5)

This subtle passage sets the groundwork for the system of associations
Brathwaite seeks to elaborate, among mythology, politics, and art. A
reference to the Mau Mau uprising[29] in Kenya "uncurls" as the genesis of African struggles against colonialism. The mention of trumpets
emphasizes the artistic role played in these social struggles: the cultural upheavals in Havana and Harlem, evocations of a socialist Caribbean, and the civil rights movement in the United States assemble to
articulate an approach to social change that echoes La Rose's politically
committed definition of culture as the inaugural platform for social activism. In a word, then, Jah is *power*: whether this is the power to subjugate or the power to resist, Jah is the power to organize and control.
    Next comes Ananse, the Ashanti trickster figure, depicted both as
man and spider, and known for cunning, subtlety, and survival. In
Brathwaite's poem he is depicted "[w]ith a black snake's un- / winking
eye," his mouth "a black pot / grinning / grinning." But behind this
exterior, there lies a "brain green, a green chrysalis / storing leaves"
("Ananse" [1969] *A* 1–2, 43–5, 7–8). Rohlehr remarks that Ananse "survived the fire of history, but with a burnt-out, transformed sensibility"
(*Pathfinder* 182). A famous Akan legend holds that there are no stories
in the world. The sky god, Nyame, has hoarded them all for himself.
Ananse approaches Nyame wishing to purchase the stories on behalf
of the world. Nyame stipulates that before he will share the stories Ananse must fulfil a series of tasks. Through trickery, Ananse must capture, in turn, the Python, Onini, the Leopard, Osebo, Mmoboro, the
Hornets, and the invisible Fairy, Mmoatia. Brathwaite makes Ananse
the populist god of literary and cultural knowledge. He is a giver like
Prometheus, but unlike the thief of fire, Ananse chooses compromise
and circumvention over agonistic self-sacrifice.[30] A rhetorician, Ananse

    ... squats on the tips

    of our language
    black burr of conundrums

    . ...

he spins drum-
beats, silver skin
webs of sound
through the villages[.]   (12–14, 17–20)

Associated with transformation, appropriation, and counter-insur-
gency, Ananse is the trickster figure who enters the web of power and
reweaves its narratives into something useful for the community.

In a note to *Arrivants*, Brathwaite explains that Legba is the Daho-
mean/Haitian "god of the gateway," or crossroads, who forms the
"crucial link between man and the other gods" (*A* 273). For this reason, Legba is the first god to be evoked at Vodun ceremonies. Said
to know all human languages, Legba is depicted as the facilitator of
communication, speech, and meaning. A "lame old man on a crutch,"
he has nevertheless known "Burma, Malaya, and has been / to Sin-
gapore" ("Legba" [1969] *A* 2, 5–6). Presiding over the boundaries between worlds – the mythological and the earthly, the Caribbean and
the African, and so on – Legba personifies a simultaneous moment
of cultural fracture and potential reconnection. Though he takes the
form of a broken being, he possesses the capacity to shepherd the diasporic community through the "maimed world of banks, books, [and]
insurance businesses" (27).

Ogun is the fourth of Brathwaite's principal archetypes. He is the Yoruba and Afro-Caribbean creator god, but, as Brathwaite relates in his
notes to the poem, he is "seen here in his aspect as divine craftsman" (*A*
274). The image of god as a maker or carpenter is consistent with Yor-
uban, Akans, and Christian belief systems, making the poem, in at least
one respect, a metaphor of creative process. Rohlehr reads the text as a
"magical awakening and transfiguration of Tom into Ogun; of timidity
and inertia into creative power" (*Pathfinder* 290). The Caribbean poet
who formerly worked in Western abstractions, and according to predetermined European poetic models, articulates a different vision from
the materials of the island he inhabits:

And yet he had a block of wood that would have baffled them.
With knife and gimlet care he worked away at this on Sundays,

explored its knotted hurts, cutting his way
along its yellow whorls[.]   ("Ogun" [1969] *A* 27–30)

Rohlehr further observes the multiplicity of meanings implicit in a phrase such as "knotted hurts": the knots "which occur in wood wherever the limbs of trees have been amputated," the "psychic maimings" of slavery, and an image of complexity pertaining to the interlacing of New World cultures. One might additionally speak of creole as the creative knotting of language, in such a way that makes its symbolic codes difficult to unravel. Yet there is a subtle political component to the poem. As I have remarked before, *Arrivants* consistently links the artistic, religious, and political; the Haitian adaptation of Ogun depicts him as a god presiding over the political realm, who is said to have possessed the slaves of the Haitian Revolution. In contemporary worship, Ogun is summoned whenever the community wishes a more democratic society.[31] Nowhere in the poem is it explicitly stated that the carpenter is Ogun; instead, an unnamed speaker describes his "uncle," a "knock-knee'd" old man found among the "canefield mulemen" and "lorry drivers." By the end of the text, he transforms the wood, "eaten by pox, ravaged by rats," into the "emerging woodwork image of his anger" (1–10, 42, 46). The Everyman of the poem, somebody's uncle and the descendant of slaves, constructs and wears the mask of Ogun.

The principal gods of Brathwaite's New World pantheon come to symbolize power (Jah), appropriation and reversal (Ananse), connection and communication (Legba), and revolutionary change (Ogun). Stripped of their religious associations, these concepts could easily substitute for a manifesto enumerating the principles of a social movement:

(1) know the system of power and how it operates to subjugate peoples;
(2) work to manipulate this system to one's advantage;
(3) establish a community of like-minded individuals and organizations prepared to resist subordination, building networks of communication between them; and
(4) only when these conditions are met can individuals become possessed as revolutionary subjects of change.

These principles cannot, however, exist independently; the "celebrant's body," Brathwaite instructs, "acts as a kind of lightning conductor for the god" ("Glossary" *A* 271). The question for Brathwaite is one of subjectivation: the subject frees oneself from the constraints set by individualism, becoming, as Alain Badiou would say, an "element of another body" (*The Communist Hypothesis* 236). The godly is none other than the truth of an emancipated existence, the individual becoming a militant embodiment of this truth at precisely the moment she relinquishes her individual subjectivity and commits to this political project.

Possession and Revolt

Brathwaite was not naïve in his commitment to anti-colonialist revolt. Among those revolutionaries he names, most had either died in battle, were imprisoned, or were assassinated. So, too, collective mobilization of the population had as much to do with material necessity as any intellectual principle of freedom: "Ninety-five per cent of my people poor / ninety-five per cent of my people black / ninety-five per cent of my people dead." The speaker of "Caliban" so proclaims, "you have heard it all before O Leviticus O Jeremiah O Jean-Paul Sartre" ("Caliban" *A* 1–4). Well before the catastrophic storm of 2008, the international community routinely described Haiti as the western hemisphere's poorest country. Although a detailed history of Western intervention in Haiti is beyond the scope of the present study, it is imperative to remember that much of Haiti's "deliberate impoverishment" is the "direct legacy of perhaps the most brutal system of colonial exploitation in world history, compounded by decades of systematic postcolonial oppression … [and] neoliberal intervention" (Hallward, "Our Role" n.p.). Art is, for Brathwaite, a central activity through which historical memory is preserved and collective action is realized; it is during precisely those moments of crisis and catastrophe that Brathwaite suggests one must embody the gods.[32] In "Ananse," the "webs of sound" reverberate "through the villages" via the drum (the inaugural word of *Arrivants*). A symbol of rhythm, communication, and rebellion (Rohlehr, *Pathfinder* 164 ff.; Lee, *The Language of Caribbean Poetry* 97), the circular form of the drum has additional significance for African culture: "with africa [*sic*] its chief subsistence source and model … is the circle …. [T]he drums are round, its dancers dance a circle; the villages and their houses: also round" ("Metaphors of Underdevelopment" 251). Further still, in the contemporary context the drum is the accompaniment of the protest march. Brathwaite, in beginning with this instrument, is evoking a multiplicity of "time centres" and connecting African religious practice with the contemporary civil rights movement. The "webs of sound" echoing through villages (and throughout the trilogy) find their way to figures of historical change: "Tacky heard him / and L'Ouverture" ("Ananse" *A* 21–2). As the epigram to this section suggests, Brathwaite's appropriation of Afro-Caribbean religions has no value as an abstract system alone; the gods are significant insofar as they are "possessed" by a subject. The energies of rebellion and community are "grounded" in the bodies of "ordinary, believing, participating, individual[s]" ("Glossary" *A* 271).

Wherever Brathwaite evokes his New World mythology, the spiritual principles they represent are "grounded" in social action. I have already mentioned Bussa, among others. Toussaint L'Ouverture appears in these poems, both as an Ananse trickster figure and as the embodiment of Ogun. C.L.R James's *The Black Jacobins* was a foundational text for Brathwaite and La Rose, and thus Toussaint's exploits were well known to both poets. Born into slavery, he led a successful rebellion against European colonial power: he expelled French and British authorities, abolished slavery, and established an independent colony in Haiti in 1797. Toussaint initially fought with the Spanish against the French. Once France abolished slavery in 1794, he promptly switched sides (making the switch from royalist to republican), mobilizing his army of liberated slaves against the Spanish and English, and winning the forts of the Cordon de L'Ouest for the French Republic. By 1798, acting as commander-in-chief of the French Army in Haiti, he successfully forced the withdrawal of Spanish and English forces, but negotiated the continuance of commercial trading with the latter. As a military and political strategist, Toussaint was capable of diplomacy and compromise. He invited former white plantation workers to remain in the country, and encouraged reconciliation between African, mixed-race, and white communities. (He was, for instance, decidedly opposed to the extremist position of French commissioner Léger-Félicité Sonthonax, who proposed the extermination of all Europeans on the island.) And while his newly drafted constitution effectively muted all influence from French authorities, Toussaint expressed superficial allegiance with France's Napoleon Bonaparte.[33]

That such a figure should appear in Brathwaite's trilogy in a poem entitled "Ananse" is no coincidence. Brathwaite saw the revolutionary leader as a trickster, playing the colonial powers against one another while he plotted the end of slavery. Complementing his military prowess, Toussaint spoke French, had the benefit of an education, and was well versed in the ideas of the Enlightenment. The slave uprisings in

Haiti were precipitated in part by the French Revolution. The principles of liberty, equality, and fraternity promised by the *Declaration of the
Rights of Man* had reached the colonies, and leaders like Toussaint were
quick to apply these declarations to black and mixed-race peoples. Just
as Toussaint cleverly mobilized colonial armies against one another, he
exposed the hypocrisy of his colonial oppressors by appropriating and
reversing their most prized texts. Finally, given Brathwaite's penchant
for puns and linguistic detours, he would have certainly taken note of
Toussaint's name. His given name means "the awakening of all saints";
L'Ouverture, his adopted surname, was coined for his capacity to exploit "openings" in the defences of his political and military opponents.
If Toussaint was the first successful slave to overthrow a colonial power
in the Caribbean, then perhaps he is also the first to subject the colonial
language to productive corruption.

Returning to the reading of Brathwaite's trilogy at the London Tra-
verse Theatre Company, it might be said that the poet was constructing
a "magical event," indeed, the creolization of time itself, whereby the
mythic Ananse and the historical Toussaint and a community of activists and artists converge. "So the god," Brathwaite instructs, is "the
mask of dreamers" ("Masks" [1968] *A* 41–2):

> … I can show
> you what it means to eat
> your god, drink his explosions of power
>
> and from the slow sinking mud of your plunder, grow.
>
> ("Eating the Dead" [1969] *A* 70–3)

Eating the Dead: The Trickster Figure as Poetic Discourse

The passage cited above is taken from "Eating the Dead," a practice with
origins in both the Catholic Eucharist and the African-Haitian voudun
ritual of "manger les morts." In both religions, the ritual symbolizes the
embodiment of spiritual communion; in its original context, however,
the Akan ritual was performed in order to express allegiance to one's
community. Its intent formed bonds that are both spiritual and political.
The "drinking of the gods" is a crucial element of the ceremony, whereby
the oath taker drinks from a source of water first poured over an object sacred to an ancestral god.[34] The poem summons two figures specifically: Ananse ("Brother Spider" of "enduring cunning" [17, 20]) and

Ogun ("the iron stranger" [23]). Thus Brathwaite is aligning the trickster storyteller with the god of revolutionary defiance. The poem expresses the speaker's commitment to rebuild his community by collecting "drift-words" and assembling anew. As I remarked earlier, Brathwaite consistently exposes the subtexts of words, transforming negative into positive terms: submerge, underground, subterranean. These terms, which suggest marginalization and subordination, come to emphasize a communal network operating under the surface of the dominant culture. Brathwaite's evocation of the dead assembles an underworld of associations that establishes continuity with an ancestral past. Yet the poet's emphasis on consumption and creative process has another feature. Brathwaite's poetic practice should also be understood as eating colonial discourse: the poet appropriates, consumes, and extracts that which is regenerative and discards its fecal remains. It is in this context that the reader must approach the otherwise puzzling lines: "I must devour it all like a bank, / cell by cell, vault by vault, blinding to the void" (61–2). Why would Brathwaite suggest that the creative process and political role of the artist emulate the capitalist's exploitative consumption of the island? Consumption is here understood as linguistic recycling: the colonial discourse must be internalized, broken down, and recombined. This is the essential first step of resurrection.

It should be said, however, that CAM never understood language to be an autonomous realm. For Brathwaite, it was "in language that the slave was perhaps most successfully imprisoned by his master and it was in his (mis-)use of it that he perhaps most effectively rebelled" (*Development of Creole Society* 237). This is a tantalizing assertion for literary critics who wish to make claims for the revolutionary possibilities of language as such, but his caveat to this statement is equally important. Although language "helps to inform action," it alone does not constitute a platform for change. Successful challenges to power involve linguistic, ideological, and physical revolts in unison. It is in precisely this sense that one may begin to understand Brathwaite's contention that CAM is integral to the poetics its members were building. The poetic "mis-use" of language must be understood as the linguistic component of CAM's productive mis-use of Western educational and institutional models. The micropolitical lines of the poem extend to these macropolitical configurations.

From the appearance of *The Arrivants* trilogy and onward to *X/Self*, Brathwaite appropriates and recycles several poetic styles influenced by jazz, slave songs, calypso and African drum rhythms, sermons, call-and-response "hollers," forms of visual poetry enabled by computer fonts (which he calls his "Sycorax video style"), and techniques of collage. In an interview with Nathaniel Mackey, the poet refers to his signature "(mis)use" of words through "linguistic turns and detours" as a "calibanization" of language (Brathwaite, "Interview" by Mackey 15). The prominence of the figure of Caliban as an allegory of colonial oppression in Caribbean writing has drawn critical response from Octave Mannoni, Frantz Fanon, Aimé Césaire , Philip Mason, Nathaniel Mackey, Rob Nixon, and M. Nourbese Philip, among others.[35] Perhaps it is not too obvious to point out that "Caliban" is a near anagram of "cannibal." Brathwaite's description of his poetic techniques as calabanisms suggests the cannibalization of language – strategies of appropriating, detouring, revising, and redefining. These poetic techniques are also Ananse's, the trickster figure who spins a "black burr of conundrums," "word-breaking" and "creat[ing]" anew. Similarly, Toussaint knew the value of renaming, taking on the avatar "L'Ouverture," a political and military "opening" akin to the significatory openings Brathwaite creates at the level of the sign. Toussaint's identity is a detour, from slave to free being, an "opening" for Black Haitian subjects. I do not wish to belabour the point here, but it is absolutely essential that the principles of survival, cunning, and protest, embodied in the trickster god and the actions of rebels, are exactly those principles informing Brathwaite's poetry.

Techniques of line and word breaking not only expose a word's polysemic possibilities, but expose a sign's subtext, in effect, mobilizing an irreconcilable secondary sense against its primary meaning. A word is momentarily broken, and then its signifying chain reassembled. Here is an early example from *Arrivants*:

they go to school to the head-
master's cries,

read a black-
board of words, angles,

lies;
they fall

over their examinations.
It is a fence that surrounds them.   ("Legba" *A* 17–24)

Brathwaite's form of line breaking is an exaggerated version of what critic Derek Attridge calls "meaning in process," a term he derives from Milton's description of lineation as "sense variously drawn out" ("Preface" to Milton, *Paradise Lost* 4).[36] Attridge explains that in the "transition from one line to another, where the reader usually attempts to establish some coherent meaning," sense can be "modified or contradicted a moment later" (*Poetic Rhythm* 17–18). Mackey thoughtfully observes that Brathwaite's method is a "graphic departure from [a] standard, presumably stable procedure[,] ... remind[ing] us, at the graphic level, of the divisibility and alterability of words" ("Wringing" 139). In the poem cited above, the school system is an institution seeking to regulate and standardize language, to give its expression the precision of geometry: "words, angles, / lies." Of course, the line break exploits a different meaning, just as the forced pause between "black" and "board" provokes consideration of race before a school lesson. Brathwaite would subsequently apply his technique of lineation in more graphically radical ways to words themselves, so that by *X/Self*,

$$\mathcal{X}\text{-}$$

plosions of mad-
rigal gas tar

bines. the car
bides of bhopal.   blitzkriegs of mein kampf.   fake satellites
like discoteques departing up. wards[.]   ("Nuum" 77–82)

A "carbide" is a chemical compound and an important constituent of metal, but here refers to the Union Carbide Corporation's subsidiary pesticide plant in Bhopal, India, where one of the worst industrial disasters in history took place.[37] "[G]as tar" and "tar/ bines" ("turbines") converge in a "mad- / rigal" of near insane levels of corporate recklessness. Brathwaite cuts into single words, either with a line break or with punctuation marks. For instance, "x / plosion" refers both to a disaster and the articulation of a plosive consonant speech sound produced by a closure of the oral passage and its sudden, forced release of occluded air (for instance, the "p" sound in "explosion"). The reader thus receives the harrowing image of the Bhopal community inhaling and exhaling airborne toxins.

Aside from the more apparent observation that nation language informs Brathwaite's deliberate misuse of poetic language, his "calibanizations" must further be understood in connection to historical-revolutionary themes in *Arrivants*. It is this relation between poetic technique and a mythic-political platform that is of the greatest significance. The following passage appears in "Vèvè" (1969), the penultimate poem in *Arrivants*:

> So on this ground,
> write;
> within the sound
> of this white limestone *vèvè*,
>
> ...
>
> on this ground
> on this broken ground.   (51–4, 88–9)

Once again, Brathwaite alludes to African-Haitian ritual, this time to the drawing of the *vèvè*, which involves marking the ground with chalk or flour before invoking a deity. Harold Courlander explains that "the *vèvè* is not a permanent record. It is made as an act of supplication or veneration ... In the ensuing ritual and dance, the *vèvè* is obliterated by the feet that pass across it" (*The Drum* 125). Rohlehr takes note of the symbolic reversal: Brathwaite inverts "the well-known image of the poet as a man who makes black marks on pure white paper[;] ... white symbols are sketched against a dark ground" (*Pathfinder* 306). But whereas Rohlehr contends that the white chalk symbolizes the Caribbean poet's acceptance of "English language as his 'white' medium for exploring the black ground of being," it is the movement of the community's dancing feet across the chain of signs that signals their creative modification through rearrangement and reassemblage.

The preceding passage from "Vèvè" is often taken in the broadest sense to express the poet's attempt to narrate the diaspora's fragmentary past into a "New World," but attention to the entirety of the poem suggests a specific role for poetic language. The ceremonial *vèvè*, after all, is an invocation to the gods, and they are ever present in this poem. In fact, this may be the only poem in the collection in which all of the principal gods of Brathwaite's pantheon appear together: the "black eye" of Ananse looks on and is "welcomed by / drumbeats," Legba "ragged" with his "crutch" is present, as is Ogun with his "sword" (28,

64–5, 85–6, 73). A telling stanza precedes the frequently quoted lines above, in which a "ground" for writing is prepared. The speaker describes "the slave rebellion of the rot / of dust" (41–2):

> that crusts the coral
> with foundation stone,
> that stirs the resurrection
> out of Tacky's bones.   (47–50)

Does the speaker of "Vèvè" suggest that the signs cut into the "ground" be written with the bones of dead revolutionaries? The concept of "ground" is important to Brathwaite. Like La Rose, who asserts that "home" is a "moving foothold" ("Everchanging" 1), he is cautious not to use it as a metaphor for origin, calling it, in turn, a "broken ground" or "sailing ground." Fragmentation is not a wholly negative concept; it opens up the possibility of a stable yet changeable foundation. Yet Brathwaite gives the term "ground" another sense. Recall that the "celebrant's body" acts as an electrical conductor. Thus, the body acts as "ground," which is to say it embodies the "divine electrical charge" of the deity. For Brathwaite, to be "grounded" refers to the moment of spiritual possession. "For on this ground,"

> trampled with the bull's swathe of whips
> where the slave at the crossroads was a red anthill
> eaten by moonbeams, by the holy ghosts
> of his wounds
>
> the Word becomes
> again a god and walks among us[.]   ("Vèvè" A 79–84)

What must be understood is that Brathwaite's poetic "detours" constitute the implantation of Jah, Ananse, Legba, and Ogun, and hence power, reversal, community, and collective will, into the body of words. Brathwaite's images, of cannibalism and mastication, crossroads and magic, driftwords and dancing, all point to reassemblage, but not in the sense of change for change's sake. The pantheon of gods in *Arrivants*, embodied by Tacky and Toussaint, also embodies poetic form. The trickster figure is poetic language itself, disrupting chains of signification and liberating meaning from fixity. Brathwaite's technique of line and word breaking involves at its core an infusion of an emancipatory force manifesting itself at the level of the poetic line.

To Havana and Beyond

It is no coincidence that Brathwaite, La Rose, and Salkey all used the radio at some point to promote their political and artistic objectives. Brathwaite ran a programme as the extramural director in St Lucia; La Rose directed a similar program in Trinidad; and Salkey contributed to *Caribbean Voices* in London. Although CAM never explored this option, the transition of their activities, from private sessions to public meetings to even larger conferences, resembles that of a radio wave's circumferential expansion. Their intention was to establish "spider web-like" links between political and aesthetic realms, between like-minded artists, activists, and organizations engaged in struggles for racial equality. By the late 1960s its cultural project had gained momentum and a general awareness that the objectives of CAM shared aspirations with other Third World struggles.[38] From the outset, members of the group had sought to maintain connections to artistic activities in the Caribbean, for instance, by publishing in Collymore's Barbadian-based magazine *Bim*. Moreover, the CAM newsletter featured a column designed to keep immigrant populations apprised of Caribbean cultural developments and publications. Between 1968 and 1970, members of the group travelled to Cuba, Jamaica, Guyana, and Trinidad, with serious intentions of expanding CAM activities in these centres. La Rose, Salkey, and C.L.R James attended the 1968 Cultural Congress of Havana in Cuba (an event that precipitated Salkey's subsequent travels throughout Central and South America). Brathwaite travelled to Jamaica, where he met Marina Maxwell and participated in the emergence of Yard Theatre. Gordon Rohlehr had taken a position at the UWI in St Augustine, Trinidad. And in 1970, members of CAM (including Brathwaite, La Rose, Salkey, Wilson Harris, and Aubrey Williams) would rendezvous in Guyana, at the invitation of the People's National Congress, to participate in the Caribbean Writers and Artists Convention. The results were decidedly mixed, but their successes and failures provide invaluable lessons in pan-Caribbean cultural collaboration.

Shortly after returning from the Havana Congress, John La Rose read "Prosepoem for a Conference" at the third and final CAM Conference in 1969. The poem formed part of a speech entitled "The Development of Black Experience and the Nature of Black Society in Britain." It would later appear in *Race Today* with a dedication to Salkey:

A people of exile, living in the permanence of tragedy and dispossessed hope. We are the wanderers and a wonder of this world. We have survived, deprived of pristine utterance, appropriating and welding language out of ancestral wounds and sacrifice. Wounds still fresh-cut work under my words. In the colloquy of everything, everything present lives with everything past in momentary and imperfect blindness. We are, such as we are, the living tissue of contemporaneity caught in islands, or thicker land masses, plying our own triangular trade in ourselves, exporting ourselves from hopelessness into hope, from disillusion into anaemic illusion; avoiding the pilgrimage of return into the dark unmentionable habitats that lie in ourselves; … and lived to fight. Such as we are, we are the salted embryo of a world whose fixities grow loose while ours, our world – once indecently naked and rootless – firm and gel for the encounter with history, ready. Fragments of roots – scorned in the night of self-contempt – spring to rebirth, the seed of renewal. Exile paid its premium in self awareness; we begin to know. A message of hope and contradiction, but such is my message. ("Prosepoem" [1969] 13)

The title of La Rose's essay promises a focused discussion of the Black British experience, yet his poem speaks in more internationalist terms of unspecified "wanderers" from "islands, and thicker land masses." Indeed, no "we" is named beyond a "people of exile." There is trauma, movement, reconnection, and a conditional message of hope, but these elements could easily constitute a blueprint for power struggles and diasporic movements across vast parts of the planet. Thus, his essay positions the Black British experience as one cause among a multiplicity of other struggles abroad.

One can trace the events leading up to the third CAM conference and La Rose's poem. In addition to those who were present for the very first committee meeting of the Caribbean Artists Movement, Cuban poet Pablo Armando Fernandez was also in attendance at Orlando Patterson's London flat in May 1967. He told the group of an ambitious event planned for January 1968, and invited members of CAM to attend the two-week-long congress of Third World intellectuals and artists. It attracted approximately five hundred scholars and artists from Africa, Asia, and the Americas. Orlando Patterson, Andrew Salkey, and John La Rose attended as delegates, and in April and May of the same year, they organized two symposia in London devoted to the congress for the benefit of the CAM community.[39]

In many ways the Havana Congress constituted a critical juncture for Salkey and La Rose's thought; their work with CAM, the latter explains, was a cultural "platform" they wished to merge with other literary, social, and political movements. The concluding remarks of congress organizers in Havana in many ways enumerated the principal concerns preoccupying the two activists:

(1) One should quickly cast aside the false opinion that the responsibility of the intellectual in underdeveloped countries is different from that of the intellectual in highly developed capitalist countries ...
(2) The Eurocentrist view of the world has entered a state of crisis in the last decade. Asia, Latin America and Africa in one way or another have begun to shape the history of the world ...
(3) European history and culture ... is the history of a class as far as the history of colonialism and neo-colonialism are concerned[.]
  ("El Congresso Internacional de Intelectuales Tricontinental" 873)

By the time of the Havana Congress (1968), Castro's nationalization of foreign-owned property (most of which was owned by U.S. companies), the failure of the Bay of Pigs Invasion (1961), and evidence that a U.S. embargo on the small island had not crippled the country's Soviet-backed economy signalled a victory for Caribbean, Central, and South American socialism. Castro's land reforms raised the standard of living among the country's poorest constituents, while the implementation of public health care and education won further popular support. (Despite its own categorization as a Third World country, Cuba provided substantial medical and educational aid to more than thirty underdeveloped nations.)[40] Notably, Salkey's first excursion on the island was to attend a photographic exhibition of Che Guevara. He makes a point in his symposium talk to recount his surprise at how little it mattered to his tour guides that Che was not Cuban: "I was brought up, like most of you, believing that our Anglophone societies were the only ones in the Caribbean worthy of any attention; the Jamaican thought of the Jamaican only" ("Second CAM Symposium" 1). Salkey learned to value Che, above all else, as a "figure who is an internationalist. Nationalisms were anathema to him" (1). In the years after the foiled Bay of Pigs Invasion, Che remarked brazenly, "our revolution is endangering all American possessions in Latin America. We are telling these countries to make their own revolution."[41]

Just as strikingly, Salkey found the same sense of responsibility among the Cuban intellectual and artistic community, who, citing the Cuban critic Ambrosid Fornet, had sought to link artistic activity to "'a very definite revolutionary practice'" (3). Salkey would later edit a collection that he titled *Writing in Cuba Since the Revolution* (1977); in the introduction, he observes that since early on in Cuba's national literature, its poets seem far less preoccupied with "the individual imagination" and far more focused on "putting their writing at the service of ... community problems, and in bolstering the causes and aspirations of the endemic Revolutionary Movements" (12). Salkey continues, "the Revolutionary purpose of creative writing in Cuba, today: to rid the individual and the society of alienation, through inventiveness and experimentation and conflict, and to attain the uphill road towards a better cultural life" (13). The same anthology positions excerpts from Che Guevera's *Man and Socialism in Cuba* alongside poems by writers who exemplify his notion of the artist as "a kind of cultural duty officer" ("Second CAM Symposium" 3).[42]

In 1968 the excitement of the revolutionary period was still very much in force, particularly among visiting intellectuals from the Caribbean and South America, whose adulation was rooted in a desire for home-grown political change. This was definitely the case for Salkey and La Rose. The latter had failed to implement a socialist regime in Trinidad, but Cuba proved that a Caribbean nation could not only assert its cultural legitimacy, it could also potentially gain economic autonomy. Furthermore, La Rose and Salkey learned from their Cuban experience that the nationalist aspirations of post-colonial countries could coincide with internationalist cooperation, that dialogue between communities facing common struggles – however paradoxical – led to greater national stability.[43] Salkey's "Remember Haiti, Cuba, Vietnam" (c. 1976) makes the point concisely:

Here's something folk tales tell
us about, at night, but which
we lose sight of during the day:

Giants can be surprised.

That's something three slingshots
in our third of the world gauged
and defiantly stretched to success.

What's the light like now in the dark?

Look at the untouched stones
lying on our beaches
and the idle rubber bands
in our upturned hands!   (1–12)

Brathwaite's trickster figure is seen here making friends. Just as Ogun
had fashioned new masks with African and European tools, the discarded by-product of industrialization ably hurtles indigenous projectiles. That said, not all of CAM's attempts to establish coalitions in
Caribbean nations succeeded. The internationalist scope of their activities would need to be grounded by local, self-directed political and cultural action.

John La Rose's "Welded" Poetics

La Rose was a revolutionary figure, exiled from Trinidad for his promotion of socialism. He was a publisher of subversive literature, an
education activist, and a proponent of popular Caribbean culture (La
Rose co-wrote a history of kaiso music and played in steel bands). That
said, he *did not* equate populism with popularity. He would have found
such an equation vulgar (if not inadvertently racist), since invariably
the high/low cultural distinction will subordinate Third World folk
cultures to European traditions. "I don't accept those distinctions,"
he informed one interviewer: "[h]igh culture, popular art ... my first
introduction to the art and so on was through the kaiso, through the
so-called classical music, through the literature, through popular participation in politics in the Caribbean." He "related all these things
together [in] a totally holistic approach to art, society and life, and
politics" (CAM Papers 6/44 [15]). Notably, it is Brathwaite's *Rights of
Passage* that La Rose offers as an exemplar of such a political-aesthetic
amalgam. Salkey and La Rose encountered an important distinction between populist and popular art among the intellectuals of the Cuban
Revolution. Che Guevara, for instance, proclaims in *Man and Socialism
in Cuba* that orthodox communism had "made errors ... [seeking] an
art that would be understood by everyone, the kind of 'art' function-
aries understand." Che rejected the tenets of social realism, believing
that attempts to "find the only valid prescription for art in the frozen
forms ... of realism-at-any-cost" had placed "a straitjacket" on "artistic

expression" (138–9). Ernesto Cardenal's distillation of Che's position is blunter still: "In Cuba, as contrasted with Russia, there is no attempt made to create an art that can be understood by the people, the attempt is to educate the people to the point where they can understand art" (*In Cuba* 189).[44] Salkey included this particular excerpt from Che's book in his collection of Cuban writings. The task of the poet was not to reduce the poem's function to transparent political communication. Like Brathwaite, La Rose assembles the materials of a political poetics with purpose, making clear that what interests him are those common junctures in the way different activist, intellectual, and popular discourses "conceptualize" the same challenges (CAM Papers 6/44 [18]).

That La Rose had thought to integrate his "Prosepoem" for Salkey into the body of a political essay, which he, in turn, read to the community in London that partially inspired it, provides a fitting example of his interdisciplinary approach to cultural work. The epigram links a political friend to a community of activists; the poem, embedded within the essay, links aesthetic and political discourses in and as a collective articulation of Third World unity. La Rose's poems are collected in two slender volumes: *Foundations* (1966) and *Eyelets of Truth* (1991), but many of them appear and reappear in the body of political essays, indicating persuasively that these projects were linked. "I can never think of politics without thinking of poetry ... a certain kind of poetic statement," he remarks, "[b]ecause politics is another kind of poetry" (CAM Papers 6/44 [18]). Even stylistically they are comparable. La Rose did not leave a copious body of writing; he wrote neither an epic poem nor an expansive work of political science. As a grass-roots activist, he preferred the short essay, the position paper, the manifesto, and the open letter. His writings appear in journals, newspapers, and newsletters, or as manuscripts left over from public speeches given at rallies and meetings.

La Rose understands the poem to operate within and as a nexus of cultural forces. I mentioned "Fantasy in Space" earlier on in the chapter as an example of his carefully assembled synthesis of nation language, European poetic modes, the carnivalesque, and political discourse. In "Prosepoem," La Rose describes this poetic practice through an image of linkage: "appropriating and welding language out of ancestral wounds and sacrifice." The reader may extrapolate from this proposition that (1) language is *communal*, (2) *material*, and (3) the product of *historical* forces. That is, language must be freely available for appropriation and redefinition, it is that malleable material fused and jerry-rigged from

collective articulations of meaning, and it retains the traces of experience, events, and memory. The poetic for La Rose is the construction of
precise expression welded from these elements.

More so than a writer like Salkey, whose experience at the Havana
Conference exposed the Jamaican activist to the possibilities of a Third
World revolutionary consciousness, La Rose was already receptive to
the propositions arising from the Havana Congress. He spoke Spanish
and French, and travelled widely throughout the Caribbean and the socialist states of Eastern Europe. In an unpublished essay entitled "Everchanging Immanence of Culture," the poet explains:

> diaspora is never ending; like the migration of Volga Germans and Tartars
> under the stern command of Stalin, the flight of Mexican hopefuls into the
> USA, or the arrival of guest workers and West Indians in Europe. In words
> from this poem of mine:
>
> > What we leave we carry
> > It is no mud we dry
> > On our boots.
>
> At the moment of encounter with the other, we join the dance in con-
> stant entanglement and change. The newcomer changes and the society
> changes too. ("Everchanging" 2)

The radical displacement brought on by social and economic dispossession is an intolerable condition, but so is the rigidity of cultural permanence. One is "never fixed," as the title of one of La Rose's poems
suggests, " – never fixed / in heroic pose, / but plasticine[,] ... [e]ver
reshaping" ("Never Fixed" 5–7, 15). The condition of culture is a condition of being "interlinked" by economic, social, and technological
elements of "entanglement and change": "[t]hese elements of material
culture shape our lives and we insert our meanings and aspirations
into them. We shake the tree to its roots and uproot it if we can, if in
the pursuit of that aspiration, we add our stone and mortar, our ideas
and innovations to the construction of a better world" ("Everchanging" 2). The work of poetry, of history, and of politics is not merely
about remembering or re-establishing one's roots, but of remaking social and class relations such that they aspire to radical equality.

Andrew Salkey: A Co-operative Poetics

Salkey was an accomplished freelance reporter for BBC World, a novelist, a children's fiction writer, a folklorist, and an anthologist of significant repute. His *A Quality of Violence* (1959) and *Escape to an Autumn Pavement* (1960) had earned him a reputation as a gifted prose writer, as had his later contemporary adaptations of the Ananse tale (Salkey relocates the trickster figure to America, and has him globetrotting across the planet, stealing plutonium from world powers!). He also published poetry, winning the Thomas Hellmore Poetry Prize for his unpublished epic *Jamaica Symphony* (1953). His interest in poetry was rekindled by his involvement with CAM. During the late 1960s and throughout the 1970s he edited collections of Caribbean writing (*Breaklight: An Anthology of Caribbean Poetry* [1971], *Writing in Cuba Since the Revolution* [1977]), published his first volume from twenty years prior, and wrote two others: *In the Hills Where Her Dreams Live: Poems for Chile* (1979) and *Away* (1980). The poems in these volumes were composed in an ad hoc manner over the course of the decade during Salkey's travels throughout the South American continent. Compounding his diverse repertoire of talents, he penned two accounts of his travels: *Georgetown Journal* (1970) and *Havana Journal* (1971).

In Cuba, Salkey encountered intellectuals who enthusiastically appropriated and shared intellectual resources from Caribbean and South American traditions. While in Guyana and Trinidad, he found comparable acts of collaboration. In his *Georgetown Journal*, Salkey provides meticulous accounts of the 1970 student uprisings, an event that would lead to more organized demonstrations directed by the National Joint Action Committee (a collective organization of numerous unions, cultural organizations, and student and youth groups).[45] The role of the poet, accordingly, is to participate alongside these groups engaged in opposition to common sources of exploitation. Salkey's political preoccupations are evident in his poetic writing, both thematically, as a poetics of journalistic documentation, and as a formal concern, whereby Salkey imagines the page as an "asentamiento" (work cooperative) of political discourses expressed by activists, politicians, and literary figures.

The poet explains that *In the Hills Where Her Dreams Live* was composed with all of America's subordinated others in mind:

… in terms of Cuba, Chile, and so on in search of justice, in search of equity from America's heavy imperialistic hand. When Chile was robbed of its election for the Salvador Allende socialism I said it would be a good thing to keep the faith for that which was robbed of the Chilean people by doing a poem every year … [T]he concerns of the Caribbean and South America are similar; the pockets of opposition are almost identical." ("Andrew Salkey Talks" 46)

Salkey composed a series of poems about Chile (1974–8) just after Pinochet's junta seized control of the country (1973), and then later wrote an occasional poem in each of the next five years, documenting the affects on the country's cultural climate. The evocation of a "'New Havana'" (C [c. 1974–5] 277) in Latin America's southern cone created a disconcerting image for the Nixon administration and Western multinationals. Chile had no immediate strategic geopolitical importance for the United States; granted, it was another site of Cold War tensions, but unlike Cuba and Afghanistan, which lined the borders of the United States and the former Soviet Union, or the Middle East, with its abundant oil reserves, Chile's location and natural resources seemed a less pressing matter. Yet a functional socialist system in Chile would potentially create the conditions for pan–Third World socialism in opposition to Western military and corporate exploitation.[46] The perceived threat could be plotted on a map: Cuba at the northern tip and Chile at the southern cone, a resultant spread of socialism enveloping the interiors of the Caribbean, Central, and South America. The Havana Congress was emblematic of such a dispersal of subversive ideas throughout the planet's disenfranchised communities.

The first text in Salkey's volume, entitled "Inside," contains this explanatory note: "[t]his poem was written with the following inspiring thought in mind: that the personal loss of a Jamaican woman may be of comparable quality and intensity as that of the national loss of Popular Unity to Chile" (13). Thus, according to its title, every "inside" is simultaneously an "outside":

Time and again,
she had been carelessly used,
hurt, pulped
and spat out by her friends.
…

what went wrong
with all those early
close relationships,
how things got more
and more twisted and snarled,
what caused the dislocation
and the drift[.]   ("Inside" 1–4, 21–7)

A comparable epigram to Salkey's long poem "Chile" features Pablo
Neruda's declaration, "They receive instructions against Chile":

[i]n this way they decide from above, from the roll of dollars;
in this way, the dwarf traitor receives his instructions,
and the generals act as the police force,
and the trunk of the trees of the country rots.

Salkey's paratextual note and citation contrast two forms of power: a
top-down model of organization where "mountain-men" make decisions "from above," and an ensemble of actors forced to meet within
"the silent underground" (C 205, 262): activists (Mariategui), poets and
artists (Pablo Neruda, Victor Jara), and the deposed socialist government (Allende, Popular Unity).

Salkey catalogues the components of a global state apparatus with
concision: the "correctly-dressed soldiers / sailors, airmen, police" (C
203–4), together with the "oil men, wheat men, / telephone and ca-
bles men, Pepsi Cola men, / copper men: all men of stained steel" (C
312–14),

mountain-men all in uniform,
licensed earth-quake makers,
persistent grave-fillers.

Time and again,
mountains in America
come down
and crush the people.   (C 205–11)

Like Duncan's many-headed hydra, Salkey's "mountain-men" wear
many "uniforms." The Pinochet regime appears alongside corporate

actors, the United States government, and Milton Friedman's "Chicago Boys."[47] Salkey's catalogue of atrocities carried out during the coup emphasizes a war of markets inexorably linked to a military seizure of power.[48] Although it is beyond the scope of this book to lend clarity to this complex and bloody episode of Chilean history, clearly the speaker of Salkey's poem characterizes the Pinochet junta as an illegal dictatorship and U.S. political and economic involvement as an act of state- and corporate-sponsored terrorism.

The following passage depicts this complex partnership:

> the plodding thump
> of democracy's drum,
> folded in its convoluted shell,
> sounded lost at sea;
> holding their oilskin conch, high,
> Fatherland and Liberty screeched
> their oath to burn half of Chile
> to save it from national recovery
> and Chilean ownership;
> up went the clanging threat
> of the "March of the Empty Pots,"[49]
> spick and span every middle class one[.]   (C 163–74)

The speaker of Salkey's poem offers a striking indictment of the violence and destruction that the junta justified in the name of salvation from socialization. Furthermore, lines of power connect the landowning class of Chile, the American military-industrial complex, and the right-wing academic sector. The Fatherland and Liberty Nationalist Front was a fascist paramilitary group largely composed of wealthy, private-school educated youth who initially sought to prevent Allende's presidency and later worked to overthrow the leader with fiscal support from the CIA.[50] Salkey characterizes Fatherland and Liberty as an agent of physical oppression linked to this economic project seeking to undo the work of Allende's socialist reformation.[51] Significantly, Salkey never names Pinochet in his long poem. The junta occupies a position within currents of political, military, and economic collusion that allows "Capital [to] step back into the same stream" (C 306).

Salkey also concisely names the motivation for military action against Allende's government: the nationalization of major industries and agrarian land reforms – hence, the junta's "oath to burn half of Chile / to save it from … Chilean ownership" (C 169–71). Between 1970 and 1972, industries controlled by the Popular Unity government rose from 43 to 164.[52] Chief among them was copper, Chile's most plentiful raw material and its main export. The government passed a constitutional amendment to reappropriate the U.S.-owned Gran Mineria del Cobre, Anaconda, and Kenecott, along with other foreign subsidiaries. Because the U.S.-owned mines alone controlled more than half of Chile's export earnings, and because Allende had widespread support from working- and middle-class Chileans, even the political right had to concede to the plan.[53] At the same time, Allende had proposed sweeping agrarian reforms. But whereas his nationalization of natural resources had enjoyed popular support, the Popular Unity government faced internal opposition from the country's wealthy elite and some members of the middle class. The speaker of Salkey's poem defers to a native Chilean to point out the irony: "'Seize a farm? / Where's the harm?'":

Araucanian Chileans,
first warrior-workers,
Chile's Incas,
chueca-players,
great talkers,
grooved perfectly
in their isolation,
fought and lost
but surely
must be listening, now,
and laughing their easy,
last laugh[.]   (C 35–6, 68–79)

Allende and his government passed a reform bill specifying that any privately owned farm larger than eighty hectares would be expropriated and redistributed to peasants. The redistributed land was reorganized into "asentamientos," or public cooperatives.[54] Salkey's speaker justifies the actions but resists descriptions of the native community or peasant classes as having a more sacred bond to the Chilean landscape. His mode of representation retains both the ironic critique of the colonizer claiming entitlement to land, while he insists that the question is an issue of class, accessibility, and shared resources, rather than identity. Salkey cites the Peruvian political theorist Jose Carlos Mariategui shortly after this passage, and more to the point, the activist's proposed synthesis of Che's "new man" and "Inca communalism" (C 146–7).[55] Mariategui most famously argued that South America's "Indian question" is in fact a "land problem." Reconciliation and community building, he argues, can only occur through institutional reform calling for the communization of excessive private ownership. The metropolitan and agrarian communities of post-colonial Chile had only one workable option: to share public land and profit from its resources equally. Dispossession is not merely an existential state but a condition of the relations of production; the problem of racism required a progressive, socialist solution.

Notably, Salkey's poem "Chile" bears a striking resemblance to Denise Levertov's stylistic practice in "Staying Alive." The core text in his collection of poems devoted to Chile is thirteen pages long and contains no fewer than fourteen quotations appropriated from speeches by liberator Simon Bolivar, street vendors, the Chilean constitution, an Araucanian native, Pablo Neruda, a bookseller, a lawyer, and so forth. Akin to Brathwaite's conception of the poem as an amalgam of "time centres," Salkey assembles citations, epigrams, footnotes, and paraphrase; these texts are appropriated from public documents, or spoken by citizens in public spaces. Indeed, Salkey conceptualizes the poetic page as a public space, complementing a thematic preoccupation with cooperative land ownership.

It is therefore instructive to recall the poet and editor's assessment of Cuban writers during the revolution. Salkey had been impressed by authors for whom the individual imagination never took privilege over the public good. Indeed, it is neither the poet's imagination nor merely one's discerning capacity to anticipate revolutionary transformations that Salkey focuses upon, but rather one's commitment to politics, to the other, to "community problems" beyond the self. Salkey's evocation of Neruda and Victor Jara[56] shares this sentiment. Neruda held a diplomatic position in the Popular Unity government and both he and Jara were firm supporters of the socialist coalition. There is indeed a fine line between the politically committed poet and the "state artist," the "cultural duty officer" (to use Salkey's phrase) and the literary bureaucrat. But for Salkey, the disavowal of practical politics by the artist is a cop-out. Such commitment, though the dangers are real, is a necessary risk.

A Local Internationalism?

Both La Rose and Salkey's experiences at the congress had caused a fusion of political and artistic endeavours – La Rose's "Prosepoem" and Salkey's "Chile" suggest an important intensification of their commitments to Third World struggle, and a consideration of the role of poetics in such a project. Notably, CAM's other attempts to forge connections with organizations in the Caribbean fall short. Why had CAM's successful initiatives in London not had a similar effect in most other Caribbean nations they visited? And what was different about Cuba?

Guyana had won independence in 1970, and a largely sympathetic People's National Congress had already begun to establish events such as the Caribbean Writers and Artists Convention. Alternatively, Gordon Rohlehr (who had taken up a position at UWI, in St Augustine, Trinidad) complained of general disorganization and irreconcilable political factionism among intellectuals there.[57] According to Brathwaite and Rohlehr, failure to launch CAM in these sites was either the result of too many resources already in place or not enough. Whether or not this is true, it does not explain the lack of success in Jamaica, nor Trinidad two years later during the 1970 student uprisings, where it would seem the situation invited artistic-political collaboration.

Brathwaite arrived in Jamaica to complete research at the UWI, Mona, staying from January to March 1968. He returned in October, just as the so-called Rodney Riots had begun. Walter Rodney, the Guyanese historian of Africa and proponent of the Black Power movement, had been teaching at the UWI, Mona; having attended a conference in Montreal, Canada, he was promptly refused re-entry into Jamaica afterwards. The government cited Rodney's communist sympathies (he had made trips to Cuba and the Soviet Union), but likely it was the academic's fierce criticism of the post-independence ruling elite that explains the government's actions. His expulsion from the country incited mass demonstrations by students at UWI on 16 October; more radical members of the faculty, along with artists, labour unionists, and members of the general public, soon joined the marches.[58] The context was somewhat different at Mona/Kingston than in London. Protesters in the Jamaican capital and at the Mona campus had undertaken their first major demonstration against a post-independence government composed mainly of middle- and upper-middle-class black leaders. Fear of Black Power rhetoric had, ironically, more to do with class than race, since Rodney had criticized the bourgeois elite and instilled a sense of class consciousness among poor Jamaicans.

Just as this volatile political context encouraged collaboration among activists, intellectuals and artists had begun to organize themselves. Upon Brathwaite's return to UWI, Mona, artist and cultural theorist Marina Maxwell had helped to plan an arts seminar between CAM members and the New World group. New World was similarly pan-Caribbean in its membership, but unlike CAM, it was mainly composed of political scientists, economists, and sociologists; Walmsley additionally observes that New World "had been founded, and operated, within the Caribbean alone" (*Caribbean* 195).[59] Both Brathwaite and Maxwell had plans for CAM to fuse with New World, and add an artistic component to the latter's activities. The idea was a good one, since the Caribbean organization centred at UWI was more strictly academic in scope. In fact, Maxwell's ambitions for a Jamaican artistic movement were very similar to CAM. In "Towards a Revolution in the Arts," she conceives the "whole" of the Caribbean and South America as a "store of cultural elements and patterns," advocating "a regional synthesis" of Third World artistic energies ("Towards" 28). In 1967 Maxwell had participated in the CAM symposium entitled "West Indian Theatre" at the West Indian Student Centre in London, and had since been developing her concept of the Yard Theatre. She describes the practice as "an attempt to place West Indian theatre in the life of the people[,] … to find it in the yards where people live and are." It was, moreover, an "attempt to synthesise actively in the performing arts" (30).[60] Brathwaite attended the theatre, describing Yard as a "submerged" art of "subterranean flow[s]," using language that clearly connects its activities to that of CAM and Brathwaite's poetics; his detailed accounts of these performances emphasize "the collaborativeness of the effort," a "total theatre" in which the elements of nation language, Rasta, and the "street/community" converge, "poetry extended into movement, gesture, mime … cross-rhythm: free flow: reverberation" ("The Love Axe/1 – Part Three" 182). Yard Theatre brought together Rastafarians; proponents of experimental theatre, dance, and poetry; and members of the general public. Often the events were coordinated with occasions commemorating the achievements of activists like Che, Malcolm X, and Frantz Fanon.[61]

With all of these disparate local factions poised to mobilize, Jamaica, and, in particular, the university campus at Mona seemed a perfect context for CAM to lend structural support for a fusion of art and politics.

In an article for *Bim* years later, Brathwaite recollects enthusiastically that together Walter Rodney, the students at UWI, New World, the Creative Arts Centre (CAC) at Mona, Rastafarians, and the Yard Theatre had established "the links – artistic and intellectual – " necessary for a mass movement ("The Love Axe/1" 56). Although he never explicitly states his desire for CAM to be the organizing centre of such an endeavour, in a letter to Salkey, he insinuates that CAM should act as "an invisible spark," such that it may "avoid the faction lark and still spread de INFLUENCE" (CAM Papers 3/514 [1–2]). Brathwaite had already set up a Jamaican edition of the *CAM Newsletter* earlier in March at the end of his first visit; he proceeded with an "exploratory CAM evening" with the intention of establishing a more stable organization that would bring together these disparate local activities. In a letter written to Salkey on 18 December 1968, Brathwaite recounts the disappointing night:

> Doomed to fail from the start, I know. But typical of what we're up against as you will remember from your last stint here. Amongst those present were the following, revolving poles apart:
>
> | | |
> |---|---|
> | J Hearne | Bobby Hill |
> | Cecil Gray | Marina Maxwell |
> | M Morris | Orlando Patterson |
>
> Need I go further[.]   (CAM Papers 3/496 [1])

Like Rohlehr in Trinidad, Brathwaite concludes that a "split ... [in] personalities" and a volatile political situation created irreconcilable differences between "Black Power, student power, sufferers, [and] radicalism" (CAM Papers 3/496 [1–2]).

The reasons are more complex, however. CAM's failure in Jamaica has to do with an attempt to impose organizations from outside the local communities themselves. This is not to say that all international cooperation is doomed to failure; the case of the Havana Congress suggests otherwise. Yet CAM was the consequence of a unique set of circumstances in London, a group of immigrants who forged their own community out of the makeshift resources, tactics, institutions, and histories available to them. A comparable assemblage needs to begin in these other centres, whereby the projects of disparate groups can unite only after local commitments to such a project are established. In Jamaica, an artistic community did in fact emerge through a synthesis

of Yard Theatre, Rastafarianism, the New World movement, and interested members of the UWI. CAM, too, was an element of this assemblage that came through networks of scholars and activists who had
returned from London to work at the university – but it could not succeed as a central structure organizing these other elements. CAM-Ja-
maica failed not because of irreconcilable personalities, as Brathwaite
attests, but because he had inadvertently replicated a colonialist practice of imposing external systems of organization on local populations.
Just as Brathwaite rejects the verse given to Caribbean schoolchildren
– of "snow falling on canefields" – as an assimilative transposition of
one culture onto another, CAM emerged out of a particular historical
junction that could certainly participate in but not supplant or police
the direction of cultural activities in Jamaica. By comparison, the alliances forged in Cuba were more productive because the logic ran in the
opposite direction. Just as CAM members conceptualized their practice as being akin to a community centre, Cuban artists and intellectuals suggested an approach to collaboration focused on historically
specific forms of struggle. They appropriated concepts, figures, and
so forth from abroad (e.g., Che), but they were always situated within
the Cuban context. Simultaneously, they openly encouraged delegates
at the congress to take what useful elements of Cuban culture made
sense for their own struggles. An approach to cultural activism is never
universally applicable to every situation, but it is universally transferable to any situation in which its ensemble of participants choose it
as their own. The same logic may be found in Brathwaite's *Arrivants*:
its pantheon of gods change and reconstitute to embody the demands
of London-based migrant activists. It is in this precise sense that we
must understand that the relation of the local to the international is
only valid if the allegiances of the latter preserve and defend the autonomy of the former.[62]

For the most part, CAM resisted the idea of itself as a central organization, instead choosing to function as a constituent element within
a network of movements and projects, a literary organ in this network
of emancipatory struggles. We should not overexaggerate CAM's possible reach into other spheres of activity beyond its immediate sphere
of action. This is no denigration of the role of poetry or its capacity to
enact change. Writing had to enter into these collective projects, taking a stand in the discursive environment in which it operates. If the
market-and-state framework's totalizing project had begun to enclose
and saturate everyday life, language, and affect, then like New Beacon

intervening into the publishing industry, the Community Workers Association challenging the deportation of immigrants, and the Black Parents Movement protecting youth from police brutality and classroom discrimination, poetry's terrain is language and here it must intervene. CAM was most effective when its members converged, together and with others, to *engage struggle where one was,* all the while assessing the real possibilities of change in a given situation. This, I argue, is its most important contribution: an understanding of the local nature of political struggle, manifesting itself simultaneously in action and in language.

4 The Women's Liberation Movement: A Poetic for a Common World

[T]he common world is what we enter when we are born and what we leave behind when we die … It is what we have in common not only with those who live with us, but also with those who were here before and with those who will come after us. But such a common world can survive … only to the extent that it appears in public.

– Hannah Arendt[1]

The simple phrase, 'there is only one world,' is not an objective conclusion. It is performative: we are deciding that this is how it is for us. Faithful to this point, it is then a question of elucidating the consequences that follow from this simple declaration.

– Alain Badiou[2]

[T]he task was never one of retrenching from the radical analysis of the New Left; it was simply to go further.

– Robin Morgan[3]

Devising our Networks

More than one activist in the Women's Liberation Movement (WLM) has observed the centrality of poetry in the feminist projects of the 1960s and 1970s. Historians Polly Joan and Andrea Chessman, having in 1978 assembled the most comprehensive guide to Women's publishing in North America to date, proclaim: "poetry was the medium of the movement" (*Guide to Women's Publishing* 3). Yet despite the aesthetic and political commitments linking Robin Morgan, Adrienne Rich, Gloria Anzaldúa, Irena Klepfisz, Minnie Bruce Pratt, Pat Parker, Judy Grahn, Honor Moore, June Jordan, Susan Griffin, Anne Waldman, Diane di Prima, Audre Lorde, and many others, a feminist poetic community is more difficult to "locate" than it is with the other collectives addressed in this book. Black Mountain had an alternative college in North Carolina, CAM had the West Indian Student Centre in London, while the TRG's combination of physical and discursive publics – the workshop and the Eternal Network – anchored their experiments in multi-authorship. It is too easily taken for granted that the existence of an accessible space is a precondition for collective experimentation. By contrast, women writers encountered the twin edifices of capital's enclosure of the public sphere and an oppressive patriarchal system equally evident among left- and right-wing political and cultural factions. Audre Lorde aptly registers this acute sense of dislocation:

> for the embattled
> there is no place
> that cannot be
> home
> nor is.   ("School Note" 25–9)

Many women found themselves excluded both from the official institutions of culture, as well as the counter-publics and alternative communities seeking to challenge the racist and classist policies of the nation state. Poetic groups like the Beats, BMC, the New York School, Black Arts, CAM, and countless others often echo the hypocrisy of the New Left's disregard for female oppression.

Adrienne Rich makes the point adroitly: "[d]enied space in the universities, the scientific laboratories, the professions," those affiliated with the Women's Liberation Movement had to "devise [their] own networks" in which to theorize, practice, and enact their efforts ("Conditions" 214). Joan and Chessman record no fewer than seventy-three feminist periodicals and sixty-six presses operative from the late 1960s until the mid-1970s. Magazines like *Rat*, *Speakout*, *The Second Wave*, *Moving Out*, *Aphra*, *Women: A Journal of Liberation*, *Sinister Wisdom*, along with presses such as Daughters, Diana Press, Kelsey Street Press, Shameless Hussy, and the Women's Press Collective disseminated a considerable body of work throughout the United States and Canada. By 1978 feminist small presses had collectively sold over one million books and pamphlets.[4] Anthologies like *No More Masks!: An Anthology of Poems by Women* (1973), *Rising Tides: Twentieth-Century American Women Poets* (1973), and *The World Split Open: Four Centuries of Women Poets in England and America, 1550–1950* (1974) established a counter-tradition of writing that helped readers to redress literary history by challenging its legacies of gender exclusion. Nor was the poetry anthology separate from the WLM's political work: Robin Morgan's *Sisterhood Is Powerful* (1970), for instance, includes a large section devoted to "poetry as protest," while two poets, Cherríe Moraga and Gloria Anzaldúa, edited the influential *This Bridge Called My Back: Writings by Radical Women of Color* (1981). Moreover, a "how-to" compendium like Kirsten Ramstad and Susan Ronnie's *The New Woman's Survival Sourcebook* (1975) indicates the degree to which poetic writing was linked to a broader cultural and political activism. An accessible and thoughtfully illustrated manual of resources for women looking to pursue various facets of the WLM, the book's table of contents lists chapters such as "Work," "Health," "Education," "Literature," and "Law and Politics." The sourcebook, its editors remark, "compile[s]" a working list of "women's newspapers and magazines, printing presses and publishers, anti-rape centers, health clinics, art galleries, credit unions, childcare centers, research libraries, scholarly journals, schools, bookstores, karate studios, lobbying coalitions, divorce clinics, film cooperatives, theatre groups, bands, [and] therapy collectives" (vii). Health, politics, and culture converge within the discursive sphere the *Sourcebook* assembles. Turning to the chapter titled "Literature," one encounters a conversation between Rich and Robin Morgan on the topic of poetry and community building, information about how to run an alternative press, along with brief critical studies of poets such as Susan Griffin, Judy Grahn, and Audre Lorde. The poetic, understood in this context, is carefully situated within communities of authors, editors, disseminators, and readers of books. Drawing from Grahn's formative and influential work, Adrienne Rich describes her own poetry as the "making of connections," the "drive / to connect" ("Power and Danger" 250; "Origins" 11–12).

Granted, the WLM was still very much a cosmopolitan movement, its main proponents and participants based in major cities like New York, San Francisco, Boston, and Montreal. Yet compared to Black Mountain or CAM, groups whose work was anchored by a tangible site of collaboration, the WLM's forms of solidarity echo the manifold structure of its publishing networks, magazines, and direct action protests. One should be cautious here, since there is a danger in setting up an inadvertently sexist and historically inaccurate binary opposition between supposedly male (centralized) and female (decentralized) tactics, conveniently concealed, as it were, within this ostensibly innocent discussion of place and space. In fact, countless authors and activists affiliated with the WLM echo Jo Freeman's contention that "structurelessness" too can be "tyrann[ical]." The celebration of a leaderless, provisional, impermanent collective seemed only possible among those whose access to the public sphere went unquestioned. Instead, Women's Liberation proliferates the ideal of unqualified, radical equality throughout very different feminist social structures and cultural locales. I will develop this line of critique momentarily, but for now let it suffice that WLM poetics unfolds within an expansive nexus of political formations.

A shortlist includes large, formal organizations like the National Organization for Women (NOW), the Women's Political Action Caucus (WPAC), the National Black Feminist Organization (NBFO), and Women of All Red Nations (WARN) alongside comparatively flexible networks of "consciousness-raising" and direct-action groups such as WITCH, New York Radical Women (NYRW), the Redstockings, Bread and Roses, Cell 16, The Feminists, New York Radical Feminists (NYRF), and the Combahee River Collective (CRC). Of course, these various national, regional, and local activities reflect markedly different, often incompatible positions on a variety of questions. For instance, what forms of organization and tactics are needed? How do distinctions between private and public gender politics, work, and social experience? How should a feminist project address questions of race, class, sexual orientation, ageism, regionalism, and other forms of discrimination? And under what circumstances might Women's Liberation forge alliances with other groups? One should always acknowledge from the outset that as a set of theories and practices the WLM comprises multiple discourses. While organizations like NOW sought constitutional equality for women in mainstream U.S. society through legislative reform, groups like NYRF and CRC insisted that the patriarchal foundation of society as such required radical structural change. Historians like Myra Marx Feree, Beth B. Hess, Alice Echols, and Barbara Ryan map largely persuasive distinctions between liberal, socialist, and radical feminist ideologies.[5] Often, however, matters of practical organization made these conceptual boundaries unstable, while strict distinctions between socialist and radical feminists arguably conceal an important history of feminist-Marxist alliance.

The political orientation of WLM poets and the organizational model of the small press network undoubtedly reflect the less bureaucratic and more collectivist-minded groups associated with consciousness raising. Grahn was a member of Gay Women's Liberation and helped to establish A Woman's Place and the Women's Press Collective, Morgan co-founded WITCH and NYRW, while Audre Lorde was a member of the CRC. Ambivalence was a constant, however. Musing on a reformist organization like NOW, Morgan observes: "an ecumenical view (which I hold on alternate Tuesdays and Fridays) would see that such an organization … reaches a certain constituency that is never going to be reached by, say, a group called WITCH … On certain Mondays and Thursdays," however, Morgan "fear[s] for the women's movement's falling into precisely the same trap as did our foremothers, the suffragists: creating a bourgeois feminist movement that never quite dared enough, never questioned enough, never really reached out beyond its own class and race" (*Sisterhood* xxii). In her prefatory remarks to *This Bridge Called My Back*, Moraga reveals that "the deepest political tragedy I have experienced is how with such grace, such blind faith, this commitment to women in the feminist movement grew to be exclusive and reactionary" (Anzaldúa and Moraga xiv). "The lesbian separatist utopia? No thank you," she remarks. "I want a movement that helps me make some sense of the trip from Watertown to Roxbury, from white to Black" (xiii–xiv). Jo Carrillo conveys similar frustration with attempts at inclusion by middle-class, white feminists registering symbolic gestures of solidarity only:

> Our white sisters
> radical friends
> love to own pictures of us
> sitting at a factory machine
> wielding a machete
> in our bright bandanas
> holding brown yellow black red children
> reading books from literacy campaigns
> holding machine guns bayonets bombs knives
> Our white sisters
> radical friends

should think
again.

...

We're not as happy as we look
on
their
wall.   ("And When You Leave," 1–13, 39–42)

Writing in Anzaldúa and Moraga's anthology, Carrillo asserts that as "committed feminists[,] we are challenging white feminists to be accountable for their racism because at the base we still *want* to believe that they really *want* freedom for *all* of us" ("And When You Leave" 62). The challenge is a persistent one: namely, how to generate universal solidarity, on the one hand, and properly reflect and respect cultural difference, on the other. Rachel Blau DuPlessis puts the question bluntly: how do we choose between or possibly reconcile a feminism of "sameness/equality" and a "feminism of difference"?[6]

In bringing together the work of Rich, Lorde, Morgan, Grahn, Moraga, Anzaldúa, and others – indeed, poets drawn from socio-economically diverse Latina, African American, and white feminist traditions – one risks eliding key critical differences in regional and social location. Yet nor should one ignore the material-feminist approach informing their common practice. Rich, for instance, condemns a tendency in orthodox Marxism to promote a "sexless, raceless proletariat," but she also insists that feminism "must be a socialist movement, must be an anti-racist, anti-imperialist movement" ("Notes" 219, 225). She refuses to accept the liberal solution that women need simply join the existing public sphere, nor would she espouse the classical individualist tradition from which liberalism arises. Likewise, Audre Lorde's "Notes from a Trip to Russia" echoes the CRC's socialist mandate, "that the liberation of all oppressed peoples necessitates the destruction of the political-economic systems of capitalism and imperialism as well as patriarchy" (3). The poets of the Women's Liberation Movement gradually adopted a material-feminist approach; if oppression is a manifold system irreducible to gender, race, or sexual orientation alone, then, in all of these instances of exclusion simultaneously, one must engage with the economic and social specificity of women's different experiences.

Morgan remarks that the movement could "exist where three or four friends or neighbors decide to meet … It also exists in the cells of women's jails, on the welfare lines, in the supermarket, the factory, the convent, the farm, the maternity ward, the street corner" (*Sisterhood* xxxvi). By this admittedly romanticized account, one might be tempted to describe the diverse networks of feminist activism as endorsing a nomadic, contingent, permanently impermanent collective, making it a poster child for the post-war era's ostensible incredulity towards modernity's master narratives. Yet the semi-provisional character of these networks is rather *a condition of survival* amid restricted resources and exclusion from existing institutions; one should resist a facile celebration of dispossession as if it were freedom. That which permits a heterogeneous movement such as Women's Liberation to proliferate in such radically different social, cultural, and economic locales throughout the West was and is an emancipatory ideal implemented through reproducible democratizing structures. Publications could fold, resources disappear, and groups disband, but there was always the possibility of remobilization precisely because the WLM applied an unapologetically totalizing set of prescriptions designed to achieve radical emancipation for any subject whosoever.

This is, of course, a controversial claim, because it would seem to elide the philosophies of difference, alterity, otherness, and plurality that constitute the major challenges to the second-wave's feminism of "equality/sameness." Yet, in opposing universalist conceptions of womanhood, I worry that this line of critique vitiates one the movement's most crucial contributions to political thought and activism. Consider, briefly, the following passage from Feminists member Pamela Kearon's "Power as a Function of the Group":

> the group creates its own reality and its own truth. Knowing that reality is whatever is agreed upon by society, the group creates its own society and thereby its own power. Power is the organization of many wills with a common purpose and a common interpretation. The group through its many individuals working together creates an interpretation and then stands collectively behind it. (109)

Simply put, a movement worthy of the name must commit itself to a prescriptive political truth. One need not insist that this truth is found in human nature, but simply to state it, commit oneself to it, and encourage others to mobilize behind it. Yet the axiom of emancipation that Kearon and others advance is not the abstract universal of liberal humanism precisely because it makes no pretence at being an essential principle of human nature. Barbara Smith remarks similarly: "Feminism is the political theory and practice to free *all* women: women of color, working-class women, poor women, physically challenged women, lesbians, old women, as well as white economically privileged hetero-sexual women. Anything less than this is not feminism, but merely fe-male self-aggrandizement" (qtd. in Anzaldúa and Moraga, *This Bridge* 61). One might think of such a politics as the formulation of truths from the ground up rather than from the top down. A proponent of such a political truth recognizes that it is socially produced, and must negoti-ate its implementation within radically different situations, under dif-ferent external pressures, and so on. And while "wills with a common purpose" may appear to anticipate Michael Hardt and Antonio Negri's definition of the multitude as "singularities" that "act in common," ab-sent is a celebratory rhetoric of the transitory, impermanent, and varied collectivity. The event of the group's formation becomes the ground upon which a society, a culture, a writing is formulated, fought for, and maintained through militant stewardship and protection.

Whether it is radical feminism's indictment of the New Left, or Af-rican American feminism's race and class critique of radical feminist thought, the project is to pursue emancipation towards its fullest expres-sion. Lorde remarks frequently that such a politics requires of human beings a radical openness. A writing cannot only concern the subject speaking; it must concern the "planet that we share" and the "interests of our *common* future" ("Above the Wind" 62; my italics). One hears this word with remarkable frequency: the preservation of a "common future," the "building of a common world," the "dream of a common language," the "work of common women," and the words of a poem distributed across the page, "dancing with each other in common."[7]

> I am a welder.
> Not an alchemist.
> I am interested in the blend
> of common elements to make
> a common thing.   (Moraga, "The Welder" 1–5)

Arguably no other concept is more important to the poets of the WLM (and more misunderstood) than the *common*. Many critics challenge a universalizing tendency in radical feminist art and politics, an issue I will return to throughout this chapter, but it suffices to say at this point that a poetics of the common, as writers like Rich, Lorde, Anzaldúa, and Grahn understood this principle of thought and action, had to do with the formation of a shared cultural and social space rather than a universal female identity.

To this end, three general theses guide this chapter: first, however paradoxical, it is a radically singular conception of equality that allowed feminist practices to spread in such different communities throughout North America. Choosing between a feminism of difference and a feminism of sameness obscures this crucial fact. Second, the WLM was more Marxist than New Left Marxism. I agree with scholars like Chantal Mouffe and Ernesto Laclau, who argue that sexism and racism are irreducible to class struggle; one should, therefore, militantly guard against the subordination of race and gender to class. Yet feminist interventions into Marxist thought generate renewed tactics of opposition to patriarchy and capitalism that radical feminists, and especially its poets, identify as a system of manifold oppressions. At the present moment, roughly ten years into the third millennium, is it not surprising that a turn in theory to the "commons" – and to forms of distributed creativity tasked with defending it from state authority and private enclosure – ignores the formative contributions of feminist thought to these debates? A host of theorists formulating a discourse on the commons (a list that includes Michael Hardt, Antonio Negri, Giorgio Agamben, Paolo Virno, Slavoj Žižek, and Alain Badiou)[8] choose to root such a project in the largely male-driven Autonomist and post-Workerist traditions with no mention at all of the WLM. The task at hand is not a matter of asking how feminist thought conforms to Marxism, but rather to ask how radical feminism reinvents Marxism as a gender-alert form of political practice and social existence. Faced with the total subsumption of capital saturating every aspect of contemporary life, radical feminism responds in kind: we must saturate contemporary life with the very principle of feminist liberation. Distilling the "communist hypothesis" to its skeletal core, subordination is not inevitable, and different forms of collectivity are possible, namely, organizations based on the "free association of producers." The task, as expressed by one contemporary thinker, is to bring the communist hypothesis into existence in another mode, to help it emerge within new forms of political experience" (Badiou, "The Communist Hypothesis" 35).[9]

Third, nowhere is this synthesis of Marxist-feminist practice more evident than in a poetics of the WLM focused on the concept of the "common." Here, I have in mind Adrienne Rich's *The Dream of a Common*

Language, Judy Grahn's *The Work of a Common Woman*, Lorde's *Between Our Selves*, Gloria Anzaldúa's *Borderlands/La Frontera: The New Mestiza*, Robin Morgan's *Monster: Poems* and her collaborative writing experiments with members of WITCH. But, more to the point, I mean these works understood within the small press networks, political formations, and resource centres to which a poetics of protest was intimately allied. Moreover, a theory of the common emerges in key essays, for instance, Rich's "Conditions for Work" and "Power and Danger: Works of a Common Woman," Grahn's *Really Reading Gertrude Stein*, Lorde's "Poetry Is Not a Luxury," and Morgan's *Going Too Far*.

Two interlocking conceptions of the common emerge from their poetry and poetics: the first is a radically materialist idea of the world (Arendt: "what we enter when we are born and what we leave behind when we die"). The second meaning is the common as social regime, denoting those actions taken in defence of a radically accessible, shared world. Despite temptations to read a claim for the "common world of women" out of context as validation of female separatism, a poet such as Rich distrusts such exceptionalism. The purpose of naming a group of people (women, Arabs, immigrants) is not to make a case for their exceptional status, but rather to unwork their externally imposed state of exception by defending their access to the common. The claim here is not "we are all the same"; the claim is "we share the same world." Thus, the common modifies, but it does not replace, philosophies of alterity, otherness, multiculturalism, and pluralism, whose proponents worked diligently to critique the white, male, and Western notion of subjectivity claiming universal status on behalf of everyone else. This logic need not carry out the erasure of racial, sexual, or cultural difference, but rather the common as a social practice works to create a world without material and ideological walls barring entry to the innumerably different subjects and groups that occupy the common world. To think the common, then, one must repudiate the binaric choice between sameness and difference. Finally, growing out of this synthesis of material-feminist politics and cultural work a demonstrable shift in lyric writing takes place. One might call this a poetic of the common. This tendency is most pronounced in the work of Rich, Grahn, Lorde, Anzaldúa, and Morgan, but one could also include the work of Irena Klepfisz, Cherríe Moraga, June Jordan, Anne Waldman, and several others. Much of the remaining sections of this chapter are devoted to elaborations of this concept as it materialized in various sites of WLM cultural production; let it suffice for now that the democratizing structures of feminist political action manifest themselves as the structuring principles of poetic form.

The Tyranny of Structurelessness

Jo Freeman first delivered her influential essay, "The Tyranny of Structurelessness," as a speech to the Southern Female Rights Union at an event in Beulah, Mississippi, in May 1970. The text was later published in numerous journals and anthologies, including *The Second Wave*, *Berkeley Journal of Sociology*, *Agitprop*, *Ms.*, and *Radical Feminism*. Freeman's claim is poignant: in opposition to rigid state institutions, the New Left had valorized "leaderless, structureless" group formations (285). I have argued that this binary opposition pitting the rigid structure of society (*gessellschaft*) against a romanticized notion of community (*gemeinschaft*) produces an untenable and reductionist oppositional logic. Community without structure, as this imperative materialized in the post-war era's hippie culture for instance, was admittedly an understandable counterbalance to an age dominated by total war, totalitarian regimes, and the onset of the Cold War's inflexible ideologies. Structurelessness, however, is an organizational impossibility, and when one perpetuates the myth that groups can operate according to no set of rules or regulating practices, it becomes a "way of masking power" (286). (Note that one could apply the very same logic to the structure of poems; from Olson and Levertov to Rich and Lorde, "open form" does not mean a structureless writing, but instead a practice that foregrounds the "relations between things," between the elements that compose in and as a field of action.) A genuinely democratizing organization must instead work to make its own structure recognizable: "the rules of decision-making must be open and available, and this can happen only if they are formalized" (287).

Several WLM activists have sought to formulate strategies of consciousness raising – among them, Kathie Sarachild, Jo Freeman, Irene Peslikis, Pamela Allen, and members of the Chicago Women's Liberation Union (CWLU).[10] Sarachild's "A Program for Feminist 'Consciousness Raising'" was prepared for the First National Women's Liberation Conference in late November 1968 in Chicago. Like Freeman, she outlines a program striking for its attention to basic axioms and tactics that enable open group participation. The following is a condensed version of the manifesto:

I.   The "bitch session" cell group
    A.   Ongoing consciousness expansion
    B.   Class forms of resisting consciousness

C. Recognizing the survival reasons for resisting consciousness
D. "Starting to Stop"
E. Understanding and developing radical feminist theory
F. Consciousness-raiser (organizer) training

II. Consciousness-raising Actions
A. Zap Actions
B. Consciousness programs
C. Utilizing the mass media

III. Organizing
A. Helping new people start groups
B. Intra-group communication and actions   (79–80)

This organizing technique attracted ridicule from men within the New Left. Of course, when Chinese radicals used a comparable method, Speak Pains to Recall Pains, it was, as Morgan observes, "right-on revolutionary"; when women employed this tactic, "it was 'group therapy' or a 'hen party'" (*Sisterhood* xxiii). Notably, personal testimony marks only the very beginning of the process, such that by 1 (A) of the expanded program, participants move from testimony to group interaction, and then to the naming of common oppression. "There is only collective action," Carol Hanisch claims, "for a collective solution" ("The Personal Is Political" 76). The sessions are used to create resources (e.g., newspapers, posters, films, etc.), organize events and protest actions, and develop communication strategies for engaging (often hostile) mass media. Several activists rightly object that consciousness raising has its limits. Group discussion is only meaningful if it leads to concrete political action, institutional changes, and so forth; yet planning these types of actions composed an important part of this process. Consciousness-raising sessions involved creating the resources and conditions for interested parties to start new groups. In this regard, radical feminists build something akin to the TRG and Fluxus's Eternal Network, creating a common conceptual model to be freely appropriated and adapted by other feminist groups.

Pamela Allen describes a similar procedure in "Free Space," in which participants engage in a four-part process of "opening up," "sharing," "analysing," and "abstracting." The first phase is meant in two interrelated senses: opening up as personal testimony and as the social space needed for communal participation. The second phase, sharing, is akin to "building a collage of similar experiences" (275). The linked process of opening up and sharing has less to do with its cathartic value than with exposing a situation of common discrimination. By analysing these conditions, the group develops concepts meant "to define not only the why's and how's of our oppression," but also "ways of fighting that oppression" (276). Activism synthesizes theory and practice: just as concrete experience must anchor all theory and analysis, understanding the systems of power that shape everyday experience requires abstract critique. Like Freeman, Allen explains that since "we are a group that believes that there is always a structure," the abstraction of a group's methods and forms of organization foregrounds the power dynamic that shapes its approach to collective action.

The consciousness-raising models advanced by Freeman, Sarachild, and Allen afford a sample of comparable strategies evident in groups as diverse as the Red Stockings and the Chicago Women's Liberation Union, for whom consciousness raising constituted an integral intersubjective strategy for naming objective conditions of dispossession. Despite ideological differences among many of these consciousness-raising groups, an attempt is evident among them to formalize a process of open, egalitarian decision making. This commitment to structural and organizational scrutiny was less prevalent among the male-dominated New Left. Sarachild's program (and numerous like it) provides an obvious practical solution: its flexible and adaptable structure can materialize and rematerialize anywhere the collective energies are present to put such action into practice. It bears repeating, feminist action proliferates rhizomatically (to use Deleuze's term) only because it commits itself to a singular political precept. Indeed, what enables the WLM's network logic – its emphasis on distributed creativity and group autonomy – is an unabashedly intransigent commitment to unqualified equality one should not shy from calling absolute.

Usurping the Left's Mimeograph Machine: Robin Morgan, WITCH, and Poetic Insurrection

One thing I know: There is no atom that is not political[.]

– Robin Morgan[11]

Robin Morgan's "Goodbye To All That" appeared in the first issue of *Rat* in January 1970. Its publication, together with the first seizure of a male-run leftist newspaper, marked a crucial moment. Of course,

Morgan was not the first feminist activist to proclaim a break with the New Left, but the concision and elegant delivery of her tract quickly popularized a position held by numerous proponents of the Women's Liberation Movement. Morgan records the unsuccessful efforts by the leftist media to mute its far-reaching critical reference;[12] soon after its publication, a feminist collective in San Diego adopted "Goodbye To All That" as the title of their newspaper, while numerous other women's groups and gay organizations acknowledged its influence. Morgan's indictment is particularly striking in that her denunciation moves much further than the familiar catalogue of outrageously sexist claims by New Left leaders. It was not simply that a few sexist men happened to occupy positions of power within an otherwise egalitarian movement; rather, the very form of leftist organization was structured on a model of exclusion: "[a] genuine Left doesn't consider anyone's suffering irrelevant or titillating; nor does it function as a microcosm of capitalist economy, with men competing for power and status at the top, and women doing all the work at the bottom (and functioning as objectified prizes or 'coin' as well). Goodbye to all that" (123). It was likely the comparison of leftist organizations to the capitalist mode of production that earned Morgan more than one death threat.[13] One should also take pause at her poetic sensibility, her knack for just the right word: "goodbye." Although radical feminist groups often employed tactics of direct action and active confrontation, the value of withholding one's participation in struggle was never more evidently powerful than when a significant portion of the Left up and left.

When "Goodbye To All That" appeared in print, below her byline, Morgan identified herself as a member of WITCH. The Women's International Terrorist Conspiracy from Hell first congregated in the autumn of 1968 in New York. Robin Morgan, Florika, Peggy Dobbins, Jo Freeman, and Naomi Jaffe (later a member of the Weather Underground) rank among its initial participants. WITCH "covens" staged public actions, or "hexes," blending elements of guerilla theatre and poetry with political protest. Yet their goal was expansion. On Mother's Day one WITCH collective became Women Infuriated at Taking Care of Hoodlums. Amid the tedium of corporate office work, provisional communities formed Women Indentured to Traveler's Corporate Hell and Women Incensed at Telephone Company Harassment. There was also Women's Independent Taxpayers, Consumers, and Homemakers; Women Interested in Toppling Consumption Holidays; and, in the case of Morgan's byline for *Rat*, Women Inspired to Commit Herstory. Covens spread throughout the country, and, in so doing, sought to multiply their "insouciance, theatricality, humor, and activ-ism" ("WITCH" 538). In fact, the modular structure of WITCH reflects a central characteristic of the WLM in general: it was neither a rigid or-ganization, nor did it suffer from what Freeman would later dub "the tyranny of structurelessness." The viral quality of WITCH – its capacity to modify and adapt as specific actions and political situations required it to – proved a valuable tactic for feminist authors and organizers. A simple name and a flexible organizational model facilitated the disper-sal and reconstitution of like-minded groups committed to the move-ment. Akin to consciousness-raising techniques, a structured process paradoxically facilitates spontaneous action.

For audiences today, references to witchcraft are more likely to con-jure images of Harry Potter, All Hallows' Eve, and mainstream cul-ture's habitual satire of Wiccans than one of the hundreds of thousands of women tortured and executed in Europe and North America over a period of several hundred years. Of course, humour is a strategy used to cope with trauma and to undermine the authority of official cultures; one need not look far into Jewish and African American comedy to find racist symbols repurposed and deflated. Yet the ease with which this symbol is absorbed into popular culture with little satiric reference to an original context of exploitation is telling. For the general pub-lic in 1960s America, the term would have also resonated poignantly with McCarthyism, and the mass hysteria of 1950s communist "witch-hunts." Freeman, Morgan, and other members of WITCH sought to *de-tourn both* of these images. That is, as "agitators and as targets" (543), witches analogize the position women had to take up in radical poli-tics, flanked on both sides by American conservatism and New Left hypocrisies. The ironic choice of leftist activists to appropriate the term "witch hunt" would not have been lost on WLM members. The recla-mation of this cultural symbol comments on both the conservative tra-ditions and institutions that vilify independent women, and the failure of the male Left to register the historical associations of the term with female oppression.

One WITCH collective in Washington, DC, targeted the United Fruit Company's oppressive treatment of Third World employees abroad and secretaries at home. Groups in Chicago pelted the University of Chicago Sociology Department with hair and nail clippings for firing a radical feminist professor, while various covens routinely disrupted bridal fairs across the country.[14] But perhaps the most infamous dem-onstration took place at the 1968 Miss America Pageant in Atlantic City, where members crowned a live sheep. Recollecting years later, Morgan surmised that many of their strategies still "identified politically with the confrontational tactics of the male Left and stylistically with the clownish proto-anarchism of such groups as the Yippies" (*Going Too Far* 72). There were other missteps. At one bridal fair, for instance, a coven circulated stickers that read: "Confront the Whore-makers at the Bridal Fair." Members of WITCH had used the slogan as a pun on the well-known anti-war message "Confront the Warmakers," but many simply interpreted it as the "pillorying of women" (74). Morgan admits that the group erroneously assumed that the general public would recognize that their critique was directed at systemic forms of sexism.

Morgan's own acknowledgment of the group's mistakes has arguably led critics to over-exaggerate these shortcomings. For instance, in *Motherhood Reconceived: Feminism and the Legacies of the Sixties*, Lauri Umansky objects that WITCH "decr[ies] motherhood as a patriarchal ruse" (96). Yet the group had not meant to denigrate motherhood as such, but rather the patriarchal institutions that render maternal commitment and conventional gender roles as obligatory social norms. In fact, while WITCH might have been clearer on this point at bridal fairs and other demonstrations, the passage Umansky has in mind appears in "Mother's Day Incantation": "Become a *liberated mother* / a woman, not a 'mom'" (550; my italics). A parody of Hallmark ("Hellmark") cards, the text was written by Women Interested in Toppling Consumption Holidays. Far from denouncing motherhood, a "liberated mother," according to WITCH, rejects the commercial exploitation of the mother-child relationship. Likewise, in *Hearts and Minds: Bodies, Poetry, and Resistance in the Vietnam Era*, Michael Bibby points to a WITCH poem targeting the incarceration of several female protesters at New Haven's Niantic state prison in 1969: "women as represented in the poem appear classless and raceless even though the prisoners of Niantic were Black Panthers. What ultimately links the oppressed," Bibby explains, "is biological gender; the victims of oppression are female, and by implication, oppressors are male" (96). It is no doubt true that many white feminists associated with the WLM subordinated race and class to a universalizing definition of "sisterhood," yet here are the final lines of the poem's opening verse paragraph:

All 6 are black.
All 6 are Panthers.
All 6 are sisters.   ("Pass the Word, Sister" 8–10)

Questions of race figure prominently in the poem from the very beginning. What is more, WITCH members point out that since activist Rose
Smith had given birth in Niantic prison, the incarcerated also includes
a newborn baby (a gesture fully recognizing motherhood):

> Children oppressed:
> on welfare, in orphanages,
> in schools, in foster homes;
> by poverty, by routine,
> by racism, by male supremacy.
> Therefore,
> WITCH curses the State
> And declares it unfit.   (52–9)

WITCH characterizes patriarchy as a multifaceted system of sexism,
racism, and economic disenfranchisement. Certainly the concept of sisterhood that Morgan advocates runs the risk of privileging gender, but
we should read these decisions in context, since this tendency is in large
proportion a response to the New Left's subordination of gender to
class and race issues. White radical feminist groups indeed deserve criticism if they express a coalitional politics as a mere symbolic gesture;
however, the implied distinction between cultural (symbolic) production and structural-economic critique deserves further consideration.

The term "cultural feminism" was first proposed by members of the
Chicago Women's Liberation Union to name an emerging schism in the
WLM: between those celebrating femaleness on the one hand, and those
engaged in analysis of the economic factors oppressing women on the
other. Alice Echols extends this analysis, arguing that by 1975, "with the
rise of cultural feminism," the creation of "a female counterculture" replaces the central goal of opposing "male supremacy" (*Daring to Be Bad*
5). Echols is correct – and her book is excellent – but the term "cultural
feminism" is an unfortunate one, since it would seem to implicate all
cultural production in the turn from a political project bent on ending
economic dispossession to a supposedly genteel culture of "lifestyle"
preferences. For poets like Rich, Grahn, Lorde, Anzaldúa, and Morgan,
questions of culture and class are intimately connected. Rich proclaims:
"if we care about the imagination, we will care about economic justice"
("Arts" 165). For Morgan's part, she does not mince words indicting the
underlying "classist" and "elitist" assumptions that denigrations of art
invariably imply: "I think the notion that culture is irrelevant basically

… assumes out of guilt, and I must say stupidity, that poor people don't care about art, therefore it is counterrevolutionary to like art to be an artist – unless, of course, it's socialist realist art" ("Poetry and Women's Culture" 109). Instead, Morgan and her collaborators insist that a feminist intervention must take place simultaneously in economic and cultural spheres.

Attention to the work of the Guerilla Girls and the Chicano ASCO make clear WITCH's considerable influence on feminist street theatre and performance art. And while recognition finds its way into histories of performance,[15] the revisionist texts of WITCH play an important if rarely acknowledged role in advancing a highly politicized appropriative literature akin to Fluxus, conceptual, and situationist poetics. I mention at several stages in this book that such tactics emerged – often independently of one another – as central features of Cold War–era poetic and cultural movements throughout the West. The situationist practices of *détournement*, *dérive*, and psychogeography spring readily to mind.[16] Given the present study, one should not overlook CAM's signature repurposing of "Standard English," a hallmark of Caribbean, Black British, and African Canadian and American verse. Looking ahead to the TRG, a litany of similar practices of creative misprision, parodic translation, and forms of appropriation colour their work, as well as that of Fluxus, pop art, conceptualism, and concrete and sound poetry. Many of these appropriative tactics evolve from avant-garde traditions, yet consider that similar approaches to language and art may be found in leftist poetry and culture in America dating to the slave song, *The Little Red Songbook*, and the work songs of Woody Guthrie, Langston Hughes, and the Harlem Renaissance.[17] Similar tactics were also found in the militant activism of the Brown Berets, the American Indian Movement, post-Stonewall gay activism, and the Black Arts Movement.[18] For Morgan and others, poetic discourse must insurrect, transform, and permeate everyday language.

The group's work synthesizes the poem with the pamphlet, the chant, and the open letter. Circulated at rallies, consciousness-raising meetings, and through small-press networks, these collaboratively written "non-poem non-letters" (Morgan, "Letter" 32) were dispersed through the channels of the WLM. And while such a gesture evokes the conflation of art and everyday life, members of WITCH insist that "everyday" should never imply "neutral," as the most prosaic and banal communications often express the subtly internalized ideologies of gender oppression. In a song lyric, for instance, playing on a jukebox –

To be sung to the tune of "A Pretty Girl Is Like a Melody"

A pretty girl is a commodity
With stock to buy and sell.
When the market is high,
Count up your shares
In what she wears
That pay you dividends.

A pretty girl in this society
Is judged by looks alone.
What you see on her face
Is often the waste
Of chemicals developed for the war.   (1–11)

This playful yet invective revision of Irving Berlin's popular song is typical of many parodies sung at rallies.[19] Resonating with the TRG's playful homophonic translations of Catullus and other canonical texts, members of WITCH were more likely to target the artefacts of mass culture, given its increasingly expansive reach and particularly formative influence on young people. Moreover, the little magazines and anthologies of the WLM frequently challenged conventional approaches to canonicity and aesthetic criteria by integrating radically different writing communities. Morgan's *Sisterhood Is Powerful*, for instance, collects the work of established poets such as Sylvia Plath alongside this offering from an anonymous seven-year-old:

A hen
is useful to men.

She lays eggs
Between her legs.   ("Anonymous Poem" 504)

In *The Art of Protest*, T.V. Reed draws a distinction between "women's movement poetry" and the "feminist poetry movement." Whereas the former privileges the movement's political concerns over aesthetics, with the latter "poetry comes first and the central concern is to establish a new kind of poetry" (95). Although Reed admits the distinction is "partly artificial," such a categorical division would seem typical of the formalism that so many feminist poets sought to challenge by fusing art and politics.

Like their appropriations of popular ballads, WITCH frequently conflates the poem with the political tract. Cited earlier, "Pass the Word, Sister" documents the struggles of fourteen members of the Black Panthers detained at Niantic prison in 1969. Five of the members were women, of whom two were pregnant, one giving birth in prison:

How does New Haven's Niantic State
Woman's Farm treat women
in confinement?
They are:
isolated form other prisoners;
denied sleep by the continual noise
of walkie-talkies
and constant bright lights;
denied their constitutional right
to prepare their case;
denied their legal right
to choice of counsel ...[.]   (18–29)

Anticipating the "drive to connect" in the work of Rich and Grahn, such conditions of incarceration frequently symbolize the separation and desired unification of white middle- and working-class women, minorities in the West, and women in the Global South:

We women are:
In jail at Niantic
In the mud of vietnam
In the slums of the cities
In the ghetto-sinks of suburbia
at the typewriters
of the corporations
at the mimeograph machines
of the Left[.]   (65–73)

To this end, the text combines the declarative axioms of the manifesto with the liberating versification of open form practice. And like their song parodies, the group's techniques of appropriation expose the gender bias of seemingly neutral language:

CONFINEMENT: 1. The act
of shutting within an enclosure;
the act of imprisoning.
2. The state of being restrained
or obliged to stay indoors.
3. A woman's lying-in;
childbirth. – *Standard College Dictionary*[.]   (11–17)

Taken in isolation, the poem might be interpreted to mean that childbirth makes a prison of the female body. One should take note of the "speaker," however; the portable dictionary, with its codification of meanings uncluttered by historical usage, still appears to its readers as the reliable narrator of a culture's language (every recorded instance in the *OED* depicts the mother as the sentence's object).[20] Language as an environment can be a space of interaction and open exchange; it can also be a jail cell and a tool for repression. The gesture here is *not* to replace direct action with critique of culture as such, but rather to expose how a logic of containment and enclosure operates in the cultural as well as the socio-economic sphere, and usually in concert. Recalling the function of the consciousness-raising session, "Pass the Word" attempts to open up a space in language that can only be achieved through the occupation and dismantling of those discursive barriers that thwart community building.

It is within these networks of political struggle that WITCH's challenge to the art object's aesthetic autonomy should be understood. In publishing "Goodbye to All That" in the pages of *Rat*, members of WITCH had usurped the Left's "mimeograph machines." Yet the same was beginning to happen to poetic language as such. In "When We Dead Awaken: Writing as Re-vision," Adrienne Rich outlines one aspect of a feminist poetics as the "act of looking back, of seeing with fresh eyes, of entering an old text from a new critical direction" (11). In evoking the poet as (re-)visionary, the gesture is not a mythologizing one, but precisely the opposite: to confront and denaturalize the ostensible timelessness of a patriarchal past and present. Such a method is more than a "chapter" in feminist cultural history; it is a tactic of survival for navigating the immanent terrain of an inherited language: "until we can understand the assumptions in which we are drenched we cannot know ourselves" (11). Rich's metaphor is carefully chosen. Naming the world "afresh" is, indeed, the work of literature, but this act takes place within a system of patriarchy-capital whose total subsumption saturates language as such. WITCH constitutes an instance of counter-response, in which the role of art should be an equally total-izing project to proliferate and infuse culture, ideology, and language with the principles of common emancipation.

The Location of the Commons: Adrienne Rich, Judy Grahn, and the Building of a Common World

We need to begin changing the questions. To become less afraid to ask the still-unanswered questions posed by Marxism, socialism and communism. Not to interrogate old, corrupt hierarchical systems but to ask anew, for our own time: What constitutes ownership? What is work? ... How can we move from a pro-duction system in which human labor is merely a disposable means to a pro-cess that depends on and expands connective relationships?

– Adrienne Rich[21]

Decades before the commons became a fashionable object of study for post-autonomist Marxists, Continental philosophers, and legal schol-ars, WLM poets anticipate what Slavoj Žižek calls the *"new forms of apartheid"* dividing the excluded from the included (*First as Tragedy* 91). WITCH names this logic of enclosure the material as well as the ideo-logical-discursive "containments" that slowly erode the public spaces, cultural resources, and means of assembly that facilitate democratic ac-tion. A history of the commons cannot be written without the crucial intervention of feminist activism and its poetics.

Critics of Adrienne Rich's critical and creative work during the 1970s and 1980s typically emphasize the following ideological shift: what begins as a tendency to essentialize womanhood in collections like *Dream of a Common Language: Poems 1974–1977* (1978) and non-fiction studies like *Of Woman Born* (1976) gradually gives way to col-lections exhibiting a conscious awareness of race, gender, and class diversity in *Time's Power: Poems 1985–1988* (1989) and essays such as "Notes Toward a Politics of Location" (1984). Jan Montefiore, for in-stance, insists that Rich's formative texts of the early 1970s seek to liberate a female literary tradition from patriarchal models by docu-menting a common tradition of women's writing, but, in so doing, she invariably "subsume[s] all particular histories" into a single "rep-resentative fable" (*Feminism and Poetry* 58). By the outset of the 1980s, Montefiore continues, Rich's work demonstrates a "much-needed cor-rective to the possible essentialism implied in the myth of a timeless female world" (89). We are told that difference replaces similitude; plurality replaces commonality.

Yet an important question arises: what does Rich mean by "common"? And what does the term mean for others, like Judy Grahn, Robin Morgan, Audre Lorde, and Gloria Anzaldúa? In Rich's case, is the dream of a common language the tower of Babel re-erected? Does the idea of a "common woman" invoke a fixed, homogenous category of female identity? Although texts such as "Notes Toward a Politics of Location" (1984) and "Blood, Bread, and Poetry" (1984) have since become the touchstones framing critics' assessments of Rich's poetic practice over several decades of prodigious work, it is striking that other essays, composed during the mid-1970s, rarely receive mention. In particular, "Conditions for Work: The Common World of Women" (1976) and "Power and Danger: Works of a Common Woman" (1977) contextualize the poetry of this period, yet these essays also develop a very precise concept of the "common" – one that will persist as a consistent feature of Rich's writing for the next three decades (in texts like "Defying the Space that Separates" [1996], "Arts of the Possible" [1997], and "Poetry and the Public Sphere" [1997]). The titles of her earliest papers alone are evocative: the "common," for Rich, is carefully and inextricably linked to "work." Indeed, when Rich evokes the term "common," she has in mind *a way of working together*, such that work names the project of "building" the shared resources of "a common world" ("Conditions" 205).

The term "commons" in contemporary usage can refer to natural resources, public spaces, social institutions, information and research, and government and communicational infrastructure. A motley array of meanings converge within its signifying power, such that we feel compelled always to pluralize the word. The commons contains material assets (e.g., parks, forests, water), intangible resources (e.g., the public domain, government research), and virtual environments (e.g., public radio, the internet). Yet we also allude casually to the "commonplace" to denote the familiar, the ordinary, and the demotic. The commons is difficult to articulate because it is everywhere and nowhere; legal scholars have the peculiar habit of defining the commons by what *it is not*: i.e., that which is not owned.[22] The terms "private" and "public" fail to register the meaning of commons, since in its purist sense the concept refers to a space unenclosed by market economies or the authority of the state. Beyond this range of meanings, the commons, from at least the fourteenth century onward, affords a synonym for community (L. *communis*).

Rich could not be more adamant that the creation of "community" consists not in formalizing a universal identity, but in "sharing" the task of building and defending a "common world." For Rich and her collaborators, this activist undertaking must also lay the groundwork for a cultural poetics. In organizing a women's clinic, a law collective, a writing workshop, in editing a magazine, or in running a centre for artistic work, a women's prison project, or a crisis centre, "we come to understand at first hand not only our unmet needs but the resources we can draw on for meeting them" amid poverty and institutional hostility ("Conditions" 208). Rich calls this the "work of connection," a phrase which appears in her 1997 lecture, "Arts of the Possible." Yet what makes this claim so striking is its consistency with the focus of her politics-poetics more than twenty years earlier:

> the true nature of poetry. The drive
> to connect. The dream of a common language.
>
> ("Origins and History" 11–12)

The "making of connections" ("Power and Danger" 250), which Rich asserts is the defining feature of Judy Grahn's poetry and activism, comes to constitute by the mid-1970s a central focus of very different poets associated with the WLM, including Rich, Anzaldúa, and Lorde.

Grahn's *The Common Woman Poems* (1969) and *She Who* (1977) were read widely among activists in the WLM, mainly through readings and events – for instance, the Westbeth Artists' Project, where Rich first heard Grahn read "A Woman Is Talking to Death."[23] In 1978 Diana Press collected her writing in the aptly titled *The Work of a Common Woman*. This was an idea Grahn had been developing since the *Common Woman Poems*, "using the idea of commonality means standing exactly where you and/or your group (of whatever current definition) are, and noticing what part of you overlaps with others who are standing exactly where they are" (289). Subjects are in a continual state of becoming; what anchors the alliance of subjects working in common are the shared conditions that either enable or necessitate their solidarity as groups. It cannot be said enough that what is "common" is not necessarily an identity, but shared social space, institutions, language, and the *work* undertaken collectively to bring about change. Like Grahn's notion of commonality, *conocimiento* ("relatedness") for Anzaldúa should not be mistaken for sameness. "When you relate to others," she explains, "not as parts, problems, or useful commodities, but from a connectionist view," one creates the conditions in which different individuals and groups generate an "unmapped common ground." *Conocimiento*, a form of collective consciousness, "advocates mobilizing, organizing, sharing information, knowledge, insights, and resources with other groups" ("now let us shift" 199–201). Once again, we find among these different factions of the Women's Liberation Movement a notion of the common that focuses not on identity but on the shared resources and tactics of collective labour. The common signifies both the shared world that any of us inhabits and the platform from which the "alliance" of "'us' and 'others'" enacts the universal *not as an identitarian* category of being but as a *political category* of action.

Audre Lorde contends that the poem must form "future worlds": poetry involves the "transformation of silence into language and action" ("Transformation" 43). In reading this, one of Lorde's most frequently quoted maxims, one should also be mindful of her terminological precision. Action, she states, involves "collective responsibility – the decision to build and maintain ourselves and our communities together and to recognize and solve our problems together." Identification with others is not then predicated on an a priori essence anterior to race, gender, class, and so forth, but on the principles of cooperative work necessary to bring about equality.

Notably Lorde, along with Barbara Smith, was a member of the Combahee River Collective (CRC), a black feminist organization credited with popularizing the term "identity politics." In light of legitimate criticisms that identity politics fetishizes difference and diverts attention from class conflict, it is instructive to read the CRC's particular "concept of identity" in its original context:

> We realize that the liberation of all oppressed peoples necessitates the destruction of the political-economic systems of capitalism and imperialism as well as patriarchy. We are socialists because we believe that work must be organized for the collective benefit of those who do the work[;] … material resources must be equally distributed among those who create these resources. We are not convinced, however, that a socialist revolution that is not also a feminist and anti-racist revolution will guarantee our liberation … We need to articulate the real class situation of persons who are not merely raceless, sexless workers, but for whom racial and sexual oppression are significant determinants in their working/economic lives. Although we are in essential agreement with Marx's theory … we know that his analysis must be extended further …

We reject pedestals, queenhood, and walking ten paces behind. To be recognized as human, levelly human, is enough." ("Statement" 275–6)

The CRC's "identity politics" is not conceived as a "cultural feminism" (to use Echols's term). In fact, the claim to be recognized as "human, levelly human" edges closer to a feminism of sameness than to an identity politics with which the group is usually aligned. Nor was "biological determinism" a valid "basis upon which to build a politic" (277); the group categorically opposed any form of sexual or racial separatism. The CRC instead insists that race and gender oppression are irreducible to class oppression, but this line of reasoning was meant to expand, not replace, the critique of the capitalist mode of production. Here we find once again that naming an oppressed group confers no essential or exceptional status on that community. The CRC's axiom of collective emancipation bears something in common with the mantra of the French *sans- papiers*: "everyone who is here is from here." For the Combahee, the question is not how do we simply respect difference, but how might one proceed from the prescriptive claim of an unqualified equality and build a world faithful to this political axiom. The Combahee Statement and Rich and Grahn's concept of the common demonstrate important points of convergence. The presently fashionable alter-globality of plural, coexisting social worlds is not a viable end in itself. Decades ago Anzaldúa had already grown suspicious of a conciliatory and increasingly quietistic liberal pluralism taking hold both in feminism and among the New Left more broadly. "Can you assume," she asserts, "that all of us, Ku Klux Klan and holistic alliances members, are in it together just because we're all human? … It's impossible to be open and respectful to all views and voices" (203).

There is instead one world within which an unlimited set of differences exists. The work of community is the bringing into being of new forms of relation, but ethical recognition of the other can only take place under the condition that the axiomatic truth of a common world accessible to all is first honoured. We hear frequently, of course, that contemporary capitalism facilitates a single global order, yet billions of people have only limited access to this world. Such a system depends on this exclusion. Insofar as commonality names a collective subject, it is one based on the cooperation of an ensemble of different individuals and groups labouring to defend our common existence in the shared world.

Consciousness Raising as Poetic Discourse

[I]n a paragraph ... the word chair is alive the word the is alive the word is is alive and the word alive is alive and they are all dancing with each other in common.

– Judy Grahn[24]

The term "radical feminist lyric" describes a range of techniques that put into practice consciousness raising as poetic discourse. This form of writing is neither the mid-century anecdotal lyric, nor is it commensurate with the confessional mode to which a feminist poetics is no doubt partly indebted. In employing such a phrase I have in mind M.H. Abrams's canonical statement on the "greater Romantic lyric," a term he uses to denote a set of common features among the poems of Wordsworth, Coleridge, Keats, and Shelley. This lyric mode (which critic Corey Marks also calls the "descriptive-meditative structure")[25] typically unfolds in three parts: (1) a speaker encounters a physical scene, which (2) functions as a trigger for interior contemplation (a thought, a memory, a feeling, and so on), followed by (3) a movement towards epiphanic disclosure, resolution, or consolation. Such poems involve a processual movement from the material-particular to the abstract-general. And though a silent auditor is often implied, this is strictly a rhetorical devise; the greater romantic lyric is a record of the mind in conversation with itself. In regards to what I will call the radical feminist lyric, there are ostensible similarities: in particular, a speaker is depicted within a particular locale, while such poems record a processual transformation of thought. Yet unlike the Romantic lyric Abrams formalizes, the lyric I am attempting to locate within a range of post-war feminist poetry typically features an alternative three-part structure: (1) a speaking subject (not always the author) is situated in a time and place in which power relationships are as palpable as a tangible locale; (2) the speaker forges connections with a community facing subjugation, typically women, but also other groups facing similar oppression; and, finally, (3) the naming of a common project of opposition. The lyric mode in question draws upon practices of consciousness raising and community building as the processual logic of its poetic method. In a word, the poem records not a mind talking to itself, but *a transformation of I's into we's.* Lorde could not be more precise: if the poem is a distillation of "our hopes and dreams toward survival and change," if indeed the poem is a laboratory for a "future world," then its movement involves a "transformation of silence into language" and from language into "action" ("Transformation" 43). The poem is still revelatory, in that it is *consciousness raising*, but it jettisons transcendent generalization; from a gender-alert, materialist poetic stance, the poem moves not towards universal knowledge but towards collectively forged actions.

As a preliminary example, consider Honor Moore's "Polemic #1." The opening lines announce a potential alliance between reader and writer: "[t]his is the poem to say 'Write poems, women' because I want to / read them" (1–2). The poem traces a movement from the speaker's drive "to connect" to the manifesto-like axiom its title promises: "we can't be stopped." In effect, the text attempts to devise a network that circumvents the disciplinary institutions of cultural production that women are normally forced to navigate. The "Art Delivery Machine" is that diffuse apparatus of the state that

> ... instructs
> by quiet magic women to sing proper pliant tunes for
>   father, lover, piper who says he has the secret, but
>   wants ours; it teaches us to wear cloaks labelled
>   Guinevere, become damsels, objects in men's power joustings
> like her: lets us shimmer, disappear, promise to rise like a
>   Lady of the Lake, but we drown – real, not phantom.
> The Art Delivery Machine is ninety-nine and forty-
>   four hundredths percent pure male sensibility, part of
>   a money system ninety-nine and forty-
>   four hundredths percent pure white-male-power-structure controlled. So
> you may wonder why I write this poem and say "Write your own poems,
>   women!" Won't we be crushed trying? No. We have more
> now, fifty-six hundredths percent of the Art Delivery
>   Machine. We can't be stopped ...[.]   ("Polemic #1" 35–49)

The speaker invents no illusory "outside" of the system; rather, like Allen's claim, women must forcibly open up a space in which to occupy and to advance an emancipatory politics. Appropriately, this poem appears first among documents collected in the "Literature" chapter of *The New Woman's Survival Sourcebook*. Readers in 1975 who encountered Moore's poem in the *Sourcebook* would have turned the page and found an interview with Robin Morgan and Adrienne Rich about the relationship between art and activism. Next, readers would have encountered an article entitled "An Alternative Network for Sharing Our Poetry," replete with photographs of Madwoman: a Feminist Bookcenter and information about do-it-yourself publishing.

It will be argued perhaps that the procedural logic of the radical feminist lyric depends upon a highly selective reading of WLM poets, that in fact much of the poetic output of this moment generates as many examples of poetry indicative of the inward-looking anecdotal lyrics Ron Silliman calls the "school of quietude" or political poems that inadvertently essentialize identity. In Donna Kate Rushin's "The Bridge Poem," for instance,

> The bridge I must be
> Is the bridge to my own power
> I must translate
> My own fears
> Mediate
> My own weaknesses
>
> I must be the bridge to nowhere
> But my true self[.]   (Donna Kate Rushin, "The Bridge Poem" 45–52)

As I have argued earlier in this chapter, competing theories of subjectivity among members of the WLM were more prevalent than subsequent post-structuralist and third-wave feminists acknowledge. Recent efforts to collect Anzaldúa's earlier writings from the 1970s, for instance, clearly reveal a preoccupation with social location and the transformative nature of identity:

> "Reincarnation" (1974)
>   I
>   slithered shedding
> my self
>   on the path
>   then
>   looked back and
>   contemplated
>   the husk
>   and wondered
>   which me
>   I had discarded

> and was it the second
> or the two thousand and

thirty-second

> and how many me's
> would I slough off
> before voiding
> the core
> if ever[.]   (1–19)

Most of the critical attention to Anzaldúa's body of work specifically attends to her exceptional long poem, *Borderlands/La Frontera: The New Mestiza* (1987), an ambitious multilingual text investigating the complex social and linguistic landscape of the United States/Mexico border region. The text deploys no fewer than eight identifiable languages and dialects in conjunction, weaving Mexican and *tejana* history and personal testimony in what constitutes a hybrid lineage of shifting *mestizos* geography, language, and identity.[26] Like the description of subjectivization above, such an emphasis on nomadism and hybridity makes the critical space of the text safe for post-structuralists to enter – indeed, to declare Anzaldúa's project in step with the radical critique of the subject undertaken in the post-war years by Continental thinkers. Two contextualizing observations about Anzaldúa's poetics are key: first, her understanding of the subject is local to a site of cultural displacement, movement, and synthesis specific to the borderland. Second, and this is crucial, for Anzaldúa simply declaring the subject is without essence *is not enough*. Recalling *conocimiento* as a practice of consciousness raising, the question is always how does the perpetually "reincarnat[ing]" subject enter into communal formations with others? What are the possibilities of this political subject? Like Rich and Grahn in their respective social locations, the question always regards the "I" becoming "we" both in language and in action:

> Some of us are still hung-
> up on the art-for-art trip
> and feel that the poet
> is forever alone.
> Separate.
> More sensitive.
> An outcast.

...

But what we want
– what we presume to want –
is to see our words engraved
on the people's faces,

...

We don't want to be
Stars but parts
of constellations.   ("The New Speakers," 22–8, 36–9, 45–7 [c. 1975])

A poetic of consciousness raising develops from the collectivist spaces of
activist networks, in which opening up, sharing, and organizing come to
constitute the principles of a poetic mode developed and expanded by a
community of poets associated with the WLM. The anxiety that "we's"
produce receives considerable attention in this study: Olson asks, "[i]
nside totality, where are we, who are we?" For Duncan, "we must begin
where we are ... entering and belonging to a configuration being born
of what 'we' means." Rich is as insistent on this question: "who is *we*?"
How do "we's" form, and how might we form them otherwise?

A brief assessment of Rich's work from the 1950s onward to the late
1970s aptly demonstrates how this question informs her poetics. As
many critics note, she gradually abandons the well-wrought, formally
chiselled verse of *The Diamond Cutters* (1955) for the open form techniques and historical themes particularly evident in *A Will to Change*
(1971). The following two passages illustrate this transition:

"A Walk by the Charles"

Finality broods upon the things that pass:
Persuaded by this air, the trump of doom
Might hang unsounded while the autumn gloom
Darkens the leaf and smokes the river's glass.   (1–4)

"November 1968"

Stripped
you're beginning to float free
up through the smoke of brushfires
and incinerators

the unleafed branches won't hold you
nor the radar aerials[.]   (1–6)

The technically proficient metres, rhythms, and rhymes, which had won
Rich so much early praise, are subsequently "stripped." The ground
upon which so many of Rich's contemporaries learned their practice had
been sufficiently "cooked," to use Robert Lowell's phrase. Morgan is decidedly less cryptic: "I don't write what I once called poems anymore
– / the well-wrought kind that you and I / might once have critically
discussed over a gentle lunch." Instead, she asserts, the text ignites "a
fuse," "a small ticking insight / from the page" that can "flash into an action" ("Letter" 10–12, 18–22). Olson's influence on feminist poetics is an
ambivalent one. Scholars such as Duplessis, Libbie Rifkin, and Michael
Davidson aptly observe that open form was conceived within the hyper-
masculine milieu of 1950s culture, yet undoubtedly this appropriation
afforded many women writers a set of poetic techniques enabling a synthesis of poetic form and cultural activism. Susan Howe maintains that
despite Olson's heterosexist attitudes, his "writing encouraged me to be
a radical poet. When I was writing my first poems I recall he showed
me what to do" ("Since a Dialogue We Are" 166). The practice variously
called open form, projectivism, and field composition had sought to
enact democratizing social structures at the level of poetic form; to borrow Morgan's evocative phrase once more, Olson, Creeley, and others
associated with BMC failed to "go far enough." Almost immediately Levertov understood the value of Olson's "relations between things" as an
axiom of poetic activism, which she expresses through polyphony, appropriation, and intermedia in "To Stay Alive." Likewise, Lorde will remark: "There are many kinds of open" ("Coal" 4 [1968/1976]).[27]
    If Rich's work indicates a shift from well-wrought to open form
verse, then several critics also observe a gradual shift from the self-ex-
ploratory lyrics of "confessional" poetry in the early 1960s to a dialogic-
epistolary form in feminist writing of the late 1960s.[28] Accordingly, a
conversant poetics emphasizing common struggle and social themes
typified by poems like Morgan's "Letter to a Sister Underground" and
"Portrait of the Artist as Two Young Women," Honor Moore's "Polemic
#1," and Adrienne Rich's "Coast to Coast" gradually replaces a preoc-
cupation with loneliness and isolation in texts by Anne Sexton, Maxine
Kumin, and certain of Sylvia Plath's poems. Plath's influence on Rich,
Moore, and others deserves pause, however; though indeed some of
her poetry reflects the lyric of private reference that Rich and others

subsequently challenge, few poets in the English language comment on state oppression with such efficacy. Recall that a poem like "Daddy" (1962) unfolds as a series of private references to a father/husband figure that are filtered through the following cultural signs (god, Nazi, devil, vampire, teacher). In this regard, Plath, more capably than nearly anyone in post-war verse, demonstrates the meaning of the "personal *is* political," not by opposing private to public spheres of life, but rather *by exposing an identical patriarchal logic governing them both*. The domestic sphere joins the school, the prison, the media, the church, and the court as one more state apparatus socializing Western subjects. Though "Daddy" was composed in 1962, the text would not appear in print until the posthumous publication of *Ariel* in 1966, amid rapid changes in feminist politics and aesthetics. Moore's Art Delivery Machine applies Plath's institutional critique to the publishing industry, while forging alternative cultural networks.

Yet this transition from a lyric of private reference to an epistolary form too seems an incomplete characterization of the poetry of the WLM. One might conclude, for instance, that poets involved in the WLM staged an intervention in lyric writing, whereby the mind speaking to itself now speaks to another. Kim Whitehead argues that, like the confessional group, the "banishment of persona … proved to be particularly important to women finding their voices as feminists" (4). Yet the convention of personae is readily evident in Morgan's "Voices from Six Tapestries" and Rich's "Paula Becker to Clara Westhoff," poems that construct imaginary encounters between female historical figures. A collection like Rich's *A Wild Patience* employs appropriative methods akin to Salkey and Levertov's expansive use of citation, while in Grahn's *The Common Woman Poems* and *She Who* social location (rather than the person of the poet) replaces persona, whereby a multiplicity of race, class, and gender positions encounter one another on the page. Just as Denise Levertov's participation in the New Left provoked a noticeable shift in her work from anecdotalism to dialogic collage, radical feminist activism contextualizes the contestatory formal politics of these works. Indeed, these poems are not private communiqués between individuals; they instead document the complex formation of collective subjects. But whereas Levertov's work is still very much couched in a New Left project of alliances between the student movement, Vietnam protest, and Black Power, the work of Rich and Grahn formulates a critique of the patriarchal models informing conservative and New Left politics alike.

Rich's "Culture and Anarchy" provides a useful illustration. The title is an obvious allusion to Matthew Arnold's work of criticism. Although innumerable challenges to Arnold's "touchstone" aesthetics by feminist, Marxist, post-structuralist, and post-colonial theorists are well documented, it is worth noting Terry Eagleton's poignant observation that Arnold's advocacy for a depoliticized national culture is "refreshingly unhypocritical" in its political motivations. According to Arnold, marshalling the energies of the middle class to pacify the poor is a necessary precondition for stabilizing class hierarchies: "[l]iterature was in several ways a suitable candidate for this ideological enterprise. As a liberal, 'humanizing' pursuit, it could provide a potent antidote to … ideological extremism." Because literature trades in "universal human values rather than in such historical trivia as civil wars, the oppression of women or the dispossession of the English peasantry, it could serve to place in cosmic perspective the petty demands of working people for decent living conditions or greater control over their lives" (21–2). Rich counters Arnold's own position as touchstone of high Victorian criticism with a multitude of early suffragist texts written at the end of the nineteenth century. Like the "Alabama woman still quilting in her nineties," the text "stich[es] together" (13, 42) the diary and letters of Susan B. Anthony, Jane Addams's *Twenty Years at Hull House*, Elizabeth Barrett's correspondence with Anna Brownell Jameson, Anthony and Ida Husted Harper's *The History of Woman Suffrage*, and Elizabeth Cady Scanton's speech "On Solitude of Self." Notably, none of these texts are fictional; Rich is mindful to incorporate a litany of documents into the body of her poem, thus purposefully contaminating the literary with the non-literary, the aesthetic with the political. For Rich, all literature is collage in flux:

> Rough drafts we share, each reading
> her own page over the other's shoulder
> trying to see afresh[.]   ("Culture and Anarchy" 34–6)

The poem becomes increasingly populous, linking suffragist activism with abolitionists such as Harriet Tubman, Sojourner Truth, and Maria Mitchell, native activist Matilda Joslyn Gage, journalist Ida B. Wells-Barnett, and "all those without names" (116). Preceding this passage, Elizabeth Barrett's letter to Anna Jameson appears italicized:

> *and is it possible you think*
> *a woman has no business with questions*

like the question of slavery?
Then she had better use a pen no more[.]   (95–8)

The assemblage of appropriated texts in Rich's poem analogizes a transformation in mid-century poetic writing I have been calling the radical feminist lyric: a diary becomes a letter, and a letter becomes a collectively authored political tract. In the most concrete terms, "Culture and Anarchy" follows this sequence: from Anthony's diaries (a conversation with the self) to the correspondences between Anthony, Harper, and others (communication with another), to a work such as *The History of Woman Suffrage* (a political thesis). Rich documents the becoming-political of the speaker. Like Olson, she is grappling with the problem of the one and the many. Collectivity in the poem appears as neither the homogeneously singular culture of Arnold's civilized citizenry nor a celebration of structurelessness as such. The textual collage brings together individuals, groups, and texts in a methodical distillation of the principles of female liberation, aimed at "complete emancipation" (150).

Rich's preoccupation with community formation, in many ways, stems from her engagement with the work of Judy Grahn, arguably one of the most undervalued American poets of the second half of the twentieth century.[29] The *Common Woman Poems* was produced and disseminated as a mimeograph edition in 1969. Passages from these poems were frequently circulated and recited at WLM events, such that the text became an "anonymous talisman for the women's liberation movement as a whole" ("The Common" 55). For instance, the final passage of "Vera, from my childhood" appeared on various posters in slightly altered forms:

A common woman is
As common as a common loaf of bread –
AND WILL RISE.

"Well, the quote is *sort of* correct," according to Grahn (55). Both accurate and slightly misleading versions of the passage circulated among members of the WLM. Here is the original version from *The Common Woman Poems*:

the common woman is as common
as good bread
as common as when you couldnt go on

but did.
For all the world we didnt know we held in common
all along
the common woman is as common as the best of bread
and will rise[.]   (20–7)

Of course, these forms of adaptation are not problematic as such; WITCH used the permutation of its acronym to expand the sphere of possible actions it undertook. But here, a precise meaning is lost. A "common woman" can indeed "be any woman, but the bread is not just any bread … The *best* of bread is the most carefully made" and it "feeds everyone" (Grahn, "The Common" 55). Both versions yoke the domestic image of the loaf with the "rising up" of a female underclass. Yet in the original poem considerable emphasis is placed on action. The "best," for Grahn, is she who offers herself up to others – after all, bread provides sustenance and rises to be shared. "Common," she carefully maintains, "steps outside of our factory driven lives to honor and treasure each of us, and in our commonality, to call for collectivity, alliance" (55). In brief, this seemingly minor additional meaning explains so much misinterpretation of Grahn's poetic output. "Common," as we have said, is not a category of identity; it describes the work of connection, of "collectivity" and "alliance," between subjects that act, build, and create in common. Anticipating the potentiality implied in the Stein-inspired use of the phrase "She Who," the common woman is "She Who increases / what can be done" ("She Who increases" 1–2).

  The Common Woman Poems comprises seven interlocking texts. The title of each names a specific woman in a particular location – for instance, "Ella, in a square apron, along Highway 80" and "Nadine, resting on her neighbor's stoop." At first glance, the texts depict portraits of working-class, lesbian, and ethnic women within these respective communities:

Her grief expresses itself in fits of fury
over details, details take the place of meaning,
money takes the place of life.
She believes that people are lice
who eat her, so she bites first …[.]   ("I. Helen" 19–23)

She holds things together, collects bail,
makes the landlord patch the largest holes.

At the Sunday social she would spike
every drink, and offer you half of what she knows, ...

                    ... The neighborhood
would burn itself out without her ...[.]   ("III. Nadine" 1–4, 14–15)

          She has taken a woman lover
          whatever shall we do
          she has taken a woman lover
          how lucky it wasnt you ...

On weekends, she dreams of becoming a tree;
a tree that dreams it is ground up
and sent to the paper factory, where it
lies helpless in sheets, until it dreams
of becoming a paper airplane, and rises
on its own current ...[.]   ("IV. Carol" 1–4, 13–18)

The meticulous documentation of commonplace life and the terse, gritty
character of the poetic sequence mark its most emphatic characteristics. Grahn maintains that she sought to represent "regular, everyday
women without making [them] look either superhuman or pathetic"
(60). More so than other mid-century poets who sought to challenge
Eliot's objective correlative by capturing the minutiae of daily experience, Grahn manages to reveal the macropolitics of every micropolitical
moment. Same-sex love and abortion were particularly controversial
topics, but so were representations of underclass aspiration. *The Common Woman Poems* evokes at once Plath's teeming dissension, Langston Hughes's exploding dream, and Rich's collective imperative. Note
that the first-person pronoun appears only in the text's final five lines
of the sequence. Until this point, the third-person feminine "she" links
speaker, character, and reader. Yet the relation between these agents is
never specified in advance; or rather, the work of the common reader
involves mapping the potential connections between these changing
subject positions, positioning the reader as one more agent within the
network of writers, small press editors, disseminators, and activists
who make up a WLM poetic culture.

By the publication of *She Who*, the role of the reader as agent of an
emancipatory politics is rendered all the more striking:

She Who continues.
She Who has a being

named She Who is a being
named She Who carries her own name.
She Who turns things over.
She Who marks her own way, gathering.
She Who makes her own difference.
She Who differs, gathering her own events.
She Who gathers, gaining
She Who carries her own ways,
gathering She Who waits,
bearing She Who cares for her
own name, carrying She Who
bears, gathering She Who cares[.]   ("She Who continues" 1–14)

Grahn's previous strategy of naming individual women in *The Common Woman Poems* gives way to the repetitive use of the third-person feminine pronoun. "She Who" is a position in language that can be taken up by any woman, but there is an important precondition. The "She Who" of Grahn's text is she who "turns things over," who collects those who "wait," and who "makes her own difference." The operative term "continues" affords an evocative pun. While the prefix "con-" intimates its Latin origin, "together with, in combination or union" (*OED*), its suffix "-eus" mixes with its homonyms "you's" and "use." Continuity, collectivity, and purpose converge in the poem's opening line only to proliferate. Hence, Grahn's clever adaptation of Stein's axiom: "the difference is spreading" ("A Carafe" 3).

One may choose to read *The Common Woman Poems* as a simple affirmation of difference. If so, the text will likely be read in support of the imperative of identity politics, its celebration of diverse subject positions. Depending on one's definition of "common," however, the reader may also conclude that the text evokes such attention to difference only to assimilate these socially located identities within a unifying notion of womanhood that, in the final analysis, subordinates class and race to gender. Yet Grahn ultimately advances an alternative to this familiar deadlock. Close attention to the aforementioned passage from "Vera" indicates that what we *hold* in common, in the most concrete possible sense, is "the world" understood in its radically material openness. In naming the subject's race, gender, and socio-economic position, Grahn's text is not merely celebrating difference; rather, her goal is to locate specific sites of dispossession – in this case the challenges of poor women – and to demand for these subjects the access to a common world enjoyed by anyone at all.

Morgan's proclamation is the correct one: the task, whether in art or in politics, must not be to retrench from the Left, but rather to "go further" in demanding radical equality as the necessary precondition for any community that dares call itself one. It is not, of course, enough simply to declare one's commitment to an idea, but to locate and install this idea in precisely those historical movements and moments in which real antagonisms give rise to actual change. The presence of racism in the community is enough evidence that it had serious shortcomings, but notice the response from Chicano and Black feminists: radical feminism did not go far enough in its bid for unqualified equality. They sought to take it even "further." The WLM's most controversial and difficult claim to accept – its declared commitment to the category of universality – is precisely that aspect of the movement we must revive today. Yet I reiterate that the universality proposed by the WLM is of a particular character incompatible with the abstract universality of liberal humanism, the latter's rigid application of a rule imposed upon any and all situations. Instead, the WLM invite us to reimagine community in terms of the desires and hopes of those excluded from it. Let us call this the universality of the common world.[30] To be sure, poetry alone is hardly a substitute for political action, but one challenges the autonomy of art by expressing this very fact, by situating the poetic text within a larger field of commitments. If capital has come to saturate every aspect of contemporary life – our affects, our desires, our knowledges – then, for the WLM, a material-feminist poetics demands that we challenge this development by saturating poetic language, indeed all language, with the demand for radical equality. This is a project that should not be relegated to the cultural sphere only, but it should happen there as well.

Turning now to the Toronto Research Group, and a host of activities undertaken with members of Fluxus, visual and sound poets, and conceptual artists, we undoubtedly encounter a very different scene of collective literary experimentation, yet the WLM's preoccupation with a shared culture will likewise constitute an important concern among a group of poets rightly credited for their prescient anticipation of the digital age's participatory cultures. If Black Mountain, CAM, and the WLM, in their respective locations both social and geographic, engaged questions of community largely in terms of places and publics, then the TRG's work affords an important shift towards discursive and transnational communities. As a group preoccupied with ideas and practices of collaboration and appropriation, it also marks a moment in which the advanced West would drastically re-define its very notion of property, as market consortiums began to radically expand their efforts to control and enclose information, knowledge, and culture as such.

5 The Toronto Research Group: A Poetic of the Eternal Network

The relationship of the community to the world of things remains that of private property ... Let us now picture to ourselves, by way of change, a community of free individuals, carrying on their work with the means of production in common, in which the labor-power of all the different individuals is consciously applied as the combined labor-power of the community.

– Karl Marx[1]

[I]f language were made either private or public – that is, if large portions of our words, phrases, or parts of speech were subject to private ownership or public authority – then language would lose its powers of expression, creativity, and communication.

– Michael Hardt and Antonio Negri[2]

Until looking into the mirror just now ... I'd never met a Marxist with a sense of humour.

– Steve McCaffery[3]

The Institute of Creative Misunderstanding

The "Toronto Research Group" usually refers to a series of research reports and associated activities conducted by Steve McCaffery and bpNichol from 1972 to 1982, the dates of their first manifesto and the last of their investigations into creative translation, the material production of the book, and non-narrativity.[4] Throughout this chapter, the name Toronto Research Group (TRG) will refer to these activities, though one should bear in mind that these investigations did not take place in isolation. TRG research is an important component of a constellation of integrated critical and creative collaborations by several experimental poets during the 1970s. These activities were undertaken both at the local level of a scene within the Toronto literary community and as part of a larger international network of poets with whom McCaffery and Nichol kept in constant contact. At approximately the same time that they began their work together, Nichol and McCaffery formed the sound poetry collective the Four Horsemen with fellow poets Paul Dutton and Rafael Barreto-Rivera. McCaffery and Nichol composed several poems together, including "Parallel Texts," "Collboration" [sic], and "In England Now that Spring," the title piece of a co-authored book also containing their tandem gestural scores. McCaffery undertook similar projects with Steve Smith (*Crown's Creek*, *Edge*) and with members of the Language Group (*Legend*), while bpNichol worked on numerous intermedial projects, including the Seripress collaborations with Barbara Caruso. In addition to the more celebrated albums by the Four Horsemen (*CaNADAda*, *Live in the West*), McCaffery and Nichol's experiments with creative translation would occasion several multi-authored projects, most notably *Six Fillious* (with Robert Filliou, George Brecht, Dieter Roth, and Dick Higgins), but also McCaffery's *8 × 8: La Traduction à L'Epreuve* (a bilingual composition involving Michel Beaulieu, Cécile Cloutier, Michel Gay, Alexander Hutchison, Daphne Marlatt, André Roy, and George Stanley) and Nichol's *Translating Translating Apollinaire* (a similar translational work that features collaborative sections with McCaffery, Higgins, Karl Young, Hart Broudy, and Richard Truhlar).[5]

The poet and editor Karl Young would remark of Nichol that "he was Toronto's most innovative poet at a time when that city could claim more innovative poets than any other in the English speaking world."[6] Perhaps Young exaggerates, yet it is likely that readers familiar with mid-century North American writing may have never heard of the TRG, despite the fact that its members made sizeable contributions to sound poetry, visual and concrete poetry, Fluxus, Language writing, and conceptual art. Further attention to the relationship between Fluxus and the TRG is warranted if for no other reason than Dick Higgins was active in both groups. But then, so was McCaffery, who composed the intermedial piece *Scenarios* (1978) at the "Flux-Wedding" of George Maciunas and Billie Hutchins.[7] Many of the ideas McCaffery co-developed with Nichol and Higgins anticipate aspects of Language writing. The TRG occupies a nebulous position in the history of experimental poetics, insofar as its members participated simultaneously in a variety of artistic movements during the 1960s and 1970s. In his role as editor of *Ganglia Press*, *GrOnk*, and *The Cosmic Chef*, Nichol made concerted attempts to expose different literary communities to one another. Unlike the majority of American magazines associated with the "Mimeograph Revolution" of the 1960s, *GrOnk* brought together British, Czech, American, Canadian, French, and Austrian concrete and experimental practitioners, using a technology for disseminating texts usually associated with smaller scenes of writing and pamphleteering. Although Nichol was the principal editor, editorial control changed hands among several writers, and the mimeo editions were often mailed free of charge to subscribers worldwide.

Despite the interest in such experiments among members of the Toronto literary scene, critical attention to this aspect of their combined practice is noticeably absent beyond preliminary assessments of the Four Horsemen's sound poetry.[8] Certainly Nichol's role as a facilitator of community during these years receives comment, but such observations are typically relegated to his work as an editor or the consequence of biographical readings of *The Martyrology*. In his introductory remarks for the *Open Letter* special issue "bpNichol + 10," Frank Davey asserts that the critical industry devoted to Nichol's work had tended to deify the personality of the poet by conflating 'bp' the person and the body of texts associated with his name.[9] In the same issue, commentators such as Lori Emerson, Darren Wershler-Henry, and Christian Bök echo Davey's complaint; the latter two indicate that such celebratory criticism has taken *The Martyrology* as the centrepiece for a largely anecdotal and honorific approach to his oeuvre, precisely because his long poem, Bök argues, "lends his life work an imaginary coherence, unifying his career under the reassuring, but inhibiting, aegis of humanistic legitimacy" ("Nickel Linoleum" 66).[10] Bök and Wershler-Henry call for critics to explore the rich heterogeneity of Nichol's literary practice, finding alternative paths through his early concrete texts in *Journeying & the Returns* and *Konfessions of an Elizabethan Fan Dancer*, the 'pataphysical experiments collected in the *love/zygal/artfacts* trilogy, and *The Adventures of Milt the Morph in Colour*. This is not to suggest simply that an alternative set of texts should usurp *The Martyrology* as the privileged "centre" of Nichol's canon; rather, these critics indicate that a more comprehensive approach is needed to identify the complex array of practices collected under the proper name known as "bpNichol." A comparable tendency can be found in the critical attention paid to

McCaffery's literary career. Interest in his work has come mainly from critics of the Language Group, and thus his single-authored texts from the late 1970s and early 1980s such as *Panopticon* tend to receive disproportionate attention.[11] Following from Davey's assertion, if the goal of earlier criticism had been to distinguish 'bp' the person from the "author function" that marks a body of literary texts, then as critics we should insist upon a further step: to acknowledge the frequency with which "bpNichol," "McCaffery," Higgins," "Barreto-Rivera," and others signify as proper names dispersed and reconstituted as other *collective* nouns – the Toronto Research Group, the Four Horsemen, or Six Fillious.

In the three previous chapters, I have sought to establish a crucial connection between the social organizations that poets create and the methods of writing they adopt: collaboration at BMC and the development of open form writing, CAM's anti-racism activism and the history of nation language, consciousness raising in the WLM and a poetic of the common. The TRG's social poetics by comparison involves a more radical experiment in form, whereby collaboration constitutes the hallmark of their literary practice – in sound poetry, creative translation, collaborative poems, intermedial texts, and conceptualist-inspired performance art. For the sake of clarity, it is possible to extrapolate from the many texts mentioned above a list of four broad and often overlapping areas of work: (1) research (e.g., the TRG reports), (2) textual composition (e.g., "In England Now that Spring"), (3) performance (e.g., the Four Horsemen), and (4) creative translation (e.g., *Six Fillious*). Some of these practices are dynamic, involving real-time acts of spontaneous exchange, while others are appropriative, insofar as they involve the modification of another poet's work. Moreover, these four modes involve no implicit sequence from one to the next. The TRG did not precede the Four Horsemen in a fixed trajectory, but instead they were a "community of two alongside of which grew that community of four ... extend[ing their] range and interest in collaboration" (McCaffery, "Interview" by Jaeger 91). Although multi-authored poetry is, generally speaking, a marginal practice, it appears with frequency among numerous twentieth-century literary movements including the Dadaists, Surrealists, Beat poets, the New York School, the Oulipo Group, members of the St Mark's Poetry Project, the Language Group, and Spoken Word poetry, in addition to forms such as Renga or Chaining, and strategies of textual appropriation and sound poetry more generally. One might also point to digital poetries, whose complex algorithms and new media design often occasion collaborations between poets and programmers. Speaking once again to the unacknowledged importance of the TRG, undoubtedly it is the primary poetic forerunner to twenty-first-century digital, flarf, and conceptual poetries. If this is indeed the case, it is because the TRG, more than any other Cold War–era movement, anticipates the pending war over information that will constitute a central feature of what is now dubbed "the knowledge economy." In the introduction to this book, I list among the Cold War's chief socio-economic developments the radical transformation and globalization of intellectual property standards. The TRG's experiments in multi-authorship, I argue, constitute a poetic activism challenging proprietary definitions of authorship.

"Setting Up" an Institute

Reflecting on the importance of collaboration, McCaffery would observe years after his work with the TRG that by the late 1960s Toronto had become a tangible site of "'community building.'" "With the Vietnam War driving loads of American poets to Canada, Toronto felt something like a 1916 Zurich at the time of the birth of the Dada sound poem" (McCaffery, interview by Ryan Cox). What he also encountered was a resurgent interest, particularly among the youth, in the possibilities of radical leftist action. Bryan D. Palmer observes the "breathtaking explosion" of Trotskyist, Maoist, and revolutionary protest groups that came into being from roughly 1967 to 1977 across the country, but especially in the nation's largest city (*Canada's 1960s* 280–1). A shortlist includes the New Left Caucus, Red Morning, Rising Up Angry!, Canadian Party of Labour, Progressive Worker, Communist Party of Canada/Marxist-Leninist (formerly the Internationalists), Socialist League/Forward Group, Spartacist League (later the Trotskyist League of Canada), Revolutionary Marxist Group, Revolutionary Workers League, En Lutte/In Struggle, and Workers Communist Party. (Keep in mind the population of Canada in 1970 was barely 20 million, and the population of Toronto was just over seven hundred thousand.)[12] Invited to speak at a conference arranged by the Student Union for Peace Action in December 1966, Black Mountain expat Paul Goodman expressed his surprise that "in Canada, of all places, there seemed to be a lot of Marxism" (the students apparently grew impatient with Goodman's "subjective orientation") (qtd. in Palmer, *Canada's 1960s* 274). Writing for the magazine *Canadian Dimension*, Cy Gonick persuasively argues that the Canadian

public was at least marginally more receptive to the possibilities of socialism, lacking the United States' legacy of anti-communism and its
tradition of fierce liberal individualism (evident on both the Left and
the Right).[13] Yet McCaffery's injunction, that until peering in the mirror
he had never met a Marxist with a sense of humour, registers both an
ironic playfulness and a serious reprisal of the intransigent programs of
China's Cultural Revolution and the social realism demanded in Eastern Europe. By the early 1970s, Olson's provocative allusion to Mao
meant something altogether different; not unlike the Cuban socialists
Salkey encountered, the TRG's "Kommunism" sought to advance the
principles of an egalitarian economic model with open, local, and playful experiments in artistic collective life.

At the same time, however, the British-born McCaffery, having arrived
in Canada in 1968, also encountered a "backward and repressive"[14] preoccupation with national identity, one that ironically established continuity between the Diefenbaker and Trudeau eras of Canadian politics.
He recounts a humorous but telling anecdote in which the poet Dorothy Livesay poked him in the stomach with an umbrella for taking
up space in "Canadian" literary magazines. More disconcerting, however, was the prevalent and polemical ant-Americanism of the period.
One commentator indicts the United States as a "sick society," citing
its rampant inequality, lust for profit, and use of violence. The obvious
objection is not whether or not evidence of such systemic greed and dispossession exists, but rather how Canada was different.[15] Many on the
Left in Canada were justifiably opposed to foreign control of industry
and the expropriation of natural resources. But this debate might instead have emphasized the threat economic dependency posed to political autonomy, while engaging Canada's own ruling elite – its growing
complicity in exploiting the developing world as well as its labouring classes at home. Invariably, essentialist and moralizing arguments
often obfuscated what Marxist commentators insisted was an issue of
class amid a distracting nationalist rhetoric.

Marshal McLuhan nearly predicts this contradictory milieu years
earlier in a remarkable self-published manifesto entitled *Counterblast*
(1954):

B L A S T
  england ancient GHOST of culture
  POACHING the EYES of the
  canadian HAMLETS

USA

    COLOSSUS of the South, horizontal
    HEAVYWEIGHTS flattening the
    canadian imagination

...

B L A S T (for kindly reasons)

      C A N A D A

    The indefensible canadian border
The SCOTTISH FUR-TRADERS who haunt
the trade routes and Folkways of the
canadian psyche

B L A S T   all FURRY thoughts
         The canadian BEAVER,
submarine symbol of the
    SLOW

        UNHAPPY

                subintelligentsias.

...

      Oh BLAST

The MASSEY REPORT damp cultural igloo
for canadian devotees of
          T I M E
           &
          L I F E

...

B L E S S

      The MASSEY REPORT,
      HUGE RED HERRING for
derailing Canadian kulcha while it is
absorbed by American ART & Technology.   (2, 3, 4–5)

McLuhan republished a greatly expanded version of this obscure mimeographed volume in 1969 with Toronto press McClelland and Stewart
(making it likely that Steve McCaffery and bpNichol encountered it).
Historian Bryan D. Palmer describes the text as "almost Beat-like" in

its "countercultural anticipation of the 1960s" (147), although the title makes it clear the new media theorist had Futurist-Vorticist typography and Dadaist collage centrally in mind. McLuhan explains in the preface to the 1969 edition: "the term COUNTERBLAST does not imply any attempt to erode or explode [Lewis's] BLAST. Rather it indicates the need for a counter-environment as a means of perceiving the dominant one" (5). McLuhan's explanatory note aside, "counterblasting" preserves Lewis's violent masculinization of artistic discourse. Such bombastic language resonates with Olson's rhetorical "projectiles," along with others among the American post-war avant-garde. Arguably, however, analysis of Cold War masculinity plays out slightly differently in the Canadian context. McLuhan's missive to blast (in precise order) England and then the United States lists English Canada's two principal cultural-economic influences over the course of the nation's history. Yet so too McLuhan sets his sights on the Massey Report of 1951 (more formally, the Royal Commission on National Development in the Arts, Letters and Sciences). The government-appointed commission made recommendations for state patronage, leading to, among other things, the formation of the National Library of Canada and the Canada Council for the Arts. Blasting the Massey Report meant challenging Canadian cultural nationalism, since the commission's endorsement for state support was largely a gesture of independence from the United States' formative influence. In turn, McLuhan objects to nationalism in both its imperialist and indigenous-reactionary forms, one based on colonial exploitation, the other on a collective "psyche" linking the land to a single ethnic or racial history (e.g., "Scottish").

For the British-born McCaffery, none of this was particularly interesting. He and Nichol shared a deep suspicion of nationalism. Their collaborations with poets such as Dick Higgins, Robert Filliou, and Dieter Roth traversed not only national but linguistic borders, countering such parochialism with their transnational literary commitments. One should not conclude, however, that the TRG promoted a vague conception of cosmopolitanism at the expense of locality and place. The name chosen for their research site was the *Toronto* Research Group; Four Horsemen albums featured the titles *Live in the West* and *CaN-ADAda*; while McCaffery's major collection of essays is cleverly titled *North of Intention*. Not only does this collection playfully reference the neighbour to the south, it also applies large portions of Continental philosophy to anglophone Canadian writers (a fusion of French theory and English poetry not lost on Canadian audiences). The playful subversion of *CaNADAda* surely conjures McLuhan's *Counterblast*, opening up a "counter-environment" within the nation ("NADA"). The TRG's linked localities will present a better framework for understanding the digital public spheres it anticipates, namely, by demonstrating that communication technologies supplement rather than replace tangible sites of community building.

Their Fluxus co-collaborators Filliou and Brecht jointly developed the concept of the Eternal Network[16] with similar ideas in mind. Conceived, according to Filliou, as a "more useful concept than the avant-garde," he offers the following definition:

> There is always someone asleep and someone awake
> someone dreaming asleep, someone dreaming awake
> someone eating, someone hungry
> someone fighting, someone loving
> someone making money, someone broke
> someone traveling, someone staying put
> someone helping, someone hindering
> someone enjoying, someone suffering
> someone indifferent
> someone starting, someone stopping
> The Network is Eternal (Everlasting)[.]   ("Research" [c. 1970] 1–11)

The two poets conceived of the Eternal Network during the late 1960s as an international community of artists working together by way of correspondence. The idea grew out of their "non-shop" in the south of France, the "Cédille qui Sourit," "an international center of permanent creation," where the two "played games, invented and disinvented objects, corresponded with the humble and mighty, drank and talked with [their] neighbors, manufactured and sold by correspondence suspense poems and rebuses" (*Teaching and Learning* 198). According to Filliou and Brecht, art should be collaborative and egalitarian, it should challenge the distinction between art and daily life, and it should emphasize process over product. Since the initial formation of Filliou and Brecht's Eternal Network, critics in art circles have arguably applied the term too narrowly to a tradition of correspondence or "mail art" codified in collections such as Chuck Welch's edited collection *Eternal Network: A Mail Art Anthology* (1995), and Michael Crane and Mary Stofflet's *Correspondence Art: Source Book for the Network of International Postal Art Activity* (1984). Filliou and Brecht's initial purpose hints at a broader usage. The works circulating through the Eternal Network tend to be the ephemeral materials of Fluxus multiples, mail art, language-focused conceptual art, and a large body of poetry increasingly incapable of definition via traditional generic distinctions: sound, visual and concrete, creative translation, and procedural verse. What is more, the two men proclaimed that an art network should have no final autonomy, that such collectives are connected with yet other aesthetic and political assemblages: "we have thought of advocating an International Nuisance Network, composed of people from any walk of life, regardless of nationality." They might demand a new deal for artists and non-artists alike, housing for the poor, "access to Parks and other public places – free time on radio, television, [and] newspapers" (204). Hence, the Eternal Network was not merely to be a system of correspondence but a political community – one focused on promoting public access, collective ownership, and a transgeographic commons of interaction and shared resources.

One of McCaffery and Nichol's most important collaborators, Dick Higgins, frequently referred to their group practice as the Institute of Creative Misunderstanding. Higgins expands upon this notion in an interview:

> To broaden my perspective I conceived of a community of artists and thinkers who could take conceptual models and, with good will (my assumption, like Kant's in his ethics), transform these models – evoking not simply intellectual discourse but humor or lyrical effects which would otherwise not be possible. This is, of course, my Institute of Creative Misunderstanding ... I would not describe the Institute for [sic] Creative Misunderstanding as a "fake institute" ... so much as an abstract entity and process of existence which creates a paradigm of community of like-minded people by its very name and mentioning.[17]

Higgins, like McCaffery and Nichol, conflates community with practice. More than simply a "likeminded group of authors," Higgins has in mind the communal development of a common "conceptual model" – echoing his Exemplativist manifesto, in which the poet states that art is always a process of "model-making and model-using" ("Six Trivial" 114). In their introduction to Open Letter's special issue on Canadian "Pataphysics,[18] McCaffery and Nichol remark that their investigations had spawned several institutes of advanced poetic study: l'Institut Onto-Genetique, the Institute of Hmmrian Studies, and (borrowed from Dick Higgins) the

Institute of Creative Misunderstanding. The authors also hint playfully the "pending existence of a Centre for Marginal Studies" and the possible formation of a "non-College of Epistemological Myopia" (8). Like Jarry's 'pataphysical[19] science of imaginary solutions, their intended goals are both playful and parodic. Yet the idea of an institute was something that Higgins, McCaffery, and others used quite seriously to think through the social production of their poetics – what the former in a letter to his friend calls their common "investigat[ions]" into "methods and implied processes" (Dick Higgins Papers, Box 21, Folder 41).[20] Their co-developed notion of social space and shared ideas applied to material sites as well: the laboratory settings of the TRG and the rehearsal sessions of the Four Horsemen.

The etymology of the term "institute" helps to clarify their dual use of the word as conceptual space and physical place. As a verb, the word dates to at least c. 1325, meaning "to set up" or "cause to stand," while the term's meaning as a type of "organization" dates to the founding of the Institut National des Sciences et des Arts in France. Proposed during the revolutionary Convention Nationale on 8 August 1793 and established two years later in 1795, the "Institut National" was conceived as an alternative to the academies and learned societies endowed by the monarchy as a site of advanced training in science, politics, and literature. There is likely also an element of parodic disenchantment here directed at the unsustainability of the May 1968 revolution, and perhaps also the Cultural Revolution in China, which had taken aim at cosmopolitan intellectualism. Ultimately, Higgins, McCaffery, and Nichol found the concept useful for conceptualizing a poetic laboratory free of the avant-garde's militarist and nationalist connotations; in both its verb and noun senses, the institute is a concept that, for the TRG, combines sustainable collective organization and the experimental production of literary techniques.

In their 1973 manifesto, TRG members make two principal claims about the nature of research: first, "research is symbiotic" (RG 23). That is, research is the product of an interdependent relationship between persons or groups, although Nichol and McCaffery may have in mind the stricter scientific definition: "the living together of two dissimilar organisms," their interaction and adaptation within a shared environment (OED). Second, "[R]esearch can function to discover new uses for potentially outdated forms and techniques" (23). Echoing Adrienne Rich's "writing as re-vision," their reports involve re-*searching* the past. McCaffery and Nichol eschew the myth of pure innovation. They advocate a poetics predicated not on the "new" but on "new uses" for pre-existent literatures. Hence, by the title of their collected reports, *Rational Geomancy*, they mean "a mastery of, or at least familiarity with a multiplicity of techniques[,] an acceptance of the past that we inherit as the earth we realign, the macrosyntax from which we foreground ... In ancient China," they explain, "one form of geomancy involved the actual realignment of topographies, the construction or removal of whole hills to assist the flow of telluric currents" (153–4). Since "geomancy" is an art of divination, Caroline Bayard argues that the TRG erroneously sutures two incompatible models of thought: one that is animistic and the other indebted to a deconstructive reading practice (via Barthes and Derrida).[21] Like many North American poets of the 1960s and 1970s (the Beats, the San Francisco Renaissance, and Naropa), the TRG often naïvely celebrated Eastern cultures, particularly as an alternative model to Western capitalism. Although accusations of exoticism are justifiable, their point here has to do with a critique of the modern book, and the narrow definitions of "author" and "text" it has produced. An example offered in D.F. McKenzie's *Bibliography and the Sociology of Texts* provides an instructive point of comparison. He cites the Australian Arunta Aborigines, for whom the landscape serves a "textual function." He inquires "if there is any sense in which the land – not even a representation of it on a map, but the land itself – might be a text" (31). Both McKenzie, and the TRG more than ten years earlier, argue that the book is but one type of textual artefact. As McKenzie states concisely: "[t]he argument that a rock in Arunta country is a text subject to bibliographical exposition is absurd only if one thinks of arranging such rocks on a shelf and giving them classmarks" (33). By analogy, Chinese geomancy suggests a topographical approach to history, whereby literary tradition is conceived as a plane of surfaces which authors appropriate, "realign," and reuse. The writer is always confined by a literary tradition she inherits, but can reconfigure its elements to forge adaptive practices. The practice of geomancy and the Institute of Creative Misunderstanding – as concepts used by the TRG – both suggest that literature is a history of techniques and materials, and the common "property" of all poets. That which is brought into the institute, into poetry's laboratory, must be made available to all.

Multi-Authorship and Labour Relations

As Roland Barthes and Michel Foucault both argue in their foundational studies of authorship, the notion of an author as the sole creator of a work is a fairly recent formation, as are the attendant institutions that codify this prevailing definition into laws of copyright. Martha Woodmansee and Peter Jaszi argue that the legal category of the author is "informed by the Romantic belief that long and intense legal protection is the due of creative genius" and that "the notion that the writer is a special participant in the production process – the only one worthy of attention – is of recent provenience" (*The Construction* 5, 16).[22] Their definition of romanticism is not without problems, but the radical changes to intellectual property standards during the years of McCaffery and Nichol's creative output is undeniable. The U.S. congress extended what had been a modest term of protection (twenty-eight years plus an optional twenty-eight-year term of renewal) several times during the 1960s and early 1970s, culminating in the Copyright Act of 1976, at which point the term of protection now covered the life of the author plus an additional fifty years (a term that has since been extended to seventy years).[23] Echoing Barthes's assertion that the author is the "epitome and culmination of capitalist ideology," one legal scholar explains that "unrewarded authorial genius was used as a rhetorical distraction," as courts and corporations colluded in undermining an approximately two-hundred-year-old system that had sought to balance the concerns of authors, publishers, and the general public (Barthes, "Death" 143; Vaidhyanathan, *Copyrights* 11). It is no coincidence that by the 1970s powerful lobby groups like the Recording Industry Association of America (RIAA) and the Motion Picture Association of America (MPAA) began focusing their efforts on intellectual property regulation.

Canada would not pass similar legislation until the 1980s, but it was clear that the United States and other rich countries were moving towards a global standard designed to commodify and police a newly emerging information economy. If the "singular genius" model of authorship codified into law conceals the social production of literature, then the TRG insists that such a logic is built into "[o]ur current books"; by relegating reference to the text's appendix, we "have converted context into index … where what is 'old' is buried beneath what is 'new'" (*RG* 132). It is with this emphasis on an approach to the book that foregrounds its own collective modes of production that the TRG gives the avant-garde renewed purpose: "avant-garde work," McCaffery and Nichol insist, does not consist of the "push towards chaos and oblivion it is so often seen as, but rather the drive towards a reassertion of context" (132).

A qualification is necessary: if the TRG broadly distrusts a "Romantic" theory of the isolated genius, then which romanticism is this?

Olson knew better than to generalize in this way, indicating that an egoless poetics would find a useful starting point in Keats's notion of "negative capability" as an alternative to the Wordsworthian "egotistical sublime." Moreover, if the lyrical self is the object of disdain, then McCaffery and Nichol might also have begun with Shelley's conception of poems as "episodes to that great poem, which all poets, like the co-operating thoughts of one great mind, have built up since the beginning of the world" ("Defence" 493). Despite the sometimes haphazardly conceived effort to "get away from that romantic ideologeme of the lyric self," McCaffery and Nichol's creative texts often suggest a more complex engagement with romanticism.[24] McCaffery produced a series of textual appropriations of Wordsworth's poems, for instance, calling them "performance transforms," "extractions," and "treatments." The purpose is ably summarized in a poem entitled "An Afterthought" (1978):

<blockquote>

... go to

the remains of
            Form
in the eye
            the elements
of future Function,   Form

a brave something in the hands
or a stream to guide

this hand in the act of that

hand.   (1–10)

</blockquote>

The point is not merely to insist on the inherent instability of a text's meaning, but also actively to morph past traditions, choosing not to denounce but rather to redeploy the latent possibilities of canonical texts. Wordsworth's enthusiastic promotion of copyright law aside,[25] his understanding of the writing subject was never as rarefied as McCaffery assumes, as this well-known sonnet indicates:

<blockquote>

Nuns fret not at their convent's narrow room;
And hermits are contented with their cells;
And students with their pensive citadels;

...

</blockquote>

In truth the prison, unto which we doom
Ourselves, no prison is: and hence for me,
In sundry moods, 'twas pastime to be bound
Within the Sonnet's scanty plot of ground;
Pleased if some Souls (for such there needs must be)
Who have felt the weight of too much liberty,
Should find brief solace there, as I have found.

("Nuns Fret Not" [1804] 1–3, 8–14)

There is no doubt that Wordsworth mythologizes the author's work as a labour of solitude, despite the collaborative nature of his own work with Samuel Taylor Coleridge and his sister Dorothy.[26] Indeed, the writer – like the nun, hermit, and student – is isolated, but not unencumbered by material or formal constraints. Nor are these constraints irrevocably detrimental to the poem. Wordsworth's gesture is more than just a metaphorical connection between the room and the formal constraints of the sonnet; he is acknowledging the material, if not the social, conditions of artistic work. In the introductory essay of their third research report, "The Language of Performance of Language," the TRG asserts: "[w]e are entering this *room* as if it were an inner ear; a hollow space, cavernous, labyrinthine, in which certain intronuclearities might participate" (*RG* 227). One might choose to think of the TRG's practice as an attempt to make communes and institutes of Wordsworth's cells and convents.

With this qualification in mind, it is nonetheless significant that the prevalence of collaborative authorship among many twentieth-century avant-garde poets has gone largely unnoticed, despite significant experiments with collaboration as a means to subvert conventional theories of authorship. Intriguingly, both Foucault and Barthes mention this phenomenon, the latter stating that the Surrealists, seeking the "desacrilization of the image of the Author[,] ... accept the principle and the experience of several people writing together" (Barthes, "Death" 14). Barthes has nothing more to say about collaborative writing, only that it problematizes the author's deification; yet his allusions to the "exquisite corpse" games and co-authored automatic writings of André Breton, Paul Eluard, and Philippe Soupault invite comparison with the TRG. In a short piece entitled "Notes on a Collaboration," Breton and Eluard seem to confirm Barthes's assumption by stating that "to be two together ... is as good as being everyone, being the other *ad infinitum* and no longer oneself" (159). Contrast this assertion with an interview conducted by Pierre Coupey, Dwight Gardiner, Gladys Hindmarch, and Daphne Marlatt, in which bpNichol describes the initial response to the performances of the Four Horsemen:

> When, for instance, The Four Horsemen started, the first thing we had to overcome was that everybody knew my name and nobody knew the rest of the group's names. Okay, so what you have is 'bpNichol and The Four Horsemen.' It sounds like I got this back-up group of Motown singers tapping their toes ... no way – group, group, group, group, you know, think of it as a group. This was a very hard process. People don't want to think of writers as groups. They're fixed on writers as the single consciousness[.] ("Interview" Coupey et al., 148)[27]

The collaborative dynamic of performance differs from the automatic writing of the Surrealists, but notably both groups reject the author as a "single consciousness." Yet, whereas Breton and Eluard want to obliterate the writer altogether, Nichol is more interested in foregrounding the presence of a plurality of writing subjects perpetually interacting. In their TRG reports, McCaffery and Nichol contend that their research is the product of a "We-full, not an I-less paradigm" (*RG* 11, 149). The former insists elsewhere that collaboration involves a "therapeutic antidote to the private, writing self. It demands interaction and renunciating single control" ("Annotated" 74). Such tactics disturb the supremacy of univocality, problematize intentionality, and discredit the proprietary nature of authorship. Nichol and McCaffery's "we-full" (not "I-less") paradigm, however, stops short of a wholesale erasure of the author, advancing instead a poetics of authorial assemblage and synthesis. Rather than eradicate the writing subject, McCaffery, Nichol, and their various collaborators foreground a mode of writing that announces its own communal process.

One should, however, be wary of sentimentalizing community and communal writing. It is enticing to remark, as one commentator does regarding the Four Horsemen's performances, that its members worked in "absolute trust and awareness of each other" (Scobie, *bpNichol* 19). On the contrary, Barreto-Rivera recalls the group's initial naïveté and the gradual recognition that "the process of understanding one another might take ostensibly longer than [they] had expected" (*CaNADAda*, n.p.). McCaffery is far less euphemistic. Objecting to the opinion that their performances were the product of a harmonious synthesis, he observes in an interview with Peter Jaeger: "[t]he workshops and practices were the sites of tremendous labor and disagreement; there were extreme differences in personality and opinions" (McCaffery, "Interview" by Jaeger 90–1). Akin to the processes adopted by radical feminists, members of the TRG quickly learned of the "tyranny of structurelessness." Their work almost always employs some strategy of collaborative research, writing, and performance that consciously foregrounds the organizational principles enabling their multi-authorial experiments.

But if his contention is that collaboration is a formally radical redefinition of authorship and an affront to intellectual property regimes, then one need only cite corporate and legal writing, TV and film scripts, advertising copy, pulp fiction, and romance novels as contemporary examples of multi-authorship that are not only stylistically conventional, but which also perpetuate notions of intellectual property. Authors of these cultural artefacts are no less "alienated" from the object of their labour, according to Marx's definition. Moreover, is factory labour a form of collaboration? If so, the assembly line – the apotheosis of the industrial mode of production – rather than disrupting property ownership, merely renders it more efficient. Collaboration has only the sort of political merit that the TRG hopes to ascribe to if it constructs non-alienated modes of communal labour.

Whether in his early writings on alienated labour in the *Economic and Philosophical Manuscripts*, or later in *Capital*, Marx is most distressed by the erosion of labour's social function, and the relation of this phenomenon to private property. Capitalism subjects labour to continuously greater and more rigidly demarcated "separations": the worker is separated from the product of her work, from other workers, and from the capitalist who appropriates her work, just as capital is separated from labour and different classes from one another. "Man – and this is the basic presupposition of private property – only produces in order to have. The aim of production is possession." Marx continues,

I have produced for myself and not for you, as you have produced for yourself and not for me. You are as little concerned by the result of my production in itself as I am directly concerned by the result of your production. That is, our production is not a production of men for men as such, that is, social production. Thus, as a man none of us is in a position to be able to enjoy the product of another. ("On James Mill" 129–30)

Labour production is inexorably bound up with the production of communal relations. In his work with Engels, he asserts that the production of all activity, labour or otherwise, is generated through social relationships: "it follows from this that a certain mode of production … is always combined with a certain mode of cooperation" (*The German Ideology* 157). In effect, capitalist modes of production create modes of cooperation that paradoxically isolate human subjects, subordinating their own existence to the objects they create.

The question of writing and community is typically brought to bear on issues of publication and dissemination of literary works. Like many other writers during the twentieth century, the TRG created alternative presses to evade the restrictive markets of mainstream publishing, enabled in part by the affordability of mimeograph and photocopying technologies. A magazine like *GrOnk*, with its alternating editorial staff, sought to create community on paper. The TRG was imagining ways to apply the same principles to writing itself. For this to work, they would have to develop modes of poetic writing in step with Marx's communist axiom: a practicable form of organization based on the free association of producers that eliminates divisions of labour and private appropriation of wealth. Hence, the Toronto Research Group had to commit itself to a poetics of open and non-proprietary appropriation.

The Kids of the Book-Machine

The Toronto Research Group began with impromptu conversations between Steve McCaffery and bpNichol that materialized into written reports addressing a variety of issues. In particular, the two poets privileged three areas of investigation: the materiality of the book, non-linear narrative, and the process of translation. (One should add to this list of concerns a crucial contribution to the study of non-canonical twentieth-century writers.) The TRG research sessions functioned as testing sites for a number of co-developed poetic experiments, including homolinguistic translation, the post-semiotic poem, gestural semiotics, 'pataphysical poetics, and conceptualist and intermedial performance. Some involved language in performance, some used handwritten notation and visual scoring, while others required unbound pages and irregular materials for their construction.

The TRG's multivalent approach to poetic experimentation reflexively challenges the boundaries of the book as traditionally conceived. I hold on to Jerome McGann's definition of the poetic: "to display the textual condition … [as] language that calls attention to itself, that takes its own textual activities as its ground subject" (*Textual Condition* 10). Thinking of the poem as a textual activity – and not an autonomous artefact – helps to determine its various functions in an era of artistic experimentation increasingly dominated by what Dick Higgins calls "intermedia." Once the critic accepts that any poem belongs to a context of social production and reception, a more pertinent question presents itself: how does the poetic operate within a particular context of writing, one that may include other forms of artistic, cultural, and social commitments.

In a rather inconspicuous footnote to the preface of *Black Riders*, McGann insists that "[a]n indispensable point of departure for investigating the future of the book in the age of media and electronics is the Collected Research Reports of the Toronto Research group" (181). Between *The Textual Condition* (1991) and *Black Riders* (1993), studies that investigate the effects of modern printing technologies on the practice of reading and the presentation, transmission, and distribution of texts, and *Radiant Textuality* (2001), the first comprehensive analysis of "literature after the world wide web," there is no other mention of the TRG reports. Where does one situate the self-styled "kids of the book-machine" in the history of print culture? Surprisingly little has been said about the TRG in relation to the history of the book, even among excellent scholars like McGann, Johanna Drucker, and Marjorie Perloff, who otherwise afford considerable attention to McCaffery's single-authored works. Perloff, for instance, astutely argues for *Carnival* (1967–70) as a benchmark example of a poem that "challenges the sequentiality of the normal book" ("Signs" 111). Yet the co-authored reports helped to fashion these activities; they constitute an integral part of the same scene of collaboration. The TRG itself claims in its 1973 manifesto that "all theory" comes "after the fact of writing" (*RG* 23). This proclamation is one of the few wrongheaded assertions made by the group, and it misrepresents McCaffery and Nichol's own contribution to twentieth-century poetics. According to their approach to writing as the recontextualization of literary resources, traditions, and techniques, theory and research are coextensive with creative practice. There is no act of writing independent of an approach to or re-*searched* history of texts.

More than a decade before the critic D.F. McKenzie pronounced that bibliographic analysis should be synonymous with the "sociology of texts,"[28] McCaffery and Nichol had undertaken their research into "non-book texts" (McKenzie's term), not for the purpose of bibliographic study, but as a means to enlarge the arena of literary experimentation beyond the constraints of the book proper. McGann argues that "textual studies remain largely under the spell of romantic hermeneutics. In such a view texts, and in particular imaginative texts, are not imagined as certain kinds of social acts." One "breaks the spell," he argues, "by socializing the study of texts at the most radical levels" (*Textual Condition* 12). Indeed, the TRG had this very project in mind for its creative practice. Although their work might be understood as poetic acts designed to give textual critics severe headaches, their intent is to forge a materialist hermeneutics that foregrounds the social act of all writing. To do so, they argue, one needs to expand and transform the material features of the book itself.

In part 1 of the second report, "The Book as Machine," McCaffery and Nichol address the physicality of the book and its implications for the experience of writing and reading. By "book-machine" the authors mean its "capacity and method" of linguistic information storage and retrieval; a book activates when a reader opens it and begins to read (*RG* 60). The conventional book, they argue, features three "modules" that predate even Gutenberg's printing press: the "lateral flow of the line," the "vertical or columnar build up" of lines on a page, and a linear movement "organized through depth" (by which they mean the sequential ordering of "pages upon pages") (60).[29] Of course, these are socially constructed conventions that have since fixed and normalized reading practices. That texts departing from linearity are typically called "typographic experiments" indicates as much. It is the kind of reading the traditional book manufactures that is precisely what the TRG contests. McCaffery and Nichol observe a dichotomy in readerly reception: the book as "machine of reference" and the "book as a commodity to be acquired, consumed, and discarded" (62). It should be clear which of the two the TRG privileges, yet their rationale bears spelling out. The conventional book-machine, argue Nichol and McCaffery, essentially replicates an oral activity. Although for reasons of practicality a book is organized into lines, columns, and pages, it imagines a single line of text that "reconstitutes the duration of a 'listening'" (62). The book as reference-machine, on the other hand, reimagines the page as a site that accommodates a "reader's free, non-lineal eye movements" across its "multi-activating surface" (62).

In their research, the TRG privileges a trajectory of writing that explodes the imposed linearity of the traditional book, their antecedents and contemporaries including Gertrude Stein's *Tender Buttons* (1914), Madeline Gins's *Word Rain* (1969), B.S. Johnson's novel *The Unfortunates* (1969), Ferdinend Kriwet's architectural poetics, John Furnival's language constructs, Ian Hamilton Finlay's textual landscapes, and McCaffery's own visual works. This shortlist of avant-gardists, concretists, and conceptual artists certainly suggests the TRG's non-canonical proclivities, but it is important to remember that they also cite the newspaper, demotic forms such as the comic strip, and pop cultural genres such as board games as examples of artefacts that condition very different practices of reading. Their research into unconventional material production and narrativity constitutes a rejection of the conventional book's teleological unfolding in favour of texts that explore the book-machine's spatial and temporal possibilities. This approach to the book's materiality refuses the implicit assumption that the page is a neutral surface upon which a content is expressed, conceiving of it instead as "a spatially interacting region": the "[p]age becomes an active space, a meaningful element in the compositional process and the size and shape of it become significant variables" (*RG* 65). Hence, the book becomes a significant aspect of narrative presentation, reflexively alerting the reader to the labour involved in its construction and the reader's participation in its building. By reworking the bibliographic and textual codes involved in conventional techniques of narrative presentation, the reader is forced to generate new methods of reading, becoming a participant, indeed a collaborator, in semantic production.

In an interview with Caroline Bayard and Jack David, Nichol describes the TRG's symbiotic approach to writing:

> We've always typed. We type with maybe one of us typing what's in our mind and then we kick an idea around. And then maybe I dictate to Steve while he types. And maybe I'm typing, and he's dictating to me. And I'm adding something as I think of it. And then we go over it, and go over it. So it happens at the time of writing. And part of it is just getting that moment together. ("Interview" 31)

A frequent consequence of this synthesis is the introduction of errancy and spontaneity into their discourse – what both men refer to in the reports as the "particle drift" between a "mini-community of two" (144). Just as one records the thoughts of the other, the writer might deviate into his own personal discourse, unbeknownst to the speaker. Thus, their technique involves elements of indeterminacy and playfulness that generate a final postulation based on approximations that belong exclusively to neither. Yet the function of indeterminacy in the TRG reports is decidedly different than, say, the "writing through" procedures of John Cage or Jackson Mac Low, writers who diminish authorial intention through aleatoric operations. Instead, Nichol and McCaffery's method seeks to preserve in print the provisional event of thought and discussion between them.

Critics typically gloss over the implications of this process for reading the reports. Caroline Bayard briefly mentions "the peculiar quality of being a tightly structured text in which neither contributor is identifiable" (*The New Poetics* 60). Susan E. Billingham concedes that their method of transcription "constitutes a dialectical dialogue" that explores "the interpersonal relations" involved in group activity, yet their co-authored research merely provides her with a convenient point of division between their divergent "theoretical positions" in later writings (*Language and the Sacred* 98).[30]

Regardless of any prior knowledge of their method of dictation, the reader encounters no less than four identifiable strategies of co-authorship. Some reports feature an ostensibly *unified* voice: the earliest report on translation (1973), for example, employs a conventional essay format. Based on these preliminary research sessions, it became clear to both writers that a crucial element of their collaboration should be "to stretch the formal parameters" of the reports (*RG* 10). In subsequent sessions, Nichol and McCaffery introduce unattributable voices in *dialogue* as a means to mark disagreement or to steer their research in a particular direction (e.g., "The Book as Machine" [1973] and "Interlude: Heavy Company" [1976]).[31] In other reports, such as "Rational Geomancy: A Re-Alignment of Kinship (II)" (1978),[32] a double-band structure separates two discrete texts in juxtaposition, reorganizing the page to accommodate multiple systems of inscription.[33] The dialogic and heteroglossic structure of the page is clearly indebted to Bakhtin. The two bands alternate positions of master and supporting discourses, exploiting points of convergence and interplay. The reader invariably undergoes an experience of cognitive disorientation, an affliction the TRG refers to as "paralirium": the state of being "paralysed ... beside a reading" (*RG* 169). The reader is confronted with a choice: though she cannot activate the bands simultaneously, she can read them succes-sively (in any order) or she can read the pages continuously, whereby the bands are woven like a double helix. The authors contend the "bands" function as discursive "binds" and writerly "bonds" (168), evoking a notion of the page not as linear sequence but as a *paratextual* space of interaction. Adeena Karasick remarks that "[f]rom 1970–1976, concern shifts ... from ('work' to 'text') decipherable machine to a poly-semic plurality" ("Tract Marks" 94). Certainly this is true, but the TRG would later expand the report into more *performative* activities, includ-ing a collaboratively produced photo comic strip, a series of 'pata-physical games, while the third report ("Language of Performance of Language" [1978–82]) features an assemblage of collaborative writing, conceptualist performance, and intermedia composition.

The four discursive modes I refer to as (1) *unified*, (2) *dialogic*, (3) *pa-ratextual*, and (4) *performative* each (to varying degrees) transforms the expository function of the essay-report into a dialogic event, so that the page is conceived as a space of multiple inscriptions. These investiga-tions provide a platform on which Nichol and McCaffery devise sev-eral techniques that extend writing beyond the conventional structure of the book. Consider two examples: "Collboration No. 2" [*sic*] (c. 1978), a conceptual-intermedia work, and "The Body: In Light" (1980), a ges-tural text.

In "Collboration No. 2," the first of sixteen "performed essays" form-ing the third of the TRG reports, performers are instructed to sit facing one another at identical typewriters. A roll of paper is "fed through the carriages of both machines forming a connected paper chain," after which, "[e]ach performer types the phrase 'WHAT ARE THE LIMITS OF COLLABORATION?' At the completion of each phrase the type-writer carriage is returned and the phrase is repeated on a new line. The piece ends when the roll of paper tightens and snaps in two" (*RG* 228). One might take this single piece to homologize the principal concerns of the TRG reports: while the page is wrested from the constraints of the codex, the movement of text proceeds in opposite directions simul-taneously. The page is both shared and torn. Rather than characterize their efforts as the symbiosis of an ideal community of writing subjects, the page is conceived as an intensive field of action, a performative site of divergent inscriptions dramatized by their coming together and moving apart. A single page might accommodate a unified assertion; it might also feature disagreement. The missing "a" of the title succinctly expresses this point on a micro-poetic level: all collaboration func-tions within an economy of addition and loss. An integrative writing generates a productive third space of creativity, but only insofar as one is prepared to relinquish authorial control. In this sense, McCaffery and Nichol suggest that collaboration takes on ethical and political dimensions, as they conceptualize the page as a shared space where in the labour process is understood as a practice of intersubjective exchange.

In a brief essay entitled "Performed Paragrammatism," McCaffery describes a "hybrid" of visual and textual materials he and Nichol use to complicate the formal purity of a work. "[T]he tracing of a hand, a drawn letter, comic strip balloon, or cloud," for example, work "to interrupt techno-typographic layout with a kind of gestural semiotics. The presence of two different … writing systems inaugurate a dialogue that complicates the spatio-temporal dimension in reading" (361). The purpose of this practice is not a Luddite's suspicion of technology but rather an attempt to disrupt the "social neutrality of type" by way of a chirographic intervention (361). In "The Body: In Light," Nichol and McCaffery employ physical interference as a collaborative technique.[34] Requiring two "composers," the first begins to write a letter as the second interrupts and "distorts" it; as a result, "any intentional gesture" is "thwarted and rerouted into a different mark" (*RG* 245). Next, the piece undergoes a second deformation during performance as one performer coerces the other's body in order to transform the sound she produces – for instance, by "a bending of A's mouth by B, a hammering on B's back by A … designed to delay, accelerate or reshape the sound" (245).

Consequently, both grapheme and phoneme undergo a process of disfigurement by gestural intervention. So why bother to do this? Clearly Nichol and McCaffery accentuate the role of physical bodies in the process of language making, but this is in no way a notion of the "natural" body in opposition to the technology of writing. Instead, theirs is a materialist poetics calling attention to the configuration of bodies, performance space, page, writing instrument, and sign system constituting a complex machine of language production. Emphasis on "coercion" and "disfigurement" reinforces the notion that the speaking subject is never free from social intervention by external discursive and material forces that inform the process of writing/speaking. The reader confronts a pen forming a linguistic sign, produced through the tension between the writing subject and the multiplicity of force relations that inform the mark of her writing.

The book is transformed from an artefact that replicates the "duration of a listening" (*RG* 62) to an interactive and multiplicitous zone – a

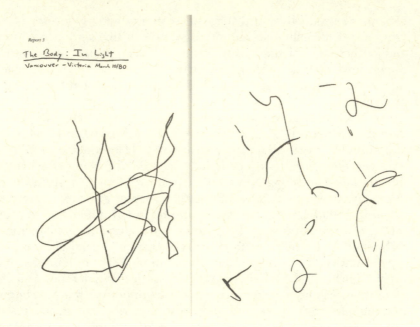

Fig. 2. The Toronto Research Group, "The Body: In Light," performed on 10 March 1980, Vancouver, British Columbia, *RG* (Vancouver: Talonbooks, 1992) 246, 251. Used with permission.

machine generated by authors and activated by readers. If the production of the modern book, its gradual displacement of contextual knowledge to the text's index, replicates a process whereby the author comes front and centre as the sole inventor of an original idea, then the TRG's poetic techniques explode the book's linear design to reveal the multifaceted contributions of editors, collaborators, disseminators, and so on.

A Realignment of Kinship: The Four Horsemen

In "A Taxonomy of Sound Poetry," Dick Higgins defines the genre in its broadest terms as "poetry in which the sound is the focus, more than any other aspect of the work" (40).[35] Such an intractable definition might include the non-semantic choruses of Aristophanes's plays,

nineteenth-century nonsense verse, or the chant structures and incanta-
tions of numerous indigenous peoples of Asia, North America, and Africa, in addition to the avant-garde traditions typically associated with
the genre. Among practitioners of post-war sound poetry, a stricter definition seems appropriate: "it is no longer de rigeur [*sic*] that a poem
must attempt to be powerful, meaningful or even necessarily commu-
nicative (a main assumption of the 18th and 19th century poetries)" ("A
Taxonomy" 43). The zaum poems of the Russian Futurists, the brutist
poems of the Dadaists, and the simultaneous poems of the Italian Futurists had disturbed conventional expressive and mimetic theories of
literature. By the 1950s, many sound poets had sought to emphasize the
most radical suggestion of early twentieth-century practice: a poetics
divorced from the referential function of literature.[36] McCaffery is one
of the most vocal proponents of this conception of sound poetry, while
Richard Kostelanetz offers perhaps its most cogent definition as "language whose principal means of coherence is sound, rather than syntax
or semantics" ("Text-Sound Art" 14).

   Although Higgins's broad assessment of the genre ultimately points
to this more strict definition, he prefers an encompassing taxonomy of
"classes": (1) works in an invented language ("purely without reference to any known language," e.g., Iliazd's "zaum" poems); (2) near-
nonsense works (those involving the "interplay between semantically
meaningful lines" and "nonsense," e.g., Kurt Schwitters's "To Anna
Blume"); (3) phatic poems ("poems in which semantic meaning, if any,
is subordinate to expression of intonation," e.g., Antonin Artaud, "To
Have Done with the Judgment of God"); (4) un-written-out poems
(a sound poem that is improvised, e.g., Henri Chopin's tape-recorder
pieces); (5) notated ones (a sound poem that is notated, e.g., Kurt
Schwitters's Ur Sonata).[37] A historian of sound poetics might take issue
with certain aspects of this list. For instance, it is perhaps more accurate
to describe these not as "classes" but as modes, since several pieces involve these features in combination. And while the first three categories
cite stylistic differences, the last two consider methods of transcription.
This is not a problem per se, but the examples he cites in order to dif-
ferentiate between notated and unnotated sound performance falters
for the simple reason that the tape recorder is a system of information
storage. Magnetic tape is in fact another form of inscription, reproducing a phonetic rather than a graphematic signifier.[38] It would perhaps be more accurate to distinguish – as musicologists do – between
"free" and "structured" improvisation; the former denotes unplanned

performance, while the latter usually employs a loose form of notation within which a performer is free to improvise as he chooses. Aside from these specific issues, however, Higgins draws a coherent and accurate trajectory from the historical avant-gardes to post-war practitioners, bearing in mind also the more explicit resonations with pre-twentieth-century precursors.

Taken in conjunction, Higgins's taxonomy and the stricter McCaffery/Kostelanetz definition of sound poetry as verse divorced from its semantic function provide a useful framework in which to situate the poetics of the Four Horsemen. Ironically, by McCaffery's own postulation many Four Horsemen pieces are not "sound poetry" properly speaking. A poem such as "Matthew's Line" (1972) affords an example. During the performance, McCaffery reads the nineteenth-century poet John Clare's "I Am"; Paul Dutton and Rafael Barreto-Rivera alternate readings of an incantatory phrase borrowed from a "groovy" three-year-old, "My shoes are dead, oh microphone" (Dutton in English, Rivera in Spanish); while Nichol verbalizes an abstract and undulating "eeeee" sound. Leaving aside for now the relationship between these elements, according to Higgins's taxonomy this single poem employs no fewer than four of his delineated categories. McCaffery's appropriation of Clare's poem involves a sound collage of found materials; the chant-like repetition of a three-year-old's phrase, although absurd, consists of comprehensible words that subsequently undergo a phatic expulsion of meaning; while Nichol's more abstract vocalizations conform more readily to the strict definition of sound poetry that McCaffery and others advance. Furthermore, not only are some Four Horsemen texts improvised ("Stage Lost," "In the Middle of a Blue Balloon") while others are notated ("Seasons," "Matthew's Line"), but some involve elements of both notated and improvised components (e.g., "Mischievous Eve"). The Four Horsemen's oeuvre is difficult to categorize precisely because it combines postmodernist strategies of appropriation and non-Western chant structures, manifesto-like axioms and non-referential grunts, improvised texts and pre-transcribed materials. If one prefers a stricter definition of sound poetry, then the Four Horsemen are better understood as a performance ensemble.

Yet perhaps the most significant distinction – one left unconsidered in Higgins's survey – is the function of the sound poetry *ensemble* or *collective*. Within the tradition of sound poetry, multi-voice improvisation is infrequent but can be traced to Dadaist simultaneous works such as Richard Huelsenbeck, Marcel Janko, and Tristan Tzara's "L'amiral cherche une maison à louer" (1916).[39] The practice gained popularity during the 1970s, mainly in Britain and North America. In addition to the Four Horsemen, several collectives explored the collaborative possibilities of the genre: in Canada, the ensemble Owen Sound; in New York, the simultaneous works of Jackson Mac Low and the multi-voice texts of Jerome Rothenberg; and in Britain, the group performances of Koncrete Canticle and JGJGJGJG. Multi-voice performance introduced the possibility of dialogism, polyphony, and a mode of improvisation closer to musical models and intermedial practices like that of Fluxus happenings. The Four Horsemen, in particular, conceived of their practice from the outset as an experiment in collectivity, whereby multi-voice composition articulates community at the level of the poem's performance.

Nichol describes the laboratory conditions that enabled the creation of their pieces: members of the group would "bring fragmentary lines, half-formed ideas, dreams, works in progress ... out of which, thru [sic] a kind of bricolage, the compositions take shape" (Four Horsemen, *Prose Tattoo* 3). Echoing Barreto-Rivera's account of the group's inaugural activities, Nichol recalls that the preliminary workshop sessions mainly consisted of the four poets improvising. Only after early pieces such as *Seasons* (c. 1971) – the first of their jointly conceived works – did they begin to conceptualize the poem as a "consciously group-conceived, group-written composition ... the idea of the poem as product of a community" (*CaNADAda*, n.p.). Their first performance together on 23 May 1970 at the *Poetry and Things* reading series illustrates this transition. The reading comprised solo-composed pieces by each performer, while the other three members of the group provided improvisational accompaniment. This form of interaction preserves the status of a single author, while relegating the group to a secondary and corollary role. Shortly thereafter, the group shifted their focus to a process that would eliminate the latent privileging of a single speaker in favour of a practice that explores the collective energies of the group.

A significant development to emerge from their rehearsals is the construction of a system of inscription. Not unlike John Cage's use of time brackets for his proto-Fluxus performance at Black Mountain (see chapter 2), the Four Horsemen employed a four-part "grid" that operated like a set of "traffic lights" within a performance, indicating "transition points ... [that] define who's doing what when, with whom, & what elements they have to work with" (3). Within this structuring frame, however, elements such as pitch, rhythm, duration, and colouration remained unstable and unrepeatable. In a certain sense, the transition that Nichol describes from an ad hoc method of group performance towards a form of flexible systematization of group pieces provides an excellent example of the problem of community formation applied to aesthetic practice. The group began with a somewhat utopian idea of collaboration as a series of direct and spontaneous relations unencumbered by organizational structures (*gemeinschaft*). They determined thereafter that an organizing system need not crystallize into a rigid formula ordering and regimenting their performance (*gesellschaft*). By adopting a method of structured improvisation, certain flexible constraints frame a field of action, wherein, paradoxically, spontaneity is permitted to take place. Whereas in their first reading, the group used a solo piece to anchor their collective performance, the grid operates by decentring the individual and redistributing the poem's collective labour.

Nichol insists that the group wrote no central text; "the center," rather, "is an ongoing compositional workshop" that integrates the labour of four writer-performers (*Prose Tattoo* 4). In some cases, the group created pieces communally from the beginning; other times, a piece might develop by reworking an individual contributor's solo composition. The example of "In the Middle of a Blue Balloon" (1972) is instructive. This piece began as Barreto-Rivera's solo-authored text, which was then adapted by the group into a multi-voice performance. The piece was recorded several times and then subsequently transformed once again, this time replete with props: "in the most recent version … Rafael, its originator, stand[s] silently (almost invisibly) in the background as bp & Paul fight in the foreground & Steve appears to be attempting to watch the original piece on a television whose back is toward the audience" (3–4). In a sense, this anecdote exemplifies a key element of their process. By the end of the piece, its originator is the one furthest removed from its execution; in the foreground, the other members jostle ceaselessly to modify and transform it. The workshop operates as a site of exchange, in which the subject both exerts power and relinquishes it. McCaffery's part in the performance playfully calls attention to the unrepeatability of the original: even the television, a technological means of visual reproduction, remediates and thus alters the original live performance.

In an important manifesto from the late 1970s, "Discussion … Genesis … Continuity," McCaffery expands on Barreto-Rivera's contention that the poem is a communal product, suggesting further that the poem-in-performance imitates certain communal formations: "We structure our pieces very much along the lines of a piece of string containing a series of knots. The knots," he explains, "have a double function as both points of coherence (where everything comes together) and as points of transition (where everything changes)" (34). The audience member of a Four Horsemen piece negotiates the interaction of its morphing elements; these "knots" or clusters fuse provisionally in "collectivizing structure[s]" – each time in different multiplicities of bodies, sounds, and sign systems that disperse and re-assemble. Hence, McCaffery argues, their aesthetic practice "homologizes" certain states of collectivity: "the movement from isolation into community, the problematics of community … [and] the collectivization of the self" (33). The metaphor of a piece of string is only partly successful, since it suggests a monolinear image. Each Four Horsemen performance might be thought of in terms of an assemblage, as a particular sort of social formation involving actors, networks, and technologies.

This last observation is more obvious when applied to "In the Middle of a Blue Balloon," but each Four Horsemen piece foregrounds a process of elements assembling. It is instructive to consider "Matthew's Line" once more. The poem that McCaffery reads, John Clare's "I Am" (c. 1864), was composed while Clare was incarcerated in the Northampton General Lunatic Asylum:

I am – yet what I am, none cares or knows;
My friends forsake me like a memory lost:
I am the self-consumer of my woes –
They rise and vanish in oblivion's host
Like shadows in love-frenzied stifled throes –
And yet I am and live – like vapours tossed

Into the nothingness of scorn and noise,
Into the living sea of waking dreams
Where there is neither sense of life or joys
But the vast shipwreck of my life's esteems;
Even the dearest that I love the best
Are strange – nay, rather, stranger than the rest.

I long for scenes where man hath never trod,
A place where woman never smiled or wept,
There to abide with my Creator, God,
And sleep as I in childhood sweetly slept,
Untroubling and untroubled where I lie,
The grass below – above, the vaulted sky.   (1–18)

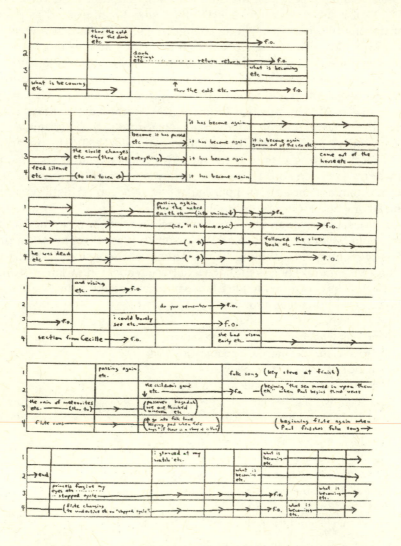

Fig. 3. The Four Horsemen, "Seasons," c. 1971, *The Prose Tattoo: Selected Performance Scores* (Milwaukee: Membrane P, 1983) 25. Used with permission.

The poem features several prominent romantic tropes: an outcast figure ("the self-consumer of my woes"); Blake-like apocalyptic imagery ("oblivion's host"); a "sweetly" and "untroubling" childhood (echoing Wordsworth's "simple creed / of Childhood … Delight and liberty" ["Intimations" 136–7]); and a preoccupation with the divine properties of nature. In the vein of Wordsworth's ode "Intimations of Immortality," the poet's isolation and the dissipating genius give way to the potential consolation of transcendence, or as Stephen Scobie remarks, the speaker's transition "into a pantheistic unity of Nature" (*bpNichol* 73). Yet the TRG's expressed objection to the "romantic ideologeme of the lyric self" begs the question: why would the Four Horsemen use a poem such as this, and how is it transformed in the group performance? Pausing at the title "I Am," perhaps the Four Horsemen seek to enact the obliteration of the speaking "I," bringing together a convergence of voices into a perfect transcendent unity. Given McCaffery and Nichol's claims elsewhere for a "we-full paradigm," one that neither erases the subject nor treats the group as a fixed, totalizing structure, this argument seems unconvincing. What happens next in "Matthew's Line" helps to resolve this conflict. At no point do the four voices align, but instead they remain a polyphonic medley of sounds that explode the "I am" that Clare's poem enunciates. McCaffery's reading, Dutton and Barreto-Rivera's repetition of a nonsense phrase, and Nichol's non-semantic hum advance simultaneously, until the penultimate line of the Clare poem, at which point Nichol repeats after McCaffery in a series of echoes: "so let me lie," "the grass below," "the vaulted sky." The singular poetic voice bifurcates and multiplies. McCaffery stretches the final word "sky," as three of four voices blend as a hybrid of abstract yet discernibly different undulations and reverberations, while Dutton repeats the word "dead" until the end of the piece. Instead of launching into "the vaulted sky," the performers remain on "the grass below." The individual's death is announced, as the communion undertaken is not with a divine "Creator," but a movement from isolation into community, just as a text is transformed and reconstituted.

As a further illustration, "Mischievous Eve" (1977) from the *Live in the West* album provides a very different type of social formation. The piece begins with a cacophony of laughs that gradually grows to a harmonic cohesion of chant-like rhythms. Just as the incantation reaches a fever pitch, McCaffery interrupts loudly by shouting the conspicuously gendered word "Gentlemen." After a moment of silence, he then delivers a speech entitled "History of North American Respiration" in a didactic tone, as Barreto-Rivera and Dutton begin to chant a phrase with increasing speed. The phrase becomes perceptible only halfway through the speech, gradually overpowering all other sounds: "one voice alone saying many things still cannot say what two voices together saying one thing can." The chant gradually hushes and the listener can once again make out the speech in progress. By this time, McCaffery has begun a similar credo: "get them speaking your way." He repeats this line and the four performers once again explode semantic meaning with uncontrolled laughter.

The title of the piece introduces several possible readings of one of the Four Horsemen's most challenging works. "Mischief Eve" takes place on the night before "Guy Fawkes Day," a British holiday commemorating the failure of a plot by Catholic dissidents to blow up the House of Parliament on 5 November 1605. On the night before the festival, youths play pranks and vandalize property in what would seem a counter-tradition that reverses the spectacle of nationalism that marks the official celebration. Implicit in this reading of the title is a dialectic between performances of the dominant culture and pockets of resistance to its official mandates. Yet the title intimates an alternative meaning. The grammatical form of the word "mischievous" is adjectival, and since the word typically describes human behaviour, there is reason to believe it modifies a proper noun. "Mischievous Eve" might then be a reference to Eve's transgression in Genesis. The two readings collude in significant ways: both involve a transgression against property by figures whose traditional status as villains is challenged. Like Prometheus's theft of fire, Eve's choice to consume the fruit of the tree (and thus the knowledge it contains) effectively allegorizes an act of appropriation by rejecting God's proprietorship over meaning. If Adam names the objects of the world, securing, in turn, each sign its referent, then Eve prefigures the public domain, infringing heroically against Adam's right to exclusivity.

To this point, one encounters a truly dizzying array of mutative practices variously called geomantic research, collaborative scores, performance transforms, extractions, treatments, intermedia, and gestural works. From the shared conceptual models of an Eternal Network, texts appear only to be disfigured, transformed, and playfully adapted. The TRG's geomantic analogy is fitting: the reader encounters a text's continuous realignment, its energies redirected and its tactics put to new uses. One rightly locates the TRG at the intersection of many important mid-century experimental groups: Fluxus, language-based conceptual work, sound and visual poetries, and the origins of Language writing, yet the post-structuralist model of authorship typically offered to account for the respective practices of these groups fails to account for McCaffery and Nichol's "we-full, not I-less" mode of writing. One witnesses not authorial erasure but the communalization of literary artefacts. The reader becomes part of this network of actors, intertexts, technologies, and spaces engaged in the production process of a culture.

The Eternal Network

Tell a thing.
Translate it. Let others translate it too.
Destroy the original.
What have you destroyed? What remains?

– Dick Higgins[40]

– what happens here?
– a translation? or an allusion?
– perhaps the translation of translation itself?

– Steve McCaffery[41]

The TRG's first research report on translation advances the following proposition: "[i]f we no longer consider translation as being necessarily an information service – the one tongue's access to other tongues – then it can become a creative endeavour in its own right" (*RG* 32). Translation might be thought of as a point of departure from the original, rather than its exact reiteration in a foreign sign system. Nichol and McCaffery produced a sizeable body of translational works;[42] many were conceived as collaborative projects, in which a single text was subject to multiple translations by several poets. Given the sparse critical attention to this aspect of their work, it will be useful to describe the normative concept of translation they oppose and a taxonomy of the alternative translational methods they invent. Principal among these procedures are homolinguistic, allusive-referential, and post-semiotic translation.

The "Equivalent Message" Theory of Translation

The basic distinction between *literal* ("word for word") and *free* ("sense for sense") translation dates to the theoretical writings of Cicero and

Horace,[43] although it is Saint Jerome who famously coins the phrase in a defence of his Latin translation of the Greek Septuagint Old Testament: "[n]ow I not only admit but freely announce that in translating from the Greek … I render not word-for-word but sense-for-sense" ("The Best Kind of Translator" 25). A literal approach to translation involves a one-to-one substitution of words in the source text with its closest equivalent in the target language. Citing Cicero's earlier efforts to replace "word for word" translation with an approach that attempts to capture the "general style and force" ("The Best Kind of Orator" 364) of the original, Jerome argues that the unavoidable syntactical incongruities of literal translation produce awkward and nonsensical texts. Employing a military metaphor, "like a conqueror," the translator marches "the meaning of his originals … into his own tongue" (115).

Later theorists of translation would expand on the "literal versus free" translation debate. Dryden, for instance, constructs a tripartite model of methods – *metaphrase*: "word by word, and line by line"; *paraphrase*: "translation with latitude, where the author is kept in view by the translator … but his words are not so strictly follow'd as his sense"; and *imitation*: "the translator … assumes the liberty not only to vary from the words and sense, but to forsake them both as he sees occasion: and taking only some general hints from the original" ("Preface to Ovid's *Epistles*" 38). Dryden's concepts of metaphrase and paraphrase are largely recapitulations of the literal and free methods of translation outlined by previous classical orators and religious scholars. His additional category of imitation, however, is formulated in response to his contemporary, Abraham Cowley, who in his preface to *Pindaric Odes* (1656) endorses a mode of translation that reaches far beyond paraphrase or free translation to invest the target text with the "wit or invention" of the translator, importing the source text and its author into the cultural and historical moment of the target language. In reference to his own translation of Pindar's odes, Cowley freely admits that he has "taken, left out, and added what [he] please[s]" ("Preface to Pindarique Odes" 175). Dryden rebukes both the extreme literalism of metaphrase and the "forsaking" of sense by imitation; the former method makes a "verbal copier" of the translator, while the latter's tactics of derivation obfuscates the original. Opting for paraphrase as the appropriate approach, Dryden provides a more elaborate taxonomy of translational practices; although fully aware of the particular problem for poetry to convey both form and sense, he ultimately reinforces the same approach advanced by his predecessors.[44] The same might be said for the imperialist project underscoring Jerome's "sense-for-sense model." Lesley Higgins observes that Victorian scholars Matthew Arnold, Benjamin Jowett, Edward Fitzgerald, and Walter Pater were involved in "an intense intellectual and ideological struggle for control over the Platonic canon [and Greek classics]"; translation was yet another activity bound up with "imperialist praxis" (Higgins. "Jowett and Pater" 44). Although Fitzgerald's racist view of Persian poets is an extreme case,[45] Arnold certainly shares his elitism, distrusting both the "ordinary English reader" and the critic's "individual caprices" (*On Translating Homer* 4). If there is a "touchstone" to be found in a translation, he argues, it will be discerned by "ask[ing] how his work affects those who both know Greek and can appreciate poetry" – namely, his equally well-educated contemporaries (4).

A twentieth-century linguist such as Roman Jakobson makes similar assumptions about the intent of translation as the maximal transference of sense. In "On Linguistic Aspects of Translation," Jakobson admits that comparative analysis of languages often reveals incomplete or partial "equivalence between code-units," or definable terms within the lexicon of a sign system. He offers as an example the Russian word for "cheese." Because its Russian heteronym, "сыр," includes only those foods made from compressed curds that are also fermented, the Russian definition excludes cottage cheese. This example, albeit prosaic, expresses the intimate relationship between the discursive production of language and the systematization of objective phenomena specific to any linguistic community. Yet, despite the cultural specificity of the "code-units" that constitute a given language, Jakobson nonetheless insists that the function of translation must be to locate equivalence between messages in distinct sign systems:

> Translation from one language into another substitutes messages in one language not for separate code-units but for entire messages in some other language. Such a translation is a reported speech; the translator recodes and transmits a message received from another source. Thus translation involves two equivalent messages in two different codes. ("On Linguistic Aspects of Translation" 139)

Jakobson's structuralist approach affords greater descriptive rigour, but the function of translation is effectively the same as that of Dryden, advocating a translational approach that decodes and recodes at the level of holistic sense. Theories of translation, from Cicero to the prevailing models of the 1970s, tend to debate the most effective approach to transfer the maximum retention of *meaning* from the source text to the target language. In each case, translation as a theoretical problem addresses the signified, with only varying degrees of attention to the signifier as a secondary matter of importance. But what is more, each theorist colludes in the assumption of an ultimate Signified; the role of the translator is thus to reach *behind* the linguistic sign to a universal and fixed meaning.

Despite this recapitulation of classical translation theory, Jakobson usefully extends translation beyond a properly linguistic domain. Consider his instructive typology – *Intralingual*: "interpretation of verbal signs by means of other signs of the same language"; *Interlingual*: "interpretation of verbal signs by means of some other language"; *Intersemiotic*: "interpretation of verbal signs by means of signs of nonverbal sign systems" ("On Linguistic" 139). According to his classification, translation occurs within a single language, between different languages, and between verbal and non-verbal sign systems. Like George Steiner, Jakobson observes the crucial epistemological affinity between translation and interpretation, namely, that any interpretative act involves a translational one, even within the same language. To interpret a poem, for instance, might involve a translation of a figurative economy of linguistic signs into a metacritical one. It is likely that McCaffery and Nichol read Jakobson's essay, given the similarity of their own terminology, although the two poets modify his terms somewhat, replacing intralingual and interlingual translation with homolinguistic and heterolinguistic translation.[46] Likewise, it is Jakobson's notion of intersemiotic translation that informs their notion of the post-semiotic poem. I shall discuss the TRG's use of these translational methods momentarily; for now, it suffices that although McCaffery and Nichol borrow Jakobson's terminology, they reject his imperative of message retention.

In the first of their research reports, the TRG expose the Judaeo-Christian presuppositions that underlie normative theories of translation. They point to its origins in the story of Babel, whereby linguistic diversity replaces a singular, universal language in order to prevent the perceived threat of humanity's usurpation of heaven. Traditional theories of translation, argue Nichol and McCaffery, hinge upon a principle of semantic similitude – that *behind* any signifier, in any number of sign systems, there exists a common, stable meaning that a translator seeks to reveal and transfix. Though specifically a parody of Chomskean grammar trees, McCaffery's poem ably dramatizes this approach:

The Letter 'a' According to Chomsky

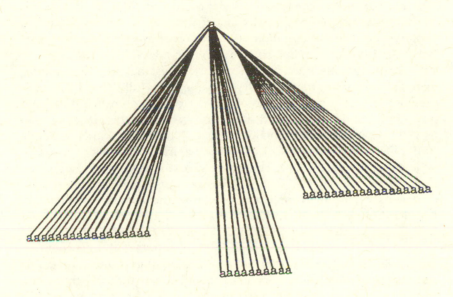

Fig. 4. Steve McCaffery, "The Letter 'a' According to Chomsky," 1975, *Seven Pages Missing: Volume Two: Previously Uncollected Texts* (Toronto: Coach House Books, 2002) 54. Used with permission.

Translation is predicated on a paradoxical double gesture: as it diversifies it homogenizes, as it reproduces a linguistic artefact in another language, it nonetheless mobilizes meaning back towards a purported universal origin. In "Unposted Correspondence," composed in 1981, McCaffery states that his research with Nichol sought to expose the "pathology of translation … its mythic support of an ultimate signified that acts as the source text's transported truth" (355). The various translational techniques that McCaffery and Nichol employ "take as a central concern the elimination or limitation of this problem: the post-Babel condition of man that so many mythologies reflect" (*RG* 31–2).

Granted, McCaffery and Nichol do not suggest that normative modes of translation are outdated or unadvisable; they fully admit that conventional translations often succeed in reproducing sense. It is that poetry's foregrounding of sound shape and verbal rhythm, its emotional as well as propositional function, and its tendency towards semantic multiplicity, make the efficacy of normative translation not only unfeasible but misapplied as well. Between the extreme view held by Benedetto Croce, for instance, that poetry is untranslatable, and those who erroneously elide the problem of semantic and formal reproduction, translation might serve a different function.[47] The role of the translator, rather than to preserve and fix a poem's semantic content, might involve augmenting and multiplying a text's potential. Like their experiments altering the textual codes of the book in order to reveal its communal artistry, McCaffery and Nichol assert that the translator, rather than look to make her work invisible, should be understood as a participant in a work's linguistic migration. Translation then becomes the work of community, one that acknowledges its transformation of sense and intercultural exchange.

Translation as Mutation: Three Procedures

(I) *Homolinguistic / Heterolinguistic / Homophonic*. In their first research report, Nichol and McCaffery introduce their terms "heterolinguistic" and "homolinguistic" – which broadly correspond to Jakobson's distinction between *interlingual* and *intralingual* translation – or translation between different languages and translation within a single language. A third term requires definition, however. In order to contest normative translation's privileging of meaning retention as the major function of translation, Nichol, McCaffery, Dick Higgins, and others employ translation homophonically. *Homophonic* translation involves a process in which the poet translates the sound of a language instead of its sense (privileging the signifier instead of the signified). The following lines of Catullus's poem, when transformed homophonically from Latin into English by Nichol, generate humorous results: "Pisonis comites, cohors inanis, / aptis sarcinulis et expeditis" becomes "Piss on his committees, cohorts in inanities / apt as sarcasm & as expeditious" (Green, *Poems of Catullus*, 72; Nichol, "from Catullus XXVIII" [1984] 1–2). Peter Green translates these lines to read: "Piso's flacks, poor empty-handed staff-ers / loaded up with your piddling little backpacks" (*Poems of Catullus* 73). The poem is addressed to Catullus's long-time friends Veranius and Fabullus, who likely had enlisted in Calpurnius Piso Caesoninus's regiment. Catullus inquires whether they have encountered the same thrift and negligence that he himself had endured as an aid to Mem-mius, propraetor of Bithynia (both he and Piso were notorious for their profiteering and corruption). Critics of Catullus frequently contrast this poem with "XXIX," in which he reprimands Mamurra, Caesar's chief engineer, who was infamous for his lavish expenditures. Green and others point out that Catullus seems only to object to such govern-ment corruption when members of staff are not given a just share of the takings. Nichol's homophonic transformation of the poem's mate-rial sound seems to distil the poem to pure expletive and sarcasm. It is likely that Nichol's choice of Catullus's verse is playfully satiric. Catal-lus will sanction Rome's imperial exploits provided he gets his share; Nichol plunders the textual riches of the Latin poet's work in turn. Al-beit Nichol's purpose is altogether different. Just as radical feminists were claiming at approximately the same time, language must be, for the poet, a shared resource.

The following is a homolinguistic example from McCaffery's re-working of Shakespeare's 105th sonnet, "Let Not My Love Be Called Idolatry" (1972):

> lay it in hot
> mile of a beak
> all died
>   hollowtree ...   (1–4)

Phonetic literalizations of certain words and recombinations of sylla-ble clusters create playful misreadings: "my love" becomes "mile of" while the vowel combination "ie" and the second "d" in "died" blends into "hollowtree," echoing the word "idolatry." Nichol and McCaffery's translation method shares an affinity with a tradition of literary appropriation that includes Tom Phillips's *A Humument* (1980), Ronald Johnson's *Radi os* (1977), and Burroughs and Gysin's cut-up methods. But whereas Phillips employs a technique of concealment, Johnson proceeds by deletion, and Burroughs and Gysin permutation, Nichol and McCaffery's translational procedures are best described as mutations.[48] As the source text travels to its target language, it undergoes the corruption of authorial contamination; the result is a hybrid of written readings. A work such as *Six Fillious* (1978) implies this trope of (per) mutation by its very title. A limit case of translation as cross-cultural collaboration, the text consists of five translations of Robert Filliou's *14 Chansons et 1 Charade* (1968) by George Brecht, Dieter Roth, Nichol, McCaffery, and Dick Higgins, composed in three languages using normative, homophonic, and homo-heterolinguistic techniques.[49] Here is an example from the poem's opening interlude:

Filliou	Brecht	Roth
c'est l'hommage dansant	here's an homage in dance	hier wird ein tier gefeiert
au **m**ammifere **m**	to that **m**ammal **m**	und zwar der säuger **m**
m le **m**alheur **m**onsieur	**m** for **m**isfortune **m**an	**m** meine herren !
madame le **m**alheur **m**	**m**a'am **m**isfortune **m**	der missgriff **m** meine
		damen !

Nichol	McCaffery	Higgins
sailor magic dance on	air song imagine dense	here's weird, a deer's
tho momma fear him	target may maul him	a-feared.
emily my whore my sewer	infamous fortune my en-	and what's with the soy,
my dame'll lure him	ema amiss farts your name	dear? *i am.*
		i am. mine the heron,
		the mischievous *i am.*
		mine the dumb one!
		(46, 52, 57, 2, 18, 31)

McCaffery's contribution consists of a homolinguistic transformation of Brecht's normative translation of Filliou's poem. The refrain repeated throughout Filliou's version, which Brecht translates literally to read either "here's" or "it's an homage in dance," is repurposed by McCaffery seven times: "air song imagine dense," "it's sane imagining a dunce," "hits a numb urge intense," "hats on oh midget ants," "i'd sign him agendas hence," "eats sand or margined hens," and "hitch a name merge intense" (18–19). This multi-authored experiment treats Filliou's poem as public property, creating wild permutations that destabilize and mutate its original meaning. The author becomes one in a series of filters through which the poem's sound/meaning travels and transforms. Unlike the authors' methods of research and performative collaboration, both of which unfold in real time and involve a mutually conceived act of community formation, creative translation is more properly an appropriative strategy. *Six Fillious* is composed of discrete contributions by several authors and thus fails to achieve the same level of subjective integration. That said, the title might be read one of two ways. Either the translator provisionally embodies the author whose work he translates (hence each translator becomes a distinct version of "Filliou"), or Filliou, a proper name signifying a body of work, becomes a different sign each time his poem is translated into another sign system. If these two readings are conjoined, then translation is understood to collectivize the writing subject/text, multiplied at the moment of intercultural contact. A new language creates a new Filliou. The text invites the reader to reconsider appropriative strategies as collaborative writing, dramatizing the communal production of meaning involved in such practices.

(II) *Allusive referential*. It is clear from Higgins's letters to McCaffery that his practice is informed in part by his readings of the TRG reports on translation, and conceived, according to McCaffery, as a key element of their Institute of Creative Misunderstanding.[50] Variously referred to as "fractured translations" or "transforms," Higgins offers the following description of the processual act involved in allusive referentialist writing:

> 1) I think *a*. Let us call *a* my "object." 2) As artist, I observe that though I try to think *a* simply, I find that my mind moves on to *b*. I could fight this and insist upon mentioning *a* only … Instead I accept the displacement. *B* now becomes the new object, which I will call a "referential." 3) But I find that when I refer to *b* in my original context, that the sense of *a*, if the intuition has been a close one, remains. ("Towards an Allusive Referential" 68–9)

There is certainly overlap between homophonic procedures and allusive referential ones. In fact, Higgins provides a homolinguistic translation as one of several examples of his method. There are, however, key differences. Though both exploit the aleatoric possibilities of translating the sound of the material signifier instead of the signified, allusive referentialist procedures function according to broader associations at the level of sense and, more specifically, the slippage or displacement of thought that generates a new text that nonetheless bears the trace of its source. In *Classic Plays* (1976), for instance, Higgins takes as his source text the Persephone story from the *Homeric Hymn to Demeter*. Rather than recount the narrative content of the myth, Higgins instead transforms the principal figures of the story – Persephone, Demeter, and Hades – into complexes of signs:

per se
    phone
                   is sound(ed by)
per se
    phony
                   is bound(ed by)
per sé
    fun
                   is phone(d by)
persephone

phonos
phone
    us

phone
    us
persephone[.]   (*Classic Plays* 1–15)

Forced to travel between the company of the gods and the underworld, Persephone occupies a liminal space between two realms. The reader of Higgins's text encounters not a proper noun so much as a site of multiple significations achieved through homophony, pun, and permutation. Higgins suggests that words "might be taken as … radicals with great polyvalence, capable of entering into a vast variety of identities which are, presumably, difficult to explain hierarchically" ("Towards" 68). Isolated into phonetic units, "per se" (by itself) and "phone"(from the Greek meaning "sound, voice" and *phonetos*, "to be spoken, utterable") are suggestive of the one that forms speech, a reading reinforced by the pun on "se/say." Like the goddess that moves between worlds, "Persephone" the signifier occupies multiple realms of meaning, never resting at one for very long. Given that the goddess is associated with nature and her abduction functions as an origin myth accounting for seasonal change, it must also be concluded that Higgins unavoidably genders language, associating mutability and polyvalence symbolically with the female body. Although these are positive qualities for Higgins, the "transform" of the myth involves an ideological move that in part stresses the liberation of meaning from a fixed sign, while it, too, abducts a female-gendered sign, previously associated with nature. Ultimately, this strategy liberates the signifier from a fixed chain of signification, while it still bares the faint traces of Saint Jerome's imperialist project, in which translation is a form of abduction.

In an exchange of letters during the summer of 1977, McCaffery expresses his interest in the concept as a more "embracing" economy of metaphoricity (Dick Higgins Papers, Box 21, folder 41), although he also partially rejects the "a to b" associational model Higgins advances as being too Aristotelian in its preservation of the metaphor's structural integrity.[51] That is, implicit in Higgins's formulation (and the Persephone myth as well) is a dyadic structure that regulates the interplay between the literal and the figurative, between surface and depth. Instead, he likens the concept to Derrida's notion of the trace, insisting that allusive referentiality functions by a "chain of deferrals and postponements" that "deflects one signifier into a second signifier and that way by-passes the ideationality of the signified" (Box 21, Folder 41). An example elucidates McCaffery's claim:

"23"	"Twenty Three"
And their feet move	the move(meant) of the foot from Crete
	in rhythm, not
Rhythmically, as tender	
feet of Cretan girls	in a tender rhythm
danced once around an	but intending rhythm crush
altar of love, crushing	a soft calligraphy
a circle in the soft	of O's
smooth flowering grass[.]	
	into the grass[.]
(Barnard, *Sappho*, 1–7)	(McCaffery, *Intimate Distortions*, 1–7)

McCaffery's poem is one in a book-length sequence entitled *Intimate Distortions: A Displacement of Sappho* (1979), a text he dutifully dedicates to Higgins (the "allusive referentialist") and for which he takes as his source text not the original Greek but Mary Barnard's 1958 English translation of Sappho. In McCaffery's text, proper nouns such as "Cretan girls" and "altar" are deleted; although the words "Crete" and "grass" provide the reader with a sense of place, given the position of the former in the poem's first line, it is likely that the "move(meant) of the foot from Crete / in rhythm" puns instead on a "cretic" line. The emphasis is shifted from the static thing to the rhythm of movement. McCaffery's revision is potentially jarring for the reader because he mainly refuses to allow a signifier its corresponding signified, occupying instead a nebulous zone of signification. A combination of alliterative "o" sounds in the final stanza of Sappho/Barnard's text ("love," "soft," "smooth," "flow-") and the image of a "circle" becomes a "calligraphy / of O's," at once suggesting a fixation on the material letters and the form of one's lips expelling breath. McCaffery's title – with its explicit use of the word "displacement" – emphasizes that aspect of Higgins's practice that foregrounds the "deferring action of signs in movement, to the actual leap from being one thing to another" (Box 21, Folder 41). The metaphor is apt: McCaffery defines Higgins's "transforms" as the leaping of signifiers. Therefore, a more open concept of metaphoricity is proposed: one unconfined by the dyadic structure that restricts the two figurative terms in conventional theories of metaphor to a two-way association, a practice that encourages further adaptations, making the translated text the source for yet another creative translation.

(III) *Post-semiotic*. Jakobson's observation that translation occurs between verbal and non-verbal sign systems occasioned a number of experiments in intermedial poetics. In their first research report, Nichol and McCaffery acknowledge Decio Pigniatari and Luiz Angelo Pinto, members of the Brazilian Noigandres literary collective, as the inventors of the semiotic or "code" poem. Their aim, the TRG notes, is a universal language that seeks to "bypass the need for translation" by employing "non-verbal pragmatic sign formula[s]" (*RG* 34). An example clarifies their otherwise abstract definition (see figure 5).

The weakness of this type of poem is its unavoidable recourse to a lexical grammar in which to decode its non-verbal function. There is, of course, an implicit translation process – "from words *into* semiotic signs

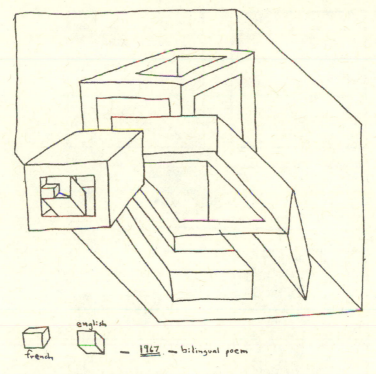

Fig. 5. bpNichol, "Bilingual Poem," 1967, in "Research Report 1: Translation," *Open Letter* 2, no. 4 (Spring 1973): 85. Used with permission.

back into words" (RG 34). What is more, the authors' wish to "bypass" translation altogether merely echoes a nostalgia for a pre-Babel Adamic language, naïvely thought to have been achieved through the universality of visual signs. There is also a certain closure in this method, a complementary entrapment of meaning within two corresponding sign systems. During the summer of 1970, the TRG jointly conceived of a "post-semiotic" poem, in which the "lexical conversion of non-verbal code back into words is eliminated." A procedure of "semantic suggestion" (35) replaces the search for a metatranslational text. McCaffery's "A Translation of Sir Philip Sidney's Sonnet XXXI from 'Astrophel and Stella'" (1972) provides a useful example:

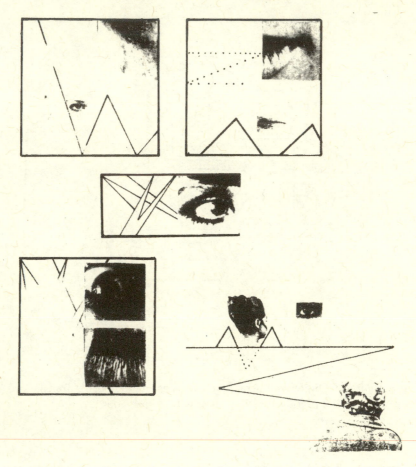

Fig. 6. Steve McCaffery, "A Translation of Sir Philip Sidney's Sonnet XXXI from 'Astrophel and Stella,'" 1972, *Seven Pages Missing: Volume Two: Previously Uncollected Texts* (Toronto: Coach House Books, 2002) 163. Used with permission.

The original poem is not a direct address to the beloved, but rather an invocation to the moon, whose "sad steps" across the sky and pale "face" prompts the speaker to "read" in "thy looks" a familiar experience of unrequited love. The moon, too, he conjectures, has been struck by cupid's arrow, but to no avail; thus, the speaker concludes, in heaven as in earth, "beauties ... love to be lov'd, and yet / Those lovers scorn whom that love doth possess" ("Sonnet XXXI" 1–2, 11–13).[52] Comparing the "vocabulary" of the post-semiotic translation, the reader should be struck by its visual synecdoche, its sexual fixation on bodily apertures, and the voyeuristic subject position of the speaker/viewer. The moon, in McCaffery's version, comes to signify the body as pure surface upon which the lover projects his own perceptions on a "beloved" never empowered to speak. McCaffery's choice to remediate his translation as a comic strip – a demotic genre – comments on the popularity of Sidney's subject matter and the courtly love tradition itself as a "cartoonish" overembellishment of sensual desire. Yet the organization of comic frames is more diagrammatic than cartoon-like. Cupid's arrows become those in a diagram mapping modes of perception and cognition, speaking perhaps to the procedural nature of the sonnet form and the conventions of courtly love.[53] The post-semiotic poem establishes an intertextual connection between a source text and its adaptation. But instead of a closed relationship between the two, one finds a remediation executed to adapt while it permits – perhaps invites – further adaptation.

Translation and the Politics of Appropriation

Among the dominant theories of translation I discussed previously, the problem of the translator's status is simply elided by ignoring her contribution to the creative act. The translator is understood as a transparent medium, through which the sense of one language enters the form of another. McCaffery and Nichol insist, conversely, that the translator becomes a "living force within the work" (*RG* 29) and a collaborator in its augmentation and modification, as reading itself becomes a writerly activity. That is, the translator becomes another writer in the multivalent and social production of texts. In a conversation recorded in the pages of *Open Letter*, both authors agree that translation and collaboration share a governing logic:

B: ... collaboration is also a way of bringing a kind of readerly activity into the writing process ... It certainly relates nicely to what you and i have talked about for years in terms of homolinguistic translations and, too, what i've ended up calling 'conversations with the dead' (viz your Sappho displacements and my Catullus 'translations').

s: Yes, both translation and collaboration suggest that creativity is not integral
    / expressive but dialogic / relational. (Nichol, "The Annotated" 75)

Not only are many of their pieces multi-authored, several of the strategies they invent are as well. The *post-semiotic* poem, McCaffery recounts, was a concept Nichol and he "arrive[d] at together (I can almost remember the brand of wine we drunk [*sic*] that evening rapping together)" (McCaffery, "Interview" by Jaeger 80). Dick Higgins's notion of the *allusive referential* is partly adapted from his readings of the TRG reports and his correspondence with McCaffery during the mid-1970s. McCaffery's homolinguistic rewriting of the *Communist Manifesto* (see below) into the dialect of his native West Riding of Yorkshire was the suggestion of Robert Filliou, during a trip he, McCaffery, and Allan Kaprow had taken to Roberts Creek, British Columbia (*Wot We Wukkerz Want*, n.p.).[54] In accordance with the principles of the Institute of Creative Misunderstanding, these authors were building and adapting "conceptual models" for communal use.

    McCaffery, Nichol, and Higgins worked to shift emphasis from object to process, defining the poem as a unit in the continuous mutation and infinite proliferation of a sign's semantic content. All objects instead become provisional points in an infinite series, emphasizing not its being as such but its continuous potential for transmutation into or as part of another object. The title *Six Fillious* elegantly expresses this mutant proliferation of an object's infinite possibility. Yet the Eternal Network is also meant as a model of communal interaction, calling for a similar approach to community formation as a continued openness to transformation. This principle is evident in their communication network, the Four Horsemen's "ongoing compositional workshops," and the TRG's "we-full (not I-less) paradigm." Appropriative activities as diverse as collage and montage, mash-ups and machinema, found art and sampling, creative translation and theatrical adaptation, occur within marginal communities of avant-gardes, activists, and sub-cultures. There are several reasons for the relationship between appropriation and communal art production, but if artistic appropriation operates by effacing property ownership, it follows that the cultural objects they create can no more be owned than the objects they take. Prevailing explanations of appropriation highlight concepts of piracy, theft, and plagiarism, a gesture that inadvertently criminalizes such practices. The TRG instead proposes a model of shared culture, in a sense seeking to realize Rich's "dream of a common language." An integral part of artistic appropriation involves an ethic of sharing, of making one's cultural production infinitely available to others for use.

The political undertones of this practice are brought forward in McCaffery's *Wot We Wukkerz Want* (1977). This is the opening section of Samuel Moore's 1888 English translation of *The Communist Manifesto* followed by McCaffery's version in Yorkshire dialect:

> Two things result from this fact:
> 1. Communism is already acknowledged by all European powers to be itself a power.
> 2. It is high time that Communists should openly, in the face of the whole world, publish their views, their aims, their tendencies, and meet this nursery tale of the Spectre of Communism with a manifesto of the party itself.
>
> To this end, Communists of various nationalities have assembled in London, and sketched the following manifesto, to be published in the English, French, German, Italian, Flemish, and Danish languages. (78)

> Nahthuzzuh coupler points ahm goointer chuckaht frum awl thisseer stuffidge:
>   Wun: Thadeelin wear reight proper biggun inthiseer kommunizum.
>   Too: It's abaht bluddy time thut kommunizum spoouk its orn mind, unwarritsehbaht, un edder reight set-too we awl this youngunz stuff ehbaht booergy-misters, wee uh bitter straight tawkin onnitsoowun.
>   Un soourt kommiz frum awlort place uv snugged it up dahn in Lundun, un poowildahl the buk lernin tehgither un cummupwithisser Manifesto, unnitz innuzoowun un int' froggy, unt' jerry, un i-ti, unt flemmy unt dayunish.
>
> (171)

In the liner note of the 1979 audio tape, MyCaffery explains his rationale for accepting Filliou's proposal to write the poem. "How," he inquires, "can a manifesto designed to inspire the working class to a world revolution be effectively conveyed in Stunted Victorian English prose?" (373). What he and Filliou imagine instead is a "dialect materialism" (liner note) specific to the varied historical conditions of numerous working communities – a "soft manifesto" malleable enough to mutate into Jamaican patois, Nuyorican Spanglish, or English cockney. McCaffery suggests that this movement across geography and across nation state requires a similar transition into the language and dialect specific to language users. Amid their discussions at Roberts Creek, Filliou, Kaprow, and McCaffery agreed that such a translation would be a poetic realization of the Eternal Network. *Wot We Wukkerz Want* imagines that the propositions contained in its content belong to a social continuance – an everlasting network or infinite series. Thinkers like Slavoj Žižek and Alain Badiou insist that the truth of communism can be found in its axiomatic "hypothesis": that class subjugation is not inevitable, that a form of collective organization based on the freely associated labour of producers is possible. Drawing many of the same conclusions as CAM members after attending the Havana Congress, in moving from "communist" to "Kommunist," the eternal status of this claim is never universal in the liberal-humanist sense of an abstract generality applied to any situation, but *universally transferable*, in that it may be taken up and reinvented infinitely by a community according to the specifications of its culture, language, and history.

McCaffery understands that at the core of Marxist discourse are competing notions of appropriation: one that appropriates the labour of the other for himself and a communal sharing of resources produced and redistributed for the good of the community. The text of the *Communist Manifesto* itself should be understood as such. Unalienated labour is that which is mutually appropriatable by a community of members who understand their production as a production for the other. T.S. Eliot's witty observation that immature poets borrow and mature poets steal makes no sense within this poetic economy. To borrow implies a predetermined condition of return. No such precondition exists within an infinite series, in which the "borrowed" phrase is always already "borrowed" from elsewhere. The Eternal Network, then, should be understood as an approach to aesthetics and sociality: the poem and the community as the unpropertied resource of all.

Practices of appropriation have become an increasingly dominant feature of recent experimental verse, for instance, in constraint poetry, conceptual writing, Flarf, and digital poetries – all of which, I would argue, productively appropriate from the TRG. Whether its members were collaborating in the tactile, real-time environments of performance spaces, workshops, and research labs, or whether these activities happened as a part of a transgeographic institute of shared conceptual models and techniques, the principal value of the TRG is its practice of appropriation, understood not merely as the transgressive act of censorial concealment to which Bloom gives the name "anxiety of influence," but instead a poetic economy of mutual use, a view of the text's value being its capacity for adaptation, modification, reframing, amplifying, and repurposing. Darren Wershler has coined the term "conceptualism in the wild" to denote popular cultural practices that (often unknowingly) appropriate and disperse ideas drawn from the avant-garde.[55] Such tactics become *memes* perpetually adapted and recontextualized elsewhere. It is often said of McCaffery and Nichol that their overlapping bodies of work resist generic classification. Their practice drifts in and out of visual, sound, performance, procedural verse, Language writing, Fluxus practice, and conceptualism. That said, we should be wary of celebrating such diversity for its own sake. McCaffery's translation, and the Eternal Network from which it arises, invites us to imagine the texts produced within the Toronto Research Group as memes that install, replicate, and proliferate the communist hypothesis as an imperative of literature. The motley patchwork of experiments they undertook should not distract us from the unwavering political project underscoring the TRG's activities. Let us even call it unabashedly the *truth* of the TRG's oeuvre: to defend a public cultural domain from proprietary enclosure.

Epilogue   Community as an Eternal Idea

The goods of the intellect are communal.

– Robert Duncan[1]

Robert Duncan often called himself a derivative poet, a fact usually glossed over as mere cleverness. But perhaps he affords the most lucid critique of originality among poets writing during the second half of the twentieth century. Implicit in such an idea is a notion of aesthetic production forged relationally among a community of others who copy and extend, mutate and redirect the material of a collective practice. One may object that in defining a practice we regulate its aesthetic principles and police its transformation. Certainly this can and does happen. Yet the alternative is rarely preferable. To suggest that one is simply an individual writer without allegiance to a tradition is to abjure the influences and ideological principles that frame all aesthetic activity; it is to ignore the community of those who enable one's own creativity. At the very least, the author who self-identifies with a common noun acknowledges that her poetry is always situated within traditions and modes of writing, shared methodologies, and common ideas. From this point of view, the poet participates in and contributes to a practice of writing that is never entirely one's own, insisting, as Duncan does, that the "goods of the intellect are communal."

Yet one still frequently hears the complaint: to what extent can a poet's writing change things? What political consequences arise from the alternative practices of community that these poets imagine? This is a valid question, but I suspect that it is made with certain fallacious assumptions in mind; in particular, one should remember that it virtually never occurs that a single individual implements radical change (nor would we likely want this to be the case). This claim is in no way a declaration of nihilistic entrapment, but simply an acknowledgment of how power, agency, and culture operate. If one agrees with theorists like Michel Foucault, Louis Althusser, and Judith Butler that power is diffuse and multifaceted, then it makes sense that change always requires a collective will of singularities that act in common. One might reformulate rather than reject Shelley's claim that the poet is "the unacknowledged legislator of the world" ("Defence" 508). Instead, one should ask how this legislation is collectively written and rewritten by the authors of a culture, how literature participates in this multiform conception of agency by constituting one element of a broader aesthetic network, which in turn is part of an even larger socio-economic one. The role of art, from this vantage point, is the permeation of an egalitarian ideal prescribed, incorporated, and dispersed into the body of all cultural activity.

In this sense, the succinct expression Eternal Network articulates an underlying theme of this book. The word "network" evokes the many participants who create art and their channels of distribution; networks remind us that the world is composed of difference and multiplicity. Any action, text, or principle bears the trace of a heterogeneous collective that labours in its creation. But what does one make of the other term, "eternal"? This word seems strangely out of place amid a consortium of mid-century avant-gardes for whom the demotic, the impermanent, and the ephemeral are said to constitute their central traits. Filliou and Brecht translate this word from the French, *permanent*, to render a lasting attention to the networks on which we rely for our existence, wishing to transmit this commitment "everywhere and everytime a mutation can be accomplished" ("La Fête est Permanente" 204). In calling community eternal, an axiomatic claim is never universally applicable to every situation, but it is universally transferable to any situation in which an ensemble of participants chooses it as their own. Political experience is singular and local, but the wealth of their intellectual and artistic production is infinitely renewable ("mutation-al"). We choose to establish an axiomatic claim: the right, say, for local autonomy, or that racism is violently oppressive, sexism is equally oppressive as racism, ideas belong to everyone, and so on. We need not believe a universal claim is discoverable in human nature or metaphysically anterior to human knowledge. We need only to declare it, commit to it, to become such a claim – just as so many individuals in Brathwaite's *Arrivants* come to embody the principle of emancipation represented by revolutionary figures. Badiou calls this "the local construction of the True" (*Communist* 255). We could easily extrapolate from the case studies in this book a set of prescriptive axioms: (1) the *BMC Axiom*: like the elements (Olson calls them "participants") in a poem, all subjects in a just society must count equally. (2) The *CAM Axiom*: all political action is local, but such actions are infinitely transferable to other localities. (3) The *WLM Axiom*: there are different identities, cultures, and so on, but the world we share must be singularly accessible and common. (4) The *TRG Axiom*: cultural production, like any other form of production, must aspire to the ideal of freely associated labour.

Given the sheer volume of studies addressing early twentieth-century avant-gardes, it is striking that so few critics attempt comparative studies of literary movements in the contemporary era. Recalling Raymond Williams's poignant observation, "we find histories of particular groups, but little comparative or analytic history" ("Bloomsbury" 148). Indeed, what we find is suspicion, even embarrassment. If the phrase "avant-garde movement" resonates with the recalcitrant ideologies that earned high modernism the unenviable subtitle "Age of Isms," then most studies of post-1945 literary movements highlight the heterogeneity such groups are said to celebrate. The poetic communities discussed in this book are variously structured through a combination of avant-garde formations, activist collectives, African communitarian models, laboratories, workshops, and communes. Yet such valorizations of diversity as such fail to explain the *particular* synthesis of social models, philosophical principles, and aesthetic practices that a group adopts. CAM's synthesis of West African religion, creative uses of Caribbean dialect, and Marxist theory consists of a specific assemblage solidifying its challenge to race subordination and the colonial logic of market capitalism. The WLM's synthesis of open form tactics and consciousness raising simultaneously appropriates and contests the New Left's artistic and political projects. Like CAM, their most radical gesture is not only a defiant act of self-definition, but also an act denying male culture the exclusive right to define their own traditions. This is the central function of Rich's "writing as re-vision."

Poetic Community begins in the rural United States; it then moves to cosmopolitan London (while assessing the post-war diaspora en route); the study circles back to America, this time to its urban centres; and then finally shifting to Toronto (a city positioned at the borderline of its superpower neighbour), at which point the book ends with a transnational community untethered to a tangible scene of cultural production. Generally speaking, it is an accurate contention that practices of community are becoming increasingly discursive; digital cultures undoubtedly facilitate these new forms of social experience. Yet, just as claims for an "information economy" risk ignoring the massive outsourcing of industrial production to under-developed nations, digital cultures are largely confined to the middle and wealthy classes in the West. Moreover, the new tactics that digital networks create typically transform and supplement tangible sites of social creativity. One may still locate the political in locality. The example of a collective like UbuWeb is instructive. Strongly influenced by the TRG, Fluxus, and conceptualism, the group's website (ubuweb.com) effectively digitizes the Eternal Network. Readers and writers use the site both as an archive of avant-garde art and literature, and as a forum through which to organize readings and other activities. Its members belong to collectives like ArtMob, Information As Material, and the Poetic Research Bureau, tangible scenes with an online presence whose activist work involves defending artistic appropriation and the public domain from the same intellectual property regimes that the TRG presciently anticipate.[2] Just as this cross-cultural research documents the Cold War's influence on poetic culture from a global perspective, mapping its implications among U.S., post-Commonwealth, and diasporic communities, it traces a lineage to late twentieth- and twenty-first-century writing that defines its central objective as the defence of public culture.

Although it is enticing to argue that subversive writers work "outside" of the official institutions and ideologies of a dominant culture, apart from questions regarding the epistemological validity of an ideological "outside" or a "beyond," post-war writing had no choice but to confront the apparatuses that regulate politics and aesthetics from a position immanent within a socio-political totality. The 1950s, 1960s, and 1970s witnessed renewed ethnic and racial conflicts, the radical displacement of populations across the globe, intensified military-corporate collusion, and hence increasingly more sophisticated modes of domination. The political and cultural fronts had not evaporated but were being redrawn. In opposition to the radical subjection of our social relationships to capital – what Olson describes as a total enclosure and Creeley a surrounding darkness – mid-century poets sought to intervene in the ideological fields that compete for our precepts, our affects, our everyday practices. Within these shifting enclosures, creativity becomes a matter of adapting, contesting, and transforming the dominant ideologies that shape culture. It is striking that so many of the concepts and techniques we associate with mid-century art and literature emerge from the kinds of collaborative networks discussed in this study: open form, nation language, re-vision, the *détournement*, creative translation, the new sentence, intermedial art, performance poetry, appropriative strategies, polylingualism, and so on. Poets were increasingly appealing to social models and collective labour to explain the poetic object: the field (Olson, Creeley), the park (Levertov), the commune (Duncan), the cooperative (Salkey), the laboratory/institute (McCaffery, Nichol, Higgins), and the workshop/stage (Four Horsemen). By evoking these public spaces and social sites, these poets emphasize that all aesthetic production occurs as a result of interaction, cooperation, and contestation. Shorthand descriptions of poetry in the post-1945 era typically involve a shift from product to process, from an emphasis on the poem's aesthetic autonomy to the foregrounding of a text's construction. Whether it is McCaffery and Nichol's "We-full" writing or Duncan's emphatic claim for a "derivative poetics," the construction of literary practices was undertaken collectively and the materials used to create poetry were conceived as shared resources. These developments have important consequences for the study of twentieth-century poetics: namely, many of its most significant tendencies challenge conventional notions of authorship and originality not by announcing the author's death, but by "communalizing" literary artefacts. When texts combine media, genres, and languages, they map convergences between the communities who create, use, circulate, and interpret these artefacts. In a word, they make communities of these objects. The purpose of this book, therefore, has been to reveal the networks that texts create and the modalities of social existence they enact.

Which leads, in the final analysis, to the following claim: if an avant-garde is to intervene in the realm of ideological production, if it is to stage what might be thought of as an appropriation of capital's subsumptive enclosure of knowledge and affect, then it will not only have to inscribe in literature the chief task of imagining new modalities of being; further, it will have to remake the philosophical category of the universal. As I have claimed throughout this book, the concept of eternal community need not make recourse to essentialist conceptions of gender, ethnicity, or race, nor does it need to claim that its axioms exist in human nature. It must, however, having declared its principal truths to be socially constructed, then proceed to the more admirable work of actually socially constructing them, and hence making a *practice* of such axioms. With the precondition that such truths are not universally applicable but are universally transmittable, then a cultural politics based on radical equality, autonomy, accessibility, and free association seems, as Rich might suggest, a viable ground on which to "reconstitute the world."

The so-called Information age has no doubt generated unbridled enthusiasm for transnationalism, interdisciplinarity, and cultural syncretism. Certainly this book, in addressing Cold War–era cultures from a global (rather than a strictly American) perspective, makes use of such tropes and approaches. Yet reading across national boundaries signals no fundamental good for its own sake – after all, nothing is more rhizomatically multinational than capital at the end of the twentieth century. Cross-cultural study, therefore, should not elide ethnic, racial, and gender differences but instead engage the specificity – indeed, the locality – of cultures in the plural, their formation, and their development. Rich was adamant that her search for a common language sought not erasure but respect and acknowledgment of difference – that, indeed, what is common is not who we are but what we share. Awareness of social location notwithstanding, one should neither rarify difference nor pathologize all forms of appropriation as the work of cultural colonizers and thieves. Creeley's pledge to "hand everything over" to "whomever ... might *use* it" serves as a model of the open, collective, and non-proprietary making of art based on the notion that his creative output belongs to a community beyond the self.

Although this book retains the broad segmentarity of a literary epoch (1950–80), the division is a porous one. Black Mountain has clear affiliations with Pound and W.C. Williams; the TRG appropriates elements of New York and Zurich Dada; while CAM treats history as a collagic assembly of "time centres," the rebellion of Toussaint having as much importance as yesterday's news. The modern/postmodern divide has never really worked for poetry. For instance, American modernism arguably features a continuous trajectory from Pound and Williams to the objectivists, and on to groups such as the Black Mountain poets, the New York School, and the San Francisco Renaissance. Concrete and sound poets link avant-garde modernisms with contemporary experimental poetry. The divergent rhythms of Harlem Renaissance writers generate the blues- and jazz-inflected poetics of the Beats, the Black Arts Movement, and spoken word. Similarly, Fluxus and conceptual art has had a profound influence on twenty-first-century poetries. Of course, any classification by epoch, nation, or genre generates divisions and marks both inclusions and exclusions. But perhaps the concepts of *community* and *practice* afford another way to periodize literary tradition. Instead of further dividing history into yet smaller and more precisely delineated epochs, critics might choose to trace practices, mapping generative constellations of authors, groups, social spaces, events, texts, and technologies. If one insists upon the connection between experiments in forms of writing and experiments in forms of living, it is because poetry does.

Notes

1: Introduction

1 Williams, "The Bloomsbury Fraction," 148.
2 Creeley, "Alex's Art," 63.
3 Altieri describes the immanentist mode in his *Enlarging the Temple: New Directions in American Poetry during the 1960s*: "if he [the poet] stresses the revelatory power of the poem's distinctive properties, he can imagine the primary function of poetic imagination as disclosing aspects of numinous experience not available to discursive acts of mind, which are trapped in a logic unable to capture the act of perception and thus incapable of reconciling fact and value" (31).
4 Consider how pervasive this tendency was among those philosophers still willing to evoke the term "community" after the Second World War. Examples include Georges Bataille, Jean-Luc Nancy, Maurice Blanchot, Georgio Agamben, Alphonso Lingis, and Jacques Derrida, who each had sought to reorient thinking of the ontological "ground" from whence theories of community arise. Perhaps most apparent in the discourse that emerges among them is a common suspicion of community's reduction to a singular and totalizing essence. Nancy is perhaps most direct in *The Inoperative Community*: "[t]he community that becomes *a single* thing (body, mind, fatherland, Leader ...) necessarily loses the *in* of being-*in*-common. Or, it loses the *with* or the *together* that defines it ... [H]ow can the community without essence (the community that is neither 'people' nor 'nation,' neither 'destiny' nor 'generic humanity,' etc.) be presented as such? That is, what might a politics be that does not stem from the will to realize an essence?" (*Inoperative* xxxix–xl). Bataille speaks

aporetically of a "community without community"; Blanchot similarly evokes the "unavowable community"; while Agamben names an "unrepresentable community"; Lingis the "other community"; Anderson the "imagined community"; and Derrida, the "indefinitely imperfectable" community "to come." In each formulation, however different they may be in many respects, a discernible anxiety shades any and all talk of group formations. Derrida's admission, for instance, is telling: "I was wondering why the word 'community' (avowable or unavowable, inoperative or not) – why I have never been able to write it, on my own initiative and in my name, as it were. Why? Whence my reticence?" (*Politics of Friendship* 304–5).

The quotation attributed to Bataille appears as the epigram to Blanchot's *The Unavowable Community* (Derrida discusses the passage in *Politics of Friendship*, 48–9 and 295); the remaining passages appear in Blanchot, *The Unavowable Community*, 1–26; Georgio Agamben, *The Coming Community*, 86; Lingis, *The Community of Those Who Have Nothing in Common*, 10; Anderson, *Imagined Communities*, 6; and Derrida, *Politics of Friendship*, 306.

5 Among the numerous post-colonial scholars who address strategies of neocolonialism, see Kwame Nkrumah (Ghana's first post-independence leader), *Neo-Colonialism: The Last Stage of Imperialism*.

6 In particular, see David Harvey, *The Condition of Postmodernity: An Enquiry into the Origins of Cultural Change* (1991) and *A Brief History of Neoliberalism* (2005).

7 See, for instance, Paul Hoover, ed., *Postmodern American Poetry: An Introduction*, 3.

8 See Arthur Redding's exemplary use of the term "cultural fronts" in *Turncoats, Traitors, and Fellow Travelers: Culture and Politics of the Early Cold War*, 3–36.

9 Gilles Deleuze and Félix Guattari's theory of nomadology has proven particularly influential for critics who emphasize a celebratory rootlessness in contemporary literature. Édouard Glissant, for instance, valorizes the nomadic traveller of the French Caribbean: "exhaust[ing] no territory, he is rooted only in the sacredness of air and evaporation" (*Poétique de la Relation* 224). See Édouard Glissant, *Poetics of Relation*. See also, Pierre Joris, *A Nomad Poetics*; and Hakim Bey, *T.A.Z: The Temporary Autonomous Zone*. Yet Deleuze and Guattari advance a much more cautious explanation. The nomadic, Deleuze explains in an interview with Claire Parnet, has its "dangers." Any "line of flight" capable of deterritorializing a rigid organization also has the capacity to replicate and maintain its violent hierarchies,

and, "which is perhaps the worst of all[,] … they have yet another special risk: that of turning into lines of abolition, of destruction, of others and of oneself" (*Dialogues II* 140). In a word, there is always the possibility that Marinetti's "words in freedom" will reterritorialize as so many fascistic slogans. See *A Thousand Plateaus*, 227–31, and *Dialogues II*, 124–47.

10 Badiou's own political group, L'Organisation Politique (OP), may at first glance appear to qualify as the sort of network Hardt and Negri promote in *Multitude*, insofar as the group marshals political force without recourse to the state party or its general political program, assembling only to intervene in specific confrontations (such as their solidarity with the *sans-papiers*). Yet Badiou is just as sceptical of the spontaneous and unsustainable character of mass movements, their incapacity to establish organizing structures and non-exploitative forms of economic cooperation. He insists that political thought must be both local and axiomatic; only a prescriptive assertion expressed in a concrete situation can generate a sustained project of emancipation. For Badiou, the foundational axiom of an emancipatory politics is unqualified equality. However rhizomatic, heterogeneous, or dispersed the composition of a collective subject may be, the measure of any political sequence is its fidelity to the prescriptive truth that brings such a sequence into existence. See, *Being and Event*, *Metapolitics*, and *The Communist Hypothesis*.

11 By now the militaristic origin of the term *avant-garde* is well known. Derived from the French, the name designates a small faction of soldiers deployed ahead of an advancing army to map an unknown or dangerous terrain; in aesthetic terms, the *avant-garde* refers to artistic forerunners that test and traverse the boundaries of acceptable theories of literature and art – therefore, creating art "ahead of its time." The hallmark of its practice is thus novelty in opposition to what it perceives as the static machinations of past traditions: "why should we look back," Marinetti exults, "when what we want is to break down the mysterious doors of the Impossible?" ("Founding Manifesto" 187). Nowhere is this central modernist axiom declared with greater concision than in Ezra Pound's dictum to "make it new": "[m]y pawing over the ancients and semi-ancients has been one struggle to find out what has been done, once for all, better than it can ever be done again, and to find out what remains for us to do" ("A Retrospect" 11).

12 The pronoun "we," riddled throughout the copious numbers of modernist declarations, elicits perhaps more controversy today than any other convention of avant-garde declarations. In *Manifestoes: Provocations of the Modern*, Janet Lyon observes that subsequent feminist and post-colonial

theorists have called into question the presumptuous deployment of the pronoun "we" as "an inherently colonizing construction" that homogenizes socio-cultural difference within societal groups (26). This contradiction characterizes the turbulent conflict within avant-garde formation in general between fierce individualism and collective praxis.

13 See, for example, Peter Bürger, *Theory of the Avant-Garde*; Terry Eagleton, *The Ideology of the Aesthetic*, 341–417; and Lawrence Rainey, "The Cultural Economy of Modernism," 33–69.

14 Despite a growing industry of criticism devoted to historical avant-gardes, Poggioli's agonistic account of group practice has enjoyed a notable degree of continued acceptance. Rosenberg argues that "'avant-gardes are by nature combative'" (qtd. in Lehman, *The Last Avant-Garde* 286). Describing the historical avant-gardes' preferred genre, Mary Ann Caws remarks that the manifesto engages in "We-Speak": "[g]enerally posing some 'we,' explicit or implicit, against some other 'they,' with the terms constructed in a deliberate dichotomy … set up like a battlefield … Its oppositional tone is constructed of *againstness*" (*A Century of Isms* xx, xxiii).

15 For an excellent account of the hierarchical social dynamics of the pre–First World War avant-garde, see Milton A. Cohen, *Movement, Manifesto, Melee* [sic]: *The Modernist Group, 1910–1914*.

16 For a comparison of the movement and the salon, see Voyce, "'Make the World Your Salon': Poetry and Community at the Arensberg Apartment," 630–4.

17 Silliman is quick to point out that both scenes and networks manifest certain assumptions about class. These organizing structures differ by virtue of their members' access to technologies of communication, requiring different amounts of capital. The fiscal disparity between a scene organized through a poetry reading, say, and a network through a system of correspondence may seem relatively minor, but the cost of producing an anthology or magazine may very well establish hierarchies of cultural dominance based on comparative capacities to disseminate materials. The academic poetry workshop, for instance, constitutes a scene according to Silliman's distinction, but because it functions as an organ within a degree granting institution, the required capital to participate in such communities and the cultural currency it garners is of course considerably different than a poetry reading.

18 For an excellent reassessment of the gender politics of this era, see Davidson's latest book, *Guys Like Us: Citing Masculinity in Cold War Poetics*. See also Rachel Blau DuPlessis, "Manhood and its Poetic Projects: The Construction of Masculinity in the Counter-Cultural Poetry of the U.S. 1950s."

19 See, for example, Amiri Baraka's critique of mid-century poets such as O'Hara and the politics of Bohemian culture, "Cultural Revolution and the Literary Canon," 150–6.

20 For instance, Michael Davidson's groundbreaking book, *The San Francisco Renaissance: Poetics and Community at Mid-Century*, and other studies by critics like Daniel Kane (*All Poets Welcome*), Anne Dewey (*Beyond Maximus*), Thomas Fink (*A Different Sense of Power*), and Paul Hoover (*The Last Avant-Garde*) do not define this principal term, nor trace its discursive formation.

21 See Williams, *Keywords*, 75–6.

22 See Ferdinand Tönnies, *Community and Society*.

2. Black Mountain College: A Poetic of Local Relations

1 Charles Olson, "Culture and Revolution," manuscript of *Culture and Revolution*, c. 1952, Charles Olson Research Collection, Box 29, Archives and Special Collections at the Thomas J. Dodd Research Center, University of Connecticut Libraries.

2 Robert Creeley, interview with Martin Duberman, 3 October 1967 (Audio tape). See Duberman, *Black Mountain: An Exploration in Community*, 390.

3 Olson first began teaching at Black Mountain in 1948, but would not become a full-time faculty member until the summer of 1951.

4 Paul and Percival Goodman argue that the monumentalist designs of Ebenezer Howard, Le Corbusier, and Frank Lloyd Wright forced preconceived models of society onto populations without consideration of the pragmatic ways in which individuals and groups occupy cities. Instead they privilege a model of "regional self-sufficiency … where the producing and the product are of a piece and every part of life has value in itself as both means and end … and each man has a chance to enhance the community style and transform it" (*Communitas* 220). In the preface, Paul Goldberger aptly summarizes the project of the Goodmans' study: the book, he remarks, "is a testament to the idea that the city is a collective, shared place, a place that is in the most literal sense common ground" (xi).

5 Martin Duberman records in his biography of the college that by 1950 many of the members of the community were openly gay, but Goodman's "ostentatious homosexual[ity] … was too much, even for Black Mountain" (331). Many at the college defended Goodman, including Dan Rice, Robert Creeley, Ed Dorn, and Joel Oppenheimer; nevertheless, the faculty voted against his full-time appointment.

6 The first twenty sections of Olson's long poem, most of which is composed of "letters," was first published in two runs by Jonathan Williams's Jargon press: *The Maximus Poems / 1 – 10* in October 1953 and *The Maximus Poems / 11 – 22* in the fall of 1956. Olson read these selections in their entirety at Black Mountain College in August 1953.

7 The draft of this letter was composed 12 January 1945, and appears in Olson's notebook, "Key West I, 1945," Charles Olson Papers, University of Connecticut Libraries, Storrs. The cited passage also appears in Tom Clark, *Charles Olson: The Allegory of a Poet's Life*, 94.

8 For an extended account of the administrative history of the college, see Martin Duberman's cultural biography, *Black Mountain College: An Exploration in Community*.

9 Fielding Dawson and Dan Rice make almost identical remarks: "Black Mountain was the people who were there, which explains its sudden changes. From 1950 or, for sure, '51, it was Olson's ... as Dan [Rice] has said, ... [i]t had an organic understanding of itself being transient. People came and went" (Dawson, "Black Mountain Defined" 273).

10 See Richard Kostelanetz, *Conversing with Cage*, 265.

11 Don Byrd, Robert von Hallberg, and Rosemarie Waldrop comment on Olson's reliance on Whitehead's *Process and Reality* as a formative text for the poet's writing and thought. Hallberg deftly summarizes the aspects of Whitehead's ontology that Olson would certainly have accepted: "[a]ction and motion, in Whitehead's philosophy, supplant the Aristotelian concept of matter as substance. At the center of the object is no nucleus of tangibility but instead a system of relationships" ("Olson, Whitehead, and the Objectivists" 93). Such statements help to clarify Olson's concept of process and his emerging social theory of interrelations, but it is important to remember that Olson did not read Whitehead's philosophy until 1955, almost half a decade after he had written his major theoretical prose relating to projective practice. Hence, Olson would have welcomed Whitehead's materialist ontology as a parallel endeavour to his own.

12 A former friend of Olson's during his involvement in the Roosevelt administration, Wilbur Hugh Ferry was the director of public relations for the CIO Political Action Committee and founded the center for the Study of Democratic Institutions in New York.

13 Commenting on an essay Olson penned in 1965 entitled "The Projective, in Poetry and in Thought; and the Paratactic," Donald Allen observes that increasingly Olson's interest in the projective became broadly "phenomenological" (*Collected Prose* 424), ranging beyond the catechism of Olson's

literary focus. These documents suggest that this was not a later development in Olson's thought, but his motivation from the very outset.

14 For an excellent assessment of Fenollosa's influence on Olson, see Sherman Paul, *Olson's Push: Origin, Black Mountain, and recent American Poetry*, 40–3.

15 Duncan's "Equilibrations" and his lecture with Michael Palmer entitled "Field Theory," Denise Levertov's "On the Function of the Line," Amiri Baraka's "How You Sound??" and several of Creeley's poetic statements, but in particular, "Notes for a New Prose," "To Define," and "A Note on Poetry," affords a shortlist of manifestoes that illustrate the use of field composition.

16 See Charles O. Hartman, *Free Verse: An Essay on Prosody*; Robert Frank and Henry Sayre, eds., *The Line in Postmodern Poetry*; and Rory Holscher and Robert Schultz, eds., "Symposium on the Theory and Practice of the Line in Contemporary Poetry," 162–224. Frank and Sayre's collection included several excellent articles by Perloff, Caws, Sandra M. Gilbert, Charles Bernstein, James Scully, and others. Holscher and Schultz's symposium collates brief statements on the poetic line by approximately thirty poets.

17 Olson explains the role of the typewriter in notating voice: "[i]t is the advantage of the typewriter that, due to its rigidity and its space precisions, it can, for a poet, indicate exactly the breath, the pauses, the suspensions even of syllables, the juxtapositions even of parts of phrases" (*PV* 245).

18 Reference to the "Projective Verse" essay appears in their first exchange of letters (albeit with a slightly altered title); it does not appear in *Poetry New York* until October 1950. Creeley's contribution to the final draft of the manuscript is substantial. The first version contains three sections and approximately 1750 words, while the final draft contains only two sections, extending to more than 4500 words in length. Fewer than 700 words from the original text (less than half) remain either verbatim or partially revised in the final essay. Most notably, Olson's objectist stance is present in the early manuscript, along with a somewhat less clearly articulated statement on the significance of the typewriter for notating the rhythms of poetic speech, but the principles of field composition had not yet been written. He had formulated objectism as a stance towards reality, but he had not yet devised a system of versification that would correspond to his theory of being in the world. Analysis of Creeley's letters to Olson during the intervening months demonstrates a substantial contribution in regards to this issue exactly. Between the time the first of their letters was sent on 21 April 1950, and the last time either poet mentions the "Projective Verse" essay before its publication, the two men had already exchanged a total of

sixty-four letters. No fewer than sixteen of these afford substantial discussion of the essay and poetic method.

19   Olson relies on Pound's concept of the "musical phrase," a prosody the latter contrasts with verse composed "in the sequence of a metronome" ("A Retrospect" 3). In *The Dance of the Intellect*, Marjorie Perloff argues quite rightly that Pound's aesthetic influence on a generation of American poets is radically undermined in subsequent decades by critics embarrassed by Pound's valorization of Italian fascism. Both Olson and Creeley did understand the value, but neither could be apologists for Pound's fascist sympathies or his anti-Semitic remarks. Olson might have simply disavowed Pound's political leanings and appropriated elements of his aesthetic method, but to do so would presuppose that the political and aesthetic are separate spheres; instead, he affords a competing politicization of Pound's method. In the passage cited above, Olson substitutes the "metronome" for the military "march," giving Pound's famous dictum "to break the pentameter" (LXXXI, *Cantos* 553) an additional meaning: poetic feet, like actual ones, are policed when subject to predetermined metrical formations.

20   Derek Attridge introduces the term "four-by-four" to describe all metrical stanzas in English containing four lines and four beats per line. See Attridge, "Dancing Language," *Poetic Rhythm: An Introduction*, 43–62.

21   See Ralph Maud, *What Does Not Change*, 37; George Butterick, "Charles Olson's 'The Kingfishers' and the Poetics of Change," 56.

22   The excerpted letter also appears in Butterick, "Charles Olson's 'The Kingfishers' and the Poetics of Change," 58, n.15.

23   Butterick notes that Olson's acquaintance and expert on Chinese politics Owen Lattimore was systematically alienated by the "power anti-Communist 'China Lobby'" for pro-China remarks ("Charles Olson's 'The Kingfishers'" 40), while his friend and colleague Ben Shahn (with whom Olson would undertake an artistic collaboration at BMC) was investigated by the FBI and eventually blacklisted for making political posters dubbed "pro-communist." See George Butterick, "Charles Olson's 'The Kingfishers' and the Poetics of Change," 28–69, and Frances K. Pohl, *Ben Shahn: New Deal Artist in a Cold War Climate, 1947–1954*, 1–2. For an account of the FBI's investigation of BMC, see Duberman, *Black Mountain College: An Exploration in Community*, 495.

24   Cage describes the visit in an interview with Mary Emma Harris in 1974: "[t]hey agreed to put us up and to feed us … We had parked it in front of that building where the studies were, and hadn't used it while we were there. So that when we drove it back, we discovered this large pile of

presents that all the students and faculty had put under the car in lieu of any payment. It included, for instance, oh, paintings and food and drawings, and so on" (*Conversing with Cage* 14). Richard Kostelanetz's *Conversing with Cage* collates numerous interviews with the artist over the course of his life. This very useful book for Cage scholars is organized thematically (excerpting no fewer than one hundred sources), many of which remained unpublished until the publication of Kostelanetz's collection. To avoid confusion, I cite the original interviewer and give page numbers for Kostelanetz's book.

25 Allan Kaprow coins the term in "18 Happenings in 6 Parts" (1959).

26 Faculty members at Black Mountain would have certainly been aware of Robert Motherwell's *The Dada Painters and Poets*, published just one year earlier in 1951.

27 For general studies of the happening within the context of Fluxus, see Jon Hendricks, *Fluxus Codex*; Hannah Higgins, *Fluxus Experience*; and Ken Friedman, *The Fluxus Reader*. For studies that situate the emergence of the happening in relation to mixed media, assemblage, and environment art, see Allan Kaprow, "Assemblages, Environments, & Happenings," 235–45; Adrian Henri, *Environment and Happenings*; and Mariellen R. Sandford, ed., *Happenings and Other Acts* (in particular, Michael Kirby's article, "Happenings: An Introduction," 1–28). For a study of the happening within the context of contemporary theatre, see Richard Kostelanetz, *The Theatre of Mixed Means: An Introduction to Happenings, Kinetic Environments, and other Mixed-Means Performances*.

28 In "McLuhan's Influence" Cage makes a similar contention: "When, in 1961, I wrote my lecture *Where Are We Going? and What Are We Doing?*, which is four lectures heard at one and the same time, it was in awareness of McLuhan's point that nowadays everything happens at once, not just one thing at a time." See *John Cage: An Anthology*, 170.

29 The following description of Cage's happening at Black Mountain is indebted to several sources. The most consistent representation of events comes from Cage himself, in a series of interviews I cite throughout this chapter. I am also indebted to accounts provided by five participants and audience members: Katherine Litz, Merce Cunningham, Francine du Plessix Gray, Carroll Williams, and David Weinrib. Martin Duberman assembles these crucial early records from various interviews. See his *Black Mountain: An Exploration in Community*, 352–7.

30 Foremost among these conventions is plot structure. The happening indeed has a beginning and an end, but it lacks linear progression and narrative closure. Michael Kirby aptly observes that traditional theatre

virtually always "functions within (and creates) a matrix of time, place, and character," realist conventions that ultimately assemble a "manufactured reality" ("Happenings: An Introduction," 5).

31   Charles Olson, "The Present is Prologue," 39–40.

32   The letter in question was sent to several poets, but only a few copies are extant. I quote from the letter Ignatow sent to Langston Hughes, dated 22 January 1960. Passages from the letter are reproduced in Brett Miller, "*Chelsea* 8: Political Poetry at Midcentury," 93–4.

33   Readers can trace the poem's genesis by consulting Olson's notes and essays written between 1945 to 1953, collected in *OLSON: The Journal of the Charles Olson Archives* 5 (Spring 1976). The following selections are particularly useful: "Key West I" and "Key West II" (1945), "An Outline of a Projected Poem called WEST" (c. 1946), "WEST" (1948), "West" (1953), and "POST-WEST" (c. 1953).

34   Olson's resistance to the totalizing project of the conventional narrative is equally apparent in the text's structural logic. Olson would follow the first volume of *The Maximus Poems* with two more: *The Maximus Poems IV, V, VI* (1968) and *The Maximus Poems: Volume Three* (1975), the latter of which was published posthumously with Olson's instructions. The 1960 edition of the first volume contains no explicit division into three sections, which would indicate continuity with the second volume. Similarly, volume three is not enumerated but written as a word, again disrupting any clear sequential logic with the preceding volume. Olson's long poem bears no symmetrical structure or preconceived system; instead, the poem mutates formally along its own trajectory.

35   The inscription is taken from the nineteenth-century American poet Emma Lazarus's poem "The New Colossus." In the text, the quoted lines are spoken by the statue.

36   Butterick records the slogans from advertisements in *Time* magazine, published on 16 March and 13 April 1953.

37   For an extended account of Olson and Corman's discussion of *Origin* and the implications of the little magazine for the literary community, see George Evans, ed., *Charles Olson & Cid Corman: Complete Correspondence, 1950–1964*, 27–82.

38   In *Career Moves: Olson, Creeley, Zukofsky, Berrigan, and the American Avant-Garde*, the critic Libbie Rifkin chooses to read Olson and Creeley's "alliance" as "a key axis of power in the poetry wars of the next decade and following," arguing further that the impetus for their literary ambitions were "driven ... by professional imperative" (44, 54). Rifkin's method is to begin, as it were, toward the end of Olson's literary career,

taking his "Berkeley Lecture" as a key, reading backward through the development of his and Creeley's sociopoetics. This method allows her to conclude that Olson's plan to secure a spot in the canonical ranks of American verse is at the core of his poetic ambitions. Any act of community formation – by way of their correspondences, the *Black Mountain Review*, or Black Mountain College – she interprets as actions meant to promote their careers. Rifkin's generally excellent book is meant to counter the honorific criticism of the American mid-century avant-garde, and should be read in this precise context. Yet it should be said that Black Mountain College functioned on the most modest of operating budgets, affording salaries to its faculty members that barely covered the cost of living. Accusations of careerism seem an exaggeration. Rifkin is talking of course about cultural currency, yet the poets under consideration were not canonized in Donald Allen's anthology until 1960. The Berkeley lectures that Rifkin cites as evidence for their professional ambitions takes place in 1965, while the "years of Olson and Creeley" in the critical presses does not happen until 1979, almost twenty full years after their first contact. In contrast to this assertion, consider the following statement by Brian Kim Stefans: "I would ask you to return to the numerous staple-bound, yellowing and otherwise low-tech and low-print-run publications that were circulating in the 70s and 80s when they were first looking at each other's poetry and seeing a common set of interests developing, and cite those instances where you think (1) any of the those poets thought they were writing in a style that would eventually become something like the norm in academic studies, [and] … (2) where you think that this 'careerism' seriously or even moderately compromised the general goal, aura or collective effort at investigation [?]" (http://www.writing.upenn.edu/~afilreis/88/stefans-institutionalization.html). Stefans's comment is directed at Standard Schaefer's critique of the Language Group, yet his incisive questions are equally relevant here. (The essay in question is Schaefer's "Preliminary Notes on Literary Politics.")

39 Series 2, Box 4, Folder 8, Robert Creeley Papers, Stanford University Library, n.d.
40 After substandard performances in his course work, Creeley decided to take a leave of absence. Although the request was granted by the administration, university representatives later informed him that readmission was unlikely. See Ekbert Faas, *Robert Creeley: A Biography*, 27–31.
41 See Creeley's essay, "On the Road: Notes on Artists & Poets, 1950–1965," 367–76.

42   The perceived anecdotal quality of the lyrics in *For Love* prompts critics
     like Bernstein to favour those later texts that establish a clearer lineage
     with the "radical poetics" of the Language Group, or von Hallberg to read
     For Love's formal procedures as nascent examples of the more mature se-
     quential logic of texts such as *Numbers*. See Bernstein, "Hearing 'Here':
     Robert Creeley's Poetics of Duration," 87–95; von Hallberg, "Robert Cree-
     ley and the Pleasures of System," 365–79; and Marjorie Perloff, "Rob-
     ert Creeley's Radical Poetics," http://www.electronicbookreview.com/
     thread/electropoetics/commodious.

43   In "Hart Crane and the Private Judgment," Creeley quotes a lengthy yet
     telling passage from Crane's letters to Allen Tate: "[i]t is a new feeing, and
     a glorious one, to have one's inmost delicate intentions so fully recognized
     as your last letter to me attested. I can feel a calmness on the sidewalk –
     where before I felt a defiance only. And better than all – I am certain that a
     number of us at last have some kind of community of interest. And with
     this communion will come something better than a mere clique. It is a
     consciousness of something more vital than stylistic questions and 'taste,'
     it is vision, and a vision alone that not only America needs, but the whole
     world" (14). Crane's "vision" of a "community of interest" likely fore-
     grounds his "visionary company of love" in "The Broken Tower." Rather
     than probe "inward," seeking a psychological explanation for Crane's sui-
     cide, Creeley presses outward towards an external context for his suffer-
     ing – to the community that let him down.

44   Otto Rank was a noted Austrian psychoanalyst and one of Sigmund
     Freud's closest colleagues. Creeley's letters to Leed suggest that he had
     read Rank's *Art and Artist* in 1948.

45   Creeley rightly rebukes Grover Smith, who offers the irresponsible com-
     plaint "that the neurotic irresponsibility of his [Crane's] private life and
     loves was directly synchronous with the undisciplined fancy manifest in
     his poetic images" ("Hart Crane" 14). The reader should note the subtext
     of homophobia in such a proclamation.

46   For extended bibliographic studies of Creeley's earlier work, see Timo-
     thy Murray and Stephen Boardway, "Year By Year Bibliography of Robert
     Creeley," 313–74, and Mary Novik, *Robert Creeley: An Inventory, 1945–1970*.

47   For a complete list of Creeley's collaborations with artists, see the excel-
     lent exhibition catalogue by Amy Cappellazzo and Elizabeth Licata, *In
     Company: Robert Creeley's Collaborations*, 102–7. See also Creeley's most can-
     did assessment of the artists who influenced his work during the 1950s
     and 1960s: "On the Road: Notes on Artists & Poets, 1950–1965," 367–76.

48 Marjorie Perloff, "Robert Creeley's Radical Poetics," http://www.elec-tronicbookreview.com/thread/electropoetics/commodious.

49 Novik records the following bibliographic description: "*A Snarling Garland of Xmas Verses.* By Anonymous. [Palma de Mallorca: The Divers Press, Xmas 1954.] 'Handset in Menhart and Grasset Antijua types and printed on laid papers in a limited edition. This is a Wallet pocket-book.' Booklet of poems, mainly for friends. *Ca.* 100 copies; unpaged, one sheet folded into several pages, attached to paper wrappers. MS: 1103. Contents: Poems: *Chanson, *Hi There!, *Don't Sign Anything, *Sopa, *The Conspiracy" (*An Inventory* 5).

50 Creeley remarks to Olson: "yrself, one of the damn few concerned with a method/ that can get to the shape, be the shape, of yr content. Just there, for that reason, is my respect. Not knowing you, but for these letters, and they, much help tho they are, cannot make the point altogether. Well, that is why I should like to see you/ if & when you will be in NE" (*Correspondence* 1:118).

51 Gerhardt translated and published works by T.S. Eliot, William Carlos Williams, Ezra Pound, Basil Bunting, and Creeley, among others.

52 Creeley and his wife Ann had moved to France in the spring of 1951, just as *Origin #1* appeared in print – first to Paris for a few days before settling in Fontrousse in the south of France. While in the city, Creeley encountered a multinational group of poets, which included the "obdurate and resourceful Scot" Alexander Trocchi; the British poet Christopher Logue; the eventual editor of Grove Press, Richard Seaver; and translators Austryn Wainhouse and Patrick Bowles (the latter of whom translated Samuel Becket's first novel into English), who together published in the little magazine, *Merlin* ("On *Black Mountain Review*" 254). Creeley was most interested in the function of their magazine as a site of literary exchange and community; there was a collective will among the members of the Paris group, recounts Creeley, "to change the situation of literary context and evaluation … [T]heir brilliant critical writing, which extended to political thinking as well as literary, made them an exceptional example of what a group of writers might do" (254).

53 For an extended account of Creeley's experience in post-war Germany, see Ekbert Faas, *Robert Creeley: A Biography*, 107–14.

54 Duncan makes this remark in the jacket copy of *Roots and Branches* (New Directions, 1969): "I am not an experimentalist or an inventor, but a derivative poet." This assertion echoes his claim in "Pages from a Notebook" (1953), which appeared just after Olson's "Projective Verse" in Donald

Allen's formative anthology, *The New American Poetry*: "I am ambitious only to emulate, imitate, reconstrue, approximate, duplicate" (406).

55 Duncan continues, "there is a *virtu* or power that flows from the language itself, a fountain of man's meanings, and the poet seeking the help of this source awakens first to the guidance of those who have gone before in the art" (*The HD Book* 63–4).

56 On the subject of this correspondence, see Marjorie Perloff, "Poetry in Time of War: The Duncan-Levertov Controversy," in *Poetry On & Off the Page: Essays for Emergent Occasions*, 208–21; Anne Dewey, "Poetic Authority and the Public Sphere of Politics in the Activist 1960s: The Duncan-Levertov Debate," 109–25; and Michael Davidson, "A Cold War Correspondence: The Letters of Robert Duncan and Denise Levertov," 538–56.

57 Levertov explains to Duncan in a letter dated December 1967: "[l]ecture and poetry-reading engagements provide an excellent opportunity for war-resisters to tell potential sympathizers what is going on, to activate the apathetic, to encourage isolated activists, and to alleviate their isolation by helping to put them in touch with one another" (*The Letters* 597).

58 The Public Broadcast Lab was a precursor to the Public Broadcast System.

59 Seth Rosenfeld, "The Governor's Race," http://www.sfgate.com/cgi-bin/article.cgi?f=/c/a/2002/06/09/MNCF3.DTL.

60 The Berkeley Manifesto, "What People Can Do," and Black Panther support button appear on pages 46 and 68 in Levertov's *To Stay Alive*. The button has the words "Free All Political Prisoners"; the manifesto:

WHAT PEOPLE CAN DO
1. Be in the streets – they're ours!
2. Report any action you have witnessed or been involved in that should be broadcast to keep the people informed. Especially call to report the location of any large group of people, so those people who may have been separated may regroup …
3. The Free Church and Oxford Hall medical aid stations need medical supplies, especially:
   -gauze pads
   -adhesive tape
   -plastic squeeze bottles
4. PLEASE do not go to the Free Church unless you have need to.
5. Photographers and filmmakers: Contact Park Media Committee
6. Bail money will be collected at tables outside the COOP grocery stores:
   -Telegraph Ave. store: Monday

-University Ave. store: Tuesday
-Shattuck Ave. store: Wed. & Thurs.
7. BRING YOUR KITE AND FLY IT. Use nylon strings. Fly it when you are with a crowd. A helicopter cannot fly too near flying kites.
8. Be your brothers' and sisters' keeper.
9. Take care.

61 See Robert J. Bertholf, "Decision at the Apogee: Robert Duncan's Anarchist Critique of Denise Levertov," 1–17, and Andy Weaver, "The Political Use of Formal Anarchy in Robert Duncan's *Ground Work* Volumes" (conference paper).

62 R.J. Bertholf offers an excellent historical account of the anarchist influences that inform Duncan's critique of Levertov's protest verse, drawing from a host of writings from Trotsky, Kropotkin, and Rudolph Rocker. One should be cautious, however, not to assume that anarchism is a homogenous and organized body of thought. It is more accurate to say that Duncan synthesizes elements of individualism and social anarchism, but given his suspicion of highly organized forms of rebellion, its tendency to model the forms of oppression it sets out to oppose, it is unlikely he would have supported radical anarchist-syndicalism.

3. The Caribbean Artists Movement: A Poetic of Cultural Activism

1 Stuart Hall, "On Postmodernism and Articulation," 141.

2 Kamau Brathwaite, "Interview," by Anne Walmsley, Papers of the Caribbean Artists Movement, 6/9 (35–6), George Padmore Institute, London, UK.

3 One might also point to the similarities between it and Foucault's distinction between "subjugated" and "erudite" knowledges, by which the theorist refers "to a whole series of knowledges, as insufficiently elaborated knowledges: naïve knowledges, hierarchically inferior knowledges, knowledges that are *below* the required level of erudition or scientificity. And it is thanks to the reappearance of these knowledges from *below* … a particular knowledge, a knowledge that is local, regional, or differential, incapable of unanimity and which derives its power solely from the fact that it is different from all the knowledges that surround it, it is the reappearance of what people know at a local level, of these disqualified knowledges, that made the critique possible" (*Society Must Be Defended* 7–8; my italics).

4 Brathwaite frequently enjambs single words, either by line break or period stop, in order to accentuate a sign's multiple, often contradictory,

significations. Often this strategy exposes the power relations at play in a single word. See my extended discussion of this convention later in the chapter.

5 The older generation of Caribbean writers in London, such as V.S. Naipaul and George Lamming, expressed little interest in the group. Among the principal forerunners of Caribbean-born, London-based writers, C.L.R. James is the exception. Although he was not a regular participant, he gave enthusiastic encouragement to Brathwaite and others, and delivered a lecture at one of CAM's public meetings.

6 S.K. Ruck, ed., *The West Indian Comes to England: A Report Prepared for the Trustees of the London Parochial Charities by the Family Welfare Association*, 51. Peter Fryer puts the numbers at roughly 125,000. See *Staying Power: The History of Black Power in Britain*, 372.

7 The novels of Colin MacInnes document the racially mixed communities of Notting Hill during the 1950s and 1960s. See, in particular, *City of Spades* (1957), *Absolute Beginners* (1959), and *Mr. Love and Justice* (1960).

8 In the following year, Claudia Jones began the West Indian Culture in St Pancras event, which would be the key predecessor for the Notting Hill Carnival. These events were conceived in response to the 1958 riot.

9 Brathwaite at this time published *Four Plays for Primary Schools* and *Odale's Choice*.

10 For a fuller biographical account of Brathwaite's activities during the 1950s and 1960s, see his "Timehri," 35–44; Louis James, "Caribbean Artists Movement," 209–27; and Anne Walmsley, *The Caribbean Artists Movement, 1966–1972: A Literary & Cultural History*, 39–43.

11 While in St Lucia, Brathwaite met and collaborated with Roderick Walcott, Dunstan St Omer, and Harry Simmons.

12 See Bridget Jones, "'The Unity is Submarine': Aspects of a Pan-Caribbean Consciousness in the work of Kamau Brathwaite," 86–100.

13 Salkey would interview King, Jr three times.

14 See Walmsley, *Caribbean Artist Movement, 1966–1972: A Literary & Cultural History*, 20.

15 See Walmsley, *The Caribbean Artists Movement, 1966–1972: A Literary and Cultural History*; Louis James, "The Caribbean Artists Movement," 209–27; The John La Rose Tribute Committee, eds., *Foundations of a Movement: A Tribute to John La Rose on the Occasion of the 10th International Book Fair of Radical Black and Third World Books*; and Brian W. Alleyne, *Radicals Against Race: Black Activism and Cultural Politics*, 31–40.

16 New Beacon relocated to 76 Stroud Green Road in 1973, and is still open today.

17   For a comprehensive account of the Black Parents Movement and the
     George Padmore Supplementary School, see Brian W. Alleyne, "Cultural
     Revolutionaries," in *Radicals Against Race*, 51–78.
18   Hall states further: within "black cultural production, we are beginning to
     see … a new cultural politics which engages rather than suppresses *differ-
     ence* and which depends, in part, on the cultural construction of new eth-
     nic identities" ("New Ethnicities" 446).
19   I use Peter Hallward's translations of Glissant. See Hallward, "Édouard
     Glissant between the Singular and the Specific," 441–64.
20   Brathwaite's terminology shares features with "transculturation," a term
     originally coined by the Cuban sociologist Fernando Ortiz during the
     1940s, and later adapted to literary study by critics like Angel Rama, Mary
     Louise Pratt, and Michael Taussig. The concept refers to the ways in which
     subordinate groups select and modify materials imposed on them by
     dominant cultures. Thus, Pratt describes the reciprocity between cultures
     as "contact zones," where "disparate cultures meet, clash and grapple
     with each other, often in highly asymmetrical relations of dominance and
     subordination" (*Imperial Eyes* 7). See Fernando Ortiz, *Contrapunto Cubano*;
     and Mary Louise Pratt, *Imperial Eyes: Travel Writing and Transculturation*.
21   Nancy remarks: "[I]n a *mêlée* there are meetings and encounters; there are
     those who come together and those who spread out, those who come into
     contact and those who enter into contracts, those who concentrate and
     those who disseminate, those who identify and those who modify – just
     like the two sexes in each one of us." He continues, "[c]ultures, or what
     are known as cultures, do not mix. They encounter each another, mingle,
     modify each other, reconfigure each other. They cultivate one another;
     they irrigate or drain each other; they work over and plough through each
     other, or graft one onto the other" (*Being Singular Plural* 151).
22   John La Rose, "Poetry" (A reading and discussion), Papers of the Carib-
     bean Artists Movement, 5/3/2 (2), George Padmore Institute, London,
     UK.
23   See Gates Jr, *The Signifying Monkey: A Theory of Afro-American Literary Criti-
     cism*, 44–88.
24   Kamau Brathwaite, "Glossary," 271.
25   For accounts of Brathwaite's treatment of historical themes, see Paul Nay-
     lor, *Poetic Investigations: Singing the Holes in History*, and Gordon Rohlehr,
     Pathfinder: Black Awakening in The Arrivants and "The Rehumanization
     of History: Regeneration of Spirit: Apocalypse and Revolution in Brath-
     waite's *The Arrivants* and *X/Self*," 163–207; for studies that place Brath-
     waite's work in relation to Caribbean poetics, see Jahan Ramazani, *The*

Hybrid Muse: Postcolonial Poetry in English, Edward Chamberlin, *Come Back to Me My Language: Poetry and the West Indies*, and Emily Allen Williams, *Poetic Negotiations of Identity in the Works of Brathwaite, Harris, Senior, and Dabydeen*; for T.S. Eliot's influence, see Lee M. Jenkins, "The t/reasonable 'English' of Kamau Brathwaite," 95–125, and Charles W. Pollard, *New World Modernisms*; for an appraisal of Brathwaite's use of the epic form, see June D. Bobb, *Beating a Restless Drum: The Poetics of Kamau Brathwaite and Derek Walcott*. Additionally, editor Stewart Brown's *The Art of Kamau Brathwaite* and Timothy J. Reiss's *For the Geography of a Soul: Emerging Perspectives* both contain excellent essays devoted to a wide range of works spanning several decades, while editor Emily Allen Williams's *The Critical Response to Kamau Brathwaite* collects contemporary reviews of the author's major collections.

26 Sometimes referred to as "Bussa's Rebellion," the leader was born a free man in Africa, captured by slave traders, and sold to a plantation owner in Barbados. The revolt began on 14 April 1816, and was carried out against several sugar estates by four hundred drivers, field workers, and artisans. Bussa died during the uprising, but the symbolic value of an organized rebellion against colonial rule encouraged and emboldened future victories for equality in Barbados. Bussa later became a figure of national heroism for Barbadians.

27 See J. Omosade Awolalu and P. Adelumo Dopamu, *West African Traditional Religion*; E.A. Ade Adegbola, ed., *Traditional Religion in West Africa*; E.B. Idowu, *African Traditional Religion: A Definition*; A. Adogame, R. Gerloff, and K. Hock, eds., *Christianity in Africa and the African Diaspora: The Appropriation of a Scattered Heritage*; Melville Herskovits, *Life in a Haitian Valley*; Zora Neal Hurston, *Tell My Horse: Voodoo and Life in Haiti and Jamaica*; Roger Bastide, *African Civilizations in the New World*; and Robert Farris Thompson's *Flash of the Spirit: African and Afro-American Art and Philosophy*.

28 Ananse becomes "Aunt Nancy" in the Uncle Remus stories of southern United States folktales.

29 The Mau Mau uprising took place between 1952 and 1960, and precipitated Kenyan independence from British Colonial rule in 1963. The resistance was formed by a combination of Kikuyu, Embu, and Meru ethnic groups. Brathwaite cites the revolt as the first major African opposition to European imperialism. The author likely drew upon the pan-ethnic movement as a model for the culturally diverse Caribbean region.

30 The stories given to Ananse have come to be known as the Anansesem. See Stephen Krensky, *Anansi and the Box of Stories: A West African Folktale*.

31 For an extended account of Ogun's function in Haiti's religious and political culture, see Sandra T. Barnes, ed., *Africa's Ogun: Old World and New*, 2nd ed.

32 Peter Hallward, "Our Role in Haiti's Plight," http://www.guardian .co.uk/commentisfree/2010/jan/13/our-role-in-haitis-plight. See also Hallward, *Damming the Flood: Haiti, Aristide, and the Politics of Containment*.

33 See Aimé Césaire, *Toussaint Louverture: La Révolution Française et le Problème Colonial*; and C.L.R. James, *The Black Jacobins: Toussaint L'Ouverture and the San Domingo Revolution*.

34 I paraphrase Rohlehr's description of the ceremony, who in turn cites Robert S. Rattray, *Ashanti*, 109–10.

35 See Octave Mannoni, *Prospero and Caliban: The Psychology of Colonization*; Frantz Fanon, *Black Skin: White Masks*; Philip Mason, *Prospero's Magic*; Aimé Césaire, *Une Tempete: Adaptation Pour une Théâtre Negre*; and Rob Nixon, "Caribbean and African Appropriations of *The Tempest*," 185–206. For specific reference to Brathwaite's work, see, in particular, Silvio Torres-Saillant, "Caliban's Betrayal: A New Inquiry into the Caribbean," 221–44, and Gordon Rohlehr, "'Black, Sycorax, My Mother': Brathwaite's Reconstruction of *The Tempest*," 277–96.

36 Milton justifies his choice of blank verse in a prefatory note to *Paradise Lost*: "Not without cause … both Italian and Spanish poets of prime note have rejected rhyme both in longer and shorter works, as have also long since our best English tragedies, as a thing of itself, to all judicious ears, trivial and of no true musical delight; which consists only in apt numbers, fit quantity of syllables, and the sense variously drawn out from one verse into another, not in the jingling sound of like endings, a fault avoided by the learned ancients both in poetry and all good oratory" (4).

37 Forty-two tonnes of toxic methylisocyanate gas was released in a densely populated city of more than half a million people. See Ingrid Eckerman, *The Bhopal Saga: Causes and Consequences of the World's Largest Industrial Disaster*.

38 I retain the term "Third World" where members of the Caribbean Artists Movement employ this term, and also to reflect the significant role of globalization in Cold War politics.

39 The Havana Cultural Congress took place in 4–11 January 1968 in Cuba's capital city. The two symposia, "Cuba of the Third World" and "Second Symposium on Havana Congress," took place on 5 April and 3 May 1968 at the West Indian Student Centre.

40 See David Craven's excellent survey, *Art and Revolution in Latin America, 1910–1990*, 92.
41 Brandon, "Attack us at your peril, cocky Cuba warns US."
42 For an excellent assessment of the internationalist project of Cuban painters and poster art, see David Craven, *Art and Revolution in Latin America, 1910–1990.*
43 This transition from national to international concerns is best demonstrated by comparing Salkey's first book of poems, an epic entitled *Jamaica Symphony* (1953), with his poetic writings from the 1970s. His collections *Away* and *In the Hills Where Her Dreams Live* typify a new internationalist politics.
44 For surveys of Caribbean and Latin American Marxism, see Donald C. Hodges, *The Latin American Revolution: Politics and Strategy from Apro-Marxism to Guevarism*; Armando Hart, *Marxism and the Human Condition: A Latin American Perspective*; Michael Löwy, ed., *Marxism in Latin America from 1909 to the Present: An Anthology*, trans. Michael Pearlman; Charles D. Ameringer, *The Socialist Impulse: Latin America in the Twentieth Century*; and Holger Henke and Fred Réno, *Modern Political Culture in the Caribbean*. For a study of the socialist impulse in Latin American literature, see David Craven, *Art and Revolution in Latin America, 1910–1990.*
45 For a concise account of the organization and its effects on Trinidad's history, see Colin A. Palmer, *Eric Williams & the Making of the Modern Caribbean*, 290 ff.
46 Salkey's allusions to a "New Havana" and the traces of "Che Guevera['s]" trip through Chile should remind readers that in addition to being fervently anti-Marxist and pro-capitalist, Pinochet drew "inspiration" from the National Security Doctrine. Historian Lois Hecht Oppenheim observes that the "U.S. anticommunist counterinsurgency training of Latin American militaries" was formulated in direct response to "the Cuban revolution of 1959" (*Politics in Chile* 111).
47 In the 1970 election, Salvador Allende, representing the Popular Unity party, led a coalition that included the Communist Party, the Socialist Party, the Radical Party, the Movement for United Popular Action, Independent Popular Action, and the Social Democratic Party. Allende's coalition won 36.2 per cent, securing a minority government (the right-wing candidate, Jorge Alessandri, received 34.9 and the centrist candidate, Radomiro Tomic, 27.8 per cent, respectively). Tomic's Christian Democrats threw their support behind Allende, casting their congressional votes on his behalf. See Lois Hecht Oppenheim, *Politics in Chile: Democracy, Authoritarianism, and the Search for Development*, 36.

48 The 1991 National Commission for Truth and Reconciliation Report put
the death toll at 2,279. Perhaps even more shocking than the number of
dead is the precision with which Pinochet's Junta targeted subversives.
Members of the Allende government, the Movement of the Revolutionary
Left, the Socialist Party, the Communist Party, union leaders, and members of peasant-run cooperatives were systematically executed, while
thousands more were subject to torture.

For studies of Chilean history and politics during the Allende and Pinochet years, see Oppenheim, *Politics in Chile: Democracy, Authoritarianism,
and the Search for Development*; Sergio Bitar, *Chile: Experiment in Democracy*;
Paul E. Sigmund, *The Overthrow of Allende and the Politics of Chile, 1964–
1976*; and Manuel A. Garretón Merino, *The Chilean Political Process*.

49 In December 1971, affluent women associated with the right-wing opposition to Popular Unity staged what is now an infamous demonstration
known as the "March of the Empty Pots." Wealthy elites protested the
so-called food shortage by having their maids march in Santiago's down-
town sector. Oppenheim recounts that "although they were far from without food, the government's policy of increasing workers' salaries, coupled
with its efforts to ensure that food reached grocery stores in popular
neighborhoods, had, in fact, decreased the food supplied to the more well-
to-do areas" (*Politics in Chile* 64).

50 The group launched a failed coup (known as the Tanquetazo) in July 1973;
attempted to sabotage government infrastructure projects; successfully
assassinated a pro-Allende naval official, Arturo Araya; and routinely received strategic and fiscal support from the U.S. government. Historians
Michael Stohl and George A. Lopez record that "at least $7 million was
authorized by the United States for CIA use in the destabilizing of Chilean society. This included financing and assisting opposition groups and
right-wing terrorist paramilitary groups such as Patria y Libertad ('Fatherland and Liberty')." See *The State as Terrorist: The Dynamics of Governmental Violence and Repression*, 51. Ex-leader of the group's military operations
Roberto Theime confessed to U.S. marine involvement in plots to destroy
bridges and pipelines. See *Confesiones de un ex Patria y Libertad*, Television
Nacional de Chile (TVN), 12 February 2006.

51 Notably, Fatherland and Liberty was created in 1970 by Pablo Rodriguez
Grez in the hallways of the Catholic University of Chile. This is important
because the Catholic University had been for twenty years the academic
front for American interference into South American economic planning.
Two decades previously, Santiago had become the centre of a post-war
Keynesian-style New Deal in the Southern Cone. Uruguay, Argentina, and

Chile elected socialist governments that drastically increased funding sub-
sidies for small businesses, funding for public infrastructure, schools, and
health care, while they implemented heavier tariffs on foreign imports.
Fearing the spread of socialist economic theory throughout the continent,
Albion Patterson, director of the U.S. International Cooperation Administration in Chile, and Theodore W. Schultz, chair of the Economics Department at the University of Chicago, sought to establish a school espousing
free-market principles in Santiago. Together the two men established a
program known as "The Chile Project." The U.S. government, along with
corporate interests such as the Ford Foundation, funded an exchange programme that brought South American students to the University of Chicago to be trained by Milton Friedman and his colleagues. Emerging from
this partnership was the Center for Latin American Economic Studies and
the "Chile Workshop." And indeed, this is what Chile became – a workshop for the Chicago School to impose its economic doctrines. By 1970,
students educated at Chicago arrived back in Santiago with Friedman's
Capitalism and Freedom as their guidebooks (in 1963, twelve of thirteen
economics professors at the Catholic University received degrees from
the University of Chicago) (Klein 72). For a concise history of the Chicago
School's activities in Chile, see Klein, "The Other Doctor Shock: Milton
Friedman and the Search for a Laissez-Faire Laboratory," *Shock Doctrine*,
56–83.

52 See Oppenheim, *Politics in Chile*, 61.

53 Unsurprisingly, the American government and the multinational concerns
were furious. The United States retaliated by attempting to destabilize
the Chilean economy: first, by withholding loans and credits from international lending organizations; and second, by secretly funding opposition groups within the country, including Fatherland and Liberty and the
right-wing newspaper *El Mercurio*.

54 Contrary to some accounts that characterized this decision as theft, farm
owners were compensated for lost land and retained all livestock and
machinery. During the initial years of Allende's rule, there were more aggressive land seizures, particularly by Mapuche Indians who capitalized
on the legal reform to reappropriate lands previously occupied by native
communities (Oppenheim 54–6).

55 Mariategui famously stated that "Inca communism ... cannot be negated
or disparaged for having developed under [an] autocratic regime."*Seven
Interpretive Essays*, 35] Clans (or "ayllus") within the Incan empire practiced communal ownership of land and resources. Often these clans
would ignore genealogical bloodlines and cooperate together. Mariategui

is specifically referencing this social structure within Incan society as a proto-communist indigenous economic system.

56 Victor Jara was a figure with whom writers like Salkey, Brathwaite, and La Rose identified. A teacher, theatre director, writer, singer, and activist, his writing was never a separate activity from politics and community, and like Neruda, he was a supporter of Allende's Popular Unity government. Along with thousands of other Chilean leftists, Jara was imprisoned in Chile's soccer stadium during the coup, where he was tortured and ultimately murdered.

57 Anne Walmsley affords a more sympathetic account of CAM's endeavours in the Caribbean. See *The Caribbean Artists Movement, 1966–1972*, 190–222.

58 See Horace Campbell, *Rasta and Resistance: From Marcus Garvey to Walter Rodney*, and Walter Rodney, *Groundings with My Brothers*.

59 The organization was founded by Trinidadian economist Lloyd Best in Georgetown, Guyana, in 1963. Walmsley quotes a passage from the New World group's membership form: "New World is a movement which aims to transform the mode of living and thinking in the region. The movement rejects uncritical acceptance of dogmas and ideologies imported from outside and bases its ideas for the future of the area on an unfettered analysis of the experience and existing conditions of the region" (qtd. in Walmsley, *Caribbean* 195). For discussions of the New World group, see also Selwyn D. Ryan, *Race and Nationalism in Trinidad and Tobago: A Study of Decolonization in a Multiracial Society*, 384 ff, and Herman L. Bennett, "The Challenge to the Post-Colonial State," 129–31.

60 For discussion of Yard Theatre's contribution to postcolonial theatre, see Christopher B. Balme, *Decolonizing the Stage: Theatrical Syncretism and Post-Colonial Drama*, 51 ff and 233 ff.

61 Brathwaite provides a detailed account of the theatre in "The Love Axe/1: Developing a Caribbean Aesthetic – Part Three," 181–92.

62 The final draft of this book will go to press just after the insurrectionary "riots" of August 2011 in London and throughout Britain. Sad, but entirely predictable, members of the ruling government and mainstream media immediately set to work dehumanizing the largely (but not exclusively) black rioters drawn from the nation's poorest communities, all the while applauding the revolutionaries in Egypt, Tunisia, and Libya taking up arms against their illegitimate, violent, and incompetent regimes. The abuse and subsequent self-immolation of a poor street vendor in the Arab world justifies insurrection on a national scale, but the fatal shooting of a young Black man in Tottenham does not. The racist polemic was

as fervent as it was instantaneous. British historian David Starkey, apparently more perturbed by the multiracial backgrounds of the rioters, decreed: "the whites have become black; a particular sort of violent, destructive, nihilistic gangster culture has become the fashion" (*Newsnight*, BBC). Of course, these actions by disaffected youth come on the heals of countless student protests, university occupations, and union marches challenging ruthless austerity measures enacted to dispossess further the very communities taking to the streets in London. Violent, destructive gangsterism aptly describes the predatory lending practices and securitization schemes of a U.S./European financial sector dutifully rewarded by the world's most powerful states. This is the backdrop to the riots the eminent British historian refuses to acknowledge. And although many commentators do indeed recognize this more immediate context, undoubtedly these events are part of a much longer political sequence. One could cite, for instance, the Notting Hill Riots of 1958 (in which four hundred white youths, many associated with neo-fascist groups, terrorized Caribbean immigrant communities), but it would seem that broadcasters at the BBC had the 1981 Brixton riots much on their minds, as Darcus Howe, a former member of the *Race Today* Collective, was summoned to play native informant to the political events unfolding. The interview is telling. What seems to rattle the interviewer most of all is Howe's comparison of London to ongoing insurrections in the Arab world, indeed, his explicit claim that these events are related.

4. The Women's Liberation Movement: A Poetic for a Common World

1   Hannah Arendt, *The Human Condition*, 55.
2   Alain Badiou, "The Communist Hypothesis," 38–9.
3   Robin Morgan, *Going Too Far*, 60–1.
4   Polly Joan and Andrea Chessman, *Guide to Women's Publishing*, 4.
5   For a historical overview of the Women's Liberation Movement, see Myra Marx Feree and Beth B. Hess, *Controversy and Coalition: The New Feminist Movement Across Three Decades of Change*; Alice Echols, *Daring to Be Bad: Radical Feminism in America, 1967–1975*; Barbara Ryan, *Feminism and the Women's Movement*; Kimberly Springer, *Living for the Revolution: Black Feminist Organizations, 1968–1980*; and Katie King, *Theory in its Feminist Travels: Conversations in U.S. Women's Movements*; for an excellent collection of autobiographical accounts, see Rachel Blau DuPlessis and Ann Snitow, eds., *The Feminist Memoir Project: Voices from the Women's Liberation Movement*.

6 See Rachel Blau DuPlessis, *Blue Studios: Poetry and its Cultural Work*, 66. No doubt antagonism between a feminism of "sameness/equality" and a feminism of "difference" persists as one of the chief debates in feminist poetics today. Kim Whitehead's critique of Alicia Ostriker's work is representative of this divide: "Ostriker assumes that a coherent, autonomous subjectivity is the only lived and poetic goal of women and that the end of the search for this subject position is the discovery of a single authentic femaleness that corresponds to an authentic maleness … While Ostriker and other critics like her consider this to be progress toward equality, I side with those critics who recognize differences among women and perceive feminist forms of liberal humanism as just additional acts of erasure" (*The Feminist*, 51).

7 Lorde, "Above the Wind," 62; Rich, "Conditions for Work" and "Origins and History of Consciousness," 205, 7–8; Judy Grahn, *The Work of the Common Woman* and *Really Reading Gertrude Stein*, 289.

8 See Michael Hardt and Antonio Negri, *Commonwealth*; Giorgio Agamben, *The Coming Community*; Paolo Virno, *Grammar of the Multitude*; Slavoj Žižek, *First as Trajedy, Then as Farce*; and Alain Badiou, *The Communist Hypothesis*.

9 In Margaret Benston's groundbreaking essay, "The Political Economy of Women's Liberation" (1970), the author sets out to critique the material conditions in capitalist societies "which define the group 'women.'" Benston points to an interesting passage in Ernest Mandel's *Workers Under Neo-Capitalism* on the unique status of domestic production: "[d]espite the fact that considerable human labor goes into this type of household production, it still remains a production of use-values and not commodities. Every time a soup is made or a button sewn on a garment, it constitutes production, but it is not production for the market." Household production has an obvious use value, but because it is not *exchanged on the market*, it is not a commodity. Household labour, Benston observes, is not only excluded from definitions of work as such because it lacks an exchange value, nor is it only that a capitalist economy is wholly dependent upon this exploited workforce, but further: such work, Benston insists, provides the very basis on which society "define[s] women," their relation to production, "as that group of people who are responsible for the production of simple use-values in those activities associated with the home and family" (18–19). Note also how this critique anticipates the autonomist Marxist notion of "affective" or "immaterial" labour.

10 See Carol Hanisch, "The Personal is Political," Kathie Sarachild, "A Program for Feminist 'Consciousness Raising,'" and Irene Peslikis,

"Resistances to Consciousness," in *Notes From the Second Year*, 76–8, 78–80, and 81. See Pamela Allen, "Free Space" and "Consciousness Raising," and Jo Freeman, "The Tyranny of Structurelessness," in *Radical Feminism*, 271–9, 280–1, and 285–99. See Hyde Park Chapter of the Chicago Women's Liberation Movement, "Socialist Feminism: A Strategy for the Women's Movement," in *Documents from the Women's Liberation Movement: An On-line Archival Collection,* Special Collections Library, Duke University. For an assessment of consciousness-raising's limitations, see Carol Williams Payne, "Consciousness Raising: A Dead End?" in *Radical Feminism*, 282–4.

11   Robin Morgan, "Letter to a Sister Underground," 24–5.

12   Morgan elaborates: "in Michigan, the denunciation of Sinclair disappeared; in Boston, ellipses replaced my attack on the Progressive Labor Party; in Berkeley, the Weatherman section was deleted" (*Going Too Far* 121).

13   See Morgan, "Goodbye To All That," 121.

14   See Morgan, "Three Articles on WITCH," 72–81, and "WITCH Documents," 538–53.

15   See, for instance, Marvin A. Carlson, ed., *Performance: A Critical Introduction*, 180–1.

16   See Debord's founding essays, "A User's Guide to Détournement" and "Theory of the Dérive," *Situationist International Anthology*, http://www.bopsecrets.org/SI/index.htm.

17   See William Francis Allen, Charles Pickard Ware, and Lucy McKim Garrison, eds., *Slave Songs of the United States* (1995) and Lauri Ramey, *Slave Songs and the Birth of African American Poetry* (2008). *The Little Red Songbook* was first published in 1909 and more than thirty-five editions have since been published; see *Songs of the Workers to Fan the Flames of Discontent: The Little Red Songbook* (Centenary Edition, 2005).

18   Baraka, like Rich, had come under the influence of Olson and Creeley's poetic technique early in his writing life. Baraka's (Leroi Jones) contribution to Donald Allen's *The New American Poetry* (1960) records: "there must not be any preconceived notion or *design* for what the poem *ought* to be. 'Who knows what a poem ought to sound like? Until it's thar [*sic*].' Says Charles Olson … & I follow closely with that" ("How You Sound??" 424–5). Historian and critic of Black Arts William J. Harris observes, "ironically, avant-garde ideas of form cohered perfectly with the new black artist's need to express his or her own oral tradition; the free verse and eccentric typography of the white avant-garde were ideal vehicles for black oral expression and experience" (xxvii).

19   The original text of the song reads: "I have an ear for music, / And I have an eye for a maid. / I like a pretty girlie, / With each pretty tune that's played. / They go together, / Like sunny weather goes with the month of May. / I've studied girls and music, / So I'm qualified to say: / A pretty girl is like a melody / That haunts you night and day, / Just like the strain of a haunting refrain, / She'll start upon a marathon / And run around your brain. / You can't escape she's in your memory. / By morning night and noon. / She will leave you and then come back again, / A pretty girl is just like a pretty tune."

20   The following records the *OED* entry: "The being in child-bed; child-birth, delivery, accouchement .... *1774* MRS. DELANY Corr. Ser. II. (1862) II. 15, I feel uncomfortable not to be able to come to her when she is under her confinement. *1811* PARK in Medico-Chirurg. Trans. II. 298 Mrs. S. whom I was engaged to attend in her first confinement. *1861* F. NIGHTINGALE Nursing 41 Women who had difficult confinements. *1870* E. PEACOCK Ralf Skirl. III. 211 Just recovered from her confinement."

21   Adrienne Rich, "Arts of the Possible," 164.

22   A consortium of legal scholars, theorists, and digital activists has recently begun to revive discussion of the commons. I am indebted to several scholars on the topic; in particular, see James Boyle, *The Public Domain: Enclosing the Commons of the Mind*; David Lange, "Recognizing the Public Domain," *Law and Contemporary Problems*; Jessica Litman, "The Public Domain," 965–1023; Lawrence Lessig, *The Future of Ideas: The Fate of the Commons in a Connected World*; Carol M. Rose, *Property and Persuasion: Essays on History, Theory, and Rhetoric of Ownership*; David Bollier, *Silent Theft: The Private Plunder of our Common Wealth*; and Elinor Ostrom, *Governing the Commons: The Evolution of Institutions for Collective Action*.

23   Rich's account of the reading appears in "Power and Danger: Works of a Common Woman," 247–58.

24   Judy Grahn, *Really Reading Gertrude Stein*, 289.

25   Corey Marks, "The Descriptive-Meditative Structure," 123–46.

26   Anzaldúa lists the following eight languages and dialects: (1) Standard English, (2) Working class/slang English, (3) Standard Spanish, (4) Standard Mexican Spanish, (5) North American Spanish dialect, (6) Chicano Spanish, (7) Tex-Mex, and (8) *Pachuco* (also called *caló*). Anzaldúa notes further: "Tex-Mex, or Spanglish, comes most naturally to me. I may switch back and forth from English to Spanish in the same sentence or in the same word ... From kids and people my own age I picked up *Pachuco*. *Pachuco* (the language of the zoot suiters) is a language of rebellion, both against Standard Spanish and Standard English. It is a secret language.

Adults of the culture and outsiders cannot understand it. It is made up of slang words from both English and Spanish" (*Borderlands/La Frontera* 77–8). *Borderlands'* publication in 1987 anticipated a burgeoning field of *estudios de la frontera* (border studies) over the course of the next decade. Héctor Calderón and José Saldívar's *Criticism in the Borderlands: Studies in Chicano Literature, Culture and Ideology* (1991); Emily Hicks's *Border Writing: The Multidimensional Text* (1991); and Ruth Bejar's *Translated Woman: Crossing the Border with Esperanza's Story* (1993) all appear within a decade of *Borderlands'* first published edition (1987).

27   "Coal" first appears in *In the First Cities* (1968), and then again in slightly altered form in *Coal* (1976). I cite the 1976 version. Revisions are largely minor, but significantly Lorde removes the period after line four. In her exemplary reading of the poem, Sagri Dhairyam refutes conventional interpretation of the text's purported celebration of "an intrinsically Black vision." She observes that the speaker's initial identification with the "total black[ness]" of the coal is immediately "sabotaged": I / is the total black, being spoken / from the earth's inside. / There are many kinds of open / how a diamond comes into a knot of flame / how sound comes into a word, coloured / by who pays what for speaking ("Coal" 1–7). "'There are many kinds of open,' the comment immediately following the opening lines, re-marks the ambivalence of their agenda." The relation between coal and the subsequent image of the diamond, Dhairyam argues, generates deliberately antagonistic associations "so likely to be passed over as different forms of the same mineral essence" ("Artifacts" 233). Indeed, according to this reading there is no carbon subject. The organic materials that make up a mineral such as coal are amorphous and take shape only according to unique geological and atmospheric pressures. Hence Lorde's clever metaphor: human subjects too are formed under historical pressures. If the association between fuel and Black bodies intimates slavery, the reference extends rapidly to include the exploitation of wage labour. Notice that in the poem "a diamond comes into a knot of flame" and "a sound comes into a word," but the transformation of coal into energy is deliberately left unspoken. The rhetoric of capitalism presents the aesthetic beauty of the diamond (and its associations with prestige and luxury) cut off from the oppressive scene of its production. Of course, presenting the process is determined "[b]y who pays what for speaking." Lorde's poem labours to expose the means of control over our mineral resources and our cultural symbols.

28   See, for instance, Honor Moore, *Poems From the Women's Movement*, xxiii–xxiv.

29 For instance, no selection of Grahn's work appears in Jahan Ramazani, Richard Ellmann, and Robert O'Clair, eds., *The Norton Anthology of Modern and Contemporary Verse*; Paul Hoover, ed., *Postmodern American Poetry*; or Dana Gioia, David Mason, Meg Schoerke, eds., *Twentieth-Century American Poetry*.

30 Slavoj Žižek has recently spoken of the "universality embodied in the Excluded" (*First as Tragedy* 100), an argument he partly draws from Susan Buck-Morss's *Hegel, Haiti, and Universal History*. Note Susan Buck-Morss's evocative reference to our "common humanity": "rather than giving multiple, distinct cultures equal due, whereby people are recognized as part of humanity indirectly through the mediation of collective cultural identities, human universality emerges in the historical event at the point of rupture. It is in the discontinuities of history that people whose culture has been strained to the breaking point give expression to a humanity that goes beyond cultural limits. And it is in our emphatic identification with this raw, free, and vulnerable state that we have a change of understanding what they say. Common humanity exists in spite of culture and its differences. A person's non-identity with the collective allows for subterranean solidarities that have a chance of appealing to universal, moral sentiment, the source today of enthusiasm and hope" (133). For Žižek's account of Buck-Morss's book, see *First as Tragedy, Then as Farce*, 111–25.

5. The Toronto Research Group: A Poetic of the Eternal Network

A section of chapter 5 appears in *Open Letter* 13, no. 8 (Spring 2009).

1 Karl Marx, *Economic and Philosophical Manuscripts*, 95–6; *Capital*, vol. 1:478.

2 Michael Hardt and Antonio Negri, *Commonwealth*, ix.

3 Steve McCaffery, *Wot We Wukkerz Want*, liner note.

4 The first TRG manifesto was composed in May 1972 and subsequently lost. A second manifesto was written 5 January 1973.

5 Dates for these poems and collections are as follows: "Parallel Texts" (1971), "Collboration" [sic] (1971), "In England Now that Spring" (1979), *Crown's Creek* (1978), *Edge* (1975), *Legend* (1980), *CaNADAda* (1972), *Live in the West* (1977), *Six Fillious* (1978), *8 × 8: La Traduction A L'Epreuve* (1982), and *Translating Translating Apollinaire* (1979).

6 Jacket copy, bpNichol, *art facts: a book of contexts*.

7 The wedding took place on 25 February 1978 at the loft of Jean Depuys. Both Maciunas and Hutchins wore gowns.

8 For scholars who give more than a marginal consideration of the TRG, see Adeena Karasick, "Tract Marks: Echoes and Traces in the Toronto

Research Group," 76–89; Caroline Bayard, *The New Poetics in Canada and Quebec: From Concretism to Postmodernism*, 60–7; Peter Jaeger, *ABC of Reading TRG*; Susan E. Billingham, "Inscription vs. Invocation: *The Martyrology as Paragram*," 85–133; Christian Bök, "Canadian "Pataphysics: A 'Pataphysics of Mnemonic Exception," in *'Pataphyscis: The Poetics of an Imaginary Science*, 81–97; and Miriam Nichols, "A/Politics of Contemporary Anglo-Canadian Poetries: The Toronto Research Group and the Kootenay School of Writing," 66–85.

Peter Jaeger provides astute readings of the TRG reports in relation to the single-authored creative texts of Nichol and McCaffery; in particular, Jaeger contextualizes Nichol's *The Martyrology* and McCaffery's *Carnival* and *Panopticon*. Christian Bök's study provides a provocative comparison between the TRG and Alfred Jarry's concept of 'pataphysics. Of equal merit is Nichols's article, which seeks historically to contextualize the TRG's rejection of nationalism in favour of a "local-global split" (68). Interestingly, this argument coheres with Silliman's distinction between "scene" and "network," the local and the transgeographic as substitutes for the movement (see my introduction for an extended assessment of these terms).

9 For examples of this tendency, see, in particular, *Read the Way He Writes: A Festschrift for bpNichol*, special issue of *Open Letter* 6, nos. 5–6 (Summer/Fall 1986), and Susan E. Billingham, *Language and the Sacred in Canadian Poet bpNichol's "The Martyrology."* Frank Davey argues that "[w]hat often happens on the death of an author is that an institutional group of textual custodians comes into being – scholars and editors who present themselves as caring as passionately about that author's text as the author once did ... Much of this kind of activity ... is celebratory rather than productive or critical, even, or perhaps especially, when it purports to offer no more than readings or explications ... Most of those interested in continuing to author Nichol texts have been other writers. Most of these have been writers of his own generation, and most have been his friends." Davey continues, "many of us in my generation need to release the texts known as 'bpNichol' from our friendships with Barrie the bpNichol author, and from the privileged place those friendships have given *The Martyrology* in many of our view of his writings, because of our continuing to read it as autobiography or as metaphors for autobiography" (8–9). See Davey, "bpNichol + 10: Some Institutional Issues Associated with the Continued Reading of Texts Known as 'bpNichol,'" 5–13. Davey makes similar arguments with particular reference to *The*

Martyrology in "Exegesis / Eggs à Jesus: *The Martyrology* as a Text in Crisis," 38–51.

10 See Lori Emerson, "Nicholongings: because they is," 27–33, Darren Wershler-Henry, "Argument for a Secular *Martyrology*," 37–47, and Christian Bök, "Nickel Linoleum," 62–74.

11 The special issue of *Open Letter* 6, no. 9 (Fall 1987) devoted to McCaffery's work features four essays that discuss his poetic texts, and, among them, three specifically address *Panopticon*.

12 See Statistics Canada, "Estimated Population of Canada, 1605 to Present," http://www.statcan.gc.ca/pub/98-187-x/4151287-eng.htm.

13 See Cy Gonick, "Strategies for Social Change," 39–40.

14 McCaffery, "Trans-Avant-Garde: An Interview with Steve McCaffery," http://www.raintaxi.com/online/2007winter/mccaffery.shtml.

15 The commentary in question comes from John W. Wornock's "Why I Am Anti-American." See Bryan D. Palmer's judicious assessment of anti-Americanism in *Canada's 1960s: The Ironies of Identity in a Rebellious Age*.

16 On the origins of the Eternal Network, see Filliou, *Teaching and Learning as Performing Arts*.

17 Higgins, "The Mail-Interview with Dick Higgins," http://www.fluxus heidelberg.org/dhint.html.

18 Nichol and McCaffery use a quotation mark rather than an inverted apostrophe ("pata- instead of 'pata-) to indicate the word's decontextualization.

19 Alfred Jarry notoriously defines 'pataphysics as "the science of imaginary solutions, which symbolically attributes the properties of objects, described by their virtuality, to their lineaments" (22). See Jarry, *Exploits and Opinions of Dr. Faustroll, 'Pataphysician*.

20 The letter to McCaffery is dated 13 April 1979.

21 Bayard makes the following claim in *The New Poetics in Canada and Quebec: From Concretism to Post-Modernism*: "what we are witnessing is a qualitative jump from one contemporary thought system (from a deconstructionist perspective which rejects the fetishism of reference) to an animistic one (wherein divination is practiced in order to interpret signs derived from the earth: topographies, soils, hills, and rivers – geomancy being the reading of the natural alignment of signs)" (64).

22 William Wordsworth advocated enthusiastically for copyright reform in the British parliament. In 1837 he lobbied on behalf of his friend Thomas Noon Talfourd, who introduced a bill that would extend the term of copyright to sixty years. For an extended account of the interconnected

development of Romantic concepts of creativity and intellectual property rights, see Martha Woodmansee, *The Author, Art, and the Market: Rereading the History of Aesthetics*. For a selection of pre-Romantic theories and practices of authorship, see Heather Hirschfeld, "Early Modern Collaboration and Theories of Authorship," 609–22. See also John Feather, "From Rights in Copies to Copyright: The Recognition of Authors' Rights in English Law and Practice in the Sixteenth and Seventeenth Centuries" and Max W. Thomas, "Reading and Writing the Renaissance Commonplace Book: A Question of Authorship," both of which appear in Woodmansee and Jaszi, *The Construction of Authorship: Textual Appropriation in Law and Literature*, 191–210, 401–16.

23 For accessible overviews of American copyright history, see James Boyle, *The Public Domain: Enclosing the Commons of the Mind*; Lawrence Lessig, *Free Culture*; Jessica Litman, *Digital Copyright*; and Siva Vaidhyanatha, *Copyrights and Copywrongs: The Rise of Intellectual Property and How It Threatens Creativity*.

24 McCaffery, "Trans-Avant-Garde: An Interview with Steve McCaffery," http://www.raintaxi.com/online/2007winter/mccaffery.shtml.

25 See note 22 above.

26 For commentaries on the influence of Coleridge and Dorothy Wordsworth on Wordsworth's writing, see Jack Stillinger, "Multiple 'Consciousness' in Wordsworth's *Prelude*," in *Multiple Authorship and the Myth of Solitary Genius*, 69–95; also, Wayne Koestenbaum, "The Marinere Hath His Will(iam): Wordsworth's and Coleridge's *Lyrical Ballads*," in *Double Talk: The Erotics of Male Literary Collaboration*, 71–111.

27 This tendency to reduce the Four Horsemen's group practice to a "single consciousness" still occurs. Recently the performance troupe Volcano staged an ambitious and largely successful show called *The Four Horsemen Project*, synthesizing their sound poetry with visually engaging multimedia and exceptional choreography; yet, among the thirty-six sound pieces, visual poems, and film footage clips used during the performance, no less than twenty were either solo-composed pieces by bpNichol or filmed interviews of him speaking.

28 McKenzie explains, "[t]he principle I wish to suggest as basic is simply this: bibliography is the discipline that studies texts as recorded forms, and the processes of their transmission, including their production and reception ... In terms of the range of demands now made on it and of the diverse interests of those who think of themselves as bibliographers, it seems to me that it would now be more useful to describe bibliography as the study of the sociology of texts. If the principle which makes it distinct

is its concern with texts in some physical form and their transmission, then I can think of no other phrase which so aptly describes its range" (*Sociology of Texts* 4–5).

29 This definition is more specifically related to prose. In the second report, McCaffery and Nichol acknowledge that poetry and prose involve distinctly different reading experiences: "[p]rose as print encourages an inattention to the right-hand margin as a terminal point. The tendency is encouraged to read continually as though the book were one extended line. In poetry, by contrast, the end of each line is integral to the structure of the poem whether it follows older metrical prosodic models or more recent types of breath-line notation … In poetry, where the individual line is compositionally integral, the page is more often than not itself integral" (60–1). Whereas in prose, the page functions as an "arbitrary receptacle," in poetry, it becomes instead a "frame, landscape, atmosphere within which the poem's own unity is enacted" (61). Poetry, therefore, is more visually oriented; prose is unavoidably linear. Importantly, McCaffery and Nichol would reject this assumption shortly after the composition of their second report, arguing that it fails to account for the prose poetry genre. See *Rational Geomancy*, 60–2, 92n.1.

30 Billingham chides Alan Knight and Caroline Bayard for failing to distinguish between TRG reports co-authored by McCaffery and Nichol and related pieces authored independently. This objection is ultimately legitimate if one acknowledges that the co-authored pieces generate a synthetic authorial subject irreducible to either author. Compromising this position is her selection of cover art – a comic piece produced collaboratively by both poets but ascribed to Nichol alone! The text in question, "Fictive Funnies," appears in "The Search for Non-Narrative Prose" in *Rational Geomancy*, 111.

31 This is a method that Jerome McGann would later employ in studies like *Black Riders*.

32 A shorter version of the report was published in *Portico* 5, nos. 3–4 (1981): 67–75. Authorial contributions are distinguished by colour: the upper band in blue, the lower band in red.

33 McCaffery expresses a similar interest in the dialogic possibilities of recension and the footnote, in which text and note occupy and compete within the same textual field of the page. See McCaffery, "Richard Bentley: The First Poststructuralist? The 1732 Recension of *Paradise Lost*" and "Johnson and Wittgenstein: Some Correlations and Bifurcations in the Dictionary and the Philosophical Investigations," in *Prior To Meaning: The Protosemantic and Poetics*, 58–74 and 75–104.

34   "The Body: In Light" is second in a mini-sequence of three that also contains "The Body: In Darkness" and "The Body: Disembodied." These gestural pieces were subsequently added to the larger sequence making up the TRG's third report, "The Language of Performance of Language" (*Rational Geomancy*, 229–38, 245–53, 255–71).

35   For a brief survey of the historical antecedents and contemporary modes of sound poetry, see Dick Higgins, "A Taxonomy of Sound Poetry," 40–52; Steve McCaffery, "Sound Poetry: A Survey," 6–18; and Richard Kostelanetz, "Text Sound Art: A Survey," 14–23.

36   McCaffery argues that "[s]ound poetry prior to the developments of the 1950s is still largely a word bound thing. For whilst the work of the Dadaists, Futurists and Lettrists served to free the word from its semantic function, redistributing energy from theme and 'message' to matter and contour, it nevertheless persisted in a morphological patterning that still suggested the presence of the word … Important too, in this light, is the way meaning persists as a teleology even in zaum. Khlebnikov, for instance, speaks of new meanings achieved through by-passing older forms of meaning, of meanings 'rescued' by 'estrangement.' Hugo Ball, too, speaks of exploring the word's 'innermost alchemy'" ("Sound Poetry: A Survey" 10).

37   Higgins formulates these categories in "A Taxonomy of Sound Poetry." Here, a slightly expanded paraphrasing: (1) *Works in an invented language*: works that are "purely without reference to *any* known language." E.g., Iliazd's "zaum" poems, Stefan George's "lingua romana" works. (2) *Near-nonsense works*: works that involve the "interplay between semantically meaningful lines" and "nonsense." Such pieces often involve strategies of collage and found materials, e.g., Kurt Schwitters's "To Anna Blume." (3) *Phatic poems*: "poems in which semantic meaning, if any, is subordinate to expression of intonation, thus yielding a new emotional meaning which is relatively remote from any semiotic significance." In this case, a semantically conventional word is expunged of its residual meaning through repetition or verbal manipulation of the signifier, e.g., Antonin Artaud's "To Be Done with the Judgment of God." (4) *Un-written-out poems*: A sound poem that is improvised, e.g., Henri Chopin's tape-recorder pieces. (5) *Notated ones*: A sound poem that is notated. As a subcategory of this class, Higgins includes vocalizations of visual poetry, e.g., Kurt Schwitters's *Ur Sonata*. See "A Taxonomy of Sound Poetry," 40–52.

38   The tape recorder has had a significant impact on developments in sound poetry – most obvious is that the sonic variations of orality become reproducible. Voice is liberated from the human body; it can be technologically

modified, reorganized, and augmented. Among the pioneers of tape-recorded sound poetry, Henri Chopin's "poesie sonore" and Bernard Heidsieck's "poem-partitions" are the most formidable. For an extended analysis of this practice, see Chopin, "Open Letter to Aphonic Musicians," 11–23. In a letter to Dick Higgins dated 21 June 1976, McCaffery records that the Four Horsemen "don't as a group use microphonic support or extension – hence our ostracisation from the poesie sonor [sic] scene by such inflexible (though respected) voices as henri chopin" (Box 21, Folder 41, Dick Higgins Papers).

39 McCaffery was also likely aware of the multi-voice compositions of Fluxus artists like Yoko Ono, La Monte Young, Phil Corner, and George Maciunas's "music for lips." Multi-voice performance was often a component within "happenings" and their collectively created "sound environments" (the latter an element of the "Flux Amusement Center"). See Jon Hendricks, ed., *Fluxus Codex*.

40 Dick Higgins, "A Commentary by the Poet on 'Conceptual Forks,'" 155.

41 Steve McCaffery, "Proem: The Logic of Frogs #383," 3.

42 See McCaffery's *Every Way Oakly* (Xerox publication by Stephen Scobie, Edmonton, 1978; selections were republished in *Seven Pages Missing: Volume One*, 97–119) and *Intimate Distortions: A Displacement of Sappho*. McCaffery also wrote a number of homolinguistic adaptations of Shakespeare, Marvell, and Sidney. Many of these poems went unpublished until the publication of *Seven Pages Missing: Volume Two*, 157–96. For Nichol's creative translations, see *Translating Translating Apollinaire*, which subjects the French poet's poem "Zone" to no less than thirty-four subsequent permutations and transformations. He also wrote a series of translations of Catullus's poems, many of which are collected in *zygal: a book of mysteries and translations*.

43 Cicero describes his approach to translation in *De optimo genere oratorum*: "[a]nd I did not translate them as an interpreter, but as an orator, keeping the same ideas and forms, or as one might say, the "figures" of thought, but in language which conforms to our usage. And in so doing, I did not hold it necessary to render word for word, but I preserve the general style and force of the language" (364). Horace's often quoted observation on the subject of translation etiquette can be found in his *Ars Poetica*: "[i]n ground open to all you will win private rights, if you do not linger along the easy and open pathway, if you do not seek to render word for word as a slavish translator, and if in your copying you do not leap into the narrow well, out of which either shame or the laws of your task will keep you from stirring a step" (461).

44 Jeremy Munday argues that despite the importance of Dryden's taxonomy for "translation theory, [his] writing remains full of the language of his time: the genius of the S[ource] T[ext] author" (*Introducing Translation Studies* 25).

45 Fitzgerald reveals in a letter to E.B. Cowell, "[i]t is an amusement for me to take what Liberties I like with these Persians, who (as I think) are not Poets enough to frighten one from such excursions, and wholly really do want a little Art to shape them." See Andre Lefevere, ed., *Translation/History/Culture: A Sourcebook*, 80.

46 Peter Jaeger argues convincingly that McCaffery and Nichol had likely read Jakobson's influential essay. Although they do not explicitly cite it, Jaeger observes that George Steiner's *After Babel: Aspects of Language and Translation* appears in the TRG's "catalogue" of jointly discussed readings, a book that gives extended consideration to Jakobson's typology. The TRG's reading list appears in *Rational Geomancy*, 313–20. For Jaeger's assessment of the TRG's translational strategies (particularly in relation to Nichol's *The Martyrology*) see his *ABC of Reading TRG*, 105–8.

47 See Benedetto Croce, *The Aesthetic as Science of Expression and of the Linguistic in General*, 76.

48 Referred to as a "treated" text, Phillips subjects the little-known nineteenth-century novelist W.H. Mallock's *A Human Document* to a process of selective concealment whereby painted images replace sections of text so that a new narrative emerges. Johnson uses a comparable method of deletion in *Radi os*, revising the first four books of Milton's *Paradise Lost*. The result, however, is decidedly more minimalist, transforming the dense columns of Milton's blank verse into the exposed page of projectivist aesthetics. William Burroughs and Brion Gysin's "cut-up" technique is more widely acknowledged due to Burroughs's comparatively greater fame; their method, which bears similarities to Tristan Tzara's early experiments, involves cutting and rearranging passages of text to generate meaning aleatorically. See Tom Phillips, *A Humument: A Treated Victorian Novel*; Ronald Johnson, *Radi os*; and William Burroughs's "cut-up trilogy" (*The Soft Machine*, *The Ticket that Exploded*, and *Nova Express*). See also Gysin's description of their method in "Cut-Ups Self-Explained," 132–5.

49 Dick Higgins records that *14 Chansons et 1 Charade* was initially conceived by Filliou as "a set of rock and roll lyrics which … proved too risqué for commercial broadcasting" ("The Strategy" 129). Alternatively, he published the poem along with English and German translations by Brecht and Roth respectively. With Filliou's involvement, Higgins, Nichol, and McCaffery expanded the text.

50 See, in particular, Higgins and McCaffery's correspondence during 1976 and 1977 in Box 21, Folder 41, Dick Higgins Papers. On 14 July 1976, Higgins observes: "you've put a real idea into my head, this intralingual translation concept, and it annoys me not to know the person who did so. As I work farther into that field, I'll send you some examples of what I come up with." In "A Note on *Intimate Distortions*," McCaffery contends: "Higgins and I saw allusive referential as a facet of a wider notion we termed 'Creative Misunderstanding'" (*Seven Pages Missing: Volume Two* 452).

51 At some point during the late summer of 1977, Higgins sent to McCaffery his essay entitled "Teleology: Some Incomplete Thoughts," in which Higgins summarily dismisses post-structuralist theory, referring pejoratively to several French theorists (including Roland Barthes and Jacques Derrida) as the "Paris Mafia." McCaffery's response to Higgins is instructive: it affords a rich account of the relationship between Derrida's theory and Language poetics. Furthermore, it aptly characterizes the mutual development of Higgins and McCaffery's thinking on the nature of language. The latter's comparison of allusive referentialist writing to Derrida's concept of the trace is convincing enough that Higgins abandons the essay (the manuscript of Higgins's essay features the following hand-written note: "trash, for reasons s.m. said" [Box 41, Dick Higgins Papers]). The letter in question is dated 30 September 1977, Box 21, Folder 41, Dick Higgins Papers.

52 The following is the full text of Sidney's Sonnet XXXI: "With how sad steps, O Moon, thou climb'st the skies! / How silently, and with how wan a face! / What, may it be that even in heav'nly place / That busy archer his sharp arrows tries? / Sure, if that long with love-acquainted eyes / Can judge of love, thou feel'st a lover's case; / I read it in thy looks: thy languisht grace / To me that feel the like, thy state descries. / Then, ev'n of fellowship, O Moon, tell me, / Is constant love deemed there but want of wit? / Are beauties there as proud as here they be? / Do they above love to be loved, and yet / Those lovers scorn whom that love doth possess? / Do they call virtue there, ungratefulness?" (49). I use the text as it appears in Sidney, *Sir Philip Sidney: Selected Poetry and Prose*.

53 In *Nicholodeon*, an elaboration of bpNichol's visual poetics, Darren Wershler-Henry offers the following sonnet (which readers can find online: http://www.chbooks.com/archives/online_books/nicholodeon/sonnet.html):

$?^8$

u^6

This playful poem aptly demonstrates the logical progression of a Pe-
trarchan sonnet: its organization into octave and sestet (the number of
lines represented by its accompanying exponent), and an initial invocation
by the speaker, followed by an address to the beloved.

54 McCaffery also cites this trip to Robert's Creek with Filliou and Kaprow
in a letter to Dick Higgins dated 7 November 1977: "talk: eternal network,
the speed of art, much on performance which has certainly stretched my
mind more towards performance as meta-reading" (Box 21, Folder 41,
Dick Higgins Papers).

55 Qtd. in Kenneth Goldsmith, "Meme Museum," http://www.poetryfoun-
dation.org/harriet/2011/04/the-meme-museum.

Epilogue

1 Robert Duncan, *The HD Book*, 63.
2 See Stephen Voyce, "Toward an Open-Source Poetics."

Bibliography

Abrams, M.H. "Structure and Style in the Greater Romantic Lyric." In *From Sensibility to Romanticism*. Ed. Frederick W. Hilles and Harold Bloom. Oxford: Oxford UP, 1965. 527–60.

Adegbola, E.A. Ade, ed. *Traditional Religion in West Africa*. Nairobi, Kenya: Uzima P, 1983.

Adogame, Afe, Roswith Gerloff, and Klaus Hock, eds. *Christianity in Africa and the African Diaspora: The Appropriation of a Scattered Heritage*. New York: Continuum, 2008.

Agamben, Giorgio. *The Coming Community*. Trans. Michael Hardt. Ed. Sandra Buckley, Michael Hardt, and Brian Massumi. Theory Out of Bounds Ser. 1. Minneapolis: U of Minnesota P, 1993.

Allen, Donald, ed. *The New American Poetry, 1945–1960*. 1960. Berkeley: U of California P, 1999.

Allen, Pamela. "Consciousness Raising." In Koedt, Levine, and Rapone, *Radican Feminism* 280–1.

Allen, Pamela. "Free Space." In Koedt, Levine, and Rapone, *Radical Feminism* 271–9.

Alleyne, Brian W. *Radicals Against Race: Black Activism and Cultural Politics*. New York: Berg, 2002.

Allsopp, Richard, ed. *Dictionary of Caribbean English Usage*. Oxford: Oxford UP, 1996.

Altieri, Charles. *Enlarging the Temple: New Directions in American Poetry during the 1960s*. Lewisburg: Bucknell UP, 1979.

Ameringer, Charles D. *The Socialist Impulse: Latin America in the Twentieth Century*. Gainesville: U of Florida P, 2009.

Anderson, Benedict. *Imagined Communities: Reflections on the Origin and Spread of Nationalism*. Expanded ed. New York: Verso, 1991.

Anderson, Edgar. *Plants, Man and Life*. 1952. Berkeley: U of California P, 1971.

Anon. "Anonymous Poem." *Sisterhood Is Powerful* 504.

Anzaldúa, Gloria. *Borderlands/La Frontera*. 3rd ed. San Francisco: Aunt Lute Books, 2007.

– *The Gloria Anzaldúa Reader*. Ed. AnaLouise Keating. Durham, NC: Duke UP, 2009.

– "The New Speakers." *The Gloria Anzaldúa Reader* 24–5.

– "now let us shift … the path of conocimiento … inner work, public acts." In *Fire and Ink: An Anthology of Social Action Writing*. Ed. Frances Payne Adler, Debra Busman, and Diana García. Tucson: U of Arizona P, 2009. 540–78.

– "Reincarnation." *The Gloria Anzaldúa Reader* 21.

Anzaldúa, Gloria, and Cherríe Moraga. *This Bridge Called My Back: Writings by Radical Women of Color*. Watertown, MA: Persephone P, 1981.

Arendt, Hannah. *The Human Condition*. Chicago: U of Chicago P, 1958.

Arnold, Matthew. *Culture and Anarchy*. 1869. Cambridge: Cambridge UP, 1935.

– *On Translating Homer*. London: Longman, Green, Longman, and Roberts, 1861.

Attridge, Derek. *Poetic Rhythm: An Introduction*. Cambridge: Cambridge UP, 1995.

Auden, W.H. "The Shield of Achilles." *Selected Poems*. Ed. Edward Mendelson. New York: Vintage Books, 1989. 198–200.

Awolalu, J. Omosade, and P. Adelumo Dopamu. *West African Traditional Religion*. Ibadan, Nigeria: Onibonoje P, 1979.

Badiou, Alain. "The Communist Hypothesis." *New Left Review* 49 (Jan./Feb. 2008): 29–42.

– *The Communist Hypothesis*. Trans. David Macey and Steve Corcoran. New York: Verso, 2010.

– *The Meaning of Sarkozy*. Trans. David Fernbach. New York: Verso, 2008.

– *Metapolitics*. Trans. Jason Barler. London: Verso, 2005.

Balme, Christopher B. *Decolonizing the Stage: Theatrical Syncretism and Post-Colonial Drama*. Oxford: Oxford UP, 1999.

Baraka, Amiri. "Black Art." *The LeRoi Jones/Amiri Baraka Reader*. Ed. William J. Harris. 2nd ed. New York: Thunder's Mouth P, 1999. 219–20.

– "The Black Arts Movement." In *The LeRoi Jones/Amiri Baraka Reader* 495–505.

– "Cultural Revolution and the Literary Canon." *Callaloo* 14, no. 1 (1991): 150–6.

– "How You Sound??" In Allen, *The New American Poetry* 424–5.

Barnard, Mary. *Sappho: A New Translation*. Berkeley: U of California P, 1958.

Barnes, Sandra T., ed. *Africa's Ogun: Old World and New*. 2nd ed. Bloomington: Indiana UP, 1997.

Barthes, Roland. "The Death of the Author." In *Image—Music—Text*. Ed. Stephen Health. New York: Hill and Wang, 1978. 142–8.

Bastide, Roger. *African Civilizations in the New World*. New York: Harper and Row, 1971.

Bayard, Caroline. *The New Poetics in Canada and Quebec: From Concretism to Post-Modernism*. Toronto: U of Toronto P, 1989.

Beach, Christopher. *Poetic Culture: Contemporary American Poetry Between Community and Institution*. Evanston, IL: Northwestern UP, 1999.

Belgrad, Daniel. *The Culture of Spontaneity: Improvisation and the Arts in Postwar America*. Chicago: U of Chicago P, 1998.

Bennett, Herman. L. "The Challenge to the Post-Colonial State." In *The Modern Caribbean*. Ed. Franklin W. Knight and Colin A. Palmer. Chapel Hill: U of North Carolina P, 1989. 129–46.

Bennett, Louise. "Colonization in Reverse." 1957. *The Norton Anthology of Modern and Contemporary Poetry*. Ed. Jahan Ramazani, Richard Ellmann, and Robert O'Clair. New York: Norton, 2002. 173–4.

Benstock, Shari. *Women of the Left Bank: Paris, 1900–1940*. Austin: U of Texas P, 1986.

Benston, Margaret. "The Political Economy of Women's Liberation." In *Materialist Feminism: A Reader in Class, Difference, and Women's Lives*. Ed. Rosemary Hennessy and Chrys Ingraham. New York: Routledge, 1997. 17–23.

Bernikow, Louise, ed. *The World Split Open: Four Centuries of Women Poets in England and America, 1550–1950*. New York: Vintage, 1974.

Bernstein, Charles. "Hearing 'Here': Robert Creeley's Poetics of Duration." In Terrell, *Robert Creeley: The Poet's Workshop* 87–95.

– ed. *The Politics of Poetic Form: Poetry and Public Policy*. New York: Roof, 1990.

Bernstein, Michael. *The Tale of the Tribe: Ezra Pound and the Modern Verse Epic*. Princeton, NJ: Princeton UP, 1980.

Bertholf, Robert J. "Decision at the Apogee: Robert Duncan's Anarchist Critique of Denise Levertov." In Bertholf and Gelpi, *The Letters* 1–17.

Bertholf, Robert J., and Albert Gelpi, eds. *The Letters of Robert Duncan and Denise Levertov*. Stanford, CA: Stanford UP, 2004.

Bey, Hakim. *T.A.Z.: The Temporary Autonomous Zone, Ontological Anarchy, Poetic Terrorism*. 3rd ed. New York: Autonomedia, 2003.

Bibby, Michael. *Hearts and Minds: Bodies, Poetry, and Resistance in the Vietnam Era*. New Brunswick, NJ: Rutgers UP, 1996.

Billingham, Susan E. *Language and the Sacred in Canadian Poet bpNichol's The Martyrology*. Lewiston, NY: Edwin Mellen P, 2000.

Bilski, Emily D., and Emily Braun. *Jewish Women and Their Salons: The Power of Conversation*. New Haven, CT: Yale UP, 2005.

Bitar, Sergio. *Chile: Experiment in Democracy*. Trans. Sam Sherman. Philadelphia: Institute for the Study of Human Issues, 1986.

"Black Mountain Advertising Flyer" (unsigned). 1950. Black Mountain College Collection, State Archives of North Carolina.

"Black Mountain College Bulletin" (unsigned). Vol. 8, no. 1, 1950–1. Black Mountain College Collection, State Archives of North Carolina.

Blanchot, Maurice. *The Unavowable Community*. Trans. Pierre Joris. New York: Station Hill P, 1988.

Bobb, June D. *Beating a Restless Drum: The Poetics of Kamau Brathwaite and Derek Walcott*. Trenton, NJ: Africa World P, 1998.

Bök, Christian. "Nickel Linoleum." *Open Letter* 10, no. 4 (1998): 62–74.

– *'Pataphysics: The Poetics of an Imaginary Science*. Evanston, IL: Northwestern UP, 2002.

Bollier, David. *Silent Theft: The Private Plunder of our Common Wealth*. New York: Routledge, 2003.

Boyle, James. *The Public Domain: Enclosing the Commons of the Mind*. New Haven, CT: Yale UP, 2008.

Brandon, Henry. "Attack us at your peril, cocky Cuba warns US." *Sunday Times* 28 Oct. 1962.

Brathwaite, Edward Kamau. "Ananse." *Arrivants* 165–7.

– *Ancestors*. New York: New Directions Books, 1977.

– *The Arrivants: A New World Trilogy*. Oxford: Oxford UP, 1973.

– "Caliban." *Arrivants* 191–5.

– "Cane." *Arrivants* 225–9.

– "Caribbean Report, January/March, 1968." *CAM Newsletter* 6 (Jan.–Mar. 1968): 2–5.

– *Contradictory Omens: Cultural Diversity and Integration in the Caribbean*. Kingston, Jamaica: Savacou Pub., 1974.

– "The Cracked Mother." *Arrivants* 180–4.

– *The Development of Creole Society in Jamaica, 1770–1820*. Oxford: Clarendon P, 1971.

– "Dies Irie." *Ancestors* 429–31.

– "Driftword." *Ancestors* 144–54.

– "Eating the Dead." *Arrivants* 219–21.

– "From Edward Brathwaite to Andrew Salkey." 18 Dec. 1968. Papers of the Caribbean Artists Movement, 3/496, George Padmore Institute, London, UK.

– "From Edward Brathwaite to Andrew Salkey." 23 Mar. 1969. Papers of the Caribbean Artists Movement, 3/514, George Padmore Institute, London, UK.

- "From Edward Brathwaite to Bryan King." 30 Nov. 1966. Papers of the Caribbean Artists Movement, 3/1, George Padmore Institute, London, UK.
- "From Edward Brathwaite to John La Rose." 19 Sept. 1967. Papers of the Caribbean Artists Movement, 3/190, George Padmore Institute, London, UK.
- "From Edward Brathwaite to Jon Stallworthy." 15 Oct. 1967. Papers of the Caribbean Artists Movement, 3/247, George Padmore Institute, London, UK.
- "Glossary." *Arrivants* 271–5.
- *History of the Voice: The Development of Nation Language in Anglophone Caribbean Poetry*. London: New Beacon Books, 1984.
- "Interview with Edward Kamau Brathwaite." By Anne Walmsley. Papers of the Caribbean Artists Movement, 6/9, 1986, 1–35, George Padmore Institute, London, UK.
- "An Interview with Kamau Brathwaite." By Nathaniel Mackey. Brown, *The Art of Kamau Brathwaite* 13–32.
- "Jah." *Arrivants* 162–4.
- "Journeys." *Other Exiles*. London: Oxford UP, 1975. 3–5.
- "Jou'vert." *Arrivants* 267–70.
- "Legba." *Arrivants* 174–6.
- "The Love Axe/l: Developing a Caribbean Aesthetic." *Bim* 61 (Jun. 1977): 53–65.
- "The Love Axe/l: Developing a Caribbean Aesthetic – Part Three." *Bim* 63 (Jun. 1978): 181–92.
- "Metaphors of Underdevelopment." In Brown, *The Art of Kamau Brathwaite* 231–53.
- "Negus." *Arrivants* 222–4.
- "Nuum." *Ancestors* 424–8.
- "Ogun." *Arrivants* 242–3.
- "On Gordon Rohlehr's 'Sparrow and the Language of the Calypso.'" *CAM Newsletter* 4 (Aug.–Sept. 1967): 8–11.
- "Portrait of Bussa, the Bajan Slave Rebel." *Third World Poems*. Harlow, Essex: Longman, 1983. 14–18.
- "Timehri." *Savacou* 2 (Sept. 1970): 35–44.
- "Unrighteousness of Mammon." *Arrivants* 216.
- "Vèvè." *Arrivants* 263–6.
- "X/Self xth letter from the thirteenth provinces." *Ancestors* 444–56.
Breton, André, Paul Eluard, and Phillippe Soupault. "Notes on a Collaboration." In *The Automatic Message, The Magnetic Fields, The Immaculate Conception*. Trans. David Gascoyne, Antony Melville, and Jon Graham. London: Atlas P, 1997. 159.

Brown, Stewart, ed. *The Art of Kamau Brathwaite*. Bridgen, Wales: Seren, 1995.

Buck-Morss, Susan. *Hegel, Haiti, and Universal History*. Pittsburg: U of Pittsburgh P, 2009.

Bürger, Peter. *Theory of the Avant-Garde*. Minnesota: U of Minnesota P, 1984.

Burliuk, D., Aleksandr Kruchenykh, Vladimir Mayakovsky, and Viktor Khlebnikov. "A Slap in the Face of Public Taste." Rothenberg and Joris 223.

Butler, Judith. *Bodies That Matter: On the Discursive Limits of "Sex."* New York: Routledge, 1993.

Butterick, George F., ed. *Charles Olson & Robert Creeley: The Complete Correspondence*. 10 vols. Santa Barbara: Black Sparrow P, 1980–96.

– "Charles Olson's 'The Kingfishers' and the Poetics of Change." *American Poetry* 6, no. 2 (1989): 28–69.

– "Creeley and Olson: The Beginning." *Boundary 2* 6–7 (1978): 129–34.

– *A Guide to the Maximus Poems of Charles Olson*. Berkeley: U of California P, 1978.

– ed. *Olson: The Journal of the Charles Olson Archives*. 10 vols. Storrs: University of Connecticut Library, 1974–8.

– "Robert Creeley and the Tradition." Terrell, *Robert Creeley: The Poet's Workshop* 119–34.

Byrd, Don. "The Possibility of Measure in Olson's Maximus." *Boundary 2* vol. 2, no. 1–2 (Fall 1973–Winter 1974): 39–54.

Cage, John. "Experimental Music: Doctrine." In *Silence: Lectures and Writings*. Middletown, CT: Wesleyan UP, 1961. 13–7.

– "An Interview with John Cage." By Michael Kirby and Richard Schechner. In Sandford *Happenings* 51–71.

– "Juilliard Lecture." In *A Year from Monday*. Middletown, CT: Wesleyan UP, 1963. 95–112.

– "McLuhan's Influence." In *John Cage: An Anthology*. Ed. Richard Kostelanetz. New York: DA CAPO P, 1991. 170–1.

– "Telephone Interview with Cage." By Martin Duberman. 26 Apr. 1969. Passages reproduced in *Black Mountain: An Exploration in Community*, 349.

Campbell, Horace. *Rasta and Resistance: From Marcus Garvey to Walter Rodney*. Trenton, NJ: Africa World P, 1990.

Canetti, Elias. *Crowds and Power*. 1960. Trans. Carol Stewart. New York: Penguin, 1981.

Cappellazzo, Amy, and Elizabeth Licata, eds. *In Company: Robert Creeley's Collaborations*. Greensboro: Castellani Art Museum of Niagara U/U of North Carolina P, 1999.

Caputo, John D., ed. *Deconstruction in a Nutshell: A Conversation with Jacques Derrida*. New York: Fordham UP, 1997.

Cardenal, Ernesto. *In Cuba*. 1972. Trans. Donald D. Walsh. New York: New Directions, 1974.

Carrillo, Jo. "And When You Leave, Take Your Pictures With You." Anzaldúa and Moraga 63–4.

Castle, Dave. "Hearts, Minds and Radical Democracy." *Red Pepper*. N.p. Jun. 1998. Web. 22 Dec. 2007. http://www.redpepper.org.uk/article563.html.

Catullus, Gaius Valerius. *The Poems of Catullus: A Bilingual Edition*. Trans. Peter Green. Berkeley: U of California P, 2005.

Caws, Mary Ann. "Introduction." In *Manifesto: A Century of Isms*. Lincoln: U of Nebraska P, 2001. xix–xxxi.

Césaire, Aimé. *Une Tempete: Adaptation de Pour une Théâtre Negre*. Paris: Seuil, 1969.

– *Toussaint Louverture: La Révolution Française et le Problème Colonial*. Paris: Présence Africaine, 1981.

Chamberlin, Edward. *Come Back to Me My Language: Poetry and the West Indies*. Urbana: U of Illinois P, 1993.

Chester, Laura, and Sharon Barba, eds. *Rising Tides: Twentieth-Century American Women Poets*. New York: Washington Square P/Simon & Schuster, 1973.

Chopin, Henri. "Open Letter to Aphonic Musicians." *Revue OU 33*. Trans. Jean Ratcliffe-Chopin. Paris: Cinquieme Saison, 1968. 11–23.

Cicero, Marcus Tullius. "De optimo genere oratorum." ("The Best Kind of Orator"). In *De inventione, De optimo genere oratorum, topica*. Trans. H.M. Hubbell. Cambridge, MA: Harvard UP, 1960. 347–73.

Clare, John. "Lines: I Am." *I Am: The Selected Poetry of John Clare*. New York: Farrar, Straus and Giroux, 2003. 282.

Clark, Tom. *Charles Olson: The Allegory of a Poet's Life*. New York: Norton, 1991.

Clay, Steven, and Rodney Phillips. *A Secret Location on the Lower East Side: Adventures in Writing, 1960–1980*. New York: Granary Books, 1998.

Cobbing, Bob. "Some Statements on Sound Poetry." In McCaffery and Nichol, *Sound Poetry* 39–40.

Cohen, Milton A. *Movement, Manifesto, Melee: The Modernist Group, 1910–1914*. New York: Lexington Books, 2004.

Combahee River Collective. "The Combahee River Collective Statement." In *Home Girls: A Black Feminist Anthology*. Ed. Barbara Smith. New York: Kitchen Table: Women of Color P. 272–82.

Connor, Pearl. "Interview." By Anne Walmsley. Papers of the Caribbean Artists Movement, 6/14, n.d., 1–22, George Padmore Institute, London, UK.

Courlander, Harold. *The Drum and the Hoe: Life and Lore of the Haitian People*. Berkeley: U of California P, 1960.

Cowley, Abraham. "Preface to Pindarique Odes." 1656. *Abraham Cowley: Poetry & Prose, with Thomas Sprat's Life and Observations by Dryden, Addision, Johnson and Others*. Oxford: Folcroft Library Editions, 1974. 173–5.

Crane, Hart. "The Broken Tower." *The Collected Poems of Hart Crane*. Ed. Waldo Frank. New York: Liveright Pub. Corp., 1933. 135–6.

Craven, David. *Art and Revolution in Latin America, 1910–1990*. New Haven, CT: Yale UP, 2006.

Creeley, Robert. "After Lorca." *Collected Poems* 121.

– "Alex's Art." *Echoes*. New York: New Directions, 1994. 63–4.

– *The Collected Essays of Robert Creeley*. Berkeley: U of California P, 1989.

– *The Collected Poems of Robert Creeley: 1945–1975*. Berkeley: U of California P, 1982.

– "The Conspiracy." *Collected Poems* 131.

– *Contexts of Poetry: Interviews, 1961–1971*. Ed. Donald Allen. Bolinas, CA: Four Seasons Foundation, 1973.

– "For Love." *Collected Poems* 257–8.

– "For Rainer Gerhardt." *Collected Poems* 114.

– "Hart Crane." *Collected Poems* 109–10.

– "Hart Crane and the Private Judgment." In *Collected Essays* 14–22.

– "I Know a Man." *Collected Poems* 132.

– "The Immoral Proposition." *Collected Poems* 125.

– "Interview." By Elizabeth Licata. Unpublished. 21 Nov. 1998.

– "Interview with Robert Creeley." By David Ossman. *Contexts* 3–12.

– "An Interview with Robert Creeley." By John Sinclair and Robin Eichele. *Contexts* 45–69.

– "The Memory." *Collected Poems* 223.

– "A Note." In *A Quick Graph: Collected Notes & Essays*. Ed. Donald Allen. San Francisco: Four Seasons Foundation, 1970. 32–3.

– "A Note on Poetry." In *A Quick Graph* 25.

– "An Ode (for Black Mt. College)." Series 2, Box 4, Folder 8. Robert Creeley Papers. Stanford U Libraries, Stanford, California, n.d.

– "On Black Mountain Review." In *The Little Magazine in America: A Modern Documentary History*. Ed. Elliot Anderson and Mary Kinzie. New York: The Pushcart P, 248–61.

– "On the Road: Notes on Artists & Poets, 1950–1965." In *Collected Essays* 367–76.

– "The Place." *Collected Poems* 196.

– "Rainer Gerhardt: A Note." In *A Quick Graph* 221–3.

– "Song." *Collected Poems* 142.

– "To Define." In Allen, *The New American Poetry*, 408.

– "The Wind." *Collected Poems* 164.

Croce, Benedetto. *The Aesthetic as the Science of Expression and of the Linguistic in General*. Trans. Colin Lyas. Cambridge: Cambridge UP, 1992.

Davey, Frank. "bpNichol + 10: Some Institutional Issues Associated with the Continued Reading of Texts Known as 'bpNichol.'" Spec. issue of *Open Letter* 10, no. 4 (Fall 1998): 5–13.

– "Exegesis / Eggs à Jesus: *The Martyrology* as a Text in Crisis." In *Tracing the Paths: Reading ≠ Writing. The Martyrology*. Ed. Miki Roy. Vancouver: Line/ Talonbooks, 1988. 38–51.

Davidson, Michael. "A Cold War Correspondence: The Letters of Robert Duncan and Denise Levertov." *Contemporary Literature* 45, no. 3 (2004): 538–56.

– *Guys Like Us: Citing Masculinity in Cold War Poetics*. Chicago: U of Chicago P, 2004.

– *The San Francisco Renaissance: Poetics and Community at Mid-Century*. Cambridge: Cambridge UP, 1989.

Davison, Peter. "The New Poetry." *Atlantic Monthly* 210 (1962): 85–6.

Dawson, Fielding. "Black Mountain Defined." In *Black Mountain College: Sprouted Seeds: An Anthology of Personal Accounts*. Ed. Mervin Lane. Knoxville: U of Tennessee P, 1990. 273–8.

de Certeau, Michel. *The Practice of Everyday Life*. Trans. Steven Rendall. Berkeley: U of California P, 1984.

Deleuze, Gilles. "May '68 Didn't Happen." In *Two Regimes of Madness: Texts and Interviews, 1975–1995*. Trans. Ames Hodges and Mike Taormina. Los Angeles: Semiotext(e) Foreign Agents Series, 2006. 233–6.

– "Three Group-Related Problems." In *Desert Islands and Other Texts, 1953–1974*. Trans. Michael Taormina. Los Angeles: Semiotext(e) Foreign Agents Series, 2004. 193–203.

Deleuze, Gilles, and Claire Parnet. *Dialogues II*. Trans. Hugh Tomlinson, Barbara Habberjam, and Eliot R. Albert. European Perspectives. New York: Columbia UP, 1987.

Deleuze, Gilles, and Félix Guattari. *A Thousand Plateaus: Capitalism and Schizophrenia*. Trans. Brian Massumi. Minneapolis: U of Minnesota P, 1987.

– *Kafka: Toward a Minor Literature*. Trans. Dana Polan. Minneapolis: U of Minnesota P, 1986.

Derrida, Jacques. "Autoimmunity: Real and Symbolic Suicides" (A Dialogue with Jacques Derrida)." In *Philosophy in a Time of Terror: Dialogues with Jürgen Habermas and Jacques Derrida*. Ed. Giovanna Borradori. Trans. Pascale-Anne Brault and Michael B. Naas. Chicago: Chicago UP, 2003. 85–136.

– "Nietzsche and the Machine." In *Negotiations: Interventions and Interview, 1971–2001*. Ed. Elizabeth G. Rottenberg. Stanford, CA: Stanford UP, 2002. 215–56.

– "Politics and Friendship: a Discussion with Jacques Derrida." By Geoffrey Bennington. Centre for Modern French Thought, University of Sussex.

University of Sussex. 1997. Web. 14 Aug. 2008. http://hydra.humanities
.uci.edu/derrida/pol+fr.

– *Politics of Friendship*. Trans. George Collins. New York: Verso, 1997.

– "Signature, Event, Context." In *Limited, Inc.* Ed. Gerard Graff. Trans. Samuel
Weber and Jeffrey Mehlman. Evanston, IL: Northwestern UP, 1988. 1–23.

– *Specters of Marx: The State of the Debt, the Work of Mourning, & the New International*. Trans. Peggy Kamuf. New York: Routledge, 1994.

Dewey, Anne. "Poetic Authority and the Public Sphere of Politics in the Activist 1960s: The Duncan-Levertov Debate." In Gelpi and Bertholf, *Robert Duncan and Denise Levertov* 109–25.

Dhairyam, Sagri. "'Artifacts for Survival': Remapping the Contours of Poetry
with Audre Lorde." *Feminist Studies* 18, no. 2 (1992): 229–56.

Dorn, Ed. "*The Sullen Art* Interview." By David Ossman. *Interviews*. Ed. Donald Allen. Bolinas, CA: The Four Seasons Foundation, 1963. 1–6.

Drucker, Johanna. *Figuring the Word: Essays on Books, Writing, and Visual Poetics*. New York: Granary Books, 1998.

Dryden, John. "From The Preface to Ovid's Epistles." In Venuti, *The Translation
Studies Reader* 38–42.

Duberman, Martin. *Black Mountain: An Exploration in Community*. New York:
E.P. Dutton & Co., 1972.

Duncan, Robert. *Bending the Bow*. New York: New Directions, 1968.

– "An Essay at War." *Derivations: Selected Poems, 1950–1956*. London: Fulcrum
P, 1968. 9–24.

– "The HD Book: Part 2, Chapter 10." *Ironwood* 22 (Fall 1983): 47–64.

– "Ideas of the Meaning of Form." In *Fictive Certainties*. New York: New Directions, 1985. 89–105.

– "The Multiversity, Passages 21." *Bending the Bow* 70–3.

– "Orders, Passages 24." *Bending the Bow* 77–80.

– "Pages from a Notebook." In Allen, *The New American Poetry* 400–7.

– "Preface." *Bending the Bow* i–x.

– "The Soldiers, Passages 26." *Bending the Bow* 112–19.

– "Up Rising." *Bending the Bow* 81–3.

DuPlessis, Rachel Blau. *Blue Studios: Poetry and Its Cultural Work*. Tuscaloosa:
U of Alabama P, 2006.

– "Manhood and Its Poetic Projects: The Construction of Masculinity in the
Counter-Cultural Poetry of the U.S. 1950s." *Jacket Magazine*. N.p. 31 Oct.
2006. Web. 12 Jan. 2008. http://jacketmagazine.com/31/duplessis-man-
hood.html.

– "Manifests." *Diacritics* 26, nos. 3–4 (Fall-Winter 1996): 31–53.

DuPlessis, Rachel Blau, and Ann Snitow, eds. *The Feminist Memoir Project: Voices from the Women's Liberation Movement.* New York: Three Rivers P, 1998.

du Plessix, Gray Francine. "Black Mountain: The Breaking (Making) of a Writer." In *Black Mountain College: Sprouted Seeds: An Anthology of Personal Accounts.* Ed. Mervin Lane. Knoxville: U of Tennessee P, 1990. 300–11.

Dutton, Paul, and Steven Smith, eds. *Read the Way He Writes: A Festschrift for bpNichol.* Spec. issue of *Open Letter* 6, nos. 5–6 (Summer/Fall 1986).

Eagleton, Terry. *The Ideology of the Aesthetic.* Oxford: Blackwell, 1990.

– *Why Marx Was Right.* New Haven, CT: Yale UP, 2011.

Easthope, Anthony. *Poetry as Discourse.* London: Methuen, 1983.

Echols, Alice. *Daring to be Bad: Radical Feminism in America, 1967–1975.* Minneapolis: U of Minnesota P, 1989.

Eckerman, Ingrid. *The Bhopal Saga: Causes and Consequences of the World's Largest Industrial Disaster.* Hyderabad, India: Universities P, 2005.

"El Congresso Internacional de Intelectuales Tricontinental." 1968. In *Encyclopedia of the United Nations and International Agreements.* Ed. Edmund Jan Ozmanczyk. 3rd ed. Vol. 2. New York: Taylor and Francis, 2002. 873.

Emerson, Lori. "Nicholongings: because they is." *Open Letter* 10, no. 4 (1998): 27–33.

Evans, George, ed. *Charles Olson & Cid Corman: Complete Correspondence, 1950–1964.* Vol. 1. Orono, ME: National Poetry Foundation, 1987.

Faas, Ekbert. *Robert Creeley: A Biography.* Hanover: UP of New England, 2001.

Fanon, Frantz. *Black Skin: White Masks.* London: MacGibbon & Kee, 1968.

Fast, Robin Riley. "She Is The One You Call Sister: Levertov's and Rich's Poems on Sisterhood." In *The Sister Bond: A Feminist View of a Timeless Connection.* Ed. A.H. McNaron. New York: Pergamon P, 1985. 105–22.

Feree, Myra Marx, and Beth B. Hess. *Controversy and Coalition: The New Feminist Movement Across Three Decades of Change.* New York: Twayne, 1994.

Filliou, Robert. "Research on the Eternal Network." In *Robert Filliou: From Political to Poetical Economy.* Vancouver: Morris and Helen Belkin Art Gallery, 1995. 8.

Filliou, Robert, and George Brecht. "La Fête est Permanente." In *Teaching and Learning as Performing Arts.* Koeln: Koening, 1970. 197–207.

Filliou, Robert, bpNichol, Steve McCaffery, George Brecht, Dick Higgins, and Dieter Rot. *Six Fillious.* Milwaukee: Membrane P, 1978.

Fink, Thomas. *A Different Sense of Power: Problems of Community in Late-Twentieth-Century U.S. Poetry.* Madison, WI: Fairleigh Dickinson UP, 2001.

Firestone, Shulamith, and Anne Koedt, eds. *Notes from the Second Year: Women's Liberation, Major Writings of the Radical Feminists*. New York: Radical Feminism, 1970.

Ford, Arthur L. *Robert Creeley*. Boston: Twayne, 1978.

Foster, Edward H. *Understanding the Black Mountain Poets*. Columbia: U of South Carolina P, 1995.

Foucault, Michel. *Discipline and Punish: The Birth of the Prison*. 2nd ed. Trans. Alan Sheridan. New York: Vintage Books, 1995.

– "Friendship as a Way of Life." In *Ethics: Subjectivity and Truth*. Ed. Paul Rabinow. Trans. Robert Hurley. New York: The New P, 1997. 135–40.

– "History of Systems of Thought." In *Language, Counter-Memory, Practice* 199–204.

– *Language, Counter-Memory, Practice: Selected Essays and Interviews*. Ed. D.F. Bouchard. Ithaca, NY: Cornell UP, 1977.

– "Nietzsche, Genealogy, History." In *Language, Counter-Memory, Practice* 139–64.

– *The Order of Things: An Archaeology of the Human Sciences*. 1966. New York: Routledge, 1989.

– *"Society Must Be Defended": Lectures at the Collège de France, 1975–1976*. Ed. Mauro Bertani and Alessandro Fontana. Trans. David Macey. New York: Picador, 2003.

– "Subject and Power." In *Michel Foucault: Beyond Structuralism and Hermeneutics*. Ed. Hubert L. Dreyfus and Paul Rabinow. Chicago: U of Chicago P, 1983. 208–16.

Four Horsemen, The. "Matthew's Line." *CaNADAda*. Toronto: Griffin, 1972.

– "Mischievous Eve." *Live in the West*. Toronto: Starborne Productions, 1977.

– *The Prose Tattoo: Selected Performance Scores*. Milwaukee: Membrane P, 1983.

Frank, Robert, and Henry Sayre, eds. *The Line in Postmodern Poetry*. Urbana: U of Illinois P, 1988.

Frankfurter, Marin Denman, and Gardner Jackson, eds. *The Letters of Sacco and Vanzetti*. Harmondsworth, UK: Penguin, 1997.

Fredman, Stephen. *The Grounding of American Poetry: Charles Olson and the Emersonian Tradition*. New York: Cambridge UP, 1993.

Freeman, Jo. "The Tyranny of Structurelessness." In Koedt, Levine, and Rapone, *Radical Feminism* 285–99.

Friedman, Ken, ed. *The Fluxus Reader*. West Sussex, UK: Academy Editions, 1998.

Fryer, Peter. *Staying Power: The History of Black Power in Britain*. London: Pluto P, 1984.

Gale, Matthew. *Dada and Surrealism*. London: Phaidon, 1997.

Gates, Jr, Henry Louis. *The Signifying Monkey: A Theory of African-American Literary Criticism*. Oxford: Oxford UP, 1988.

Gelpi, Albert, and Robert J. Bertholf, eds. *Robert Duncan and Denise Levertov: The Poetry of Politics, the Politics of Poetry*. Stanford, CA: Stanford UP, 2006.

Gilroy, Paul. *The Black Atlantic: Modernity and Double Consciousness*. London: Verso, 1993.

– *"There Ain't No Black in the Union Jack": The Cultural Politics of Race and Nation*. Chicago: U of Chicago P, 1991.

Ginsberg, Allen. "Howl." *Collected Poems, 1947–1980*. New York: Harper Perennial, 1984. 126–33.

Glissant, Édouard. *L'Intention Poétique*. Paris: Seuil, 1969.

– *Poétique de la Relation*. Paris: Gallimard, 1990.

Goldsmith, Kenneth. "Meme Museum." *Poetry Foundation*. 2011. Web. 4 May 2011. http://www.poetryfoundation.org/harriet/2011/04/the-meme-museum/.

Gonick, Cy. "Strategies for Social Change." *Canadian Dimension* 4 (Nov.–Dec. 1966): 39–40.

Goodman, Paul. "Advance-Guard Writing, 1900–1950." *The Kenyon Review* 13, no. 3 (Summer 1951): 357–80.

Goodman, Paul, and Percival Goodman. *Communitas: Means of Livelihood and Ways of Life*. 1947. New York: Columbia UP, 1960.

Grahn, Judy. "The Common Woman Poems." *Love Belongs* 57–65.

– *Love Belongs to Those Who do the Feeling: New and Selected Poems, 1966–2006*. Los Angeles: Red Hen P, 2008.

– *Really Reading Gertrude Stein*. 1989. *The Judy Grahn Reader*. San Francisco: Aunt Lute Books, 2009. 285–96.

– "She Who continues." *Love Belongs* 72.

– "She Who increases / what can be done." *Love Belongs* 76–7.

Guevera, Ernesto Che. "The Cultural Vanguard" (from *Man and Socialism in Cuba*). In Salkey, *Writing in Cuba* 137–40.

Gysin, Brion. "Cut-Ups Self-Explained." In *Back in No Time: The Brion Gysin Reader*. Ed. Jason Weis. Middletown, CT: Wesleyan UP, 2001. 132–5.

Hall, Stuart. "New Ethnicities." In *Stuart Hall: Critical Dialogues in Cultural Studies*. Ed. David Morley and Kuan-Hsing Chen. New York: Routledge, 1996. 441–9.

– "On Postmodernism and Articulation: An Interview with Stuart Hall." By Lawrence Grossberg. *Stuart Hall: Critical Dialogues* 131–50.

Hallward, Peter. *Damming the Flood: Haiti, Aristide, and the Politics of Containment*. London: Verso, 2007.

– "Édouard Glissant between the Singular and the Specific." *Yale Journal of Criticism* 11, no. 2 (1998): 441–64.
– "Our Role in Haiti's Plight." *The Guardian* 13 Jan. 2010. Web. 16 Jan. 2010. http://www.guardian.co.uk/commentisfree/2010/jan/13/our-role-in-haitis-plight.
Hanisch, Carol. "The Personal Is Political." In Firestone and Koedt, *Notes from the Second Year* 76–8.
Hardt, Michael, and Antonio Negri. *Empire*. Cambridge: Harvard UP, 2001.
– *Multitude: War and Democracy in the Age of Empire*. New York: Penguin Group, 2004.
Hart, Armando. *Marxism and the Human Condition: A Latin American Perspective*. London: Pluto, 2005.
Hartman, Charles O. *Free Verse: An Essay on Prosody*. Princeton, NJ: Princeton UP, 1980.
Harvey, David. *A Brief History of Neoliberalism*. Oxford: Oxford UP, 2005.
– *The Condition of Postmodernity: An Enquiry into the Origins of Cultural Change*. Cambridge: Blackwell, 1990.
Hendricks, Jon, ed. *Fluxus Codex*. Gilbert and Lila Silverman Fluxus Collection. New York: H.N. Abrams, 1988.
Henke, Holger, and Fred Réno. *Modern Political Culture in the Caribbean*. Kingston, Jamaica: U of West Indian P, 2003.
Henri, Adrian. *Environments and Happenings*. London: Thames and Hudson, 1974.
Herskovits, Melville. *Life in a Haitian Valley*. Garden City, NY: Anchor Books, 1971.
Higgins, Dick. *Classic Plays*. New York: Unpublished Editions, 1976.
– "A Commentary by the Poet on 'Conceptual Forks.'" In *A Dialectic of Centuries* 153–5.
– *A Dialectic of Centuries: Notes Towards a Theory of the New Arts*. New York: Printed Editions, 1978.
– *Horizons: The Poetics and Theory of the Intermedia*. Carbondale: Southern Illinois UP, 1984.
– "Letter to Steve McCaffery." 13 Apr. 1979. Box 21, Folder 41. Dick Higgins Papers. Getty Research Institute, Los Angeles, California.
– "The Mail-Interview with Dick Higgins." By Ruud Janssen. Fluxus Heidelberg Center, Heidelberg, Germany, 1995. Web. 15 Sept. 2007. http://www.fluxusheidelberg.org/dhint.html.
– "Six Trivial Reflections." In *Horizons* 113–15.
– "The Strategy of Each of My Books." In *Horizons* 118–36.
– "A Taxonomy of Sound Poetry." In *Horizons* 40–52.
– "Towards an Allusive Referential." In *A Dialectic of Centuries* 67–74.
Higgins, Hannah. *Fluxus Experience*. Berkeley: U of California P, 2002.

Higgins, Lesley. "Jowett and Pater: Trafficking in Platonic Wares." *Victorian Studies* 37, no. 1 (1993): 43–72.

Hirschfeld, Heather. "Early Modern Collaboration and Theories of Authorship." *PMLA* 116, no. 3 (2001): 609–22.

Hobsbawm, Eric. *The Age of Extremes: The Short Twentieth Century, 1914–1991*. London: Abacus, 1995.

Hodge, Robert, and Gunther Kress. *Social Semiotics*. Ithaca, NY: Cornell UP, 1988.

Hodges, Donald C. *The Latin American Revolution: Politics and Strategy from Apro-Marxism to Guevarism*. New York: Morrow, 1974.

Holscher, Rory, and Robert Schultz, eds. "Symposium on the Theory and Practice of the Line in Contemporary Poetry." *Epoch* 29, no. 2 (Winter 1980): 162–224.

Hoover, Paul, ed. *Postmodern American Poetry: A Norton Anthology*. New York: Norton, 1994.

Horace. "Ars Poetica or Epistle to the Pisones." *Satires, Epistles, Ars Poetica*. Trans. H. Rushton Fairclough. Cambridge, MA: Harvard UP, 1961. 442–89.

Howe, Florence, and Ellen Bass, eds. *No More Masks!: An Anthology of Poems by Women*. New York: Anchor P, 1973.

Howe, Susan. "Since a Dialogue We Are." *Acts* 10 (1989): 166–72.

Hurston, Zora Neal. *Tell My Horse: Voodoo and Life in Haiti and Jamaica*. New York: Harper Perennial, 1990.

Hyde Park Chapter of the Chicago Women's Liberation Movement. "Socialist Feminism: A Strategy for the Women's Movement." 1972. In *Documents from the Women's Liberation Movement: An On-line Archival Collection*. Special Collections Library, Duke University. Web. 8 Aug. 2010.

Idowu, E.B. *African Traditional Religion: A Definition*. London: SCM P, 1973.

Ignatow, David. "Letter to Langston Hughes." 22 Jan. 1960. Langston Hughes Papers. Yale Collection of American Literature, Beinecke Rare Book Library, Yale University.

Jaeger, Peter. *ABC of Reading TRG*. Vancouver: Talonbooks, 1999.

Jakobson, Roman. "On Linguistic Aspects of Translation." In Venuti, *The Translation Studies Reader* 138–43.

James, C.L.R. *The Black Jacobins: Toussaint L'Ouverture and the San Domingo Revolution*. 2nd ed. New York: Vintage Books, 1963.

James, Louis. "Caribbean Artists Movement." In *West Indian Intellectuals in Britain*. Ed. Bill Schwarz. Manchester: Manchester UP, 2003. 209–27.

Jameson, Fredric. *The Cultural Turn: Selected Writings on the Postmodern, 1983–1998*. New York: Verso, 1998.

Jarry, Alfred. *Exploits and Opinions of Dr. Faustroll, 'Pataphysician*. Trans. Simon. Watson Taylor. Boston: Exact Change, 1996.

Jenkins, Lee M. "The t/reasonable 'English' of Kamau Brathwaite." In *The Language of Caribbean Poetry: Boundaries of Expression*. Gainesville: U of Florida P, 2004. 95–125.

Jerome, St. "De optimo genere interpetandi." ("The Best Kind of Translator.") 395 CE. In *Western Translation Theory from Herodotus to Nietzsche*. Ed. Douglas Robinson. Manchester: St Jerome, 1997. 23–30.

— "Letter LVII to Pammachius." In *Letters and Selected Works*. Trans. W.H. Freemantle and G. Lewis. 1892. Grand Rapids, MI: Wm. B. Eerdmans, n.d. 112–18.

Joan, Polly, and Andrea Chessman. *Guide to Women's Publishing*. Paradise, CA: Dustbooks, 1978.

Johnson, Ronald. *Radi os*. Berkeley: Sand Dollars, 1977.

Jones, Bridget. "'The Unity Is Submarine': Aspects of a Pan-Caribbean Consciousness in the Work of Kamau Brathwaite." In Brown, *The Art of Kamau Brathwaite* 86–100.

Joris, Pierre. *A Nomad Poetics: Essays*. Middletown, CT: Wesleyan UP, 2003.

Kane, Daniel. *All Poets Welcome: The Lower East Side Poetry Scene in the 1960s*. Berkeley: U of California P, 2003.

Kaprow, Allan. *Assemblages, Environments, & Happenings*. New York: H.N. Abrams, 1966.

— "18 Happenings in 6 Parts." New York, Reuben Gallery, c. Fall 1959.

Karasick, Adeena. "Tract Marks: Echoes and Traces in the Toronto Research Group." *Open Letter* 8, no. 3 (1992): 76–89.

Kearon, Pamela. "Power as a Function of the Group." In Firestone and Koedt, *Notes from the Second Year* 108–10.

King, Katie. *Theory in its Feminist Travels: Conversations in U.S. Women's Movements*. Bloomington: Indiana UP, 1994.

Kirby, Michael. "Happenings: An Introduction." In Sandford, *Happenings* 1–28.

Klein, Naomi. *The Shock Doctrine: The Rise of Disaster Capitalism*. Toronto: Vintage, 2008.

Koedt, Anne, Ellen Levine, and Anita Rapone, eds. *Radical Feminism*. New York: Quadrangle Books, 1973.

Koestenbaum, Wayne. *Double Talk: The Erotics of Male Literary Collaboration*. New York: Routledge, 1989.

Kostelanetz, Richard, ed. *Conversing with Cage*. 2nd ed. New York: Routledge, 2003.

— "Text-Sound Art: A Survey." In *Text-Sound Texts*. New York: William Morrow Inc., 1980. 14–23.

– *The Theatre of Mixed Means: An Introduction to Happenings, Kinetic Environments, and other Mixed-Means Performances*. New York: The Dial P, 1968.

Krensky, Stephen. *Anansi and the Box of Stories: A West African Folktale*. Brookfield, CT: Millbrook P, 2007.

Lange, David. "Recognizing the Public Domain." *Law and Contemporary Problems* 44, no. 4 (Autumn 1981): 147–78.

La Rose, John. "Connecting Link." *Foundations* 13.

– "Everchanging Immanence of Culture." Private Collection of Sarah White, 1992. 1–3.

– "Fantasy in Space." *Foundations* 39–40.

– *Foundations*. London: New Beacon, 1966.

– "Interview with John La Rose." By Anne Walmsley. Papers of the Caribbean Artists Movement, 6/44, 1986, 1–20, George Padmore Institute, London, UK.

– "Never Fixed." *Foundations* 16.

– "Prosepoem for a Conference." *Eyelets of Truth Within Me*. London: New Beacon, 1992. 13.

La Rose, John, Tribute Committee, ed. *Foundations of a Movement: A Tribute to John La Rose on the Occasion of the 10th International Book Fair of Radical Black & Third World Books*. London: John La Rose Tribute Committee, 1991.

Larkin, Philip. "This Be The Verse." Ramazani, Ellmann, and O'Clair, *Norton Anthology* 223–4.

Latour, Bruno. *Laboratory Life: The Social Construction of Scientific Facts*. Los Angeles: Sage, 1979.

– *Reassembling the Social: An Introduction to Actor-Network-Theory*. Oxford: Oxford UP, 2005.

– *We Have Never Been Modern*. Trans. Catherine Porter. Cambridge, MA: Harvard UP, 1993.

Lecercle, Jean-Jacques. "An A-to-Z Guide to Making Dying Illegal." Introduction. In *Making Dying Illegal: Architecture Against Death, Original to the 21st Century*. By Madeline Gins and Shusaku Arakawa. New York: Roof Books, 2006. 9–23.

Lefevere, André. *Translation/History/Culture: A Sourcebook*. New York: Routledge, 1992.

Lehman, David. *The Last Avant-Garde: The Making of the New York School Poets*. New York: Doubleday, 1998.

Lessig, Lawrence. *Free Culture*. New York: Penguin, 2004.

– *The Future of Ideas: The Fate of the Commons in a Connected World*. New York: Random House, 2001.

Levertov, Denise. "Denise Levertov: An Interview." By Michael Andre. *Conversations with Denise Levertov*. Ed. Jewel Spears Brooker. Jackson: UP of Mississipi, 1998. 52–67.

– "On the Function of the Line." In *Denise Levertov: New & Selected Essays*. New York: New Directions, 1992. 78–87.

– "Some Notes on Organic Form." In *Postmodern American Poetry: A Norton Anthology*. Ed. Paul Hoover. New York: Norton, 1994. 628–33.

– "Technique and Tune-up." In *Denise Levertov: New & Selected Essays* 93–101.

– *To Stay Alive*. New York: New Directions, 1971.

Lewis, Windham. *Blasting and Bombardiering: An Autobiography (1914–1926)*. 1937. New York: Riverrun P, 1982.

Licata, Elizabeth. "Robert Creeley's Collaborations: A History." In Cappellazzo and Licata, *In Company* 11–21.

Lingis, Alphonso. *The Community of Those Who Have Nothing in Common*. Bloomington: Indiana UP, 1994.

Litman, Jessica. *Digital Copyright*. Amherst: Prometheus Books, 2001.

– "The Public Domain." *Emory Law Journal*, 39, No. 4 (Fall 1990): 965–1023.

Lorde, Audre. "Above the Wind: An Interview with Audre Lorde." By Charles H. Rowell. *Callaloo* 14, no. 1 (1991): 83–95.

– "Coal." *The Collected Poems of Audre Lorde*. New York: Norton, 1997. 6.

– "Notes from a Trip to Russia." In *Sister Outsider: Essays and Speeches*. Berkeley: Crossing P, 1984. 13–35.

– "Poetry Is Not a Luxury." In *Sister Outsider* 36–9.

– "The Transformation of Silence into Language and Action." In *Sister Outsider* 40–4.

Löwy, Michael, ed. *Marxism in Latin America from 1909 to the Present: An Anthology*. Trans. Michael Pearlman. Atlantic Highlands, NJ: Humanities P, 1992.

Lyon, Janet. *Manifestoes: Provocations of the Modern*. Ithaca, NY: Cornell UP, 1999.

Lyotard, Jean-François. *The Postmodern Condition: A Report on Knowledge*. 1979. Trans. Geoff Bennington and Brian Massumi. Minneapolis: U of Minnesota P, 1984.

Mackey, Nathaniel. "Wringing the Word." In Brown, *The Art of Kamau Brathwaite* 132–51.

Mannoni, Octave. *Prospero and Caliban: The Psychology of Colonization*. New York: Praeger, 1956.

Mariátegui, José Carlos. *Seven Interpretive Essays on Peruvian Reality*. Trans. Marjory Urquidi. Austin: U of Texas P, 1971.

Marinetti, Filippo Tommaso. "The Founding and Manifesto of Futurism." 1909. In Caws, *Manifesto* 184–9.

Marks, Corey. "The Descriptive-Meditative Structure." In *Structure and Surprise: Engaging Poetic Turns*. Ed. Michael Theune. New York: Teachers and Writers Collaborative, 2007. 123–46.

Marx, Karl. *Capital: Volume One*. In McLellan 452–3.

– *Economic and Philosophical Manuscripts*. In McLellan 95–104.

– *The Eighteenth Brumaire of Louis Bonaparte*. In McLellan 329–55.

– "The Fetishism of Commodities." In McLellan 472–80.

– "Inaugural Address to the First International." In McLellan 575–81.

– "On James Mill." In McLellan 124–33.

– "Thesis on Feuerbach." In McLellan 171–4.

Marx, Karl, and Frederick Engels. *The Communist Manifesto*. Ed. J.P. Taylor. Trans. Samuel Moore. New York: Penguin, 1967.

– *The German Ideology. The Marx-Engels Reader*. 2nd ed. Ed. Robert C. Tucker. New York: Norton, 1977. 146–202.

Mason, Philip. *Prospero's Magic*. London: Oxford UP, 1962.

Maud, Ralph. *Charles Olson's Reading: A Biography*. Carbondale: Southern Illinois UP, 1996.

– *What Does Not Change: The Significance of Charles Olson's "The Kingfishers."* Madison, WI: Fairleigh Dickinson UP, 1998.

Maxwell, Marina. "Towards a Revolution in the Arts." *Savacou* 2 (1970): 19–32.

McCaffery, Steve. "An Afterthought." *In England Now that Spring*. Toronto: Aya P, 1979. N.p.

– "The Body: In Light." *Rational Geomancy* 246–53.

– "Discussion … Genesis … Continuity: Some Reflections on the Current Work of the Four Horsemen." In *Sound Poetry: A Catalogue* 32–6.

– "A Homolinguistic Translation of Shakespeare's Sonnet 105: 'Let not my love be called idolatry.'" *Seven Pages Missing: Volume Two* 161.

– "An Interview with Karen Mac Cormack & Steve McCaffery." By Antoine Cazé. *Sources* 8 (2000): 28–47.

– "An Interview with Steve McCaffery on the TRG." By Peter Jaeger. *Open Letter* 10, no. 4 (1998): 77–96.

– "The Kommunist Manifesto or Wot We Wukkerz Want." *Seven Pages Missing: Volume Two* 171–80.

– "The Letter 'a' According to Chomsky." *Seven Pages Missing: Volume Two* 54.

– "Letter to Dick Higgins." 30 Sept. 1977. Box 21, Folder 41. Dick Higgins Papers. Getty Research Institute, Los Angeles, California.

– "A Note on *Intimate Distortions*." In *Seven Pages Missing: Volume Two* 452.

– "Performed Paragrammatism." In *Seven Pages Missing: Volume Two* 361–2.

– *Prior to Meaning: The Protosemantic and Poetics*. Evanston, IL: Northwestern UP, 2001.

– "Proem: The Logic of Frogs #383." *The Basho Variations*. Toronto: Book Thug, 2007. 3–9.

– *Seven Pages Missing: Volume Two: Previously Uncollected Texts, 1968–2000*. Toronto: Coach House Books, 2002.

– "Sound Poetry: A Survey." In *Sound Poetry: A Catalogue.* Ed. Steve McCaffery and bpNichol. Toronto: Underwhich Editions, 1979. 6–18.
– "Trans-Avant-Garde: An Interview with Steve McCaffery." By Ryan Cox. *Rain Taxi.* N.p. 2007. Web. 6 May 2008. http://www.raintaxi.com/online/2007winter/mccaffery.shtml.
– "A Translation of Sir Philip Sidney's Sonnet XXXI from 'Astrophel and Stella.'" *Seven Pages Missing: Volume Two* 163.
– "Twenty-Three." *Intimate Distortions: A Displacement of Sappho.* Erin, ON: The Porcupine's Quill, 1979. N.p.
– *"From* The Unposted Correspondence." In *Seven Pages Missing: Volume Two* 354–6.
– *Wot We Wukkers Want: One Step to the Next.* Audiocassette. Toronto: Underwhich Editions, 1980.
– "Writing as a General Economy." In *North of Intention: Critical Writings, 1973–1986.* 2nd ed. New York: Roof Books, 2000. 201–21.
McCaffery, Steve, and bpNichol. "Collboration No. 2." *Rational Geomancy* 228.
– "In England Now that Spring." *In England Now that Spring.* Toronto: Aya, 1979. N.p.
– eds. "Introduction." *Canadian "Pataphysics.* Spec. issue of *Open Letter* 4, nos. 6–7 (Winter 1980–1): 7–8.
– *Rational Geomancy: The Kids of the Book Machine: The Collected Research Reports of the Toronto Research Group, 1973–1982.* Talonbooks: Vancouver, 1992.
– eds. *Sound Poetry: A Catalogue for the Eleventh International Sound Poetry Festival, Toronto, Canada, October 14 to 21, 1978.* Toronto: Underwhich Editions, 1979.
McGann, Jerome. *Black Riders: The Visible Language of Modernism.* Princeton, NJ: Princeton UP, 1993.
– *The Textual Condition.* Princeton, NJ: Princeton UP, 1991.
McKenzie, Donald F. *Bibliography and the Sociology of Texts.* The Panizzi Lectures. London: The British Library, 1986.
McLellan, David, ed. *Karl Marx: Selected Writings.* 2nd ed. Oxford: Oxford UP, 2000.
McLuhan, Marshall. *Counterblast.* Toronto: n.p., 1954.
– *Counterblast.* Toronto: McClelland and Stewart, 1969.
Merino Garretón, Manuel A. *The Chilean Political Process.* Trans. Sharon Kellum and Gilbert W. Merkx. Boston: Unwin Hyman, 1989.
Mighty Sparrow, The. "The Slave." *120 Calypsoes to Remember.* Port of Spain, Trinidad: Caribbean Music Co., 1954. 87.
Miller, Brett. *"Chelsea* 8: Political Poetry at Midcentury." In Gelpi and Bertholf, *Robert Duncan and Denise Levertov* 93–108.

Milton, John. "The Verse." In *Paradise Lost: An Authoritative Text, Backgrounds and Sources, Criticism*. Ed. Scott Elledge. New York: Norton, 1975. 4.

Montefiore, Jan. *Feminism and Poetry: Language, Experience, Identity in Women's Writing*. New York: Pandora, 1987.

Moore, Honor, ed. *Poems from the Women's Movement*. New York: Library of America, 2009.

– "Polemic #1." In Ramstad and Ronnie, *The New Woman's Survival Sourcebook* 105.

Moraga, Cherríe. "Preface." In Anzaldúa and Moraga, *This Bridge Called My Back* xiii–xix.

– "The Welder." In Anzaldúa and Moraga, *This Bridge Called My Back* 219–20.

Morgan, Robin. *Going Too Far: The Personal Chronicle of a Feminist*. New York: Vintage Books, 1978.

– "Goodbye To All That." In *Going Too Far* 121–30.

– *Lady of the Beasts: Poems*. New York: Random House, 1976.

– "Letter to a Sister Underground." *Monster: Poems*. New York: Random House, 1972. 58–64.

– ed. *Sisterhood is Powerful: An Anthology of Writings from the Women's Liberation Movement*. New York: Random House, 1970.

– "Three Articles on WITCH." In *Going Too Far* 72–81.

– "WITCH Documents." In *Sisterhood Is Powerful* 538–53.

Morley, Hilda. "A Few Mixed Recollections." In *Black Mountain College: Sprouted Seeds: An Anthology of Personal Accounts*. Ed. Mervin Lane. Knoxville: U of Tennessee P, 1990. 317–18.

Morrison, Paul. *The Poetics of Fascism: Ezra Pound, T.S. Eliot, Paul de Man*. Oxford: Oxford UP, 1996.

Motherwell, Robert, ed. *The Dada Painters and Poets: An Anthology*. 2nd ed. 1951. 2nd ed. Cambridge, MA: Harvard UP, 1981.

Mouffe, Chantal. *The Return of the Political*. New York: Verso, 1993.

Mouffe, Chantal, and Ernesto Laclau. *Hegemony and Socialist Strategy: Towards a Radical Democratic Politics*. London: Verso, 1985.

Munday, Jeremy. *Introducing Translation Studies: Theories and Applications*. New York: Routledge, 2001.

Murray, Timothy, and Stephen Boardway. "Year By Year Bibliography of Robert Creeley." In Terrell, *Robert Creeley: The Poet's Workshop* 313–74.

Nancy, Jean-Luc. *Being Singular Plural*. Trans. Robert D. Richardson and Anne E. O'Byrne. Ed. Werner Hamacher and David E. Wellbery. Stanford, CA: Stanford UP, 2000.

– *The Inoperative Community*. Trans. Peter Connor, Lisa Garbus, Michael Holland, and Simona Sawhney. Ed. Peter Connor. Theory and History of Lit. 76. Minneapolis: U of Minnesota P, 1991.

Naylor, Paul. *Poetic Investigations: Singing the Holes in History*. Evanston, IL: Northwestern UP, 1999.

Nealon, Christopher. "Camp Messianism, or, the Hopes of Poetry in Late-Late Capitalism." *American Literature* 76, no. 3 (Sept. 2004): 579–602.

Nichol, bp "The Annotated, Anecdoted, Beginnings of a Critical Checklist of the Published Works of Steve McCaffery." *Open Letter* 6, no. 9 (1987): 67–92.

– "from Catullus XXVIII." *zygal: a book of mysteries and translations*. Toronto: Coach House P, 1985. 62.

– *An H in the Heart: A Reader*. Ed. Michael Ondaatje and George Bowering. Toronto: McClelland & Stewart, 1994.

– "Interview: with Caroline Bayard and Jack David." *Meanwhile* 168–84.

– "Interview: with Pierre Coupey, Dwight Gardiner, Gladys Hindmarch, and Daphne Marlatt." *Meanwhile* 145–59.

– "Introduction." In *The Prose Tattoo: Selected Performance Scores*. Milwaukee, MI: Membrane P, 1983. 3–4.

– *Meanwhile: The Critical Writings of bpNichol*. Ed. Roy Miki. Vancouver: Talonbooks, 2002.

– *Translating Translating Apollinaire: A Preliminary Report from a Book of Research*. Milwaukee, MI: Membrane P, 1979.

Nichols, Miriam. "A/Politics of Contemporary Anglo-Canadian Poetries: The Toronto Research Group and the Kootenay School of Writing." In *Assembling Alternatives: Reading Postmodern Poetries Transnationally*. Ed. Romana Huk. Middletown, CT: Wesleyan UP, 2003. 66–85.

Nixon, Rob. "Caribbean and African Appropriations of *The Tempest*." In *Politics and Poetic Value*. Ed. Robert von Hallberg. Chicago: U of Chicago P, 1987. 185–206.

Nkrumah, Kwame. *Neo-Colonialism: The Last Stage of Imperialism*. London: Thomas Nelson & Sons, 1965.

Novik, Mary. *Robert Creeley: An Inventory, 1945–1970*. Montreal: McGill-Queen's UP, 1973.

O'Hara, Frank. "Personism: A Manifesto." In *The Collected Poems of Frank O'Hara*. Ed. Donald Allen. Berkeley: U of California P, 1995. 498–9.

Oliva, Achille Bonito. "The International Trans-Avant-Garde." In *Postmodernism: A Reader*. Ed. Thomas Docherty. New York: Columbia UP, 1993. 257–62.

Olson, Charles. "13 Vessels." *Maximus* 2:196–8.

– *Charles Olson Reading at Berkeley*. Transcribed by Zoe Brown. San Francisco: Coyote, 1966.

– "Culture and Revolution." 1–4. Manuscript of *Culture and Revolution*, c. 1952, Charles Olson Research Collection, Box 29, Archives and Special Collections at the Thomas J. Dodd Research Center, University of Connecticut Libraries.

– "Definitions by Undoings." *Boundary 2* vol. 2, nos. 1–2 (Fall 1973–Winter 1974): 7–12.

– "For R.C." *OLSON* 6 (Fall 1976): 3.

– "The Gate and the Center." In *Human Universe and Other Essays*. Ed. Donald Allen. New York: Grove P, 1967. 17–23.

– "A Glyph." *Black Mountain College: Experiment in Art*. Ed. Vincent Katz. Cambridge, MA: MIT P, 2002. 307.

– "Glyphs." *A Nation of Nothing But Poetry*. Ed. George F. Butterick. Santa Rosa: Black Sparrow, 1989. 84–5.

– Human Universe and Other Essays. Ed. Donald Allen. New York: Grove P, 1967.

– "Human Universe." *Human Universe* 3–15.

– "I live underneath." *Maximus* 3:228.

– "I, Maximus of Gloucester, to You." *Maximus* 1:1–4.

– "I, Mencius, Pupil of the Master." *The Collected Poems of Charles Olson*. Ed. George F. Butterick. Berkeley: U of California P, 1987. 318–20.

– "The K." *Collected Poems* 14.

– "The Kingfishers." *Collected Poems* 86–92.

– "Letter 3." *Maximus* 1:9–12.

– "Letter 5." *Maximus* 1:17–25.

– "Letter 6." *Maximus* 1:26–9.

– "Letter 22." *Maximus* 1:96–8.

– "A Letter to the Faculty of Black Mountain College." *OLSON* 8 (1977): 26–33.

– "Letter to Robert Creeley." 1 Jun. 1953. Unpublished. Reproduced in Butterick *Guide to Maximus* 4.

– "Letter to Ruth Benedict." 12 Jan. 1945. In "Key West I (1945)." *OLSON* 5 (Spring 1976): 3–10.

– "Letter to W. H. Ferry." 7 Aug. 1951. *OLSON* 2 (Fall: 1974): 8–15.

– "The Long Poem." 1948. *OLSON* 5 (1976): 38–43.

– *The Maximus Poems*. Berkeley: U of California P, 1983.

– "Maximus, to Gloucester: Letter 15." *Maximus* 1:67–71.

– "Maximus, at Tyre and at Boston." *Maximus* 1:93–5.

– "On Black Mountain." By Chad Walsh. *Muthologos: The Collected Lectures & Interviews*. Vol. 2. Ed. George F. Butterick. Bolinas, CA: Four Seasons Foundation, 1979. 55–79.

– "On Black Mountain (II)." By Andrew S. Leinoff. *OLSON* 8 (1977): 66–107.

– "Post-West." c. 1953. *OLSON* 5 (1976): 51–9.

- "The Present Is Prologue." In *Additional Prose: A Bibliography on America, Proprioception, & Other Notes & Essays*. Ed. George F. Butterick. Bolinas, CA: Four Seasons Foundation, 1974. 39–40.
- "Projective Verse." In *Collected Prose: Charles Olson*. Ed. Donald Allen and Benjamin Friedlander. Berkeley: U of California P, 1997. 239–49.
- "Rev. of *The New Empire*, by Brooks Adams." *Black Mountain Review* 1, no. 2 (1954): 63–4.
- "The Song and Dance of." *Maximus* 1:54–8.
- "The Songs of Maximus." *Maximus* 1:13–16.
- *The Special View of History*. Ed. Anne Charters. Berkeley, CA: Oyez P, 1970.
- "To David Ignatow." 5 Jan. 1960. Letter 87 of *Selected Letters: Charles Olson*. Ed. Ralph Maud. Berkeley: U of California P, 2000. 267–71.
- "West." 1953. *OLSON* 5 (1976): 46–50.

Oppenheim, Lois H. *Politics in Chile: Democracy, Authoritarianism, and the Search for Development*. 2nd ed. Boulder, CO: Westview P, 1999.

Ortiz, Fernando. *Contrapunto Cubano*. Caracas, Venezuela: Biblioteca, 1978.

Ostrom, Elinor. *Governing the Commons: The Evolution of Institutions for Collective Action*. New York: Cambridge UP, 1990.

Palmer, Bryan D. *Canada's 1960s: The Ironies of Identity in a Rebellious Age*. Toronto: U of Toronto P, 2009.

Palmer, Colin A. *Eric Williams & the Making of the Modern Caribbean*. Chapel Hill: U of North Carolina P, 2005.

Patterson, Orlando. "Is There a West Indian Aesthetic?" Papers of the Caribbean Artists Movement, 5/1/2, 1966, 1–3, George Padmore Institute, London, UK.

Paul, Sherman. *Olson's Push: Origin, Black Mountain, and recent American Poetry*. Baton Rouge: Louisiana State UP, 1978.

Payne, Carol Williams. "Consciousness Raising: A Dead End?" In Koedt, Levine, and Rapone, *Radical Feminism* 282–4.

Perloff, Marjorie. *21st Century Modernism: The "New" Poetics*. Malden, MA: Blackwell Pub., 2002.

- *The Dance of the Intellect: Studies in the Poetry of the Pound Tradition*. Cambridge: Cambridge UP, 1985.
- *Poetry On & Off the Page: Essays for Emergent Occasions*. Evanston: Northwestern UP, 1998.
- *Radical Artifice: Writing Poetry in the Age of Media*. Chicago: U of Chicago P, 1991.
- "Robert Creeley's Radical Poetics." *Electronic Book Review*. N.p. 2007. Web. 12 Jan. 2008. http://www.electronicbookreview.com/thread/electropoetics/commodious.

Peslikis, Irene. "Resistances to Consciousness." In Firestone and Koedt, *Notes from the Second Year* 81.

Phillips, Tom. *A Humument: A Treated Victorian Novel*. London: Thames and Hudson, 1980.

Plath, Sylvia. "Daddy." Ramazani, Ellmann, and O'Clair, *Norton Anthology* 606–8.

Poggioli, Renato. *The Theory of the Avant-Garde*. Trans. Gerald Fitzgerald. Cambridge, MA: The Belknap P of Harvard UP, 1968.

Pohl, Frances K. *Ben Shahn: New Deal Artist in a Cold War Climate, 1947–1954*. Austin: U of Texas P, 1989.

Pollard, Charles W. *New World Modernisms: T.S. Eliot, Derek Walcott, and Kamau Brathwaite*. Charlottesville: U of Virginia P, 2004.

Pope, Alexander. "An Essay on Man." *Alexander Pope: Selected Poetry and Prose*. Ed. William K. Wimsatt. 2nd ed. New York: Holt, Rinehart and Winston, 1972. 191–234.

Pound, Ezra. *The Cantos of Ezra Pound*. New York: New Directions, 1970.

– "A Retrospect." In *Literary Essays of Ezra Pound*. New York: New Directions, 1968. 3–14.

– *The Selected Letters of Ezra Pound, 1907–1941*. Ed. D.D. Paige. New York: New Directions, 1971.

Pratt, Mary Louise. *Imperial Eyes: Travel Writing and Transculturation*. 2nd ed. London: Routledge, 2008.

Rainey, Lawrence. "The Cultural Economy of Modernism." In *The Cambridge Companion to Modernism*. Ed. Michael Levenson. Cambridge: Cambridge UP, 1999. 33–69.

Ramazani, Jahan. *The Hybrid Muse: Postcolonial Poetry in English*. Chicago: U of Chicago P, 2001.

Ramazani, Jahan, Richard Ellmann, and Robert O'Clair, eds. *The Norton Anthology of Modern and Contemporary Poetry*. 3rd ed. 2 vols. New York: Norton, 2003.

Ramstad, Kirsten, and Susan Ronnie, eds. *The New Woman's Survival Sourcebook*. New York: Knopf, 1975.

Rancière, Jacques. *Dissensus: On Politics and Aesthetics*. London: Continuum International Pub., 2010.

Rattray, Robert S. *Ashanti*. London: Oxford UP, 1923.

Redding, Arthur. *Turncoats, Traitors, and Fellow Travelers: Culture and Politics of the Early Cold War*. Jackson: UP of Mississippi, 2008.

Reed, T.V. *The Art of Protest: Culture and Activism from the Civil Rights Movement to the Streets of Seattle*. Minneapolis: U of Minnesota P, 2005.

Reiss, Timothy J., ed. *For the Geography of a Soul: Emerging Perspectives on Kamau Brathwaite*. Trenton, NJ: Africa World P, 2001.

Riboud, Jean. "Letter to Charles Olson." c. 1948. Charles Olson Research Collection, Archives and Special Collections at the Thomas J. Dodd Research Center, University of Connecticut Libraries.

Rich, Adrienne. "A Walk by the Charles." *Poems: Selected and New, 1950–1974*. New York: Norton, 1975. 29.

– "Arts of the Possible." In *Arts of the Possible: Essays and Conversations*. New York: Norton, 2001. 146–67.

– "Conditions for Work: The Common World of Women." In *On Lies, Secrets, and Silence: Selected Prose, 1966–1978*. New York: Norton, 1979. 203–14.

– "Culture and Anarchy." *A Wild Patience has Taken Me This Far: Poems 1978–1981*. New York: Norton, 1981. 10–15.

– "Defying the Space that Separates." In *Arts of the Possible* 107–14.

– *The Dream of a Common Language: Poems 1974–1977*. New York: Norton, 1978.

– "Incipience." *Diving into the Wreck: Poems 1971–1972*. New York: Norton, 1973. 11–12.

– "Natural Resources." *The Dream of a Common Language* 60–67.

– "November 1968." *Poems* 145.

– "Origins and History of Consciousness." *The Dream of a Common Language* 7–9.

– "Poetry and the Public Sphere." In *Arts of the Possible* 115–19.

– "Power and Danger: Works of a Common Woman." In *On Lies, Secrets, and Silence* 247–58.

– "When We Dead Awaken: Writing as Re-vision." In *Arts of the Possible* 11–29.

Rich, Adrienne, and Robin Morgan. Interview. "Poetry and Women's Culture." In Ramstad and Ronnie, *The New Woman's Survival Sourcebook* 106–11.

Rifkin, Libbie. *Career Moves: Olson, Creeley, Zukofsky, Berrigan, and the American Avant-Garde*. Madison: U of Wisconsin P, 2000.

Rodney, Walter. *Groundings with My Brothers*. London: Bogle-L'Ouverture Pub., 1975.

Rohlehr, Gordon. "'Black, Sycorax, My Mother': Brathwaite's Reconstruction of *The Tempest*." In Reiss, *For the Geography of the Soul* 277–96.

– *Pathfinder: Black Awakening in The Arrivants of Edward Brathwaite*. Tunapuna, Trinidad: Yee Foon Communications Ltd., 1981.

– "The Rehumanization of History: Regeneration of Spirit: Apocalypse and Revolution in Brathwaite's *The Arrivants* and *X/Self*." In Brown, *The Art of Kamau Brathwaite* 163–207.

– "Sparrow and the Language of Calypso." *Savacou* 2 (Sept. 1970): 87–99.

Rose, Carol M. *Property and Persuasion: Essays on History, Theory, and Rhetoric of Ownership*. Boulder: Westview P, 1994.

Rosenberg, Harold. *The Tradition of the New*. New York: Horizon P, 1959.

Rosenfeld, Seth. "The Governor's Race." *San Francisco Chronicle*. 9 Jun. 2002. Web. 24 Nov. 2008. http://www.sfgate.com/cgi-bin/article.cgi?f=/c/a/2002/06/09/MNCF3.DTL.

Rothenberg, Jerome, and Pierre Joris, eds. *Poems for the Millennium: The University of California Book of Modern & Postmodern Poetry*. 2 vols. Berkeley: U of California P, 1995.

Ruck, Sydney Kenneth, ed. *The West Indian Comes to England: A Report Prepared for the Trustees of the London Parochial Charities by the Family Welfare Association*. London: Routledge and Kegan Paul, 1960.

Rushin, Donna Kate. "The Bridge Poem." In Anzaldua and Moraga, *This Bridge Called My Back* xxi–xxii.

Ryan, Barbara. *Feminism and the Women's Movement: Dynamics of Change in Social Movement, Ideology, and Activism*. New York: Routledge, 1992.

Ryan, Selwyn D. *Race and Nationalism in Trinidad and Tobago: A Study of Decolonization in a Multiracial Society*. Toronto: U of Toronto P, 1972.

Salkey, Andrew. "Andrew Salkey Talks with Anthony Ilona." By Anthony Ilona. *Wasafiri* 8, no. 16 (Fall 1992): 44–7.

– "Chile." *In the Hills* 17–30.

– *Havana Journal*. Middlesex, UK: Penguin, 1971.

– *In the Hills Where Her Dreams Live*. Havana, Cuba: Casa de las Américas, 1979.

– "Inside." *In the Hills* 13–14.

– "Remember Haiti, Cuba, Vietnam." *Away*. London: Allison & Busby, 1980. 32.

– "Second CAM Symposium on Havana Cultural Congress, 1968 (Extracts)." Papers of the Caribbean Artists Movement, 5/7/2, 1–8, George Padmore Institute, London, UK.

– ed. *Writing in Cuba Since the Revolution: An Anthology of Poems, Short Stories and Essays*. London: Bogle-L'Ouverture, 1977.

Sandford, Mariellen R., ed. *Happenings and Other Acts*. New York: Routledge, 1995.

Sappho. *Sappho: A New Translation*. Trans. Mary Barnard. Berkeley: U of California P, 1958.

Sarachild, Kathie. "A Program for Feminist 'Consciousness Raising.'" In Firestone and Koedt, *Notes From the Second Year* 78–80.

Scobie, Stephen. *bpNichol: What History Teaches*. Vancouver: Talonbooks, 1984.

Sedgwick, Eve K. *English Literature and Male Homosocial Desire*. New York: Columbia UP, 1986.

Shelley, Percy Bysshe. "A Defence of Poetry." *Shelley's Poetry and Prose*. Ed. Donald H. Reiman and Sharon B. Powers. New York: Norton, 1977. 478–508.

Sidney, Sir Philip. "Sonnet XXXI." *Astrophel and Stella. Sir Philip Sidney: Selected Poetry and Prose*. Ed. T.W. Craik. London: Methuen, 1965. 49.

Sigmund, Paul E. *The Overthrow of Allende and the Politics of Chile, 1964–1976*. Pittsburgh, PA: U of Pittsburgh P, 1977.

Silliman, Ron. "The Political Economy of Poetry." In *The New Sentence*. New York: Roof, 1977. 20–31.

Smith, James K. A. *Jacques Derrida: Live Theory*. New York: Continuum, 2005.

Spivak, Gayatri. *Critique of Postcolonial Reason: Toward a History of the Vanishing Present*. Cambridge, MA: Harvard UP, 1999.

Springer, Kimberly. *Living for the Revolution: Black Feminist Organizations, 1968–1980*. Durham, NC: Duke UP, 2005.

Stein, Gertrude. "A Carafe, That is a Blind Glass." *Tender Buttons*. 1914. New York: Dover, 1997. 3.

Stillinger, Jack. *Multiple Authorship and the Myth of Solitary Genius*. New York: Oxford UP, 1991.

Stohl, Michael, and George A. Lopez. *The State as Terrorist: The Dynamics of Governmental Violence and Repression*. Westport, CT: Greenwood P, 1984.

Strong, Beret E. *The Poetic Avant-Garde: The Groups of Borges, Auden, and Breton*. Evanston, IL: Northwestern UP, 1997.

Terrell, Carroll, ed. *Robert Creeley: The Poet's Workshop*. Orono: U of Maine at Orono/The National Poetry Foundation, 1984.

Thompson, Robert Farris. *Flash of the Spirit: African and Afro-American Art and Philosophy*. New York: Random House, 1983.

Tönnies, Ferdinand. *Community and Society*. Trans. C.P. Loomis. New York: Harper & Row, 1957.

– *Gemeinschaft und Gesellschaft*. 1887. 8th ed. Leipzig: Buske, 1935.

Torres-Saillant, Silvio. "Caliban's Betrayal: A New Inquiry into the Caribbean." In Reiss, *For the Geography of the Soul* 221–44.

Touraine, Alain. *Anti-Nuclear Protest: The Opposition to Nuclear Energy in France*. Cambridge: Cambridge UP, 1983.

Umansky, Lauri. *Motherhood Reconceived: Feminism and the Legacies of the Sixties*. New York: New York UP, 1996.

Vaidhyanatha, Siva. *Copyrights and Copywrongs: The Rise of Intellectual Property and How It Threatens Creativity*. New York: New York UP, 2001.

Vendler, Helen. *Soul Says: On Recent Poetry*. Cambridge, MA: Harvard UP, 1995.

Venuti, Lawrence, ed. *The Translation Studies Reader*. 2nd ed. New York: Routledge, 2004.

von Hallberg, Robert. "Olson, Whitehead, and the Objectivists." *Boundary 2* vol. 2, nos. 1–2 (Fall 1973–Winter 1974): 85–112.

– "Robert Creeley and the Pleasures of System." *Boundary 2* vol. 6, no. 3 (1978): 365–79.

Voyce, Stephen. "'Make the World Your Salon': Poetry and Community at the Arensberg Apartment." *Modernism/Modernity* 15, no. 4 (Nov. 2008): 627–47.

– "The Practice of Community: bpNichol and Steve McCaffery in Collaboration." *bpNichol + 20*. Spec. issue of *Open Letter* 13, no. 8 (Spring 2009): 64–76.

– "Steve McCaffery's Kommunism." *Breakthrough Nostalgia: Reading Steve McCaffery Then and Now*. Spec. issue of *Open Letter* 14, no. 7 (Fall 2011): 30–41.

– "Toward an Open-Source Poetics: Appropriation, Collaboration, and the Public Domain." *Criticism* 53, no. 3 (Fall 2011): 407–38.

Waldrop, Rosmarie. "Charles Olson: Process and Relationship." *Twentieth Century Literature* 23, no. 4 (Dec. 1977): 467–86.

Walmsley, Anne. *The Caribbean Artists Movement: A Literary and Cultural History, 1966–1972*. London: New Beacon Books, 1992.

– "John La Rose: A Poet of the Caribbean Artists Movement." In La Rose Tribute Committee, *Foundations* 169–80.

– "A Sense of Community: Kamau Brathwaite and the Caribbean Artists Movement." In Brown, *The Art of Kamau Brathwaite* 101–16.

Watten, Barrett. *The Constructivist Moment: From Material Text to Cultural Poetics*. Middletown, CT: Wesleyan UP, 2003.

Weaver, Andy. "The Political Use of Formal Anarchy in Robert Duncan's Ground Work Volumes." Conf. Paper. Association of Canadian College and University Teachers of English, University of Saskatoon, Saskatchewan, 27 May 2007.

Wershler-Henry, Darren. "Argument for a Secular *Martyrology*." *Open Letter* 10, no. 4 (1998): 37–47.

Whitehead, Alfred North. *Process and Reality*. Ed. David Ray Griffin and Donald W. Sherburne. New York: Free Press, 1978.

Whitehead, Kim. *The Feminist Poetry Movement*. Jackson: UP of Mississippi, 1996.

Williams, Emily Allen, ed. *The Critical Response to Kamau Brathwaite*. Critical Responses in Arts and Letters, Number 41. Westport, CT: Praeger, 2004.

– *Poetic Negotiations of Identity in the Works of Brathwaite, Harris, Senior, and Dabydeen: Tropical Paradise Lost and Regained*. Lewiston, NY: Edwin Mellen P, 1999.

Williams, Raymond. "The Bloomsbury Fraction." In *Culture and Materialism*. 1980. New York: Verso P, 2005. 148–69.

– *The Country and the City*. London: Chatto & Windus Ltd., 1973.

– *Culture and Society, 1780 to 1950*. 1958. Harmondsworth, UK: Penguin Books, 1961.

– *Keywords: A Vocabulary of Culture and Society*. London: Fontana P, 1983.

Wise, J. Macgregor. "Assemblage." In *Gilles Deleuze: Key Concepts*. Ed. Charles J. Stivale. Montreal: McGill-Queen's UP, 2005. 77–87.

WITCH. "A Pretty Girl Is a Commodity." In Morgan, *Sisterhood Is Powerful* 554.

– "Pass the Word, Sister." In Morgan, *Sisterhood Is Powerful* 551–3.

Woodmansee, Martha. *The Author, Art, and the Market: Rereading the History of Aesthetics*. New York: Columbia UP, 1996.

Woodmansee, Martha, and Peter Jaszi, eds. *The Construction of Authorship: Textual Appropriation in Law and Literature*. Durham, NC: Duke UP, 1994.

Wordsworth, William. *The Illustrated Wordsworth's Guide to the Lakes*. Ed. Peter Bicknell. Exeter, UK: Webb & Bower, 1984.

– "Nuns Fret Not at Their Convent's Narrow Rooms." *The Selected Poetry and Prose of Wordsworth*. Ed. Geoffrey H. Hartman. New York: Meridian, 1970. 169.

– "Ode: Intimations of Immortality." Hartman 163–8.

Yau, John. "Active Participation: Robert Creeley and the Visual Arts." In Cappellazzo and Licata, *In Company* 45–82.

Žižek, Slavoj. *First as Tragedy, Then as Farce*. New York: Verso, 2009.

Index